KV-374-825

General Editors

Dr. Margaret Connolly
Dr. William Marx
Dr. Oliver Pickering
Prof. Hans Sauer

Advisory Board

Dr. A.I. Doyle
Prof. A.S.G. Edwards
Dr. Vincent Gillespie
Prof. Manfred Görlach
Prof. Anne Hudson
Prof. Linne Mooney

# The Middle English *Mirror*:

# Sermons from Advent to Sexagesima

Edited from Glasgow,
University Library, Hunter 250
by THOMAS G. DUNCAN
and MARGARET CONNOLLY

with a Parallel Text of
**The Anglo-Norman *Miroir***

Edited from Nottingham,
University Library, Mi LM 4

*to Eamon
with best wishes
Margaret.*

Universitätsverlag
WINTER
Heidelberg

Bibliografische Information Der Deutschen Bibliothek

Die Deutsche Bibliothek verzeichnet diese Publikation
in der Deutschen Nationalbibliografie;
detaillierte bibliografische Daten sind im Internet
über *http://dnb.ddb.de* abrufbar.

*In Memoriam*
ND
*et*
GBJ

ISBN 3-8253-1537-1

Dieses Werk einschließlich aller seiner Teile ist urheberrechtlich geschützt. Jede
Verwertung außerhalb der engen Grenzen des Urheberrechtsgesetzes ist ohne
Zustimmung des Verlages unzulässig und strafbar. Das gilt insbesondere für
Vervielfältigungen, Übersetzungen, Mikroverfilmungen und die Einspeicherung
und Verarbeitung in elektronischen Systemen.

© 2003 Universitätsverlag Winter GmbH Heidelberg
Imprimé en Allemagne · Printed in Germany
Druck: Memminger MedienCentrum, 87700 Memmingen

Gedruckt auf umweltfreundlichem, chlorfrei gebleichtem
und alterungsbeständigem Papier

Den Verlag erreichen Sie im Internet unter:
www.winter-verlag-hd.de

# CONTENTS

## LIST OF FIGURES AND PLATES

# ACKNOWLEDGEMENTS

For financial support of the research which led to the publication of this edition, our thanks are due to the University of St. Andrews and University College Cork; to the Royal Irish Academy, for the award of a visiting fellowship to Margaret Connolly in 1999; and to the Faculty of Arts, University College Cork, for a grant from the Arts Faculty Publications Fund to defray the expenses of preparing camera–ready copy.

For provision of copies of original manuscript material, and for permission to quote material from manuscripts in their care, the editors are pleased to acknowledge: the British Library, London; the Syndics of Cambridge University Library; the Master and Fellows of Trinity College, Cambridge; the Master and Fellows of Corpus Christi College, Cambridge; the Master and Fellows of Magdalene College, Cambridge; the Bodleian Library, Oxford; the John Rylands University Library, Manchester; Norfolk Record Office; York Minster Library; the Bibliothèque Nationale, Paris; the Huntington Library, San Marino, California; and the Ellis Library, University of Missouri, Columbia. We are glad to have had the opportunity to see manuscripts at all the UK libraries named above, and at the Bibliothèque Nationale, Paris; the reference staff in all these places have been most helpful. In addition, special thanks are due to Glasgow University Library, for permission to use MS Hunter 250 as the base text of the Middle English, and to reproduce a photograph of f. $4^v$. Special thanks are also due to the Hon. Michael Willoughby for permission to use MS Nottingham University Library Mi LM 4 as the base text of the Anglo–Norman, and to reproduce a photograph of f. $79^r$; we are grateful to the Library of the University of Nottingham for providing photographs of this manuscript.

Some of the material contained in the Introduction first appeared in a preliminary form in articles published by Thomas G. Duncan in *Neuphilologische Mitteilungen*, 64 (1968) and 82 (1981), and in essays in *Middle English Studies Presented to Norman Davis in Honour of his Seventieth Birthday*, ed. by D. Gray and E. G. Stanley (Oxford, 1983), and *The Medieval Translator: Traduire au Moyen Age 6*, ed. by R. Ellis, R. Tixier, and B. Weitemeier (Turnholt, 1998). For permission to cite and reuse portions of this material we are grateful to the editors of *Neuphilologische Mitteilungen*, Clarendon Press, and Brepols.

For advice and assistance with the Anglo–Norman text, we would like to thank Dr. A. B. Hunt, St. Peter's College, Oxford; Professor R. A. Lodge, University of St. Andrews; and Professor D. A. Trotter, University of Wales at

Aberystwyth. In addition, we would like to thank Dr A. J. Fletcher, University College Dublin, for supplying a pre–publication copy of his chapter on preaching for the Cambridge History of the Book; and Dr Scott Kleinman, State University of California, Northridge, for checking MS HM 903 for us. For guidance on many points we are grateful to the general editors of the *Middle English Texts* series.

We are grateful to the reference staff of the St. Andrews University Library and the Boole Library, University College Cork; to Julian Crowe, Computing Laboratory, University of St. Andrews; and Jill Gamble, research secretary, School of English, University of St. Andrews.

We are grateful to Karen Jankulak for serving as Assistant to the General Editors in the preparation of this volume.

This volume is dedicated to the memories of our respective supervisors: Professor Norman Davis, Merton Professor of English Language and Literature, University of Oxford, and Mr George Barr Jack, Senior Lecturer in English Language and Literature, University of St. Andrews.

# ABBREVIATIONS

This volume uses the conventional abbreviations for the *Oxford English Dictionary (OED), Middle English Dictionary (MED)* and Early English Text Society (EETS).

| | |
|---|---|
| *AND* | L. W. Stone, W. Rothwell, and T.B. Reid, *Anglo–Norman Dictionary* (London, 1977–1992) |
| ANTS | Anglo–Norman Text Society |
| BL | British Library |
| CUL | Cambridge University Library |
| *DNB* | *The Dictionary of National Biography*, 63 vols (London, 1885–1900) |
| Godefroy | F. Godefroy, *Dictionnaire de l'Ancienne Language Française et de tous ses dialectes du IXe au XVe siècle* (Paris, 1880–1902) |
| *IMEV* | C. Brown and R. H. Robbins, *The Index of Middle English Verse* (New York, 1943) |
| *IMEV(S)* | R. H. Robbins and J. L. Cutler, *Supplement to the Index of Middle English Verse* (Lexington, 1965) |
| *IPMEP* | R. E. Lewis, N. F. Blake, and A. S. G. Edwards, *Index of Printed Middle English Prose* (New York and London, 1985) |
| *LALME* | A. McIntosh, M. L. Samuels and M. Benskin, *A Linguistic Atlas of Late Mediaeval English*, 4 vols (Aberdeen, 1986) |
| MET | Middle English Texts |
| *PG* | *Patrologia Graeca*, ed. by J. P. Migne, 162 volumes (Paris, 1857–66) |
| *PL* | *Patrologia Latina*, ed. by J. P. Migne, 217 volumes (Paris, 1844–55) |
| *STC* | A. W. Pollard and G. R. Redgrave, *A Short–Title Catalogue of Books Printed in England, Scotland, and Ireland and of English Books Printed Abroad 1475–1640*, 2nd edn, W. A. Jackson, F. S. Ferguson and K. F. Pantzer, 3 vols (London, 1976–91) |
| Tobler– Lommatzsch | A. Tobler and E. Lommatzsch, *Altfranzösisches Wörterbuch* (Berlin, 1925–) |

# MANUSCRIPTS

## Manuscripts of the Middle English *Mirror*

H: Glasgow, University Library, Hunter 250
C: Cambridge, Corpus Christi College, 282
P: Cambridge, Magdalene College, Pepys 2498
B: Oxford, Bodleian Library, Holkham Misc 40
R: Manchester, John Rylands University Library, English 109
N: Norwich, Norwich Cathedral 5
Ha: London, British Library, Harley 5085
I: Cambridge, University Library, Ii.6.26

## Manuscripts of the Anglo-Norman *Miroir*

$W^1$: Nottingham, University Library, Mi LM 3
$W^2$: Nottingham, University Library, Mi LM 4
O: Oxford, Bodleian Library, Holkham Misc 44
L: London, British Library, Additional 26773
U: Cambridge, University Library, Gg.I.i
Hm: San Marino, CA, Huntington Library, HM 903
F: Paris, Bibliothèque Nationale, na fr. 11198
Mo: Columbia (MO), University of Missouri, Ellis Library, Fragmenta Manuscripta 135
T: Cambridge, Trinity College, B.14.39
Y: York, Minster Library, XVI.K.14

# INTRODUCTION

## The Text

The *Mirror* consists of a prologue and a collection of sixty sermons which were translated into Middle English in the late fourteenth century from the Anglo-Norman *Miroir*, a sermon cycle in verse composed in England in the thirteenth century by Robert de Gretham.[1] The sermons are based on the Sunday gospels, according to the Use of Sarum.

A complete Middle English sermon cycle is notable. Only about twenty such complete vernacular collections have survived even though thousands of sermons must have been written in the later Middle Ages in England. Little is known about the ownership and use of the *Mirror* manuscripts, nor can firm links be established between these manuscripts and any monastic order or house. Nevertheless, on linguistic evidence the majority of the Middle English manuscripts may be associated with the London area, which may indicate a metropolitan centre of production.

The text of this, the first edition of the *Mirror*, is based on Glasgow, University Library MS Hunter 250; the parallel text of the Anglo-Norman *Miroir* (also, hitherto, unedited) is based on Nottingham, University Library MS Mi LM 4. The extent of the textual variation among the manuscripts (especially the English manuscripts) has made it impracticable to include here a complete *index variorum*. However, full citation of relevant manuscript variants is given in the discussion of textual matters in the commentary.

None of the extant manuscripts of the Anglo-Norman *Miroir* seems to have served as the exemplar of the Middle English translator. Nevertheless, the parallel text given here from Nottingham, University Library MS Mi LM 4 offers, on the whole, a sound basis for comparison between the Middle English text and its Anglo-Norman source. Such a comparison reveals in the fourteenth-century Middle English translation significant agreements with and differences from the Anglo-Norman source of the previous century, especially in the prologue to the sermons, and particularly in matters concerning biblical translation, the status of priests, and their duties in preaching and teaching, controversial issues in the age of Langland and Wyclif.

This volume presents the prologue and the first twelve sermons (from Advent 1 to Sexagesima) of the *Mirror*. The editors decided against offering a selection

---

[1] For more information about Robert de Gretham see pp. lvi–lvii.

of sermons from throughout the cycle as it is intended that this will be the first of several volumes in which the entire text of the *Mirror* will be edited.

## Description of Manuscripts

The Middle English *Mirror* survives in six manuscripts, one of which is now divided between two locations; a seventh manuscript contains a tract based on part of the prologue. The source of the *Mirror*, Robert de Gretham's Anglo-Norman *Miroir*, survives in six manuscripts, and in two manuscript fragments; a further two manuscripts contain extracts of the *exempla* in the text. All of the manuscripts have been described elsewhere, some extensively and a number of times, others less fully and less accessibly. The following descriptions do not aim to be comprehensive, but to give the salient points.

## Manuscripts of the Middle English *Mirror*

### 1. Glasgow, University Library, Hunter 250 (H)

H has been described by Young and Aitken (1908:201). Since the catalogue description was written the first gathering has been rebound in the correct order. The manuscript is made up of vellum which is defective and patched in places; many folios are stained, dirtied and rubbbed. The manuscript is now bound in eighteenth-century millboards, covered with spattered calf and blind-tooled. It was clearly unbound for a considerable time during which it may well have lost its final folio, for the first folio has been badly soiled, rubbed, and twice torn right across; subsequent repairs with tape make this folio difficult to read. The manuscript measures 260 mm x 190 mm; there are 131 folios and foliation is in modern pencil. The flyleaves are of paper contemporary with the binding, and the first and last are paste-downs. The collation is: vi + $1^8$–$5^8$, $6^6$, $7^8$–$16^8$, $17^6$ (6 lacking after 5), iv. Catchwords occur throughout, except at the end of gatherings 7, 8, and 10; a few contemporary signatures remain, but most have been lost to trimming. Young and Aitken date the manuscript as fourteenth century. H is written in brown ink by a single clear, round, upright hand, not very formal in appearance, but not cursive, each letter being separately formed; many of its features are similar to the style sometimes called 'Chancery Hand'. The written space varies slightly between 207–216 mm x 153 mm; the text is arranged in two columns of approximately 42 lines each, with horizontal ruling and frame-lines in crayon. There is modest illumination with initials mostly in blue and paraph marks alternately in blue and red. The most elaborate initial is that of the first word where the 'M' is five lines deep, blue with red flourishes; ornamentation in red and blue continues down the left-hand margin ending with further flourishing in red at the top (now trimmed) and foot of the column. Blue

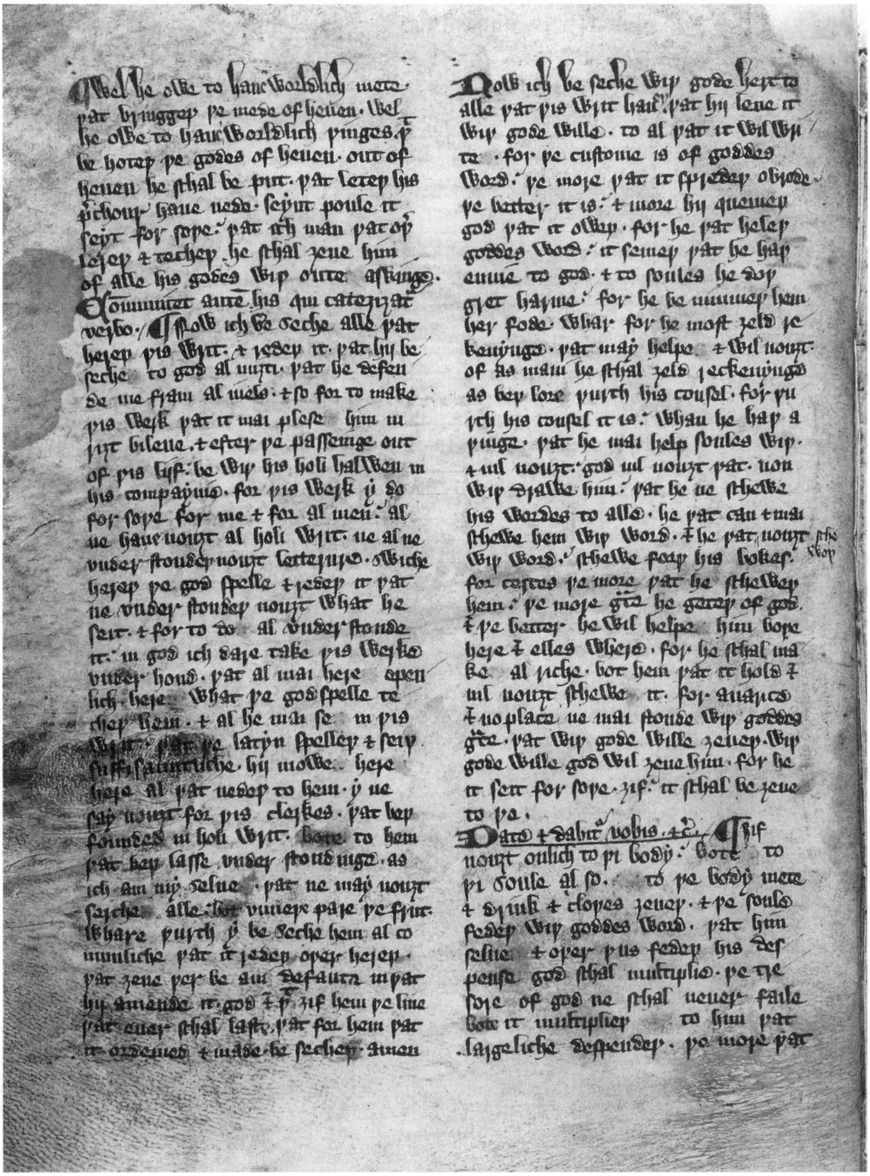

*Plate* 1   Glasgow, University Library Hunter 250 (H), f. 4ᵛ.
Reproduced by permission of Glasgow University Library, Department of Special Collections.

initials of various sizes (usually two but sometimes up to four to five lines deep), with red ornamentation and flourishes are used throughout at the beginning of sermons, and sometimes to mark subdivisions in sermons. Latin quotations are either in red or underlined in red, sometimes with small blue initials; occasionally spaces for initials have been left unfilled. On two occasions exempla are signalled by the words 'a tale' in the margin, in red on f. 28$^r$, and in brown underlined with red on f. 106$^r$. The text has been extensively altered by a reviser, whose hand is similar to that of the original scribe, and by a later hand; for discussion of the alterations see below pp. lx–lxiv. The name 'John Hyll' occurs sporadically throughout the manuscript in what might be a fifteenth-century hand.[2] In addition the inscription 'Ebenr Mussell 1740' occurs on the recto of the first flyleaf. The version of the *Mirror* given in H contains a full version of the text, though sermon 60 ends incompletely on f. 131$^v$: '... wiþ god and ben hii þat ben nouȝt...'.

## 2. Cambridge, Corpus Christi College, 282 (C)

C has been described by James (1912:48). It is a vellum manuscript of i + 139 folios measuring 260 mm x 190 mm; the volume was rebound in 1956. The volume is made up of eighteen gatherings of eight; the first quire lacks its outer bifolium, and the final quire lacks the sixth, seventh, and eighth leaves. The pagination uses odd numbers only, beginning with 3, and takes no account of missing leaves; a leaf overlooked between 145 and 147 has been numbered 146(a). Catchwords are present, and two systems of medieval signatures: a complete run of letters and minims in red, and a run of numbers and minims in brown ink, many of which have been trimmed. The manuscript is written in brown ink in a single hand, dated by James as late fourteenth century; the written space is 216 mm x 143 mm, with horizontal ruling and frame-lines in brown crayon. The text is arranged in two columns of 44 lines, falling to 42 lines towards the end of the manuscript, and has modest decoration: two line deep blue initials with red flourishing are used at the openings of sermons; rubrics are in red ink, paraph signs frequently in red or blue. Exempla are indicated by the marginal note 'a tale' (p. 12, lower margin; pp. 17 and 51, central space between two columns), 'le tale' (p. 60, left-hand margin), etc. The scribal dialect has been located in Middlesex, see *LALME*:i.62. On p. 9 at the foot of column 1, where five lines have been left blank at the end of the prologue there is a two line Latin inscription in drypoint: *Laus f------ alleluia ffuit / homo missus a deo --- n- erat.* James notes the initials 'D.N.' at the extreme bottom right-hand corner of p. 278, in a fifteenth or sixteenth-century

---

[2]   See ff. 41$^v$, 49$^r$, 69$^r$, 77$^r$, 85$^r$ and 110$^r$; some of these inscriptions have been partly erased. Partial forms of the name, or sometimes just the initials, may also be detected on ff. 21$^v$, 51$^v$, 63$^r$, 74$^r$ and 91$^r$. The catalogue records the name wrongly as 'Philippus Hyll', and identifies the script as sixteenth-century in date. See also p. lviii.

hand. In general the manuscript is remarkably free from annotation or inscription; occasionally a later hand has added notes, usually very well-known Biblical quotations. The introduction to the *Mirror* begins imperfectly on p. 3: *...prologue endeþ. nou lokeþ in þe mirour. for al þou schalt see þi figure... .* C contains part of the prologue and all sixty sermons, but sometimes the rubrics differ; for example, in C, sermons 8–10 are wrongly headed as the second, third, and fourth Sundays after the octave of Epiphany. James failed to record the presence of sermon 55 (p. 236). Sermon headings are written in English.

### 3. Cambridge, Magdalene College, Pepys 2498 (P)

P has been described several times, most recently by McKitterick and Beadle (1992:86–88); useful previous studies are James (1923:106–10), Zettersten (1976:ix–xxi), and Marx and Drennan (1987:10–11). The manuscript is on parchment, and measures 340 mm x 240 mm; the pages have been slightly trimmed. It comprises iv + 464 + iv folios; there is modern pagination. The collation is as follows: $1^8$–$2^8$, $3^6$, $4^8$–$23^8$, $24^6$ (lacks 4–6 after p. 370), $25^8$–$29^8$, $30^8$ (lacks 8). It is written by one anglicana formata hand, a clear, firm book-hand dated to the middle of second half of the fourteenth century by N.R. Ker; see Zettersten 1976:xix. The same hand has been identified in Oxford, Bodleian Library MS Laud Misc. 622 and London, British Library MS Harley 874; these three manuscripts have been located around Waltham Abbey, Essex, see *LALME*:i. 64. The written space is 292 mm x 218 mm, ruled in brown crayon; the text is arranged in double columns of between 52 and 54 lines. There are framed catchwords, slightly trimmed, but no original signatures remain. The general scheme of decoration is as follows: the initials which introduce each text in the manuscript are usually in red, six to twelve lines deep; subdivisions within each text are marked by smaller blue initials with red penwork. In the case of the *Mirror*, the initial 'M' which begins the prologue is six lines deep, coloured red and blue, with decoration in the same colours, and tracery which extends down the left-hand margin; the next letter in this first word ('Many') is oversized and also coloured red and blue. Siginificant capitals within the prologue are blue with red decoration, two to four lines deep; small blue capitals are also used, and other capitals (of normal size) are marked with red. Latin quotations are in red. The dominical occasion for each sermon is given in red, as is the Latin incipit to the gospel; the latter is introduced with a blue initial decorated with red tracery, three lines deep. Other initials within the sermons are blue with red decoration, two lines deep. Paraph marks are in blue. After the end of the sermons on p. 212b there are two blank lines and then the verse tag: *Of þe holy omelies now i wil blynne / God bringe vs to þat blisse þere ioye is euere jnne.*[3] Similar verse tags occur at the beginnings or endings (or in both contexts) of some P's other texts; McKitterick and Beadle suggest that these

---

[3]    *IMEV* 2660.1

may be an indication that the book was originally designed for reading aloud (1992:88). During the sixteenth century P was in the hands of the author, translator, and collector of manuscripts, Stephen Batman (d. 1584); he added headings to some of the texts, including, in the top margin of p. 45a the title 'Mirror, or glasse to Looke in'.[4] The manuscript had come into the possession of Samuel Pepys (1633–1703) by 1695. In addition to the *Mirror* which is the second item (pp. 45a–212b), P contains: the Harmony of the Gospels; a treatise on the Ten Commandments; the Apocalypse in English; 'The Midland Prose Psalter'; *Ancrene Riwle*; *The Complaint of Our Lady*; *The Gospel of Nicodemus*; and a number of short prayers. For a detailed list of the contents see McKitterick and Beadle (1992:86–88). The version of the *Mirror* in P contains the prologue and sermons 1–59.

## 4. Oxford, Bodleian Library, Holkham Misc 40 (B)

B (formerly Holkham Hall MS 672) was described briefly in the *Ninth Report of the Royal Commission on Historical Manuscripts, Appendix II* (1883:364), and by Paues (1904:xiv–xv), and is listed under Holkham in the Bodleian Library's typescript *Checklist of Medieval Western Manuscripts Acquired from 1916*. The manuscript is on vellum, measures 285 mm x 190 mm, and comprises ii + 260 folios. As well as modern foliation in pencil (used in references here), there is an early system of foliation which uses both Roman and Arabic numerals as follows: ff. 1–29 numbered i to xxiiii; f. 30 misnumbered xxix; ff. 31–104 misnumbered xxx to ciii; ff. 105–180 misnumbered 104–179. The volume is made up of thirty–two gatherings of eight plus a singleton, with flyleaves of modern paper at both the beginning and the end. Catchwords are present, as are contemporary signatures using letters and minims; these run from *a* to *z* in brown ink (except for *a iiii* which is in red), then from *a* to *e* in red ink, and then from *f* to *j* in brown ink; a few have been trimmed. The manuscript is dated by Paues as 'soon after 1400' and by the catalogue as 'late fourteenth or early fifteenth century'. There are five hands: (i) from ff. 1–15$^v$ line 6; (ii) from within line 6 on f. 15$^v$ to the foot of 16$^v$; (iii) ff. 17$^r$–25$^r$ line 2; (iv) from line 2 on f. 25$^r$ to the end of the epistles on f. 162$^v$; (v) from f. 162$^v$ to the end of the manuscript.[5] The last two hands are scarcely distinguishable except that one uses oblique, the other horizontal hyphens at the ends of lines. The written space varies between 219–224 mm x 132–140 mm. Initially (ff. 1–133), the text is written in long lines, 38 to the page on ff. 1–16$^v$, 45 to the page on ff. 17$^r$–133$^r$; thereafter the text is laid out in double columns, with 45 lines per column to begin with, decreasing to 37 lines by 257$^{ra}$. There is minimal decoration. The

---

[4]  On Batman see *DNB*; for a discussion of his marginalia in the *Mirror* see McLoughlin 1994:525–34.

[5]  Though the style of writing unquestionably changes on f. 15$^v$, both Paues and the *Summary Catalogue* miss the brief operation of the second hand.

prologue begins with a plain red capital 'M' seven lines deep; other capitals within the prologue are similarly plain, red, and three lines deep, and Latin quotations are also red. The initial capitals of the sermons themselves are plain, red, and usually three lines deep. The Latin incipit of the gospel pericope and the gospel rubric are in red. The dominical occasion is also in red and, unusually, is given in English. This scheme is not always fully adhered to: sometimes the Latin incipit is not rubricated beyond the initial capital; sometimes the dominical occasion is recorded in Latin as well as English. These variations are perhaps due to differences in practice amongst the five scribes responsible for the manuscript. Paraph marks are in red throughout. In 1592 B was in the hands of Johannes Forestius of Essex, as the following statement in the bottom margin of f. 7$^r$ demonstrates: *Iohannes Forestius rector de Ramseton in comitatu Essex est proprius et indubitatus possessor huius libri 1592.* By the seventeenth century both B and O were in the collection of Sir Edward Coke (1552–1634).[6] B contains the prologue and all sixty sermons of the *Mirror*, though with some variant forms of the usual rubrics. Most notably, marginal rubrics have been added to sermon 6, with the effect that the long sermon for Epiphany is divided into three parts to serve that day and the two subsequent Sundays.[7] The presence of exempla is signalled by the words 'a tale' in the margin in either brown or red ink, and the scribe has also corrected some readings. There are some annotations by a later hand using black ink. After sermon 60 B also has a considerable amount of additional material, some of which also occurs in R and Ha. From ff. 124$^v$–133$^r$ there are fourteen more items (numbered 61–74 in the checklist), which consist of other sermons and short pieces. In addition the manuscript contains: ff. 133$^r$–162$^{va}$, the Catholic and Pauline Epistles, intro-duced by the heading 'Here beginnin þe pisteles of þe ȝeer'; ff. 162$^{va}$–257$^{rb}$, the Four Gospels with prologues in the earlier Wycliffite version.

## 5. Manchester, John Rylands Library, English 109 (R) and Norwich Cathedral 5 (N).[8]

N is a fragment of eight paper leaves which were removed from R sometime between 1836–59. The relationship between R and N was noticed by Ker who describes both manuscripts in 1983:418–20 and 532–34. The prose contents of R are more extensively listed in Lester (1985:40–49). For earlier descriptions of R see James (1921:305–306) and Tyson (1929:24). R is on paper, except for ff. 75–78 which are vellum; in its present state the volume comprises vi + 123 + ii

---

6 Edward Coke's autograph is in the top margin of f. 1$^r$; the manuscript also bears the bookplate of Thomas William Coke.

7 For details see Commentary pp. 155, 157.

8 The Norwich Cathedral MSS are now held at the Norfolk Record Office; Norwich Cathedral MS 5 is now NRO DCL 5.

folios, and the manuscript measures 280 mm x 205 mm. There is modern pencil foliation, and also medieval foliation which shows that there were formerly at least 143 folios. The collation of R is: $1^{20}$ lacks 1, 16–20, $2^{19}$, $3^{12}$ lacks 2 and 12, $4^{12}$ lacks 7 and 11, $5^{12}$ lacks 2, 3, 7–9, $6^{12}$ lacks 7–9, $7^{12}$ lacks 10–12, $8^4$, $9^{14}$, $10^{12}$ lacks 5–7, $11^{16}$, $12^{10}$. There are occasional catchwords but no signatures. Ker identifies four hands, all current anglicana; the first is responsible for ff. $4^r$– $17^r$, the second for ff. $18^v$–$36^v$, the third for ff. $37^r$–$78^v$, and the fourth for ff. $79^r$–$126^r$ (dated 1432). The written space measures 215 mm x 155 mm at first, rising to 232 mm x 175 mm; the text is arranged in two columns of between 40 and 54 lines. There is minimal decoration; capitals and small letters are touched with red, and red paraph signs are used; gospel translations and other important passages are underlined in red. The final rubric on f. $126^{vb}$ reads: *Iste liber constat A[bbathie(?)] de W[elbec(?)] si quis hunc librum a predicta [abbathia(?)] alienauerit anatema sit amen et scriptus erat anno domini millesimo cccc^{mo} xxx^{mo} secundo*, i.e. 1432. The words in square brackets have been erased and replaced with the later name of 'Domino Roberto Prestwold'. The erased inscription was deciphered by James and allows the manuscript to be linked to Welbeck Abbey in Nottinghamshire, a house of the order of the Premonstratensians. This fits with McIntosh's judgment that the linguistic provenance of this copy of the *Mirror* was north Nottinghamshire; see Ker (1983:419). The manuscript also has a sixteenth-century inscription of the name 'Iohannem Voudon'. R has a table of contents on ff. 1–$2^v$ which was added at the beginning of the sixteenth century. The first part of R (ff. 4–$17^v$) contains eight sermons of the temporal, in English, for which see Lester (1985: 40–44); this is part of a sermon collection which is a derivative of the Wycliffite cycle; see Hudson (1983:i.98–123). This is followed on ff. 18–$36^v$ by seven sermons of the temporal, in Latin. The third series of sermons in R (ff. 37–126) is from the *Mirror* and represents a complete cycle which is now defective in many places. The first leaf of the *Mirror* is misbound as f. 54, and part of the first line is lost. The cycle apparently never contained sermon 5, and due to the casual loss of leaves now also lacks sermons 10, 16, 22 and 49, and parts of sermons 6, 9, 14, 15, 17, 21, 23, 32, 48, 50, 53. The eight leaves in N contain the following: all but the opening lines of sermon 11, the whole of sermon 12, and the first part of sermon 13, on ff. 5–7; the closing lines of sermon 29, the whole of sermon 30, and the opening lines of sermon 31, on ff. 1–4; and parts of the additional items 62 and 63 on f. 8. As a result the Quinquagesima (13), Trinity (29), and Pater Noster (63) sermons are therefore now divided between N and R as follows: Quinquagesima N f. 7, R ff. 52–53; Trinity R ff. 73–74, N f. 1; Pater Noster N f. 8, R f. 123.

## 6. London, British Library Harley 5085 (Ha)

Ha is briefly listed and dated as fourteenth century in *A Catalogue of the Harleian Manuscripts in the British Museum* (1808:iii.244); no detailed published description exists. The manuscript is on vellum, measures 270 mm x 205 mm, and comprises 211 folios; foliation is in modern pencil. The collation is as follows: iv, 1–9$^8$, 10$^8$ (lacks 2), 11–21$^8$, 22$^4$, 23$^8$, 24$^4$ plus a singleton added to complete a sermon and partly left blank, 25–27$^8$, 28$^4$ (lacks 4), ii. The fly-leaves (the first and last are paste-downs) are of paper except for iv, a medieval vellum end-leaf which has been cut out. There are catchwords to every gathering except the first, some partly trimmed away. The manuscript is written in brown ink; the hand, a fairly formal book hand, probably dates from the late fourteenth century. The written space is 207 mm x 140 mm with frame-lines in brown ink; the text is written in long lines. There is minimal decoration: the prologue is introduced with a plain red capital 'M', four lines deep, and large plain red initials two to three lines deep mark the openings of sermons; fairly frequently the exposition following the gospel is headed *Þe exposicion* or *Þe vndoinge* in red; red paraph signs are used sparingly. The dominical occasion of each sermon is given in red, but the Latin incipit of the gospel reading is not rubricated or otherwise distinguished; in the earlier sermons these references are not always supplied. Exempla are indicated by the words 'a tale' in the margin. The scribal dialect has been located in Middlesex; see *LALME*:i.113. In the top margin of f. 1$^r$ is written and underlined 'ye mirrur 1622', and occasional marginalia in this hand are found at the beginning of the manuscript. Other marginal additions occur sporadically throughout, mainly in a late medieval hand using very dark ink. The version of the *Mirror* contained in Ha includes the prologue and all sixty sermons, and some of the additional material contained in B. The last four sermons are misordered, and mixed in with the additional material, in the following order: sermons 58, 57, 59, 61, 66, 71, 73, 60. There is also a piece on original sin (75) which does not occur in the other manuscripts, and a sermon on the ten commandments (76), which differs from the texts on the same topic which conclude the body of additional material in B and R.

## 7. Cambridge, University Library, Ii.6.26 (I)

I is described in *A Catalogue of the Manuscripts Preserved in the Library of the University of Cambridge* (1858:iii.524–26). Hudson (1985:107) identified the eleventh tract in this manuscript as part of the prologue to the *Mirror*. Hunt (1994) edits and discusses the text. The manuscript is on vellum, measures 153 mm x 110 mm, and has 101 folios; a later hand has numbered the pages, and there is foliation in modern pencil. The volume is made up of thirteen gatherings of eight leaves; the first three leaves of the thirteenth gathering have been excised. There are no catchwords, but a series of contemporary signatures runs a–l; the second, third, and fourth leaves of each gathering are distinguished by a series of dots (1–2, 6–11) or numbers (3–5). The manuscript is written in brown ink. The written space is 105 mm x 70 mm with frame lines in brown ink; the first item regularly has 26 lines to the page, but in the second item the lines vary beween 19–26. The manuscript is very plain; there are rubrics and paraph marks in red, but spaces for capitals, usually two lines deep, have been left unfilled. The catalogue dates the manuscript as fifteenth century; Deanesly (1920:271) dates the activities of the scribe to between 1400–1430. There is an erased inscription in the bottom margin of p. 114 (f. 57$^v$), set upside down, which begins 'Jane Gr...'. The manuscript contains on pp. 1–158 (ff. 1–79$^v$) a series of twelve tracts in English in favour of vernacular scriptures; a full list of incipits and explicits is given in the Catalogue. The eleventh of these (see p. 102; f. 51$^v$), relates to the *Mirror*. This tract is introduced by the rubric: '*A comendacioun of holy writ in ouer owne langage*', and begins: *[H]oly writ haþ þe lyknesse of a tree þat bereþ fruyt note peer or appel...*, ending (p. 116; f. 58$^v$) *... in þis valeye of teris gracius god. Amen.* The author has used lines 67–74 of the prologue to the *Mirror* and, more loosely, lines 85–91, and includes three of the biblical quotations cited later in the prologue (cf. lines 107–10, 125, and 267); this material is then developed into a discourse on the merits of vernacular bible translation. This text should therefore be seen as an independent text in its own right and not as an extract of the *Mirror*. The second item in the manuscript (pp. 158–202; ff. 79$^v$–101$^v$) is a partial translation of *Elucidarium* which is ascribed to Anselm.

## Manuscripts of the Anglo-Norman *Miroir* [9]

### 1. Nottingham, University Library, Mi LM 3 (W$^1$)

Formerly at Wollaton Hall, and still the property of Lord Middleton, W$^1$ is briefly described by Stevenson (1911:220). The manuscript is on parchment. It has suffered some water damage, and is ragged at the edges on all sides; some of the initial folios are folded. The first folio is extremely dirty, the last folio less so. The manuscript consists of 101 folios, and measures 264 mm x 190 mm. It is foliated in modern pencil. The manuscript begins and ends defectively. Otherwise the collation is: 1$^8$, 2$^4$, 3–5$^8$, 6$^8$ (lacks 5), 7–9$^8$, 10$^8$ (lacks 2–7), 11–14$^8$. Catchwords, consisting of an entire line of verse, are mostly present; they are not visible at the end of gatherings 1 and 5, and that at the end of gathering 13 does not agree with what follows. There are no signatures. W$^1$ is written in black ink by two hands, the second (possibly that of a novice), contributing only on ff. 71$^v$–75$^r$. The written space is ruled in pencil and measures 168 mm x 136 mm (175 mm x 138 mm on ff. 71$^v$–75$^r$). The text is arranged in double columns of 28 lines, falling to between 20 and 23 in the section between ff. 71$^v$–75$^r$.

---

[9] Most recently listed by Dean and Boulton 1999:325–26.

Stevenson noticed only one hand which he described as early thirteenth century, but Dean and Boulton date the manuscript to the middle of the century. The dominical occasion for each sermon is given in red. The gospel readings are not rubricated, but have patterned initial capitals in blue, of two to three lines deep. The text of each sermon begins with plain red initials, two lines deep, and similar initials, alternately in red and blue, are used within each sermon. Small letters intended to guide the rubricator may be seen in the margins. There is some annotation, consisting of crude pointing hands drawn by a much later hand in brown ink. The copy of the *Miroir* contained in $W^1$ begins eight lines from the end of the sermon 1 and ends in the middle of sermon 40. There are various lacunae throughout caused by the loss of leaves. Due to losses in the tenth gathering the text lacks some of sermon 26, all of sermon 27, and all but the final 13 lines of sermon 28. A complete gathering is missing between what are now the thirteenth and fourteenth quires; this has caused the loss of the end of sermon 34, all of sermons 35–37, and the beginning of sermon 38.

## 2.  Nottingham, University Library, Mi LM 4 ($W^2$)

Formerly at Wollaton Hall, and still the property of Lord Middleton, $W^2$ is briefly described by Stevenson (1911:220–21) and by Turville-Petre (1996). The manuscript is on parchment, and is presently unbound and in a fragile condition. It has suffered some water damage, and is generally quite ragged; the final gathering is the most damaged, being folded and torn. The manuscript has been trimmed and now measures 270 mm x 180 mm; it consists of 171 folios, and is foliated in modern ink. The text ends on 171$^r$, half-way down the second column; the rest of this page and the verso are blank. A quire of at least twelve folios has been lost from the beginning. The collation is: $1$–$2^{12}$, $3^{10}$, $4^{12}$, $5$–$6^{10}$, $7$–$8^{12}$, $9^{10}$ (lacks 10), $10$–$15^{12}$. Catchwords are not present, but a system of numbers running from i–ix is visible at the bottom right-hand corner of the final leaf in each gathering. The numbers are sometimes partially or wholly lost because the manuscript is very worn at the corners. The manuscript is written in dark brown ink and is by one hand throughout. Stevenson describes the hand merely as thirteenth century, but Dean and Boulton suggest the second half of century. The written space is 210 mm x 130 mm and the text is arranged in double columns of forty-two lines each with frame-lines ruled in pencil. At the beginning of the prologue there is an elaborate capital 'A' which is six lines deep with tracery which extends the full length of the top and left-hand margins.[10] The Latin rubric for each Sunday and the gospel reference is in red. Initials used at the beginnings of the Latin pericopes are three lines deep, in blue with red penwork, but the Latin text is not otherwise rubricated and not underlined. The initial letter of the main Anglo-Norman text of each sermon is in red, but not over-sized. Paraph marks are alternately in red and blue. The

[10]   See Turville-Petre 1996 [item 10] for a facsimile illustration of this folio.

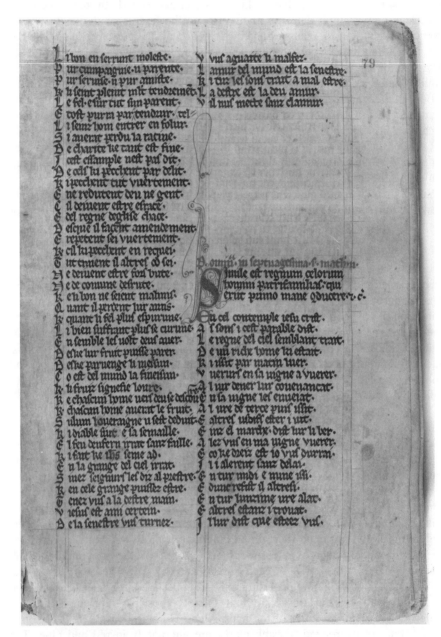

*Plate* 2  Nottingham, University Library Mi LM 4 (W²), f. 79ʳ.
Reproduced by permission of the Hon. Michael Willoughby and the University of
Nottingham Library.

scribe indicates exempla by writing 'nota' in the margins (in brown, sometimes touched up in red); he marks the beginning of the exposition of the gospel passage in each sermon by adding the marginal note 'Oml', usually in red. Small letters intended to guide the rubricator can also be seen in the margins. There are no inscriptions or signs of ownership, and no annotations beyond a few scribbles. $W^2$ contains an imperfect copy (lacking the opening 2007 lines) of the *Manuel des Péchés* by William of Waddington. The copy of the *Miroir* on ff. $57^r$–$171^r$ is complete, but there are a number of puzzling blank spaces in its copying. At the end of sermon 10 on f. $79^r$, 13 lines are left blank in the second column of text. Sermon 19 ends on f. $99^v$, almost half-way down the first column of text; the rest of this page is blank, and the following folio has been excised, but with no loss of text, and sermon 20 begins on f. $100^r$ at the beginning of the next gathering. There is another space, amounting to five lines in each column, towards the foot of $114^v$.

### 3.   Oxford, Bodleian Library, Holkham Misc 44 (O)

O (formerly Holkham Hall MS 663), is described briefly in the *Ninth Report of the Royal Commission on Historical Manuscripts, Appendix II* (1883:363), and is listed under Holkham in the Bodleian Library's typescript *Checklist of Medieval Western Manuscripts Acquired from 1916.* The manuscript is on vellum which has been mended in places; it measures 306 mm x 188 mm, and consists of ii + 64 folios, with foliation in modern pencil. The first leaf is rubbed and dirty, and seems to have suffered some water damage. The collation is: $1^8$, $2^{16}$, $3$–$7^8$(lacks 6–8). Catchwords are present but there are no contemporary signatures. The manuscript is written in brown ink and is by one hand throughout. Dean and Boulton date the manuscript to the turn of the thirteenth/fourteenth century. The written space is 220 mm x 138 mm and the text is arranged in double columns of 40 lines with frame-lines ruled in pencil. At the beginning of the prologue is a large capital 'A', four lines deep, in blue and red, with its descender and tracery extending down the left-hand margins. The initials which introduce the sermons are usually two lines deep, red with blue decoration. The Latin incipit of the gospel pericope is introduced with a blue initial decorated with red tracery and varying in size, usually two or three lines deep, but sometimes as much as twelve lines, depending on the letter. This colour scheme is not always adhered to, and sometimes the pericope initial is red and the sermon initial blue. The dominical occasion is given in red, though this rubrication has not always been supplied. Paraph marks are in brown ink. The beginning of the exposition of the gospel passage is indicated by the note 'oml' or 'omel' in red. The scribe has added occasional corrections in the margins; otherwise there is very little annotation beyond a few scribbles. The copy of the *Miroir* begins with the prologue which lacks lines 563–600 due to an error by the copyist.[11] The text of the *Miroir* ends incompletely in sermon 26; copying ceases on f. 61$^v$ after only four lines and the rest of this page is left blank, suggesting that no more was transcribed. The manuscript bears the bookplate of Thomas William Coke; his signature is in the top margin of f. 1$^r$.

## 4. London, British Library, Additional 26773 (L)

L is noted briefly in *A Catalogue of Additions to the Manuscripts in the British Museum 1854–75* (1877:ii.283), and is described by Varnhagen (1877:541–45), but note Meyer's criticisms of the latter (1878:343–47). The manuscript is on parchment of a low quality with several large splits and holes; it has been mended in places and also trimmed slightly. It measures 200 mm x 140 mm and consists of 114 folios, but is imperfect at both beginning and end; foliation is in modern pencil. The collation is: 1–3$^8$, 4$^{12}$, 5$^8$, 6–8$^6$, 9$^{14}$ (lacks 12–14), 10–11$^8$, 12$^{10}$, 13–14$^8$. Catchwords are mostly present but there are no signatures. The manuscript is written in dark brown ink and is by one hand throughout. Meyer (1886:298) dates the manuscript to the end of the thirteenth century, but Dean and Boulton suggest a date in the mid thirteenth century. The written space is 160 mm x 120 mm and the text is arranged in double columns of very variable length (between 29 and 42 lines) with frame-lines faintly ruled in pencil. Initials are two lines deep, plain and crudely drawn, in red; paraph signs are in black. Sometimes the liturgical occasions are given in red, but often these have been omitted and supplied later in light brown ink. The Latin incipit of the gospel reading at the beginning of each sermon is introduced with a red initial, but is not otherwise rubricated. Annotations are mostly confined to some crudely drawn pointing hands and some exaggerated signs for 'nota'; there are some later additions in Latin on ff. 31$^r$ and 73$^v$ in light brown ink, and on ff. 92$^{r-v}$ in red. There are two inscriptions which may indicate early owners: on f. 28$^v$ in the bottom margin is an inscription in light brown ink which when expanded reads: *A sun trecher amy Syr Thomas chapeleyn*; and on f. 75$^v$ in the bottom margin is the inscription in brown ink: *A sun trecher amy Henri de Kynto...* . The copy of the *Miroir* contained in L begins acephalously on f. 6$^r$ with the last six lines of sermon 3 and ends on f. 120$^v$ in the middle of sermon 50.

## 5. Cambridge, University Library, Gg.I.i (U)

U is described in *A Catalogue of the Manuscripts Preserved in the Library of the University of Cambridge* (1858:iii.1–8), and more extensively by Meyer (1886:283–340). It is a parchment manuscript of ii + 633 folios which measures 215 mm x 150 mm; there is modern foliation, but some traces of an original scheme of foliation remain. The collation is 1$^8$ (lacks 1), 2–21$^{12}$, 22$^{12}$ (lacks 6),

---

[11]    At the bottom of f. 4$^r$, having reached line 562, the copyist turned the leaf and erroneously re-copied lines 403–40 on f. 4$^v$. The text then resumes from line 601, with no indication that the intervening lines have been omitted.

23–30$^{12}$, 31$^{10}$, 32–35$^{12}$, 36$^{12}$ (lacks 1,11,12) 37$^{12}$ (lacks 1,4) 38$^{12}$ (lacks 3), 39–42$^{12}$ 43$^{4}$, 45–53$^{12}$, 54$^{14}$ (lacks 6), 55$^{5}$. Catchwords are mostly present but there are no contemporary quire signatures. Dean and Boulton date the hand to the first years of the fourteenth century, but after 1307, since one of the texts mentions the death of Edward I which occurred in that year. The manuscript is written in brown ink with frame-lines ruled in pencil. The written space is 160 mm x 115 mm and the text is arranged in two columns of between 37 and 40 lines. The scheme of decoration used in the *Miroir* is as follows. The prologue and first sermon are introduced by elaborate blue initial letters, six lines deep, with red, green, and gold decoration; from the letter a border in the same colours with zoomorphic motifs extends three-quarters of the way around the relevant column of text. Subsequent sermons are introduced with blue initials which are three to four lines deep, with red decoration and blue and red tracery which extends the full length of the page. Smaller initials, usually two lines deep, alternately in red and blue with contrasting tracery, are used within the text; rubrics are in red. These decorative features are used throughout the manuscript which, in some parts, also has coloured diagrams and pictures. On the verso of the first flyleaf a seventeenth-century hand has written 'bought of Mr Washington'. U contains poetry and prose, mostly in French, with some items in Latin; a full list of the contents is given by Meyer. The version of the *Miroir* included here (ff. 135–261) is complete, except for one leaf lost between f. 252 and f. 253.

## 6.  San Marino CA, Huntington Library, HM 903 (Hm)

Hm was formerly at Everingham Park, Yorkshire. Hm is described by Dutschke (1989:i.259–61); see also Laird (1942:628–37). The manuscript is on parchment and has suffered some water damage. It measures 240 mm x 167 mm, and comprises ii + 205 + ii folios. The collation is as follows: 1$^{10}$, 2–4$^{8}$, 5$^{12}$ (+ 4, f. 38), 6–7$^{8}$, 8 (ff. 64–67, uncertain structure; f. 67 cut in half vertically), 9–10$^{8}$, 11$^{6}$ (+2, f. 85), 12$^{8}$, 13$^{6}$ (+ 3, f. 101), 14–16$^{8}$ 17$^{10}$ (through f. 139), 18–21$^{8}$, 22$^{8}$ (+6, f. 177), 23$^{6}$, 24$^{8}$, 25$^{12}$ (lacks 12); quires 18–25 should have been bound between quires 8 and 9. Catchwords are present in the first two quires, and there are three runs of medieval signatures which uses roman numerals (i–vii), letters a–i, and then roman numerals again (ii–viii). The script varies but seems to be the work of one bastard anglicana hand, dated by Dutschke and Dean and Boulton as mid fourteenth-century. The written space is 180 mm x 133 mm, with horizontal ruling and frame-lines in lead. The text is arranged in double columns of between 36 and 43 lines. Initials are in blue and red; opening initials are 4–5 lines, others two to four lines deep, with alternating red and blue paraph marks. Frequent emendations in black ink have been made to sermons 7–10 and in sermons 30–53. An erased inscription on f. 139$^{v}$ in the hand of the text reads 'A Johan (?) li Romance'. On f. 1$^{r}$ is an early or mid-fifteenth century ownership note of the Benedictine abbey of St. Mary in York: *liber Monasterii beate Marie Eboracensis emptus per fratrem Clementem Warthwyk, qui Alienaverit Anathema.* The text of the *Miroir* in Hm is incomplete and disrupted by the manuscript's misbinding. It begins defectively at line 587 of the prologue and runs to sermon 28 on what is now ff. $140^r$–$205^v$. Sermons 29–53 are given on ff. 68–123, but some material is missing from the end of sermon 28 to the beginning of sermon 29. From ff. $123^r$–$139^v$ Hm contains sermons 54–58, concluding with a short prayer in English verse on f. $139^v$.[12] Hm also contains *Manuel des Péchés*, attributed to William of Waddington, ff. 1–67.

### 7. Paris, Bibliothèque Nationale, na fr. 11198 (F)

This manuscript of 68 leaves consists of a collection of fragments, both parchment and paper, which date from the thirteenth to the nineteenth centuries. The contents are listed by Omont (1915:34–35). Aitken (1922:14) noted the relevant section of two leaves (ff. 7–8), and this has more recently been described by Avril and Stirnemann (1987:91).[13] The leaves are creased and have suffered some water damage; both have been cut in half (causing some loss of text), and are now joined with transparent tape. Parts of the right-hand margins have been cut away; at their widest points the leaves measure 210 mm x 160 mm, but their dimensions are irregular. Avril and Stirnemann date the fragment to the third quarter of the thirteenth century, whereas Meyer (1903:29–31) had attributed it to the early fourteenth century; Dean and Boulton concur with Meyer's dating. The text is written in brown ink with no visible ruling. The written space varies between 140–150 mm x 110–120 mm, and the text is arranged in two columns of between 38 and 40 lines. Decoration is limited to three initials, two lines deep, alternately red and blue, and sometimes enhanced with flourishes in the contrasting colour. There are no annotations or marginalia beyond a few crude drawings. The text of the *Miroir* begins 76 lines before the end of sermon 27, and continues into sermon 28.[14] This fragment clearly derives from a copy of the complete sermon cycle.

### 8. Columbia (MO), University of Missouri, Ellis Library, Fragmenta Manuscripta 135 (Mo)

Mo is described by Baker (1928:62–67). Formerly Phillipps 15758, this single leaf is in a collection of fragments formerly owned by Sir Sydney Cockerell. The parchment leaf now measures 172 mm x 132 mm; the top of the leaf has been cut, causing the loss of approximately five lines of text. The ragged nature

---

[12]  'God almyghtfull save al rightffull', three lines, IMEV 981; see Laird 1940:601–603.

[13]  f. 6, mentioned by Aitken and by the *Catalogue général nouv. acq., IV* (1918), is a sheet of paper containing notes by Paul Meyer. According to him the fragment of two parchment leaves was discovered in an old binding and was donated by Eugene Piot.

[14]  The text begins on f. $7^r$: *A tut dis erent od Jh'u / Car sur trestuz erent eslu*, and ends on f. $8^v$: *Suuent se a uient ki li espus / E a par sa femme curius.*

of the right hand edge has obscured the beginnings of some lines on the verso. The text is copied in double columns, with 41 lines on the recto and 39 on the verso. Dean and Boulton date the manuscript to the second half of the thirteenth century. The fragment of the *Miroir* preserved here constitutes the end of sermon 15 and the beginning of sermon 16. Baker's transcription omits one line and contains several misreadings.

## 9. Cambridge, Trinity College, B.14.39 (T)

T has been described by James (1900–1904:i.438–49), and more extensively by Reichl (1973). The manuscript is on vellum, measures approximately 181 mm x 137 mm, and consists of 180 folios. The volume is in fact two volumes which have been bound together. The first section, of 87 folios, dates from the end of the thirteenth century, according to Aitken (1922:14); Dean and Boulton agree with this dating. The second section, of 93 folios, dates from the fourteenth or early fifteenth century. A transcript of almost the whole volume was made by Frederick Madden in 1843 and is now classed as B.14.40. There is one continuous modern foliation in pencil; the second section also has its own sequence of pencilled folio numbers. The collation is as follows: $1^8$, $2^{16}$, $3^{12}$ lacks 12 (? blank), $4^{12}$, $5^{10}$, $6^8$–$8^8$, $9^4$ (+2); $a^{12}$–$e^{12}$ (12 canc.), $f^{12}$, $g^{12}$, $h^{10}$. Catchwords are visible in the second part of the manuscript, but in the first part, with the exception of f. $8^v$, they have been wholly trimmed away. The first section contains material in English, French, and Latin, and is the work of several different hands. The extracts from the *Miroir* (sixteen exempla from the sermons), are copied in the sixth and seventh quires (ff. 58–72) by what James describes as a 'set hand'. Here the layout is in two columns of between 32 and 34 lines, the written space is 145 mm x 110 mm, and frame-lines are ruled in pencil; a dark brown ink is used. Each exemplum begins with initials which are alternately red or blue, with contrasting tracery extends several lines down the margin; the initial letters of each line are touched with red. In the second section of the volume a rather greenish ink is used, and there are 24 lines to a page. On f. $1^r$, is an erased fifteenth-century inscription: *...Nicholas cum aliis ... in gallico* (deciphered by Mooney, 1995:12); on f. $54^r$ in the bottom margin is *John* .... , also erased. For a full list of the manuscript's contents see James; for partial transcriptions of the extracts see Wright (1844:11) and Meyer (1903:28–37). Dean and Boulton note that the sixteen exempla do not correspond exactly to those printed by Aitken.

## 10. York, Minster Library, XVI.K.14 (Y)[15]

Y has been described by Ker and Piper (1992:731–32). It is the third part of a set of three volumes of Anglo-Norman verse (now XVI.K.12, 13, 14), which were perhaps originally independent but were put together, possibly in the

---

[15]  Aitken gives the incorrect shelfmark of XVI.K.19.

Middle Ages. They formed a single volume, F.8.174 in the collection of Marmaduke Fothergill (d. 1731), which was given to the minster by his widow in 1737; the manuscript was rebound and divided again into three volumes in 1815 or 1816. The manuscript is on parchment and is in reasonable condition, though the last folio is creased and has a hole and a tear. Y consists of ii + 6 + xiv folios, that is, one gathering of six leaves; it measures 205 mm x 135 mm and has been trimmed slightly at the top. Foliation is in modern pencil. Y is written by a single hand in brown ink. The written space is ruled in the same ink and measures 176 mm x 114 mm; the text is arranged in two columns of 37 lines. Ker and Piper describe the hand as textura and date it to the second half of the thirteenth century; Dean and Boulton concur. On f. 1$^r$ the initials are plain, coloured red, and 2 lines deep; subsequently spaces for initials have been left unfilled, and there is no other decoration. Paraph marks occur in the margin in the same brown ink as the text. A later hand has identified the dominical occasions from which the Latin texts which precede the exempla are taken, and has added abbreviated notes to this effect in the margin, using black ink. Y contains a series of nine exempla from the *Miroir*, the last of which is incomplete.[16] Meyer (1903:29–31) prints a partial transcription.

## The Textual Tradition of the English Manuscripts

This account of the relationships of the six main manuscripts of the *Mirror* is largely based on the evidence of variant readings in the seventeen exemplary tales found in the sermons. These tales give a reasonable sample of the *Mirror* insofar as they are spread throughout the work; the first occurs in sermon 2 (for the second Sunday in Advent), and the last in sermon 52 (for the twenty-third Sunday after Trinity). Anglo-Norman quotations are taken from W$^2$. Since only substantial variants germane to the determination of the manuscript relationships are relevant to the following discussion, other variations among the manuscripts in spelling, form, and wording are usually left unrecorded in the quotations.

The stemma (see *Figure 1*) can be demonstrated, with reservations concerning γ and especially δ at which points contradictory evidence is found. Whereas numerous variants represent merely changes and errors which have arisen independently within the separate traditions of each manuscript, a pattern of readings which splits the manuscripts three against three – HCP against BRHa – is fairly frequent. It is often impossible in these cases to be sure which reading is in error since both usually make good enough sense. However, where the English follows the French closely, comparison with the Anglo-Norman text reveals what must in all probability have been the original reading of the English translation.

---

[16] Equivalent to nos. 1–9 transcribed by Aitken 1922:136–57.

*Figure 1:* **Stemma**

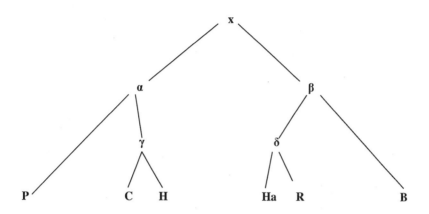

1.  The following evidence supports α:

(i) Tale XI

| | |
|---|---|
| HCP | *& held him þerfor a fole & auisard* |
| BRHa | *& holden for a fool a musard* |
| W² | *A fol le tenent e a musard.*[17] |

*Musard* is recorded in English from the fourteenth and fifteenth centuries, in some instances in collocation with the word 'fool'.[18] The error *uisard* in HCP (*uisad* in P), is surprising. It is presumably a form of 'wizard', first recorded for c. 1440.[19] The instance here is certainly earlier, towards the end of the fourteenth century at the latest.

(ii) Tale XIII

| | |
|---|---|
| HCP | *þat he nas pere to an angel* |
| BRHa | *þat he ne was pere to aungels* |
| W² | *K'il as angles per n'esteit.*[20] |

(iii) Tale XIII

| | |
|---|---|
| HCP | *as schip doþ whan it is vnder wiþ oute help* |
| BR | *as þe schip doþ whan it is vn tyed wiþ outen helpe* |
| Ha | *as þe schipp doþ whan it is vnstered wiþouten help* |
| W² | *Cum fait la nef desestachee.*[21] |

HCP are in error with the reading *vnder*; Ha has its own alteration to *vnstered*.

---

| | |
|---|---|
| 17 | W² f. 133ʳ, col b. line 9. |
| 18 | See MED *musard* n.(a). |
| 19 | See MED *wisard(e* n. |
| 20 | W² f. 150ᵛ, col. b, line 14. |
| 21 | W² f. 151ʳ, col. a, line 11. |

(iv) Tale XIII

| | |
|---|---|
| HCP | *þat vnneþe he myȝt holde hym* |
| BRHa | *þat vnneþes he wiþ held hym* |
| W² | *K' il a peine se detient.*[22] |

(v) Tale XIII

| | |
|---|---|
| HCP | *& vpon þerid day was he atrauailed* |
| BRHa | *& vpon þe þridde day he was so traueyled* |
| W² | *Al tierz iur tant fust traveille.*[23] |

(vi) Tale XIV

| | |
|---|---|
| HCP | *for to chastise ȝou of ȝour synne* |
| BRHa | *forto chastyse ȝou of ȝoure folye(s)* |
| W² | *Pur vus chastier de uos folies.*[24] |

(vii) Tale XIV

| | |
|---|---|
| HCP | *do whider þou wilt* |
| BRHa | *do it in þi celle* |
| W² | *En ta celle mette tun escleir.*[25] |

(viii) Tale XIV

| | |
|---|---|
| HCP | *ne þin honden liften toward god* |
| BRHa | *ne þin honden liften vp to ward heuene* |
| W² | *Ne de tes mains al ciel leuer.*[26] |

(ix) Tale XIV

| | |
|---|---|
| HCP | *he dede come toforn him his desciples* |
| BRHa | *he dide comen to forn hym alle his disciplis* |
| W² | *Ses disciples tuz uenir feit.*[27] |

2.   The following shared errors establish β:

(i) Tale I

| | |
|---|---|
| HCP | *& it nas nouȝt long efter þat god ne toke veniaunce on him* |
| BRHa | *& it was noȝt long aftur þat god toke uengawnce oppon hym* |
| W² | *Ne demura pas longement* |
| | *Que Deus n'en prist le uengement.*[28] |

The negative in the second clause in HCP has been taken over from the idiom of the French. The omission of 'ne' in BRHa appears to be a shared error, though such a change in favour of normal English syntax might have been arrived at independently.

---

[22]   W² f. 151ʳ, col. a, line 27.

[23]   W² f. 151ʳ, col. a, line 39.

[24]   W² f. 156ʳ, col. b, line 10.

[25]   W² f. 156ʳ, col. b, line 33.

[26]   W² f. 156ʳ, col. b, line 39.

[27]   W² f. 156ᵛ, col. a, line 10.

[28]   32/1012–13.

(ii) Tale V

The king of England had a servant good, wise, and strong. In England there could not be found his equal. But one vice he had

| | |
|---|---|
| H | *þat no man ne miʒt louen him* |
| C | *þat non ne miʒt leuen him* |
| P | *þat non ne miʒth do hym leuen* |
| B | *þat no myʒte reuen hym* |
| R | *þat non myʒt reue hym* |
| Ha | *þat noman miʒt reuen him* |
| W² | *Mais une uice male aueit* |
| | *Ke nuls hom creire nel poeit.*[29] |

It seems that the English translator misunderstood the French as meaning 'that no man might believe him' rather than 'that no one could believe'. The original English mistranslation was the reading at α and continues to C. P retains *leuen* but alters the wording and the sense to *do hym leuen*, that is 'make him abandon'. H alters *leuen* to, or misreads it as, *louen* (the letters 'e' and 'o' are easily confusable in full rounded hands such as those found in HC). BRHa share the erroneous reading *reue(n)*, presumably with the sense 'that no man might take away from him'.

(iii) Tale V

| | |
|---|---|
| H | *þe kinge tourned & went þennes* |
| C | *þe king conred went him þan þennes* |
| P | *þe king corouned went hym þan þennes* |
| B | *þe kyng wente hym þan þennes* |
| R | *þenne þe kyng went forth* |
| Ha | *þe kinge went him þennes wepinge* |
| W² | *Li reis Conred dunc se partist.*[30] |

The H reading *tourned* probably derived from a corruption of the king's name as seen in CP (the initial letters 't' and 'c' are so easily confusable as readily to lead to a misreading). BRHa omit the king's name; this may be looked upon as a shared error although the tendency to omit the name in this tale is common throughout the manuscripts.

(iv) Tale XIV

| | |
|---|---|
| HCP | *whi lestou so many soules* |
| BRHa | *why slest þou so many soules* |
| W² | *Tantes almes purquei perdez.*[31] |

(v) Tale XIV

| | |
|---|---|
| HCP | *to nemne god in þi mouþe for þi gret folie* |
| BRHa | *to nempne god in þi mouþ for þe gret folye* |
| W² | *De Deu numer pur ta folie.*[32] |

---

[29] W² f. 81ᵛ, col. b, lines 24–25.
[30] W² f. 88ᵛ, col. a, line 26.
[31] W² f. 156ʳ, col. a, line 30.
[32] W² f. 156ʳ, col. b, line 38.

3. Granted α and β alternative readings where four manuscripts agree against two should establish error for the latter. Many instances of agreement of HC against PBRHa support γ.

(i) A significant lacuna occurs in Tale XVI:

| | |
|---|---|
| HC | *to lyue & be nouʒt in doute* |
| B | *to lyue for to make vs stedefast in þe bileue þat we schul arise from deþ to lyue & noʒt ben in doute* |

PR and, with slight alterations, Ha, all contain the material omitted by mechanical error in HC. Agreements of HC against PBRHa are fairly frequent. For example:

(ii) Tale IV

| | |
|---|---|
| HC | *þe lawe* |
| PBRHa | *her lawe* |

(iii) Tale XI

| | |
|---|---|
| HC | *despeplen* |
| PBRHa | *despoilen* |

| | |
|---|---|
| HC | *þe corseintes* |
| PBRHa | *þe holy corseintes* |

| | |
|---|---|
| HC | *he said to him* |
| PBRHa | *vnto hym he seide* |

(iv) Tale XII

| | |
|---|---|
| HC | *þat held him longe* |
| PBRHa | *þat longe helde hym* |

| | |
|---|---|
| HC | *to swich point com als* |
| PBRHa | *come vnto swiche a poynt as* |

| | |
|---|---|
| HC | *schewed* |
| PBRHa | *schewed hym* |
| HC | *forsake þat* |
| PBRHa | *noman forsake þat* |

(v) Tale XIII

| | |
|---|---|
| HC | *þat be come negligent* |
| PBRHa | *þat he bicom more necligent* |

| | |
|---|---|
| HC | *he seid psalmes* |
| PBRHa | *he seide his psalmes* |

| | |
|---|---|
| HC | *þe litel harm he fel into a gretter harme* |
| PBRHa | *þe litel he fel in a grete harme* |

(vi) Tale XIV

| | |
|---|---|
| HC | *synned hou* |
| PBRHa | *ysynned wiþ me hou* |

| | |
|---|---|
| HC | *what wil tou* |
| PBRHa | *whare wiltou* |

| | |
|---|---|
| HC | *repented not* |

| PBRHa | *repented hir nouȝth* |
|-------|------------------------|
| HC | *teld it antony* |
| PBRHa | *telde it to antoyne* |

(vii) Tale XVI

| HC | *arise to liif* |
|-------|------------------------|
| PBRHa | *arise fram deþ to lyue* |
| HC | *after seid* |
| PBRHa | *after he seide* |
| HC | *soule wend fro þe bodi* |
| PBRHa | *soule wende out of þe body* |
| HC | *ne be leue y nouȝt* |
| PBRHa | *ne bileue ich riȝth nouȝth* |
| HC | *y schal* |
| PBRHa | *it schal* |
| HC | *maistrie is* |
| PBRHa | *maistrie it is* |

However, contradictory evidence linking P and C against H does occur, as in the following instance of CP agreement in error:

| CP | *ac take þe rote and let þe þorn* |
|-------|------------------------|
| HBHa | *ac take þe rose & lete þe þorn* |
| R | *but take to rose & leue þe thorne* |
| W$^2$ | *La rose met l'espine en pris.*[33] |

See Commentary, 19/13–14.[34]

## 4. In the case of δ the evidence noted is inconsistent.

(a) The tendency is for RHa to agree (presumably in error) against HCPB. For example:

(i) Tale I

| HCPB | *fote is euer lenger þe wers* |
|-------|------------------------|
| RHa | *fote was (euer) þo lenger þe wers* |
| HCPB | *his legge* |
| RHa | *þe legge* (Ha *fote*) |

(ii) Tale II

| HCPB | *of wicked liif* |
|-------|------------------------|
| RHa | *of yuel lif* |
| HCPB | *ac he nold no more* |
| RHa | *and said þat he wolde no more* |
| H | *& a mesel come þer þan* |

[33]    18/576.

[34]    Hunt (1994:206), on the basis of two lacunae found in the prologue, dismisses the relationship of H and C in favour of linking C and P.

| C | *& a mesel com þer þan* |
|---|---|
| P | *& a mesel com þan þer* |
| B | *& a mesel come þer* |
| R | *then þer come a mesel* |
| Ha | *and þan com a mesel* |

(iii) Tale XII

| HCPB | *& seyde to þe priour* (CPB *abbot*) |
|---|---|
| RHa | *& spake to þo abbot* |

(b) On the other hand there is conflicting evidence as where BHa agree against HCPR. For example:

(i) Tale XIII

| BHa | *talent for to eten* |
|---|---|
| HCPR | *talent to mete* |

(ii) Tale XIV

| B | *and leyd it al vpon an hep* |
|---|---|
| Ha | *& bren it al opon an hep* |
| HCPR | *& laid it vpon an hepe* |

(iii) Tale XIV

| BHa | *& schet þe dore harde* |
|---|---|
| HCPR | *& schet þe dore fast* |

(c) Support for a special affinity between BR, though slight, does also arise, as in the following instance:

Tale VII

| BR | *& fecch* |
|---|---|
| HCPHa | *and sech* |

The weakest point in the stemma, then, is δ. Further evidence may emerge as the whole of the text of the *Mirror* is edited; equally, arguments for independent rather than shared error, and consideration of the possibility of contamination, may lead to more persuasive conclusions. Thus, in support of δ, the reading quoted linking BR might be questioned. The relevant passage as found in H reads:

And þat large broþer bad þe oþer ʒif him bred. And he answerde: 'Þar nis non.'
'Go,' he said, 'and sech.' And he went in & fond þe huche ful of brede.

That B *fecch* and R *fecche* are in error is confirmed by the reading *quere* in the Anglo-Norman source.[35] However, it is not difficult to see how this mistake

---

[35] The corresponding lines in $W^2$ (f. 93$^r$, col. a, lines 33–37) are:

E li larges al altre dist:
'Dun li del pain.' E il respundi:  del pain] pain $W^1$UOLHm
'N'i ad point, frere.' Il dit a li:
'Va quere.' E il i entrat
E la huche plein i trouat.

could have occurred independently in two manuscripts. The long form of 's' and the letter 'f' are commonly confused; in some hands they are virtually identical. Thus *seche/secche* could easily have been read by different scribes as *feche/fecche*, and all the more readily so in a context in which either word would make sense, as here in the phrases 'go and seek' or 'go and fetch'.

However, the status of δ has no bearing on the question as to which manuscript should be selected as that most suitable to serve as the base text for an edition of the *Mirror* since, on other grounds the relative merits of B, R and Ha are not in doubt. B has many imperfections, its own share of careless errors and unique variants, a condition from which none of the *Mirror* manuscripts is free. In general, however, B offers a relatively sound text. R and Ha are of a different order. The version in Ha is partly the product of rewriting, at times remarkably maladroit; sometimes the Ha text runs parallel to that of the other manuscripts, sometimes it differs considerably. Furthermore, the gospel versions in Ha are different in origin from the translations of the Anglo-Norman text of the *Miroir* found in the other manuscripts. For its part, R is also a markedly corrupt text, though it might more aptly be described as frequently reworded and rephrased than as rewritten, a point which may conveniently be illustrated from the R version of the passage quoted above from H. R reads:

> And þe large broþer bad þat oþer ryse & gyf hym. And he grocched agayne & saide. 'Þer is non; þu has wasted alle.' 'Go & fecche,' þat oþer saide. And he ʒede inne o scorne & he fonde þe cofer ful of brede.

Compared with the H text, the substantial differences in R are: H *ʒif] ryse & gyf* R; H *bred] om.* R; H *answerde] grocched agayne & saide* R; H *Þar nis non] Þer is non þu has wasted alle* R; H *Go he said and sech] Go & fecche þat oþer saide* R; H *went in] ʒede inne o scorne* R; H *huche] cofer* R. In all these points the other manuscripts essentially agree with H.[36] In addition, of the six main English manuscripts, R is by far the most incomplete. Clearly, B alone of the β tradition could be considered as a base text.

HCP also offer substantially reliable texts, but again, like B, each with a crop of variants and errors, some shared with other manuscripts and some unique. Such errors and variants may be sampled from the comparative readings offered in the Commentary, though it is to be borne in mind that these readings are

Aitken 1922:151 mistakenly gives *pain* instead of *del pain* as the W[2] reading in the second line above.

[36]   The variants *bred]* HCHa, *sum bred* PB, om. R, may be noted. Sometimes variant AN readings offer inconclusive testimony *vis-à-vis* the original English text and its AN source reading. Here, for instance, the translator's exemplar may have read *del pain* (as W[2]) or *pain* (as do the other manuscripts). Either AN reading might have been translated simply as *bred* (HCHa) or as *sum bred* (PB). Thus, *sum* may have been added in P and in B by independent error or, again by independent error, have been omitted at γ (HC) and δ (RHa).

usually recorded only at points where difficulties arise in H. However, on balance, a manuscript from the α tradition may be preferred. HCP are all probably earlier than B. Each is copied in a single hand; B is in five hands. In addition, HCP all share the Type II form of London English of the majority of surviving *Mirror* manuscripts (four out of six), arguably, therefore, the language of the original translation.[37] P tends to offer a less reliable text than H or C. As an almost complete text, H may be preferred over the defective C. Of all the *Mirror* manuscripts, H is certainly linguistically the most interesting, for it is in H that is found the work of a uniquely thorough and systematic Middle English reviser.[38] This might be thought to count against the selection of H as the base manuscript for the present edition. However, since, on analysis, it is clear what the reviser's major changes were, the original H text may, in all but a few instances, be confidently restored.[39]

## The Anglo-Norman *Miroir* and the Middle English Translation

Robert de Gretham's Anglo-Norman *Miroir* remains unedited; only extracts from the work have so far appeared in print.[40] Of the surviving manuscripts only three, $W^2$UHm, are more or less complete. In a study of the four main *Mirror* manuscripts known to her, $W^1W^2$LU, Aitken arrived at two general conclusions:

---

[37]   H and P are listed as Type II manuscripts in Samuels 1972:166. In *LALME* the linguistic profile of C (LP 6490, *LALME* iii: 304–5) is recorded for Middlesex along with that of Ha (LP 6520, *LALME* iii: 306), also given as Type II in Samuels 1972: 166. However, there may be no justification for preferring the three α manuscripts over B on the basis of Type II attribution. As mentioned above, Ha, one of the β manuscripts, is also a Type II manuscript. In addition, significant features of the Type II language – e.g. the present participial ending -*and*, *laten* ('let'), *laden* ('lead'), *þei(ȝ)* ('though'), *þat iche* ('the same') – are found in B. An analysis of the distribution and relative preponderance of these and other Type II features throughout the manuscript to establish linguistic profiles for each of the five scribes could well lead to the classification of B (or at least, parts of B), as another version of the Type II language. In this case, granted the dating 'late fourteenth or early fifteenth century' (see p. xvi), B would represent a very late version of that language. Again, this being so, not four but five of the main *Mirror* manuscripts would fall within the Type II classification.

[38]   See pp. lx–lxiv.

[39]   A complete collation of the six main *Mirror* manuscripts has not yet been undertaken. It is to be doubted, however, if the evidence of such a collation would demonstrate any one of HCPB to be significantly less acceptable as a base text than the others. Yet on the basis of an examination of an admittedly slight portion of the *Mirror* text, the Prologue, as found in the six main manuscripts, Hunt 1994:205 also concluded that H was 'the best choice as base manuscript'.

[40]   Eight sermons were edited by Panunzio 1967. Unfortunately this work is largely derivative and marred by considerable inaccuracy; see Marshall and Rothwell 1970. Otherwise the most substantial portions of the *Miroir* so far in print are found in Meyer 1886 and 1903, and in Aitken 1922.

that these manuscripts were independent from one another, and that the contradictory nature of her sample of variant readings did not allow her to devise for them any convincing stemma. She also considered U to be the least reliable and latest of the manuscripts, the work of an extremely negligent scribe who did not always understand what he copied.[41] Laird collated the *Miroir* variants given by Aitken with the readings in Hm. On this very limited and somewhat inconsistent evidence he came to the conclusion that Hm was related to $W^1$ and U rather than to $W^2$ and L. He also judged Hm to be a late copy of the *Miroir* and one which did not offer the best available text.[42] It is to be noted that Hm is in many places difficult to make out on account of extensive alteration, and moreover, it lacks the first 586 lines of the prologue. Ideally, of course, the best manuscript for the parallel text would be the one used by the Middle English translator or the surviving manuscript closest to it. However, the relative proximity of the surviving Anglo-Norman manuscripts to the Middle English text has yet to be established. Certainly none of the three near-complete manuscripts was the English translator's exemplar. Many instances are given in the Commentary where readings in U and/or Hm as against those of $W^2$ represent those of the translator's Anglo-Norman text.[43] Although such evidence might seem to support the authority of U or Hm, it is to be noted that no account has been taken in the Commentary of readings in U and Hm which do not correspond to the English where the readings of $W^2$ clearly do. In both $W^2$ and U sermons 50 and 51 occur in the correct order; in the translator's exemplar these sermons must have appeared in reverse order.[44] There are not infrequent lacunae in both U and Hm corresponding to lines in $W^2$ which appear translated in the Middle English text.[45] As already noted, U and Hm are relatively corrupt copies. $W^2$ is not only the best complete manuscript of the *Miroir* but also, in all probability, the best witness to the translator's copy of the Anglo-Norman text even if its readings by no means always represent those of that version. It has therefore been adopted as the base manuscript for the parallel text of the Anglo-Norman *Miroir* in this edition.[46]

With what success did the translator render Robert de Gretham's Anglo-Norman verse into Middle English prose? The following passage,

---

[41]     Aitken 1922:13–14.
[42]     Laird 1942:633.
[43]     E.g. see Commentary, notes 3/25, 5/12–13, 13/28–31, 17/26, 17/31, 19/29–30, 21/34, 25/8, 27/4, 27/6, 31/8, 33/2, 39/4, 39/7, 49/12–13, 51/20, 129/2–3, etc.
[44]     See p. 171.
[45]     E.g. lines 155–56 and 2868–71 are lacking in U, and lines 609–12 and 621–34 are lacking in Hm.
[46]     Panunzio adopted $W^1$ as the base manuscript for his edition of eight *Miroir* sermons, perhaps on the basis of Aitken's opinion that $W^1$ was the oldest and best of her four main manuscripts. However, the view that $W^1$ is superior to $W^2$ has been challenged by Marshall and Rothwell 1970:315.

corresponding to 10/305–38, drawn from the discussion in the prologue of the priest's duty to teach, offers a fair illustration of his style and level of achievement. Italics are used here in Middle English quotations to indicate alterations from or additions to the Anglo-Norman text.

> In þis stede *it scheweþ þat hii han nede of brekinge of brede, þat is, vndoinge of holi writ;* ac þer nis non þat brekeþ *his* brede whan þe prist es barain, *þat [is], naked of gode werkes & of conninge,* ne vnderstondeþ nouȝt holi writ, ne ȝifeþ no kepe to hem þat ben vnder him. Þat is þe brekinge of þe brede, for to schewe wel *holi writ* & Goddes wordes, & fede þe soules wiþ gode sermouns. Þe prest ne brekeþ nouȝt þe brede whan *he ne vndoþ nouȝt holi writ as he auȝt for to don* vnto þe lewed folk *& techen hem hou þat hii miȝht comen to þe liif þat euer schal last.* How schuld he breke þis brede þat ne vnderstondeþ nouȝt holi writ, & hou schal he fede oþer þat ne can nouȝt ne wil nouȝt fede himseluen, *Y ne mai nouȝt wit hou.* As þe prophete seit: *Et erit populus ita sacerdos, þat is:* 'Swiche as þe lewed folk ben, swiche is þe preste.' *And þerfor it schal fallen of hem as God seit in þe godspelle:* 'Whan þe blinde ladeþ þe blinde, boþe fallen in þe diche.' *Swiche mantel-bond, swiche men, swiche prestes hii hiren & susten. And þerfor boþe schul gon oway bot ȝif hii amende her liif, & þat is in auntre ȝif hii schul haue þat grace. Si cecus cecum ducat, ambo in foueam cadunt.*  (11/10–27)

The English translator abbreviates, expands and modifies the Anglo-Norman text fairly fluently. The first sentence of the English largely replaces the first four lines of the Anglo-Norman text. Bodily needs are not mentioned in the English; the translator turns directly to his main theme, the spiritual need for the breaking of bread, that is, the exposition of holy writ. While the opening words of the Anglo-Norman, *Kar en cest liu*, become *In þis stede*, it is to be noted that in the Anglo-Norman, *cest liu* refers to this world and not, as *þis stede* in the English, to this place in holy writ, namely the text, *Paruuli petierunt panem & non erant qui frangerent eis,* quoted in the *Mirror*. The translator introduces clauses beginning *þat is* to clarify and emphasize his point: *brekinge of brede, þat is, vndoinge of holi writ; whan þe prist es barain, þat is, naked of gode werkes & of conninge.* He underlines what is important by brief additions: thus the Anglo-Norman *Les Deu paroles bien mustrer* becomes *for to schewe wel holi writ & Goddes wordes.* To emphasize his main concerns – at this point the duty of a priest to expound scripture and to teach lay folk how they may gain eternal life – he will modify the Anglo-Norman text, expanding one phrase and omitting another. Thus, Robert de Gretham's:

> Li prestres pain ne depescoye
> Quant par escrit ne mustre uoie
> Al lai de leisser sa folie
> E uenir al pastur de uie (10/317–20)

becomes:

Þe prest ne brekeþ nouȝt þe brede whan *he ne vndoþ nouȝt holi writ as he auȝt for to don* vnto þe lewed folk *& techen hem hou þat hii miȝht comen to þe liif þat euer schal last.* (11/16–18)

He may also add emphasis by introducing an exclamation: *& hou schal he fede oþer þat ne can nouȝt ne wil nouȝt fede himseluen, Y ne mai nouȝt wit hou.* He sometimes takes the obvious step of omitting repetitions in the Anglo–Norman verse as here in the final couplet of:

> Cest pain depescerat cument
> Ki l'escripture pas n'entent?
> Les altres pestre coment pot
> Ke sei pestre ne siet ne uolt?
> Coment pestrat altri u sei
> Qui de diuine pagine est lai? (10/321–26)

He readily expands upon and adds to the *Miroir* text to drive home a point. This is well illustrated by the final lines of the Middle English passage (not found in the *Miroir),* lines which threaten idle priests and their patrons with eternal punishment unless they reform, and conclude with the stinging observation: *& þat is in auntre ȝif hii schul haue þat grace.* From this passage it also appears that the English translator had the knack of enlivening his text and underlining his point by the introduction of a popular saying. The addition, *Swiche mantel-bond, swiche men, swiche prestes hii hiren & susten,* has the appearance of a colloquial aphorism (possibly in the form of a rhyming couplet) and, while echoing the Latin *Et erit populus ita sacerdos,* introduces yet again the issue of those who hire and sustain bad priests, a matter which is not mentioned in the *Miroir* at this point.[47]

The English translator must have been reasonably learned as seen from his introduction into the *Mirror* of the Latin texts of scriptural quotations. As already noted, he translated (presumably with approval) Robert de Gretham's condemnation of the folly of using Latin in a work addressed to lay people. Doubtless he had in mind the vanity of any gratuitous show of Latin erudition and not the perfectly proper use of Latin (accompanied by a vernacular translation), in quoting scriptural texts. Robert, indeed, may have been of this view; the absence of such Latin texts in the *Miroir* may reflect no more than the fact that it would have been difficult if not impossible to accommodate them in his rhyming Anglo-Norman verse. Scriptural texts are given in translation in the *Miroir.* However, the English translator, having quoted them in Latin, usually takes care in giving his translation in English to follow the Latin where the Anglo-Norman verse translation was less precise. Thus, in the above passage, the word order of *populus* and *sacerdos* in the Latin *Et erit populus ita sacerdos* is followed in the English *swiche as þe lewed folk ben, swiche is þe preste,* and

---

[47] See Commentary, note 11/24–25, for further discussion.

not the reversed order of the Anglo-Norman *Tels est li prestres cum est li lais –* a change in the Anglo-Norman made, no doubt, for the sake of rhyme. Again the English *whan þe blinde ladeþ þe blinde, boþe fallen in þe diche* renders the Latin *Si cecus cecum ducat, ambo in foueam cadunt* and not the Anglo-Norman *L'un cius l'altre el fosse amaine.* Of course, since these Latin quotations are all translated, they could readily have been omitted when the *Mirror* was read to an audience.

Although the translator can write with a certain fluency (evident in his interpolations), and is perfectly capable of expanding, reducing and modifying his Anglo-Norman original, he sometimes has a tendency to render the French text into English in a virtually word-for-word manner. Thus 4/85: *Cil s'entremet de fol mester* becomes *he entermetteþ him of a fole mester* (5/10); 6/167–69 (U): *E cist enseigne verreiment / De vertuz tut l'entiffement* becomes *& þis scheweþ for soþe of vertuz al þe tiffeinge* (7/5); 6/212: *Co sunt sentences de maneres* becomes *þat ben sentens of mani maners* (7/25–26); 44/1409–10 (U): *en desmesure / De orguille* becomes *into out of mesure of pride* (45/32–33); 64/1924: *Tut facent il bien lur mester* becomes *al don hii wel her mister* (65/1–2); and so on.

The influence of French idiom is reflected in various kinds of expression in the English. Thus in *And it nas nouȝt long efter þat God ne toke veniaunce on him* (33/24–25), the negative in the second clause has been taken over from the French construction in 32/1012–13: *Ne demura pas longement / Que Deus n'en prist uengement.* Three manuscripts (HCP) preserve this reading, clearly the translator's original rendering; in the other manuscripts, the negative particle in the second clause has been removed. Another instance is *He ne douted him nouȝt of Ihesu þat he nas comen to sauen þe world* (41/12–13), which renders 40/1240–41: *Il ne duta pas de Iesu / Que pur sauuer ne fust uenu.* Likewise, French idiom is not infrequently reflected in the translator's choice of prepositions: e.g. the preposition 'to' in *þat he asked to his seruaunt aske we to our soules* (99/27), cf. 98/3072–73: *E co k'il quist a sun sergant / Querum as almes meintenant;* and *He ne schal neuer fayle to non bot ȝif he faile first to him* (21/36), cf. 20/679–80: *Il ne faudra ia a nuli / Fors ki primes faldra a li;* and *and he mai þanne help to holi cherche* (125/22–23), cf. 124/3857: *Poet a eglise mult ualeir;* and the preposition 'of' in *what schal ben of vs* (93/29), cf. 92/2878: *Qe en ert de nus; Now loke ouer al, of kinge, of prince & of countour* (27/25–26), cf. 26/808–809: *Kar ore esguardez tut entur / De rei, de prince, de cuntur;* and *For he is trubled of our gode dedes, as of þe newe tidinges, Herodes* (71/19–20), cf. 70/2148–49: *Kar il est trublez de nos odes / Cum fu de la nouele Herodes.* Again, the French construction with the definite article is carried over in *hii han þe fel white* (41/34), cf. 24/1285: *Blanc unt le quir;* and with the definite article and the adjective following the noun in *so haþ þe wiked þe hert brennand* (43/1), cf. 42/1290: *Si ad li fels le quor ardant;* and *He þat haþ þe flesche slepeand* (73/33), cf. 72/2252 (U): *E il qi ad la char endormi*, and in other instances. Occasional occurrences in the Middle English of the perfect instead of the preterite tense are probably carried over here from the Anglo-Norman: e.g. *ben gon* (25/11), cf. 24/716: *sunt ale*; *han brouȝt* (25/11), cf. 24/718: *unt mene*; *han strewed* (25/14), cf. 24/726: *unt ... estrame*; *han songen* (65/12–13), cf. 64/1946: *unt chante*; *ben comen* (69/2), cf. 68/2042: *sunt uenuz*; *han sen* (69/3), 68/2043: *unt uouz*. Further miscellaneous instances of characteristically French idiom carried over into the English are mentioned in the Commentary: e.g. the genitive *child Syon* ('child of Sion') 25/9, 24/712: *fille Syon*; possible influence of French gender, see notes to 21/3, 31/23, and 93/25; the absolute use of 'his' (meaning 'his followers'), see notes to 31/22 and 109/10.

A striking feature of the English translation is the sporadic omission of personal pronouns. Although the non-expression of pronouns is characteristic of some Middle English dialects, the extent to which pronouns are omitted in this English translation suggests a marked influence of French syntax. Sometimes pronouns (especially *he*, *hii* and *þai*) have later been added in H, sometimes incorrectly as, for example, in *And God makeþ of water wyn whan amendeþ our willes* (81/22), where 'we', instead of 'he', has been interlined after *whan* (cf. 80/2518–19: *E Deus de l'ewe le uin furma / Nos uolentez quant amenda*). Twice 'we' is left unexpressed: in *þat we mai gladen þe seyntes þat ben in heuen þat ben sori for oure harmes, þat mai sai wiþ hem in her blis* 29/30–31 (cf. 28/896–98: *Que poissum faire as seinz leesce / Ki dolent sunt pur nostre peresce, / E poissum dire en lur regnee*); and in *Amende we, lordinges, our liif þat may be in compaynie wiþ Ihesus, Marie sone* 61/10–11 (cf. 34/1802–03: *Amendums, seignurs, nostre uie, / Ke seiums od le fiz Marie*). In both instances the unexpressed 'we' may be understood from the preceding 'we'. It is noteworthy that in neither case has a pronoun been added later. In *Whi baptisettow whan nart Crist* 49/10 (cf. 28/1472: *Quei baptizes quant n'es Crist grant*), *þou* is unexpressed but later added in after *whan*. Occasionally non-expression of personal pronouns in the Anglo-Norman appears to have given rise to misunderstanding on the part of the English translator. Thus, 26/766–67: *Ore auez oi de la buche / Ki en dous maners nus [vos Hm] tuche* appears as *Now ȝe han herd of mouþe, þat ich haue touched ȝou in two maner* (27/6). Here it seems that the translator has wrongly assumed an unexpressed subject 'I' in taking *Ki ... vos tuche* as meaning 'which I have mentioned to you' rather than 'which affects you'.[48]

The recognition of the extent to which the influence of French is reflected in the Middle English rendering of the *Miroir* is not necessarily to be viewed as a criticism of the translator's ability. Considerable emphasis has been placed in recent years on the trilingual character of thirteenth- and fourteenth-century

[48]   For this sense, see *MED* touchen *v.*7.(a). See further, Commentary, note 27/6.

England.[49] In this period, in contrast to subsequent centuries, language boundaries were more permeable; to a considerable extent the three languages of medieval England – English, French and Latin – 'were in practice intertwined'.[50] This is evident with respect to vocabulary; how, otherwise, could almost half of Chaucer's vocabulary have derived from French, partly from continental but, significantly, also from insular sources?[51] It is therefore unexceptional that a Middle English translator at this time should have carried over much of his vocabulary from his Anglo-Norman source. Moreover, it is to be doubted if he would have thought of words like *bordel* and *countour* as specifically French rather than English, or as having a more restricted semantic range in Middle English as distinct from Anglo-Norman.[52] Again, there probably existed considerably more overlap in ordinary French and English usage than has been commonly recognised. Thus, at first sight, the translation (quoted above) of 4/85: *Cil s'entremet de fol mester* as *he entermetteþ him of a fole mester* (5/10) might seem awkward, almost half-changed French. However, as *MED* testifies, the verb *entermeten* (used reflexively, and with the preposition 'of') meaning 'to undertake', the adjective *fol* meaning 'foolish', and the noun *mester* meaning 'task', were all well established in Middle English.[53]

On the whole, the views and concerns characteristic of Robert de Gretham's *Miroir* continue to find expression in the Middle English *Mirror*. This is hardly surprising: the translation of a text of this length must have been a daunting task and hardly to have been undertaken if the contents of the *Miroir* had not been to the translator's taste. Nevertheless, passages interpolated or omitted, and smaller additions or alterations at the level of single words or phrases, do reflect significant changes in tone, emphasis and point of view in the Middle English text. Perhaps the most valuable part of the *Miroir* is its prologue, for here central issues concerning the preacher, his task, and the relationship of priest and people are addressed. The prologue is in two parts. The first part, which ends at 6/189, is called *Li prologes*. Robert begins by addressing a certain lady Aline, at whose request he has undertaken his task.[54] Many people, he says, like poems dealing with adventure and history. Such writings are vain and false; but even if true, they are worthless as they do not benefit the soul. Robert offers as alternative reading, pleasing to God and of comfort to the soul, translations of the gospels into French followed by brief expositions based on the Church Fathers. Latin is excluded, for it is folly, says Robert, to address lay people in

---

[49] See, for example, Rothwell 1994, and Trotter 2000.
[50] Rothwell 1994:45.
[51] See Rothwell 1994:55.
[52] See Commentary, notes 19/10 and 27/26.
[53] See *MED* entermeten *v.*, fol *adj.*, and mister *n.*
[54] See 4/99–104.

Latin; everyone should be instructed in the language he understands. He invites correction of his language and rhymes and states that he will avoid misleading eloquence in favour of speaking the truth plainly. The book's title, *Mirur*, is announced and the reasons for that title fully explained. Prayers for the author are requested. In the Middle English version all mention of and references to Aline are removed. This makes little difference, however, for, in fact, Robert de Gretham aimed at a wider, largely uneducated lay audience, as did the English translator.[55]

In one respect, however, the Middle English version at this point does differ significantly from the Anglo-Norman. Robert de Gretham, anticipating a hostile reception for his work, states his wish to withhold his name.[56] The corresponding Middle English version reads:

> My name ne wil Y nouȝt say for þe enemys þat mihȝt heren it & miȝht drawen ȝour hertes fram gode þat it had wille to heren. For it is þe maner of þe enemys to ben gruchand & noyouse & wil bleþlich coniecten þe wordes of holi writte & wil tellen it forþ on her maner & ne letten nouȝt for to blame oþer. Þe wikked weneþ for to amenden it for to blamen þe gode & coniecten hem. (5/28–33)

The Anglo-Norman passage has not been carried across automatically into the Middle English. 4/144: *bons escriz* becomes specifically *holi writte*, and 4/138: *les enuius* ('the envious') becomes *þe enemys*.[57] The sense of the last couplet of the Anglo-Norman passage, 4/149–50, *The wicked man thinks to better himself by denigrating the wise*, is also altered in the English, where *amenden*, now in the sense of 'emend', has as its object 'it', seemingly holy writ, once again.[58] In order to discourage the envious 'so that they should not deprive us of that good thing [i.e. the gospel translations and simple exposition] of which they wish to say nothing', Robert de Gretham does not wish to mention his name, not, at least, 'as yet' (4/137: *encore*).[59] The translator withholds his name without qualification. He does so, he says, because of 'enemies who might hear it and draw your hearts from good who wished to hear it'. Clearly opposition to popular exposition based on scriptural translation was nothing new, but it seems that the translator was intent on safe-guarding his own anonymity, perhaps fearing even greater hostility than Robert had anticipated. Whereas Robert did

---

[55]  See 4/86 and 20/623–28. Direct address in the sermons is usually to *seignurs* (ME *lordinges*). Various other modes of address are used: e.g. 48/1498–99: *seignurs, / Prestres, e clers e sermunurs* (ME *lordinges, prestes & clerkes & prechours*) in sermon 4, and 88/2698–99: *bon enfant, / E iuuencel e enueillant* (ME *ȝe ȝonge children, ȝonge men & eld men*) in sermon 6.

[56]  See 4/137–50.

[57]  Conceivably minim confusion could have led to a misreading of Anglo-Norman *enuius* as *enemies*.

[58]  See *MED* amenden *v.* 1. (b).

[59]  For this plausible interpretation of 'that good thing' (4/139 *le bien*), see Deanesly 1920:150.

subsequently name himself, not only at the end of the homilies, but also in a request for prayers towards the end of the prologue, neither Robert's name nor that of the translator is mentioned anywhere in the English version.[60] Nevertheless, it would appear that the translator, by his use of the plural pronoun *hem*, may have intended to associate himself with Robert, albeit anonymously, in his request for prayers:

> & þat God ȝif hem þe liue þat euer schal last *þat for hem þat it ordeined & made* besechen. Amen. (21/10–12)

A sense of the translator's personal involvement in his task emerges from the two additions he makes to his abbreviated rendering of the Anglo-Norman text in the following passage:

> I ne make nouȝt for losangerie, ne for pride, ne for *to be praised þurth* clergie, ne for to haue worschip in þis liif; *I þenche to anoþer lond þer better ȝeldinge of mede is þan in þis world,* & ich it make for to aquiten me bodi & soule fram encumberment, *& to speke for me þer Y ne mai ne can.* (15/20–24)[61]

The second part of the prologue (6/190–22/694) is devoted to an exposition of such important topics as the nature of holy writ, the duties and status of preachers, the duties of lay people, God's vengeance on a sinful people, and the role of the Holy Spirit in preaching. The nature of holy writ is expounded in terms of traditional comparisons. It is like a fruit tree in which the fruit is hidden by dense foliage; as by shaking the tree the fruit falls to the ground and may be eaten, so by exposition the hidden truths of scripture are revealed. Again, holy writ is like a dark cloud; but as when it rains the earth is refreshed, so too, when the preacher expounds holy writ, what was previously obscure is revealed to man's understanding: hence the need for preachers. The translator gives a fairly close rendering of the Anglo-Norman text until Robert turns to the traditional three-fold division of society into knights, priests and the common people. At this point the translator departs from his source in the following passage:

> And þerfor God ordeined þre ordres in holi chirche, of winners, & of defendours, & *of asailours.* God haþ sette þe winners for to feden alle wiþ her trauaile, & *þat ben þe commen puple.* Þe defendours: þat ben þe kniȝtes þat schul defenden *hem & al þe lond fram iuel.* And þe *asailours:* þat ben men *of holi chirche* þat schuld techen *boþe þat on & þat oþer wiþ fair speche & wiþ reddur.* 3if þat hii deden eni sinne & trespast aȝeines God, hii it schuld adresce hem to God ward; ac as þe world scheppeþ now hii ben þe most dele rauissours & rauis þe folk fram God ward boþe wiþ her ensaumple ȝeueinge & wiþ her werkes. Ac þo þat ben gode men & trewe & kepen þe law of God, hii ben of Goddes chesinge, & God himself seit: 'He þat doþe hem ani harme, hii don it to himself.' Ac al þat ben proude, oþer coueitouse, oþer licherouse, þes ben Antecristes chesinge & haue þe toure of holi chirche aȝeines Goddes wille bot þat he suffreþ it. And who þat

---

[60]   See 20/633–34.
[61]   Cf. 14/455–64.

*mainteneþ swiche men, hii schal gon to helle wiþ hem, bot ʒif hii amenden hem.*
(9/10–25)[62]

The interpolations in the English here introduce in the strongest terms a contrast
between the *gode men & trewe* who *kepen þe law of God* and who are *Goddes
chesinge*, and the men of Holy Church who, as the world now fares, are for the
most part *rauissours & rauis þe folk fram God ward boþe wiþ her ensaumple
ʒeueinge & wiþ her werkes*. Such are proud, covetous and lecherous; they are
*Antecristes chesinge*; they occupy the tower of Holy Church against God's will.
The parallel passage in the Anglo-Norman text not only offers no criticism of
the clergy at this point, but stresses that it is an offence against God to show
disrespect for, or to fail to meet the needs of, those ordained by him. By
contrast, in the English text, it is only *the good men and true who keep God's
law* to whom harm is counted by God as harm to himself; and, having made this
point, the translator returns to 'those who are Antichrist's chosen' with the
sternest of warnings to any who maintain such men: 'they shall go to hell with
them unless they amend themselves'. Rhetoric of this kind, with its designation
of wicked priests as 'Antichrist's chosen', is typical of the translator's
interpolations.

The three orders in the Anglo-Norman are called *guaignurs*, *defendurs*, and
*conseillurs*, in the English, *winners*, *defendours* and, remarkably, *asailours*. The
word *asailour* was rare in Middle English. *MED* records only one instance in
the sense 'chastiser' required here, and that is from the *Recluse,* a late
fourteenth-century redaction of the *Ancrene Riwle*. Intriguingly, this work is
found in one of the six *Mirror* manuscripts.[63] Moreover, the very context in
which *assailours* occurs in the *Recluse* is identical – an interpolated passage
which begins *For þis londe is departed in þre in wynners & in defendours & in
assaillours*.[64] Did the interpolator in the *Recluse* perhaps use the word
*assailours* here having come across it in this same context in the *Mirror*? And
could it even have been that this word originated here in the *Mirror* from the
translator having misread an abbreviation sign for 'con' as the letter 'a' in an
abbreviated writing of *conseillurs* here in his Anglo-Norman exemplar? It is
interesting to note that in the revised version of the *Mirror* in Ha, which is
characteristically less astringent in tone, *asaillours* is replaced by *assoillours*.
Perhaps the Harley reviser did not recognise the use of *asaillour* in the new
sense 'chastiser', or perhaps he did not care for so harsh a view of the role of the
clergy, preferring the notion of 'one who assoils' to that of 'one who assails'. [65]

Robert de Gretham turns next to the duty of ordained clergy to teach. God's
judgement will be hard, he says, on those who will neither teach themselves nor

---

[62]  Cf. 8/255–68.
[63]  MS Cambridge, Magdalene College, Pepys 2498.
[64]  Quoted in Colledge 1939:134.
[65]  See further, Commentary, notes 9/11 and 9/14.

others. *He þat schuld be riȝtfulliche man of ordre, he ne most drede non of þes*, adds the translator, making the point that only when the duty of teaching is fulfilled is a cleric truly (*riȝtfulliche*) to be counted a *man of ordre*, and suggesting that such true clerics suffered hostility from their false brethren (9/29–30). However, his observation that he *ne may nouȝt say for sorowe on mani þat þer ben now swiche þat louen þe order* is translated word for word from Robert's text and has, indeed, the ring of a perennial complaint (9/33–34). The failure of many priests to teach results in a sinful people and God's vengeance. Priests, says Robert, as the eyes of the church, should guide the people by the example of their good works. However, when the clergy is blinded by the power of worldly pleasures and covetousness, it is no wonder if lay people are corrupted. In turn, because the people are sinful and truculent, God causes preachers to be silent. Again, at this point, the English translator interpolates, partly to clarify the line of thought, but typically to underline the distinction between good and bad preachers, and to accentuate his condemnation of the latter. To Robert's statement that God causes preachers to be silent, the translator adds, by way of explanation:

> þo þat ben gode men; ac þe oþer þat liuen after delices of þe world, he mai suffre hem speken ynouȝ, for fewe oþer non schal do þe better for her speche þeiȝ hii tellen hem al holi writ. And swyche prechours, ich vnderstond, be mani now, & þe folk nis neuer þe better, bot euer lenger þe wers. Ac þe gode men þat queme God, he wil do hem hold hem stille. (13/7–11)

The idea the God should silence good preachers in order to take vengeance on a wicked people may seem harsh, but the translator appears to revel in this notion to the point of losing control of his syntax:

> For þat is wratþe for soþe whan he wiþdraweþ his techinge, þat he nil nouȝt þat his folk ben tauȝt so þat he wiþdroweþ his veniaunce, þat he ne toke nouȝt wreche: & for þat he wil take wreche, he nil nouȝt þat þe folk be chastist wiþ his ȝerde. (13/28–31)

The Anglo-Norman passage rendered by these lines is:

> Kar co est ire ueiraiment
> Quant il sustrait docuement,
> Quant il ne uolt endoctriner
> Pur sa uigne eschiuer;      veniance] U
> Kar Deus cel home pas nen aime
> Qu'il par doctrine ne reclaime,
> Ki il ne uolt endoctriner
> Ne par sun flael chastier. (12/397–404)

On the assumption that the above Anglo-Norman text (with the reading *veniance* of U in the fourth line) represents the text the translator used, and that the reading of H is substantially correct, the English version of this passage seems to reveal a translator carried away with this theme of God's vengeance to the point of barely comprehensible repetition. The milder sense of the last four lines of the Anglo-Norman quotation – 'For God does not love that man whom he does not reclaim by teaching, whom he does not wish to teach nor chastise with his rod' – is lost in the harsh vengefulness of the English: 'And because he (God) wishes to take vengeance, he does not wish that the people should be chastised with his rod'.

A major theme to engage Robert's attention towards the end of the prologue is the presence of the Holy Spirit which allows the preacher to admonish the wise, to teach others even if he cannot rule himself, and which makes praise for the preacher himself inappropriate. This train of thought brings him to the traditional and orthodox concept that the preacher, even if immoral, may be considered a valid vehicle of God's word and sacraments. This view is faithfully carried over into the English as follows:

> Men owe to louen þe prechour for him, & more for þe loue of God, for þat he techeþ vs þe way to heuen. For what þat he be, ȝitte he is Goddes messanger. (19/15–17)[66]

However, recalling the translator's sternly critical views of priests and preachers, one senses that he is ill at ease at this point, for quite abruptly he launches into the following interpolation which, to say the least, fits awkwardly here and is out of keeping with the theme of loving preachers for the love of God:

> *for þe fendes ben sumtime sent for to don Godes messages. It telleþ þat þe deuel prechede on a tyme in mannes likkenes to þe folk, & so he seyd to hem whan he hade preched, þat he was a deuel & was sent þider for to prechen hem for hii had hadde so mani prechours aforn & weren euer þe lenger þe more schrewes, & were so harded in her schrewednesse, þat hii ne miȝht nouȝt ben amended, & þerfor he was sent for to prechen hem.* (19/17–23)

The same tension emerges in a much more explicit way in sermon 4, for the fourth Sunday in Advent. This sermon contains one of the seventeen exemplary tales found in the *Miroir* and, in turn, in the Middle English *Mirror*. The tale here concerns a certain holy hermit who was informed that the priest who was accustomed to say mass for him lived a wicked life.[67] He therefore decided to dispense with the priest's services. The following night the hermit dreamt that he was dying of thirst and lacked the strength to draw water from the only well to be found in the whole world. Suddenly a leper, foul, horrible and naked, appeared holding a chain to which was attached a golden cup, and drew up water and drank. But the hermit would not approach the leper. Then a voice said to him: 'Hermit, what you are thinking is foolish. Is not the cup of fine gold and the chain bright and shining, the water clear and the well excellent? Is the water

---

66    Cf. 18/579–82.
67    See 51/9–25.

any the worse on account of the person who has drawn it up? No more is God's service the worse for the priest who undertakes it.' In the brief interpretation which follows the tale in the *Miroir*, and which is carried over exactly into the English, it is stated that no priests are to be despised, that even a sinful priest may have good will towards God, and that no-one is free from sin as we were all born in sin. At this point, however, the English translator interpolates the following passage:

> *Vnderstondeþ nou3t þis tale bot for ensaumple; soþe it may wel be, bot holi writt nis it nou3t. And herfor Y telle now þis efterwarde for sum mi3t heren it & do sinne þerþurth in þis maner. As bleþliche wold a man susteine an iuel man as a gode, & so he mi3t be lorn þerþurth. And þerfor Y schal say 3ou hou 3e schal vnderstonde þis bi holi writ. 3e ne schul nou3t despise no man ne 3e ne schal nou3t lett to heren swiche a mannes masse 3if þat 3e not nou3t bi him bot gode, for to 3ou þe masse nis neuer þe wers. Ac if 3e wist it & mi3t amend him, it wer wers to 3ou; for 3e dede dedlich sinne for 3e mainten him in his sinne; for he is confort in his sinne as 3e bere him as god felawchip as anoþer man. 3ef he be a gode man þat doþ þe masse, 3our bedes ben þe better herd for his bidding; & 3if he be a sinful man, þat is to say, liþ in his sinne, his bede ne profiteþ nou3t, for God nil nou3t here him. As Ihesu Crist seyt þurth Ysaye: si extenderitis manus vestras & c – þat is, þei3 3e held vp 3our hondes & make manifold 3our bones, Y nil 3ou nou3t heren, for 3our hondes ben blodi, þat is, 3our werkes ben ful of sinne. Now Gregorii seyt also: 'As ner as 3our mouþe is worldlich filþ, as fer it is fram God whan 3e speke to him.' David also: iniquitatem si aspexi in corde meo, non exaudiet deus – 3if wickednesse be in myn hert, þat is, sinne, God ne hereþ me nou3t. More hereof Y mi3t telle 3ou michel, for God seyt: 'Drawe 3ou to holi & 3e schal ben holi: drawe 3ou to schrewes & 3e schal ben schrewes.' Hereof nil ich telle namore.*[68]

In this interpolation, the translator introduces a crucial distinction: if you are ignorant of the sins of a priest, his prayers on your behalf may be efficacious; but if you know him to be sinful, then his prayers are of no avail. Since the hermit in the tale dismissed his priest precisely because he knew he was wicked (for so he had been informed), the import of the tale – i.e. that the priest's mass was none the less valid – is, thereby, negated. But the great danger that the translator is again at pains to stress here, as he had done repeatedly in the prologue, is what he sees as the deadly sin of maintaining an evil priest.

This interpolation also raises the question of authority, scriptural or other. On the matter of authority, Robert de Gretham is clear and specific from the outset:

> Les ewangelies i uerrez
> Mult proprement enromancez,
> E puis les exposiciuns
> Brefment sulum les sainz expuns;

---

[68]    See 51/31–53/17.

> Kar sachez n'i ad nul mot dit
> Que li sainz n'aient ainz escrit:
> Io l'ai excerpe e estrait
> Des escriz ke li sainz vnt fait. (4/71–78)

His sermons were based both on the Sunday gospels which he translated into French (possibly the first gospel translations in French), and on the writings of the saints, that is, the Church Fathers.[69] The translator renders this passage as follows:

> Þe goddespelles ȝe schul finden herein, first þe tixt, & þan þe vndoinge schortlich. And wit ȝe wel, þer nis nouȝt on word writen in þat it nis *in holi writ* & out of þe bokes þat þis holi men þat weren toforn vs an made. (5/4–7)

Two points of particular interest are to be noted. The first is the English translator's emphasis on the importance of scripture as indicated by the addition of the words *holi writ* here and elsewhere in the prologue. The second, however, is his willingness to countenance the authority of *þe bokes þat þis holi men þat weren toforn vs an made*. Moreover, characteristic of the *Miroir* is Robert de Gretham's generous use of exemplary tales, and the translator makes no demur at including them in the *Mirror*. It would therefore seem that while the translator has a tendency to stress the importance of scripture, his stance on the matter of authority is, on the whole, fairly traditional and orthodox. Yet, as the interpolation in sermon 4 shows, he is ready to appeal to the primacy of scriptural authority when faced with an issue about which he has strong views: the tale of the hermit may, he allows, be true as a story, *bot holi writt nis it nouȝt*. However, in supporting his argument he is happy to quote not only scripture but also St. Gregory.

In conclusion, it is clear that many of the issues which in the thirteenth century were uppermost in Robert de Gretham's mind – a desire to offer simple and unadorned scriptural exposition based on gospel translations, an expectation that such an undertaking would attract hostility, dismissal of the folly of addressing a lay audience in Latin, condemnation of idle priests more concerned with worldly pleasures than self instruction and the teaching of others, insistence on the good standing of the devout and humble poor before God in contrast to that of the greedy, arrogant rich – were of no less concern to the later fourteenth-century Middle English translator. The latter, however, evidently feared that he and his work would meet with more virulent hostility. He more insistently focused attention on holy writ, was markedly more vehement in his condemnation of wicked clergy, 'Antichrist's chosen', and had perceptibly harsher views *vis à vis* the chastising role of the clergy and God's vengeance. He also warned repeatedly and menacingly against the sin of maintaining evil priests and had reservations concerning the traditional concept

---

[69]   See Marshall 1971:8.

of the validity of priestly efficacy by virtue of office irrespective of personal integrity.

Is there a smell of Lollardry in such views and in such language as God's *versus* Antichrist's chosen? Is the Middle English *Mirror* to be counted as a Wycliffite text? One thing is immediately evident: Robert de Gretham's thirteenth-century *Miroir* amply testifies to the fact that radical sentiments were no novelty in later fourteenth-century England. If the changes in emphasis in the Middle English *Mirror* may sometimes be harsh in tone, the translator's views, unlike those characteristic of Lollard writings, remain relatively balanced and moderate, rather than extreme. Thus, if at one point stress is placed on individual responsibility through good works in the achieving of salvation, at another, following Robert de Gretham, the efficacy of the prayers of 'priests and clerks' on our behalf is held to be important.[70] His condemnation of immoral clergy does not prevent the translator from repeating Robert's view that as clear water can be conveyed through a muddy gutter so God's word may also be channelled through an evil priest.[71] In the case of the tale of the holy hermit discussed above, the translator may have qualified Robert's view, but his position seems to be that priestly efficacy is compromised only when the recipient of the sacrament *knows* the priest to be of evil life. And though he is quick to point out that such a tale is not holy writ, he also allows that 'it may well be true'.[72] Indeed, as remarked above, the translator shows no reluctance to retain exemplary tales (little favoured by Lollards), in his translation. In placing the *Mirror* in the tradition of later fourteenth-century radical thinking some importance attaches to the view taken of its date. The *Miroir* is a long work and must have taken some considerable time to translate. The translator's work antedates any of the surviving *Mirror* manuscripts. Even though the earliest copies may have been made soon after the completed translation, if H, one of the earliest manuscripts, may be dated *circa* 1380, it would seem likely that the Middle English translation was made, at the latest, towards the beginning of the final quarter of the fourteenth century, that is, at a time which would seem too early for the *Mirror* translator to have experienced the impact of Wyclif, or, at least, of his English writings.[73] It may be added that the Type II language of four (and possibly five) of the surviving *Mirror* manuscripts is not characteristic of Wycliffite writings.[74] Langland also cried out against the *Antecrist and hise*.[75]

---

[70] See Commentary, note 37/14–17 and 37/18–22.

[71] See 17/28–19/1.

[72] See 51/31–32.

[73] See p. lxviii.

[74] According to Samuels (1963:85), Type I was the language typical of Lollard and Wycliffite texts: 'The Lollards, naturally, although they cannot be said to have invented it, were a powerful influence in spreading it, in their bibles, sermons and tracts; once they had adopted it, they copied it faithfully, probably fanatically so'.

[75] *Piers Plowman,* B-Text, Passus XIX, 220; see Schmidt 1978:242.

It may be that the changes in emphasis and attitude the translator introduced into the Middle English *Mirror* are rather to be taken as reflecting convictions of wider currency in the age of Langland than as anything that would call specifically for the label 'Wycliffite'.

## The Sermon Cycle, its Organisation and Use

The number of vernacular sermon collections extant from the late fourteenth century is not very large, and there are many more collections written in Latin than in English.[76] In terms of size the *Mirror* is comparable with other contemporary vernacular collections such as the *Speculum Sacerdotale* which contains sixty-nine sermons, and the fifty-five Middle English sermons contained in MS BL Royal 18 B.xxiii.[77] However, neither of these collections resembles the *Mirror* in terms of scope. The *Speculum Sacerdotale* is a collection of homilies on the saints, major festivals, and penitential seasons, but does not contain a sermon for every Sunday of the year, and does not base its contents on the gospel pericopes. Likewise, the collection contained in BL Royal 18 B.xxiii does not contain a coherent system of sermons for the church year either, and four of the sermons included here have been identified as the work of other authors.[78] Though these collections seem substantial in their coverage, they appear small when placed beside Mirk's *Festial* and the Northern Homily cycle, and are utterly dwarfed by the vast collection of English Wycliffite sermons.[79] In this regard the complexity of the *Mirror*'s manuscript tradition falls midway between collections such as the *Speculum Sacerdotale* which exists only in a single manuscript (BL Additional 36791), and the Northern Homily cycle which in its original version exists in twenty manuscripts.

The *Mirror* cycle consists of a prologue and sixty sermons. The survival of the full cycle in the majority of the extant witnesses is an indication of its integrity.[80] For the most part the English manuscripts of the *Mirror* regularly preserve the prologue and all sixty sermons, though exceptionally, sermon 5 is absent from R and sermon 60 from P; in each of these cases, for whatever reason, the scribe chose not to copy these sermons. Other lacunae in the extant copies of the English sermons arise from physical deficiencies in the

---

[76]   As noted by Spencer 1993:7–8.
[77]   See respectively the editions by Weatherly 1936 and Ross 1940.
[78]   Three have been identified as the work of Mirk, and one as that of Thomas Wimbledon.
[79]   The expanded versions of Mirk's collection and the Northern Homily cycle have 90 and 117 items respectively; there are 294 sermons in five different cycles in the English Wycliffite collection. For editions see respectively Erbe 1905; Nevanlinna 1972; Hudson 1983.
[80]   For a definition of the sermon cycle and its distinction from a random sermon collection, see Wenzel 1996:7–21.

manuscripts such as the casual loss of leaves; this is most extensive in the case of R which according to Lester (1985:45) has lost at least nineteen leaves in addition to the eight which survive in N. The French manuscripts of the *Miroir* have suffered more damage, and several are now clearly incomplete. The fullest version of the *Miroir* cycle is preserved in Hm, which lacks the prologue but has copies of sermons 1–58; two other manuscripts, $W^2$ and U, have the prologue and sermons 1–53; and L, though both acephalous and acaudal, nevertheless contains almost all of the cycle (sermons 3–50). The evidence of the French manuscript tradition therefore also indicates that the sermons were planned and disseminated as a coherent collection.

The scope of the cycle is made clear in the prologue. The author of the *Miroir*, Robert de Gretham, states that:

> Les ewangelies des domnees
> Io ai en franceis translatees
> E des festes as sainz partie (14/423–25).

The translator of the *Mirror* in turn says that he has translated into English *þe godspelles of sonnendays & a parti of the seyntes þat ben in heuen* (15/8–9). These statements reflect the contents of the English cycle which consists of fifty-three sermons on the Sunday gospel pericopes and seven further sermons. Of the latter, two belong to the Proper of Saints (those for the Annunciation and Christmas Day), and four belong to the Commons of Saints (those commemorating the birthdates of an apostle, a martyr, many martyrs, and a confessor and pope); the final sermon, for Quinquagesima, is a Sunday epistle rather than a Sunday gospel sermon. In the French tradition, five of these further sermons are found in Hm, and one in O. Since it seems to have been Gretham's intention to produce some sermons other than those based on the Sunday gospel pericopes (*des festes as sainz partie*), there is no reason to doubt the integrity of these sermons and their place within the sermon cycle. The apparent uniqueness of Hm may be nothing more than an accident of survival, for it is clear that at least three of the French manuscripts ($W^1OL$) are now incomplete, and we cannot therefore be sure of the extent of their original contents.[81] Alternatively, the presence of the further sermons in Hm and O alone might be attributed to circumstances of transmission. It is possible that Gretham wrote these sermons at a point when the earlier portions of the cycle had already been given out to copyists, thus giving rise to a situation where the further sermons were only transmitted in one branch of the Anglo-Norman textual tradition. Given the presence of the seven further sermons in the majority of the English manuscripts, the English translator of the text must have worked from a French manuscript which belonged to this branch.

---

[81] It should be noted that in O sermon 55 (for Christmas Day) occurs between sermons 5 and 6, that is, at the proper liturgical juncture.

For the most part the arrangement of the sermons follows the normal order of the liturgical year, beginning with Advent. The only non-dominical occasions covered are Christmas Eve, Epiphany, and Ascension. The material is for a theoretical rather than an actual ecclesiastical year, with the maximum number of lections for the periods after the octave of the Epiphany and after Trinity. Although the variation in the date of Easter makes possible a greater number of Sundays after Trinity, the Sarum missal did not provide further readings, and the material in the *Mirror* agrees with the Sarum provision. The gospel readings of the Sarum use form the basis for the sermons. Each sermon begins with a full translation of the gospel reading for the day.[82] Usually the Latin incipit of the lection is cited, and the liturgical occasion is also specified in the sermon heading, so that each sermon is firmly connected with the occasion on which the biblical passage would have been read. Robert de Gretham presumably worked from the Vulgate when preparing his translations of the gospel pericopes. The important task of transferring God's word to the vernacular carried with it the weighty obligation of achieving both clarity and accuracy, but in Gretham's case these demands were further complicated by his choice of rhyming verse couplets as a medium for the *Miroir*. The need to maintain the metre and rhyme scheme must surely have led to some compromises in terms of accuracy of translation, if only in the necessary use of line-fillers. Nevertheless the resulting versions of the gospel readings were good enough to satisfy the English translator of the *Mirror*, who relied entirely on Gretham's text when rendering the pericopes into his own vernacular of English. It is clear that this decision was not based on any linguistic deficiency on the part of the English translator. In the prologue, the English translator reinserted the Latin citations, usually scriptural quotations, which Gretham's text had expounded but not cited directly. Furthermore, the English translator then took care to match his expositions to the newly-cited Latin, rather than following exactly what Gretham had said. The only English mansucript where the Latin scriptural quotations have not been reintroduced into the text of the prologue is Ha. This omission cannot be explained as a simple failure on the part of the rubricator, since no text spaces have been left to accommodate such readings. A further distinguishing feature of Ha, and another deliberate choice of its compiler, is that in this manuscript alone, the gospel passages for each Sunday have been retranslated. Rather than risk perpetuating errors introduced by layer upon layer of translation, the Harley compiler returned to the root of the Vulgate and rendered the gospel readings anew; the resulting translations are noticeably more succint and accurate. As well as demonstrating his engagement with the text, this course of action shows that the Harley compiler was deeply conscious

---

[82]  Full translations of the gospel texts are also given in the English Wycliffite sermons, but there the translations are usually spread throughout the entire sermon.

of the responsibility to provide his readers with the best possible version of holy writ.

As noted above, the majority of manuscripts contain the full cycle of sermons. There is no instance of rogue sermons being inserted into the sequence, as happens in some of the manuscripts of Mirk's *Festial*, nor are single sermons or small groups of sermons from the *Mirror* selected for independent copying elsewhere.[83] The operation of such selection occurs only in a very minor way in each tradition. Firstly, some of the exempla from the *Miroir* are extracted and copied into two other anthologies, though the sermons themselves are not treated in this way. Secondly, part of the prologue to the *Mirror* has been used as the basis of a tract on translation, the short text entitled *A commendacioun of holy writ in our owne langage* which is found only in a single manuscript (I). After beginning with a quotation based on lines 7/19–28 of the prologue, *Holy writ haþ þe lyknesse of a tree þat beriþ fruyt note peer or appel...*, and approximating the text of the prologue, the Cambridge compiler proceeds to adapt and expand upon this until it is wholly refashioned into a different text. The adaptation is so selective that overall only about one-sixth of the tract actually depends upon its ostensible source, and the resulting text is quite different and not collatable with the relevant portion of the *Mirror*. Aside from these isolated instances, the *Mirror* cycle remains an integrated and exclusive collection, though there is one significant exception to this state of affairs. Apart from P, which is a large anthology, the manuscripts which belong to the *alpha* branch of the *Mirror*'s textual tradition contain only the sermon cycle. In the manuscripts of the *beta* branch, on the other hand, the *Mirror* keeps company with a variety of other texts, including the Catholic and Pauline Epistles and Wycliffite Gospels in B, and other, unrelated, sermons in English and Latin in R. Moreover, in the three *beta* manuscripts of the *Mirror* a substantial body of additional material occurs immediately after sermon 60.[84] This corpus consists of seventeen items, which are either sermons or shorter pieces on devotional topics. Several of the sermons belong to the Proper of Saints, commemorating the Vigil of St. Peter and St. Paul, Candlemas, the Assumption, Michaelmas, and Holy Innocents; others deal with topics such as the second coming, signs of doomsday, and the last judgment, and one is for the occasion of the dedication of a church. Some elements of basic instruction according to the model outlined by Pecham, such as the creed and pater noster, are also covered. In each manuscript the sequence ends with a discussion of the ten commandments, though the text of the latter seems to be different in each case.[85] The result is that the *beta* manuscripts might be regarded as more

---

[83]    See Wakelin 1967:93–188.

[84]    For details see the checklist of sermons.

[85]    It is interesting to note that a discussion of the ten commandments (which does not appear to be the same as any of these three) follows the conclusion of the *Mirror* in P.

complete manuals for spiritual instruction, for the laity or low-ranking clergy. Of these additional items, fourteen occur in B, thirteen in R, and six in Ha; the ordering of the material varies. There is no equivalent to this material in the *Miroir* tradition, and significantly the additional texts occur only in one branch of the English textual tradition. It would seem that at an early stage these texts became attached to the *Mirror* cycle in this branch of its transmission, and that this association was perpetuated by later copyists.

There is also something to be learned from the physical appearance of the *Mirror* manuscripts. The Anglo-Norman manuscripts (mostly thirteenth-century, some fourteenth-century) are generally finer than their later English cousins. With the notable exception of L, their compilers used better quality parchment, and added more decoration to their texts. In one instance, G, the habitual use of red and blue is varied by the addition of green, and gold is also used in the large initials which introduce the prologue and first sermon. Compared with the English manuscripts, layout seems to have been more regulated – for instance there is less variation in the number of lines per page, and all aspects of the French manuscripts seem to indicate that their production was the work of professionally-trained scribes for a well-to-do audience. An inscription in Hm records the price once paid for this manuscript: *ex pensis augusti prima septi mana xiiii s. xi d.* (fourteen shillings and eleven pence), probably an indication of its origin in a commercial or monastic scriptorium.[86] In contrast the English manuscripts are plainer, and are obviously more low-budget productions.[87] Most have the double column format, possibly influenced by the layout of the French manuscripts which all have this; only B and Ha arrange the text into a single column. The English manuscripts are also on the whole larger than the Anglo-Norman. One (P), is significantly larger than the others; otherwise there is not much variation in size, and H and C are virtual twins. Though the *Mirror* might have been read aloud, publicly, whether from the pulpit by a professional preacher, or within the household, only one of the English manuscripts, Ha, would seem to have been designed to facilitate such reading since it alone has a large, legible script. Most of the English manuscripts are the work of single hands – the exceptions are B and R which are group productions by five and four hands respectively.[88] However, the most interesting

---

[86]  f. 67$^v$, noted by Laird 1940:603.

[87]  Hudson (1983:189) comments on the unimpressive appearance of many vernacular sermon collections of this date. Whilst she is right to single out R as a typical example, the other manuscripts of the *Mirror*, though by no means luxury productions, are somewhat better than her overview might suggest.

[88]  Opinions about the appearance of B have varied. Hudson (1983:189) describes the manuscript as a 'substantial volume', but complains that it lacks the ordered regularity displayed by most of the manuscripts of the English Wycliffite sermons. More recently, however, Alan Fletcher has commented that 'the quality format and *mise en page* of certain *Myrrour* manuscripts – a notable instance being Oxford, Bodleian Library, MS

aspect of all is that the appearance of the English manuscripts confirms the split in the textual tradition discussed above.[89] The members of the *alpha* tradition, HCP, have modest decoration using blue and red, with in-filled initials decorated with flourishing and tracery, often in the contrasting colour. In contrast, the *beta* manuscripts, BRHa, are noticeably plainer, using only red, and their overall use of colour is more sparing, with such rubricated initials as are present lacking any further decoration.

Whereas many sermon manuscripts have marginal apparatus indicating the main subjects under discussion, the location of authorities, incidence of exempla, and so on, there is almost none of this in the manuscript tradition of either the *Miroir* or the *Mirror*. Sometimes the beginning of the exposition of the gospel reading is signalled in the French manuscripts by the marginal note 'Oml' (for 'omelie'), and in the English by the words 'þe exposicion' used in the main body of the text. The English manuscripts also sometimes indicate the presence of the exempla by adding the marginal note 'A tale', and very occasionally the original scribe has added the instruction 'nota' to the margin. More usually, any annotation or underlining has been carried out by later hands. The particular process of revision to which H has been subjected is discussed fully below.

The author of the *Miroir* names himself as Robert de Gretham. There have been various attempts to identify this figure, based on investigations of his Christian name, the place-name, and the name of his patron, Dame Aline. It has long been suggested that he might be the same person as the author of *Corset*, who addresses his text to *seignor alain*, and who refers to himself as *Rober son chapelain*.[90] *Corset* is a treatise on the seven sacraments, written in Anglo-Norman verse, and contemporary with the *Miroir*; linguistic studies have demonstrated that the two texts share many similarities and parallels in vocabulary, and it is now widely accepted that they are the work of the same author.[91] Recently it has been suggested that suitable real-life candidates for the *Alain* and *Aline* referred to in these texts might be Alan la Zouche and his wife Elena of Quency.[92] Alan la Zouche was one of Henry III's vassals whose career included appointments as a justice in Wales and Ireland, as sheriff of Northampton, and latterly, from 1263, as a steward in the royal household. The date of his marriage to the co-heiress Elena of Quency is not known, but it probably occurred around 1240; they had five sons. Elena seems to have been

---

Holkham Misc. 40 – recall those of certain books produced under Wycliffite auspices', in his forthcoming essay 'Compilations for Preaching' in *The Cambridge History of the Book*.

[89]   See pp. xxviii–xxxvi.
[90]   The suggestion was first made by Meyer 1880:64.
[91]   See Marshall 1971 and 1973. For an edition of *Corset* see Sinclair 1991.
[92]   See Sinclair 1992:193–208, on which the following discussion is dependent.

pious, and was patron of the Hospital of St James and St John at Brackley in Northamptonshire, a hospital which was under Augustinian rule. Alan died in 1270, Elena in 1296. Of various towns and villages with the name Greatham, the closest to this family's ancestral lands is the Greatham in Rutlandshire, and this may have been where Robert was born. Given the subject matter of his writing, and in particular the detailed knowledge of the sacraments displayed in *Corset*, he may well have been a member of a religious order. One possibility is that when Robert de Gretham wrote *Corset* he was an Augustinian canon serving as a chaplain, but by the time that he wrote the *Miroir* he had ceased to serve in this capacity – perhaps instead becoming a full-time preacher.

Although some of the above discussion is speculative, it is possible to piece together a picture of the original author of the *Miroir* and to determine some details at least of its circumstances of composition. In comparison, nothing at all is known about the figure who translated the text into English, nor can we be sure of the impetus behind the translation. It is notable that four (possibly even five) of the six English manuscripts are written in that form of fourteenth-century London English known as Type II, indicating that the capital and its surrounding area formed a significant location for the production of this text. Indeed the predominance of Type II London English in the manuscripts of the *Mirror* might also signify that the project to translate the text was begun in the metropolis.

In terms of production, two of the English manuscripts may be linked with monastic settings. The manuscript tradition of the *Mirror* contains no named scribes, but there is one whose hand has been detected in other manuscripts. The scribe responsible for P has an anglicana formata hand, a clear, firm book-hand dated to the middle of second half of the fourteenth century. This same hand has also been detected in Oxford, Bodleian Library MS Laud Misc. 622, and London, British Library MS Harley 874. These three manuscripts have been located around Waltham Abbey, the Augustinian abbey of the Holy Cross, in Essex, or at least its environs. There is therefore a tentative link to be made between P and a site of monastic production. There is possibly also a connection between the text's copying and the Augustinian order, which is interesting because one hypothesis about the original author of the *Miroir*, Robert de Gretham, is that he may have been an Augustinian canon. It has also been suggested that P may have been compiled by seculars, rather than regular clerks, and that it was made for a lay audience, 'probably for reading in a devout community or household under clerical guidance'.[93] A much clearer link between the *Mirror* and a site of monastic production is to be found in R where the final rubric on f. 126[vb] reads: *Iste liber constat A[bbathie(?)] de W[elbec(?)] si quis hunc librum a predicta [abbathia(?)] alienauerit anatema sit amen*; the words in square brackets have been erased and replaced with the later name of

[93]    Doyle 1953:i.106.

'Domino Roberto Prestwold'. The inscription links the copying of the manuscript to Welbeck Abbey in Nottinghamshire, a house of the order of the Premonstratensians. This location accords with Angus McIntosh's judgment that the scribal dialect of this manuscript belongs to north Nottinghamshire. Thus, two of the English manuscripts may be linked, with different degrees of closeness to religious houses, but there is insufficient evidence from these inscriptions to link the copying of the *Mirror* to any one monastic order, or indeed to attribute the translation of the text to any such tradition.

Indications of early owners or readers are similarly thin on the ground. There are significantly more such inscriptions amongst the French manuscripts, but these mostly contain names which can no longer be linked with any person or context. L has two inscriptions which may indicate early owners, and Hm has a contemporary inscription, now erased, at the end of the sermon cycle on f. 139ᵛ, which was written by the hand of the text and which reads: *A Johan (?) li Romance*, a reference too elliptical to be deciphered. But this manuscript also bears a later inscription which shows that in the early to mid fifteenth-century it belonged to the Benedictine abbey of St. Mary in York: *liber Monasterii beate Marie Eboracensis emptus per fratrem Clementem Warthwyk, qui Alienaverit Anathema*. T, which contains the exempla, also bears signs of later use, though again the names are too incomplete to be identified. The English manuscripts are much less annotated; in fact, they contain scarcely any inscriptions at all. Exceptionally the name 'John Hyll' has been written repeatedly in the Glasgow manuscript by what appears to be a fifteenth-century hand. This is of little use, since the name is much too common a name to be traced. There are also some sixteenth-century owners' names in B and R. Apart from these exceptions it will be clear that the *Mirror* manuscripts contain few clues about the identities of their scribes, first owners, and readers, and in this they conform to the usual pattern of silence which characterizes most sermon manuscripts. In her study of English preaching, Helen Spencer sums up the general picture in the following way, saying that:

> It is a rare stroke of luck which permits the student of medieval English sermons to identify their medieval owners and discover something about them. For the time being, not enough is known of the provenance of the books, or the identity of their compilers and scribes, to give this hazy historical picture firmer outlines.[94]

The reasons for this haziness at least seem clear. The prohibition on the production of Biblical material in the vernacular which followed Arundel's Constitutions of 1409, and the subsequent suspicion which fell upon possessors of such books, meant that it would be a very brave or, more probably, a very

---

[94]   Spencer 1993:318. Equally Hudson (1983:51) notes that almost nothing is known about the medieval owners of the thirty-one manuscripts of English Wycliffite sermons.

foolhardy reader who would commit his or her name to a manuscript which contained such material. The *Mirror* sermons, with their full English translations of the gospel readings for each Sunday, must have seemed very hot property in the fifteenth century.[95]

One factor which is notable from the admittedly slight evidence of these inscriptions is that the Middle English manuscripts show signs of reception only by a male audience. This is striking, firstly because external evidence, such as that offered by fifteenth-century wills, confirms that the members of the gentry and urban bourgeosie who favoured this type of reading material included both men and women. Bequests of 'books of the gospels' may be found in fifteenth-century wills, a formulation which Spencer has suggested may signify not just copies of the biblical text, but also expositions of the gospels such as those found in sermons. Examples include John Blount, the son of a Bristol burgess, who in 1404 bequeathed 'a certain book of mine of gospels in English'; Matilda, wife of Sir William Bowes, who left her god-daughter a 'romance boke is called ye gospelles' in 1420; and Alesia, Lady Deyncourt, whose will of 1433 mentions 'a book of the gospels in French'.[96] Such bequests suggest an image of private reading, but it is equally possible that a collection of sermons such as the *Mirror* might have been read aloud, either within the household or from the pulpit, though the format of the extant manuscripts would not seem to favour such a practice. In addition to the above, a second reason to be surprised by the apparent lack of a female audience for the *Mirror* is that the thirteenth-century Anglo-Norman text was devised for a woman. Robert de Gretham prepared his work for 'Dame Aline', as an antidote to her preferred reading of romances: *chancon de geste e d'estoire*. The English translator also frequently refers to the readers of his text as including both men and women. Doubtless the text was also available to female readers as was Robert's initial intention, but the manuscripts themselves contain no inscriptions to support this supposition.

This brief survey of the physical characteristics and literary and linguistic contents of the *Mirror* manuscripts perhaps allows the limited narrative of their production and use to be extended somewhat. Whilst in origin the *Miroir* was the product of the privileged, wealthy surroundings of an aristocratic household, probably in the Midlands, the text's subsequent translation into Middle English was very much an urban-centred exercise. Nor does the Middle English version seem to have achieved a wider dissemination. The single extant manuscript which was copied outside the greater London area may merely have been the result of the movement of texts within the closed circuit of the Premonstratensian order. The *Mirror*'s apparent movement downmarket from noble household to urban clientele may reflect the demand for spiritual reading of any

---

[95]  On the Constitutions and their impact, see Watson 1995:822–64.

[96]  See Cavanaugh 1980:116, 117, 234. These examples are cited by Spencer (1993:36 and 373–74), who suggests just such an interpretation of the term.

kind, and particularly for scriptural material in the vernacular, which existed in the capital towards the end of the fourteenth century. The *Mirror* was designed for educated lay readers, and its linguistic and social shifts may also be indicative of increasing levels of literacy. Furthermore, the fact that the Anglo-Norman manuscripts of the *Miroir* were evidently still in use in the fifteenth century is a sign that, despite the increasing ossification of Anglo-Norman into an archaic language, England remained a multilingual society whose readers could access the scriptures in more than one vernacular.

## Glasgow, University Library, Hunter 250 (H)

### i. The Scribe, the Reviser, and the Later Hand

The Hunterian scribe did not copy carefully; he corrected some of his mistakes and omissions, but not all. Quite often he misplaced words and then indicated the correct order by means of a pair of double oblique strokes. Several careless misspellings occur (eg. *falylen* for *faylen* 77/14; *slepleþ* for *slepeþ*, 107/9; *fleschcliche* for *flescheliche*, 87/28; *trulihche* for *truliche*, 109/7), sometimes with the wrong letter expuncted. He tended to confuse 'l' and 's' (eg. *þoutel* for *þoutes*, 5/36; *al* for *as*, 25/20; *alle* for *asse*, 17/1, etc.) and 's' for 'r' (eg. *besen* for *beren*, 17/7). Occasionally single letters or the beginnings of letters occur where he began to repeat or anticipate a word (eg. 69/9; 107/30; 115/22). In some cases he expuncts a mistake and interlines the correct form (eg. 77/22) or writes it after the mistake (eg. 115/6). He may delete a mistake (eg. 113/12) though where a repeated word or phrase is deleted, it is not always evident that the correction is by the original scribe. Not infrequently he omits words and parts of sentences and only sometimes makes good the omissions in the margin or above the line. In particular, it is important to note the omission of some smaller words in H, eg. *is* 73/20, 73/29 (twice on one page), *his* 3/11, *am* 91/13, *þi* 107/14, *ac* 107/24, *at* 121/7. Such words usually appear in the other English manuscripts (all the examples given do), and have been added in H, but often not by the original scribe. Clearly, the carelessness shown by the Hunterian scribe is a factor to be considered in connection with the tendency to omit pronouns – one of the striking features of this manuscript (see p. xli).

Most if not all of the alterations and additions in H (apart from those by the original scribe), are attributable to one of the two sources referred to in the following as the Reviser and the Later Hand. The Reviser's hand is similar to the original hand; he also used brown ink, sometimes, though, of a lighter shade than the Hunterian scribe's ink. Whilst some additions are clearly by the original scribe (eg. 89/9; 93/23; 113/23) and others clearly by the Reviser, sometimes – especially where smaller words have been added singly – it is difficult to decide which hand may have made them. The Reviser's hand has three distinguishing features. Firstly, it has more complete looping of ascenders (as in *b*, *l*, and *h*), whereas the ascenders of the Hunterian scribe's hand are only partly looped. Secondly, the Reviser has rather cursive forms of *w* and *þ* and a narrower, more upright, sometimes slightly angular *e* (compared with the Hunterian scribe's full, rounded form). Thirdly the Reviser's hand slopes, sometimes slightly backwards (eg. 89/23); by contrast, the Hunterian scribe's writing, if it slopes at all, does so in a slightly forward manner. Four lines in the Reviser's hand (the last partly shorn away) occur on f. 30ᵛ in the margin under the second column.

The Reviser adds or alters words fairly frequently. Many of his additions supply obvious omissions and could well have been made independently, eg. *his* 3/11, *speche* 5/15, *bore* 69/2, *is* 73/29. On the other hand, he sometimes makes alterations which are incorrect (to judge from the other English manuscripts and the Anglo-Norman source), and therefore appear to be bad guesses, eg. 31/22, see note; 69/19, see note; 71/3, see note; *is* 81/5, see note. Beside such commonplace additions, the Reviser made an exceptional series of extensive and systematic alterations affecting certain word endings (mainly inflexions) and also particular words. The main features of these alterations are listed below.[97]

1. *Alteration of final 'n' to 'þ'*. This alteration affects the present indicative plural in *-(e)n*. The bottom half of the second minim of the original 'n' was erased and an oblique stroke added to meet a descender added to the first minim to form a 'þ'.

2. *Addition of 'þ'*. Beside present plurals in *-(e)n*, the most common type, H also had plurals in *-e* and endingless plurals. To plurals in *-e* and to those ending in a stem vowel (e.g. *be, do*), a 'þ' is added fairly frequently, sometimes with a vertical line to separate the 'þ' from the first letter of the following word. Occasionally 'þ' is added over an erased 'n'.

3. *Addition of 'eþ'*. This addition is made to present plural *han* to give *haueþ*; in H 'n' and 'u' are usually identical. Two other present plurals (*vnderstond* and *susten*) have 'eþ' added; 'leþ' is added once to *wil* and once to *schul*.

4. *Erasure of final 'n'*. This, the most extensive alteration, affects infinitives, strong past participles, preterite plurals and present subjunctive plurals. Moreover, final 'n' is sometimes erased in the following words: the adverbs *often, abouen, wiþouten* (frequently), *agon, wiþinnen, bineþen, aforn, to forn* and *biforn*; the prepositions *bitwixen* and *beforn*; the conjunction *seþþen þat*; the nouns *mayden* and *morwen*; and the adjective *almiʒten*.

5. *Addition of final 'e'*. Final 'e' is added fairly frequently, sometimes followed by a thin vertical line to mark off the beginning of the next word. Many instances of the infinitive and present indicative plural form *han* ('have') are thus changed to *haue*. The adjective *god* ('good'), singular and plural, is frequently changed to *gode*. Sporadically 'e' is added to endingless infinitives of verbs ending in a consonant. Sometimes 'e' is added over erased 'n', mainly in

---

[97]     For a full analysis of this aspect of the Reviser's work, see Duncan 1981:162–74.

words with stems ending in a vowel or 'r', e.g. the infinitives *ben* ('be') and *sen* ('see') and the past participles *born* and *lorn*. Occasionally 'e' is added to other parts of the verbs (e.g. *haþ* to *haþe*, *doþ* to *doþe*), to nouns, to adjectives, to the conjunctions *bot* ('but') and to the pronoun *boþ* ('both').

6. *Alterations of 'ac' to 'bot(e'*. Whereas *ac* occurs frequently in sermons 9 and 10 (sermons which the Reviser ignored), it is systematically replaced by *bot(e* elsewhere.

7. *Alteration of 'vnto' to 'to'*. The word *vnto* occurs in the unaltered sermons only; elsewhere *to* is frequently found preceded by an erasure covering two letter-spaces.

8. *Alteration of '(vn)til (þat)' to 'or (þat/þe)'*. The alteration *or* occurs nine times on erasures which cover three or five letter-spaces. Initial 'v' and final 'l' are still visible in altered *vntil* (41/18). Apart from *til* (5/23) and *vntil* (77/32), unaltered forms are found only in sermon 10.

9. *Alteration of 'ich' ('each, every') to 'ech', and of 'ichon' to 'echon'*.

10. *Alteration of 'þis/þat ich(e' to 'þis/þat ilk(e'*. The *ilk(e* forms are always alterations in H, presumably replacing the *ich(e* forms of the other Type II manuscripts.

11. *Alteration of '-seluen' to 'selue' or 'self'*. Sometimes only the final 'n' of *seluen* is erased; sometimes -*uen* is erased and replaced by *f*.

Sermons 9 and 10 (ff. 20$^{va}$–23$^{va}$) apart, these alterations by the Reviser are found throughout ff. 1–58$^v$. The photograph of f. 4$^v$ (*Plate* 1) shows some of these changes as follows:

1. Alteration of final 'n' to 'þ': *hereþ* a12, *redeþ* a12, *beþ* a32, a34, *redeþ* a38, *hereþ* a38, *quemeþ* b6, *oweþ* b7, *beþ* b14, *fedeþ* b38;
2. Addition of 'þ': *vnderstondeþ* a21, over erased 'n': *be secheþ* a42;
3. Addition of 'eþ': *han* to *haueþ* b2;
4. Erasure of final 'n': *wiþ oute(.)* a9, *beseche(.)* a12–13, *plese(.)* a15, *do(.)* a24, *here(.)* a26, a27, *se(.)* a28, *mowe(.)* a30, *here(.)* a30, *selue(.)* a35, *serche(.)* a36, *write(.)* b3–4, *helpe(.)* b12, b24, *make(.)* b25–26, *schewe(.)* b27, *ʒeue(.)* b31 (tail of 'e' touched up after erasure), *selue(.)* b38;
5. Addition of final 'e': *han* to *haue* a1, a3, a20, *vnneþe* a36, *laste* a41, over erased 'n' *lore* b14;
6. Alteration of 'ac' to 'bot(e': *bote* a33, *bot* a36, *bote* b34, b41;
7. Alteration of 'vnto' to 'to': *(..)to* b35, b41;
8. Alteration of 'ich' ('each, every') to 'ech': *ech* a7.

The addition *scheweþ* (in the margin opposite b20) is by the Reviser; so also may be the final 'd' (on erasure) of *founded* a33. The 'þ' in *seiþ* a29 is on an erasure but is written in darker ink than that usually used by the Reviser. A loop has been added to the 'b' of *be seche* a11, also in a darker ink.

Other alterations and additions, sometimes frequent, sometimes sporadic, not by the Hunterian scribe or the Reviser, occur at intervals throughout the manuscript. At first sight several hands appear to be involved. Sometimes black ink is used, sometimes various shades of brown ink. Many of the changes are made in an informal style of writing, some are made in neat, small, upright writing (eg. *pepyll* 13/21, f. 3$^r$, and *as me list* 121/21, f. 23$^v$), and some appear in a more formal style (eg. *hyde* 15/15, f. 3$^v$; *but* 15/17, f. 3$^v$; *cold* f. 79$^v$). Yet, on examination, it is clear that one hand used both the black and the light brown inks; the fairly frequent additions of *but*, *þ$^t$* and *ħ-* ('his') are made by the same hand in various inks; the same distinctive 'humanist' *g* written in black ink on f. 24$^v$ (see 123/19), occurs in light ink in the additions *or string* (f. 31$^{va}$) and *agayn* (f. 34$^a$). Again, on f. 79$^v$, different styles of writing (informal in *ħ- land*, neat and upright in *wel* – both marginal additions – and formal in *-old*, an alternation over an erasure) are found in seemingly identical ink along with other typical changes (nos. 2, 5 and 10 below) in the same ink. Moreover, whatever the differences in ink and styles of writing, these alterations tend to occur together, concentrated in the same parts of the manuscript. It therefore seems likely that most if not all of the changes not by the Hunterian scribe or the Reviser were made by one corrector who may have made alterations on various different occasions.

In these changes, letter-forms characteristic of fifteenth-century Secretary Hand are used, for example the simple secretary 'w', unlooped 'd', and the single-compartment 'a'. Two forms of 'g' occur: an open-bottomed 'g' and the 'humanist' 'g'.[98] The word 'his' is usually written *ħ-*; *þe* and *þ$^t$* have a perpendicular form of thorn resembling a small capital 'Y', otherwise the spelling 'th' is used; the ampersand has a long initial upstroke.

Of these changes, the following are the most notable:

1. The alteration of *þei3* to *þeif*.
2. The alteration of *ac* to *ād*.
3. The alteration of *u*, the reflex of OE *y*, to 'y', eg. *brudale* to *brydale* 79/21; *fur* to *fyr* 115/4.
4. Sporadic alterations of final 'þ' to 'th', eg. *faith* probably altered from *faiþ* 25/24; *wrepth* by alteration, 89/18 – cf. *wrepþe* 63/12, *wraþþe* 125/1. Similarly, -*yth* is added to *habitt* 79/11.
5. The alteration of *hem* to *them* (frequent), and sometimes, in later folios, of *her* to *ther* (eg. f. 81$^r$).
6. Sporadic additions of pronouns, mostly *he*. The Reviser also adds pronouns.
7. Additions and alterations affecting vocabulary; eg. *lete* deleted, *for sake* interlined 71/29; *or dystroyth* in the margin after *slokeneþ* 133/17 (see note); *payn* glosses *þolemodnes* f. 54$^{va}$; *dwelleng* is interlined above *wonynge* f. 58$^{ra}$; *bidith* is interlined above *woneþ* f. 58$^{rb}$; *ryn* is interlined above *erneþ* f. 66$^{ra}$; *couþen* deleted, *knew* interlined f. 77$^{rb}$.
8. The addition of *but* – eg. 85/11; twice on f. 33$^{va}$.

---

[98]   For this 'humanist' 'g' see Ullman 1960, plates 43 and 45.

9. The occasional completion of a word at the end of a line where the Hunterian scribe has run the word over into the next line – eg. *mene* 113/15; *tunge* f.78ʳᵃ.

10. The removal of *ne* in double negatives. This is the most frequent alteration by the Later Hand. Mostly *ne* is erased but there are also a few cases where *ne* has been deleted. The extent of this change resembles that of some of the alterations by the Reviser. Several factors, however, show that this was a Later Hand alteration. Firstly, the related alteration of *nas* to *was* (109/19) is clearly in the dark ink of the later hand. Secondly, the erasure of *ne* occurs fairly frequently in sermons 9 and 10 which the Reviser left unaltered. And thirdly, the erasures occur beside Later Hand alterations and continue after f. 58ᵛ where the Reviser's alterations cease.

It would seem that the Later Hand may have been prompted in some of his alterations by changes made by the Reviser. The removal of *ac*, whether by alteration to *ād* or by erasure (as sometimes in later folios) by the Later Hand is complementary to the Reviser's alterations of *ac* to *bot(e*. So too, the sporadic alteration of an *-n* plural to *-th* (eg. on f. 81ᵛ) corresponds to the Reviser's alterations in favour of the *-þ* plural. Occasional instances of the erasure of *-n* from infinitives (eg. on f. 75ᵛ and 80ᵛ) and of the addition of an *e* to *han* (eg. on f. 75ᵛ) occurring after f. 58ᵛ (where the Reviser's extensive alterations cease) could be instances of sporadic alterations in later folios by the Reviser; but these occur in folios containing Later Hand alterations and as they are sporadic and unaccompanied by the Reviser's other changes, it seems likely that they may have been made by the Later Hand.

## ii. Language: Provenance, Date, and Linguistic Profile

The language of H is fairly homogeneous and consistent. An examination of its spellings and inflexions in terms of the phonological and morphological categories of such traditional standard authorities as Luick and Jordan reveals a fourteenth-century dialect of an east midland character. This is evident from the following predominant features.[99]

The dialect is not northern. OE /ā/ is always spelt 'o'. The third singular present indicative ends in '-þ' or, in a few instances, is contracted; the ending '-s' occurs only once, in *knows* (117/31). Nor is the dialect of H southern, southwestern or southeastern. OE initial /f/ is always spelt 'f' in H and OE initial /s/ is always 's'. The reflex of OE /y/ (long and short) is predominantly 'i' or 'y', though there are also some instances of 'e' spellings, almost all from OE short /y/, several of which occur before /r/. Of the limited number of words containing the reflex of OE /ȳ/, a few have 'u' but the majority have 'i'. OE /ēā/ and /ēō/ are spelt 'e' with the exception of four seemingly southeastern

---

[99] See Duncan 1965:xxix–lxxx for a detailed analysis of the phonology and morphology of the language of H and a full discussion of anomalous or exceptional features.

instances of the verb 'to be' as *bi*.[100]. OE /æ/ is spelt 'a'; *efter* (frequently, beside *after*) and *heruest* 'harvest' (31/13, 35/18 and 113/11) need not be reflexes of the Kentish /e/.[101] The present participle commonly ends in '-and(e'. A western provenance may be ruled out. As mentioned, the reflexes of OE /y/ (long and short) are mostly 'i' or 'y'; OE /a/ or /o/ before a nasal appears as 'a'; OE /eo/ (long and short) is spelt 'e' – apart from a few 'i' spellings for /i/ by the raising of ME long /e/; and vowels in final unaccented syllables are always spelt 'e', never 'u' or 'o'.

Other features indicate that the language of H was a southern variety of the east midland dialect. Occasional present plural indicative forms ending in '-þ' occur beside the main form in '-n'.[102] The pronouns *þair* and *þaim* are not found in H which has *her*, *here* (*hir*) and *hem* (*him*) only. The main form of the nominative plural pronoun is *hii* beside frequent *þei/þai* (especially later in the text), and occasional *he*.[103] 'Any' appears as *ani* throughout, rarely as *eni*, never as *ony*, a combination in an east midland text indicative of a southeast midland location.[104] Likewise 'e' and 'u' spellings beside majority 'i/y' reflexes of OE /y/ (long and short) and the occasional southeastern forms (such as the *bi* forms of the verb 'to be' already noted) are also characteristic of southeast midland texts.

In effect, as a southern east midland dialect, the language of H is in many ways similar to the language of Chaucer or to that of contemporary London documents. However, there are significant features which differentiate the Hunterian dialect from Chaucer's English. Thus, H has sporadic instances of the 'a' spellings for the reflex of OE long /æ/ characteristic of the earlier Essex-London dialect, as in *radinge* 'reading' (5/21), *lateþ* 'let, abandon' (27/17), *maden* 'maiden' (59/31), plural *madenes* (81/11), *ladeþ* 'lead' (11/23, 17/29, 29/12).[105] More immediately striking is the use of the '-and(e' ending for the present participle in H. This form has long been recognised as occuring in some thirteenth-century east midland texts such as the *Bestiary* and *Genesis and Exodus*. More significant for the dialect of H are the '-and(e' present participle forms in the Auchinleck manuscript. In 1922 Holmqvist, believing the main scribe of that manuscript was a Londoner, gave it as his opinion that '-*and* was at one time in current use over the whole of the East Midl. dialectal district,

---

[100] All, curiously, occur in sermon 9: *bi* as infinitive (111/12), as past participle (105/18 and 109/28), and as second plural indicative (107/18).

[101] On *efter* see Jordan 1934:§32, Anm. 3, and Luick 1914–40:§363, Anm. 5; on *heruest* see Luick 1914–40:§363, Anm. 3 and §198, Anm. 3.

[102] For the -en/-eth boundary as from Moore, Meech and Whitehall, see MED, *Plan and Bibliography*, p. 8, map 2.

[103] For the co-existence of these forms of the plural pronoun of the first person as characteristically southeast midland, see Samuels 1963:82, map 1, and *LALME* ii:26.

[104] See Samuels 1963:90, map of 'Any', and *LALME* ii:74.

[105] See Jordan 1934:§50.

even so far south as Essex (or London).'[106] Notwithstanding, it was still considered a non-southern feature by Oakden and by Moore, Meech and Whitehall.[107] In 1963 the issue was resolved by M. L. Samuels who, in characterising four types of standard written language found in fourteenth- and fifteenth-century manuscripts, demonstrated that London-Essex 'a' spellings for OE long /æ/ and the '-and(e' present participial ending were features of the written standard he designated 'Type II', a language of which 'the main hand in the Auchinleck MS may be taken as typical.' Of the seven manuscripts he then listed as featuring this Type II language he stated that:

> on linguistic grounds there seems no doubt that they must all be from the greater London area. There are certainly minor differences that probably indicate different parts of London or its surroundings; but they all agree in continuing features of that early Essex-type of London dialect that is seen in the English Proclamation of Henry III.[108]

Samuels noted twelve linguistic features which differentiated this Type II language from his Type III, the language of Chaucer. In the following table, Samuels's Type II characteristics are set out with the corresponding forms in H.

| | Type II | H |
|---|---|---|
| 1. | þat ilch(e), ich(e) | þat ich(e) or þat iche(e)?[109] |
| 2. | nouȝt, no | nouȝt |
| 3. | eld(e) | old(e), eld(e) |
| 4. | werld, warld | world |
| 5. | þai, hii | hii, þei, þai |
| 6. | þei(ȝ) | þeiȝ(e), þouȝ |
| 7. | þerwhile(s) (þat) | while(s) (þat), þarwhiles þat |
| 8. | -ande, -ende, inde | -and(e), -ende, -yng |
| 9. | noiþer, noþer | noyþer, noiþer, noþer |
| 10. | schuld | schuld |
| 11. | oȝain(s), aȝen | aȝeines, aȝain(es), oȝain, aȝen(es) |
| 12. | wil | wil, wille |

From the considerable agreement here it is clear that the language of H is to be classed more specifically as a version of Samuels' Type II standard language and to be added (along with C) to the original list of Type II manuscripts.[110] Indeed the affinity with type II is even greater than the above table would suggest. Thus, like H, other Type II manuscripts such as the Auchinleck

---

[106] Holmqvist 1922:46.
[107] Oakden 1930:34–35; Moore, Meech and Whitehall 1935:17–18. Although the latter states that 'the -nd- form survived in a continuous marginal region made up of eastern Kent, the eastern coast of Essex, Suffolk, and Norfolk, etc.' (p. 18), no distinction is made between -end and -and.
[108] Samuels 1963:87.
[109] The manuscript always has ilk(e) by alteration.
[110] Samuels 1963:87, fn 7.

manuscript, for example, have *old(e* beside *eld(e*. Again *world* beside *werld/warld* is found in most Type II manuscripts; it is the majority form in MS BL Additional 17376 and, as in H, the only form in C. Similarly *þou(ȝ)* and *aȝein(es)* also occur in some Type II manuscripts. Shared Type II status would also account for the fact that the Hunterian copyist and the first scribe of the Auchinleck manuscript both use the uncommon forms *þurth* ('through') and *seit* ('says') and that the latter's unusual spelling *wretþe* (that is with -*tþ*-) recurs in the Hunterian form *wratþe* (13/28).

Samuels originally held that on palaeographical grounds all Type II manuscripts were to be dated 'from before 1370', but subsequently revised this date, first to 1380, and then to 1390.[111] On palaeographical evidence alone it would not seem possible to do more than suggest a date for H sometime towards the end of the fourteenth century. However, there are features of the language of H which would support a date in the region of the beginning of the last quarter of the century. The conjunction *ac* ('but'), prevalent in H, fell out of use towards the end of the fourteenth century. It was not used by Chaucer or Gower and, according to MED 'ME *ac* occurs in N, EM and S texts until c. 1375'.[112] It was doubtless because *ac* appeared archaic to him that the Reviser (approximately contemporary with the H copyist, to judge from his hand) went to such lengths to erase all traces of this conjunction in H and to replace it with *bot*.[113] If on this account the language of H is not to be dated after, or much after, 1375, there are other features which would suggest that it did not belong before that date. A close examination of ff. 1–26ᵛ of H shows that in approximately the first half of this portion the plural pronoun *hii* and the conjunction *þeiȝ(e* prevail, whereas in the second half the prevailing forms are *þei/þai* and *þouȝ*.[114] The changeover is naturally more immediately evident in the case of the pronouns, beginning with a run of *þay* forms at f. 15; after this point *hii* occurs only occasionally as did *þei/þai* previously. Since there is no indication that a change in exemplar occurred at this point, it seems instead that the copyist may have chosen to modernise the language of the text, substituting the newer *þay* as being more current at his time of writing than the old-fashioned *hii*, and consequently beginning to write *þouȝ* instead of *þeiȝ(e)* as well. According to Samuels the *hii-þeiȝ(e* pair is characteristic of earlier, mainly fourteenth-century texts and the *þei-þouȝ* pair of later, mainly fifteenth-century texts. Since H has all four

111   See respectively, Samuels 1963:88; Samuels 1972:168; *LALME* i:27.
112   See under *ac* conj.
113   It is noteworthy that at the beginning of B (dated as 'soon after 1400' or 'late fourteenth or early fifteenth century', see p. xvi), *ac* is found as far as the second folio in the third hand. Then, however, as from line 11 of f. 19ᵛ, *ac* is replaced by *but*. This change (whether already in his exemplar or made by the third scribe himself), presumably reflected, as with the Reviser's alteration of *ac* to *bot* in H, a wish to replace outdated *ac* with *but* of current usage.
114   For a discussion of this pairing, see Samuels 1963:83.

forms, interestingly distributed as two pairs, it might be suggested that this manuscript lies more or less on the borderline between the earlier and the later texts, and that in effect it offers late material of the Type II language. From the linguistic evidence it may be concluded that *circa* 1380 would be an appropriate date for the language of H, and such a date would be perfectly in keeping with the palaeographical evidence.

## *Linguistic Profile*

The questionnaire was based on that used for the southern region in *LALME*. In the following list of recorded forms the dominant or only form is given first, tolerated forms which occur frequently are given in single parentheses, rare forms in double parentheses.

| | | | |
|---|---|---|---|
| THESE: | þes (þis) | AGAIN: | aʒen, oʒain (aʒein) ((aʒain, aʒeyne)) |
| SHE: | sche ((ʒhe, ʒche)) | | |
| HER: | her, hir | ERE *conj:* | ere, er, er þat, or þat |
| IT: | it ((hit)) | | |
| THEY: | hii (þai) ((he, þei)) | SINCE *conj:* | seþen þat, seþþen þat, seþ þat, siþen þat |
| THEM: | hem ((him)) | | |
| THEIR: | her (here) ((hir)) | | |
| SUCH: | swiche (swich) | YET: | ʒit (ʒete) ((ʒet, ʒitte)) |
| WHICH: | whiche, which | | |
| EACH: | ich (ech) ((iche, eche)) | WHILE: | while þat, whiles þat, þarwhiles þat |
| MANY: | mani (many) | STRENGTH: | strengþe ((stryngþe)) |
| MAN: | man | | |
| ANY: | ani ((eni)) | WH-: | wh (w) |
| MUCH: | muchel (michel) | NOT: | ne, nouʒt, ne + nouʒt ((not)) |
| ARE: | ben (be) ((beþ, bi, ar, arne)) | NOR: | ne |
| IS: | is | WORLD: | world ((worlde)) |
| ART: | art | THINK: | þenche |
| SHALL *sg:* | schal ((schul)) | WORK *sb:* | werk |
| *plu:* | schul (schal, schullen) | *vb:* | wirch- |
| | | THERE: | þer (þar) |
| SHOULD *sg:* | schuld | WHERE: | wher-, whar- |
| WILL *sg:* | wil ((wille)) | MIGHT *vb:* | miʒt (miʒht) ((mihʒt)) |
| *plu:* | wil | | |
| WOULD *sg:* | wold | THROUGH: | þurth ((þourʒ, þurʒ, þurʒh, þurʒt, þurʒth, þurht, þurtʒh, þurthʒ)) |
| FROM: | fram (fro, from) | | |
| AFTER: | efter ((after)) | | |
| THEN: | þan ((þanne, þen)) | | |
| THAN: | þan ((þanne)) | WHEN: | whan ((when)) |
| THOUGH: | þeiʒ (þouʒ) ((þeiʒe)) | *subst. pl:* | -es, -s ((-en)) |
| | | *pres. part:* | -and, -ande ((-end, -yng)) |
| IF: | ʒif ((ʒef, ʒeue, if)) | | |
| AGAINST: | aʒeines (oʒain, aʒenes) ((aʒaines, oʒaines, aʒen)) | *str pt pl:* | -en, -e |
| | | *str ppl:* | -en ((-e)) |
| | | ASK: | ask-, aske |

BEFORE *adv:*       aforn (toforn, biforn) ((bifor, before, beforn))

    *pr:*       before, afor (tofor, toforn, beforn) ((tofore, before))

BEYOND:       beȝond

BOTH:       boþe (boþ)

BRIDGE:       bregge

BURN:       brenn-

BUSY *adj:*       bisie, bisy

BUT:       ac (bot) ((bote))

CALL *ppl:*       cleped ((ycleped))

CAME *sg:*       com, come

CHURCH:       chirche (cherche)

COULD *sg, pl:*       couþe

DAY *pl:*       daies, dayes (dais)

DIE:       deye (deie, deien)

    *pt:*       died, deyde

DO *3sg:*       doþ ((doþe))

    *pt.sg:*       dede

DREAD, SPREAD:       drede, dradde, spredeþ, sprad, spradde

EITHER + OR:       oþer

EVIL:       iuel (euel)

EYE *pl:*       eiȝen

FILL:       fill-

FILTH:       filþ, filþe

FIRE:       fur, fure

FIRST:       first (ferst)

FLESH:       flesche ((flesch))

GET *ppl:*       biȝeten, geten

GIVE *pt-sg:*       ȝaf, ȝaue

    *ppl:*       ȝeuen

GO *3sg:*       goþ

HANG *pt:*       heng, hong

HAVE *inf:*       haue, han

HEAR:       heren ((here))

HIGH:       heiȝe ((heiȝ, heyȝe))

HIGHT:       hiȝt

HILL:       hil

HITHER:       hider

HOLD *pt-sg:*       held ((heeld))

HUNDRED:       hundred-, hondred-

I:       Y, ich ((i, j))

KIND *etc:*       kinde ((kynde))

LAND:       londe (lond)

LEAD *pt:*       lad

LESS:       lasse

LET *pt:*       let, lete

LIE *vb:*       lie- (liggen, liȝen, lyen)

LITTLE:       litel

LIVE *vb:*       liue, liu- ((lyue, leue))

NE + BE:       nis, nas, nart, nam

NE + WILL:       nil (ne wil) ((wil nouȝt, nel nouȝt))

NE + HAVE:       ne haþ ((naþ))

NEITHER + NOR:       noyþer (noiþer, noþer) +

NO-MORE:       nomore, namore

OR:       oþer ((or))

OWN *adj:*       owen

PRIDE *etc:*       pride ((pridde))

READ *pt:*       rede

RUN:       ern-

THE-SAME:       þat iche

SAY:       say (sai) ((sei, sigg-))

SEE *pt-sg:*       seiȝ ((seiȝe))

    *ppl:*       sen (seiȝen)

SELF:       self, selue, seluen

SILVER:       siluer, seluer

SIN:       synne (sinne)

SLAIN:       slain

SPAKE, BRAKE:       spake (spak, brak) ((breken))

STEAD:       stede

THENCE:       þennes

THITHER:       þider

TOGETHER:       togider ((togiders))

TWO:       two ((thwai, twai, tway))

UNTIL:       vntil, til

WEEK:       weke

WENT:       went (ȝede)

WHAT:       what

WHENCE:       whannes

WHO:       who

WHOM:       whom

WHOSE:       whose

WITEN:       wite, witen ((wete))

    *pt-sg:*       wist

WITHOUT *pr:*       wiþouten ((wiþowten, wiþoute))

WORSE:       wers (wors) ((worse))

WORSHIP:       worschip, worschipe

| (worchipe, | YIELD: | ȝeld- ((ȝild-)) |
| worchip) | -LY: | lich (liche) ((li)) |
| ((werschipe, | | |
| wirschipe)) | | |

## Editorial Policy

The text of the *Mirror* here is that of Glasgow, University Library MS Hunter 250 (H). Emendations have been made only where the Hunterian text is physically defective or fails to make sense. Such emendations are based on the readings of the other English manuscripts. No emendation has been attempted where a faulty reading appears to have derived from the archetype of the surviving manuscripts. All emendations are enclosed in square brackets and are discussed in the Commentary where the readings of the other English manuscripts are given along with relevant Anglo-Norman readings. Rejected readings are recorded in the notes beneath the text. Occasional obvious spelling errors, e.g. *þoutel* for *þoutes* (5/36), are corrected in the text with the manuscript forms recorded in the notes.

Some alterations in H make good obvious errors and are supported by readings in other manuscripts; these are adopted in the text. They are mostly the work of the Hunterian scribe, though in some instances one cannot be certain. In the case of other alterations it has sometimes been possible to restore the H text where some evidence of the original reading is still visible and is supported by readings in other manuscripts. Additions and alterations in H other than those by the Hunterian scribe are mainly attributable to the Reviser or to the Later Hand (see pp. lx–lxiv). In the case of the Reviser's major systematic alterations (listed on pp. lxi–lxii), the original H readings may confidently be determined and are therefore silently restored in the text. All exceptions to, or doubtful instances of, these alterations are recorded in the notes where they are labelled '*Rev.*', as are further minor changes by the Reviser; as required, these are discussed in the Commentary. Alterations judged to be by the Later Hand are marked '*l.h.*'.

The beginning of the recto and verso of each folio is indicated in the text in square brackets. Modern punctuation and capitalisation are used, and paragraphs are generally maintained as in the manuscript. Except for such commonly joined words as *atte, aman, ichon*, etc., the word-division of the manuscript (sometimes indistinct and not linguistically significant) is not reproduced. The letter 'ȝ' is rendered 'z' where it represents a sibilant. Word initial 'ff' is given as 'f' or 'F' as appropriate. Suspensions and contractions are expanded silently in both the text and the notes. The curl sometimes found on final 'r', the mark sometimes found after final 'g' and rarely after final 'k' and 't', and the occasional cross through 'l' appear to be meaningless flourishes in H; they are ignored except where (as in the stroke through 'l' in 'israel') they clearly function as marks of abbreviation; in such cases they are expanded silently. The ampersand at the beginning of a sentence is silently altered to 'And'.

The following conventions are used in the textual apparatus:

| | |
|---|---|
| *eras.* | the preceding word(s) or letter(s) erased |
| *on eras.* | the preceding word(s) or letter(s) written over an erasure |
| *ins.* | the preceding word(s) inserted above the line, in the margin, or in the interverbal space |
| *canc.* | the preceding word(s) cancelled, either by sub-punction or crossing through |
| *transp.* | the preceding words marked for transposition |
| *alt.* | the preceding word(s) or letter(s) formed by alteration |
| *alt. to* | the preceding word(s) or letter(s) altered to the reading which follows |
| *trim.* | text lost by trimming |
| *Rev.* | altered by the Reviser |
| *l.h.* | later hand |

In the notes, round brackets ( ) denote an erasure; the enclosed dots (...) indicate the approximate number of letter-spaces the erasure covers; enclosed letters (.e.) are letters written over the erasure.

The parallel text of the Anglo-Norman *Miroir* is from Nottingham University Library, MS Mi LM 4 ($W^2$). Abbreviations have been silently expanded and corrections, mainly by the $W^2$ scribe, silently adopted. Punctuation, capitalisation, and word-division have been modernised. Otherwise, apart from minimal corrections and restorations listed in Appendix One (pp. 169–70), the text is printed as found in the manuscript. Two doubtful readings are also noted in the Appendix One.

# THE MIDDLE ENGLISH *MIRROR*: SERMONS FROM ADVENT TO SEXAGESIMA

edited from Glasgow, University Library, Hunter 250

with a parallel text of

The Anglo-Norman *Miroir*

edited from Nottingham, University Library, Mi LM 4

# PROLOGUE

f. 57<sup>r</sup>

A sa trechere dame, Aline:
Saluz en la uertu diuine.
Madame, bien l'ai oi dire
Ke mult amez oir e lire
5  Chancon de geste e d'estoire
E mult i metez la memoire.
Mais bien uoil que vus sachez
Que co est plus ke uanitez,
Kar co n'est rien fors controuure
10  E folie de uaine cure;
Si l'om i troue vn bon respit
Tut li altre ualdra petit.
Co est en uair le tripot
De chescun ki mentir uolt;
15  Pur plus sourement mentir
Alcune rien dist a pleisir,
E dist alcune uerite
Pur feire oir sa falsete.
E co n'est pas chose creiable
20  Que tut seit uair k'est dit en fable.
Nun est co uair quant k'est escrit
D'estoire ke l'em en chancun dist;
Kar cil ki chancuns controuerent
Sulum lur quiders les furmerent;
25  E l'om dist en respit pur uair
Ke quidance n'est pas sauair.
Veez si co pot estre uair
Que vns enfes oust poair
Cum dist la chancun de Mainet,
30  V del orfanin Sansunnet,
V de la geste dan Tristram,

V del bon messager Balam.
Veez les altres ensement:
N'i ad celui ki trop n'i ment;
35  Ne sunt pas forstrait d'escripture,
Mais chascun fait sa controuure.
Ore seit ke tut seit ueritez,
Si est co purquant uanitez
Tels escriz oir e entendre
40  V l'alme ne poet nul bien prendre;
Kar quanque a l'alme ne fait bien
Deuant Deu ne ualt nule rien,
E cil trop laidement se sert
Ki Deu pur nule rein perd.
45  E Deu uolt de sun seruant
Qu'il seit a li tut entendant;
Tut uolt ke seit a li turne
Quanqu'il ad a chescun dune.
Il nus ad done cors e uie
50  Veer, parler, e oie,
Entente, menbres e curage,
Tut pur nus guarder de damage.
Nus eimes tuz ses despensers
Pur li seruir de ces mesters.
55  Si nus a gre bien li seruum,
Cent dubble en ert li guerdun;
E ki mesfait a escient,
Mult en ert dur le uengement.
E pur co que vus aim en De,
60  Tolir vus uoil de uanite,
Que vus li puissez rendre en bien
Quanque il demande a crestien.

# PROLOGUE

Many men it ben þat han wille to heren rede romaunce and gestes. Þat is
more þan idilchip, & þat Y wil wele þat alle men it witen; for hii ben
controued þurthჳ mannes wit þat setten here hertes to folies and trufles.
As þe leiჳer doþ, he makeþ his speche queynteliche þat it may ben
5   delicious to mennes heryng for þat it schuld be þe better listne[d]. For
Salemon seyt he had enquered & souჳt al þinges vnder sunne & þan ne
fond in al noþinge bot vanite bot þat þinge þat falleþ to Goddes worchip
and to note of mannes soule. And þerfor ich haue sette myn herte for to
drawen out a litel tretice of diuinite, þat men þat han wil for to here
10  swiche trufles, þat hii mow tur[n]en her hertes þerfro &ჳif hem to [þin]g
þat is profetabil boþe to lif & to soule. God it me grauntჳif it be his
swete wille. Amen.

    And for men seyn þat al þinges þat ben writen it ben for to leuen, & hii
gabben; for hii þat maken þes songes and þes gestes, hii maken hem after
15  weneinge, & men seit on old english þat weneinge nis no wisdome. Loke
nou to Tristrem, oþer of Gii of Warwike, oþer of ani oþer, & þou ne
schalt finde non þat þer nis mani lesinges & gret; for hii ne be nouჳt
drawen out of holi writ, bot ich man þat makeþ hem enformeþ hem efter
þe wil of hiis hert and þenkeþ þat it is soþe. And ne for þan, al is it vanite
20  for to here al swich þinges & vnderstonde hem þat þe soule ne mai no
gode leren; for al þinge þat doþ no gode to þe soule bifor God nis nouჳt
worþ, & muchel he lest of his time þat so setteþ his hert fro God &
trespasseþ gretliche. For God bit þat he schal be al atendaunt vnto him, &
he wil be turned to him al þat he haþჳeuen to ich man. He haþჳeuen vs
25  bodi & lif, sen & heren, wit & hereing & vnderstondinge in hert, & al for
to kepe þe fram harm. We ben al his spensers to serue him of his ofices;
ჳif we serue him wel, an hundredfold schal ben oure mede, & who þat
doþ iuel be his wil, ful gret schal be þe veniaunce þat schal be taken of
him. And for þat we schul ben on in God, ichil fonde to drawe ჳou fram
30  vanite þat we mai ჳeld him what þat he askeþ of cristen man &

---

7 noþinge] (.)noþinge.   11 his] *ins.*   14 english] englihs.   19 vanite] (…)vanite.
25 wit] *ins.*

Pur co vus ai fait cest escrit
V vus purrez lire a delit.
65  Ia nule rien n'i trouerez
Dunt Ihesu Crist ne seit paez,
Dunt l'alme ne seit conforte
E la char de mal turne.
Quant de lire vus prendra cure
70  Traez auant cest escripture:
Les ewangelies i uerrez
Mult proprement enromancez,
E puis les exposiciuns
Brefment sulum les sainz expuns;
75  Kar sachez n'i ad nul mot dit
Que li sainz n'aient ainz escrit:
Io l'ai excerpe e estrait
Des escriz ke li sainz vnt fait.
Point de latin mettre n'i uoil,
80  Kar co resemblereit orgoil;
Orgoil resemble ueraiement
Co dire a altre qu'il n'entent.
E si est co mult grant folie  /f. 57ᵛ
A lai parler latinerie;
85  Cil s'entremet de fol mester
Ki uers lai uolt latin parler.
Chescun deit estre a raisun mis
Par la langue dunt il est apris.
Ore vus pri, chere dame Aline,
90  Pur Deu a ki tut le mund acline,
Ke vus priez escordrement
Que Deu me doint entendement
De si traiter e de si dire
Qu'il me pardoinst peche e ire;
95  Kar lealment, sachez de fi,
En uos prieres mult me fi;
Kar bien le sai k'a bon entente
Deus s'abandune e presente.
E vus altre feiz m'auez dit
100  Que io feisse cest escrit,
Pur co, sachez, ne l'ai pas fait,
Mais nostre entente ke Deu ueit;
Vostre est li biens, uostre est li los,
Kar sanz vus penser ne l'os.
105  Si rien i ad d'amender
Del franceis v del rismeer,
Nel tenez pas a mesprisiun
Mais bien esguardez la raisun:
Deus n'entent pas tant al bel dit

110  Cum il fait al bon esperit;
Mielz ualt uair dire par rustie
Que mesprendre par curteise;
Quanque s'acorde a uerite
Tut est bien dist pardeuant De.
115  Dame, ne vus esmerueilliez
Que les lescuns ai abriggez;
Iol faz pur vus ennui tolir
E de lire duner desir,
Kar tost porreit trop ennuier.
120  L'em s'ennuie de bel chanter,
E par ennui poet l'em leisser
La rien ke plus doust aider;
Par ennui perd l'om suuent
La rien ke plus est a talent.
125  Purquant, si tut dis puisse uiure
E sanz nul entreleis escriure,
E euse la buche trestut ferine
E la lange tut ascerine,
E euse trestut le saueir
130  Quanque nul home poet auer,
Ne purrai la maite dire
De co k'apent a ma matire.
Mais mielz uoil dire acune chose
De Deu, que tenir buche close;
135  Kar suuent par petit bon dit
Tressalt li quors en grant delit.
  Mun nun ne uoil encore numer
Pur les enuius deshicer,
Qu'il ne toillent de nus le bien
140  Dunt il ne uolent dire rien.
Kar custume est as enuius,
Que grucus sunt e ennuius;
Trestuz despisent altri diz
E puruertent les bons escriz,
145  E co cuntent a grant delit
Qu'il unt en priuete u en escrit.
Ne cessent d'altres blamer
Quenses cum pur sei auanter;
Li fel se quide amender
150  Par le prudome deprauer.
  Cist liures 'Mirur' ad nun;
Ore oez par quele raisun.
Par le mirur ueit l'om defors,
E par cest escrit, alme e cors.
155  Li mirurs les tecches presente
E cist les pensers e l'entente.

woman. For þi ich haue mad þis boke þat ȝe mai reden on, for no þinge
ȝe ne schal finde herein bot þat God is wile paied wiþalle, & þat þe soule
mai ben conforted wiþal & bodi tauȝt. Whan ȝe han wil for to reden,
draweþ forþ þis boke. Þe goddespelles ȝe schul finden herein, first þe
5  tixt, & þan þe vndoinge schortlich. And wit ȝe wel, þer nis nouȝt on
word writen in þat it nis in holi writ & out of þe bokes þat þis holi men
þat weren toforn vs an made. Latin ne wil Y sette non þerin, for it semeþ
as it wer a pride for to telle anoþer þat he vnderstondeþ nouȝt. And so it
is ful gret foli to spek Latyn to lewed folke, & he entermetteþ him of a
10 fole mester þat telleþ to hem Latin. For ich man schal ben vndernomen &
aresoned eftter þe language þat he haþ lerd. Now ich besech ȝou
ententilich þat ȝe bid to God þat he ȝeue me vnderstondinge so to draw &
write þat he forȝif ȝou & me oure trespas. For vnderstonde ȝe wel, ich
afie me gretlich in ȝoure bidinges þat han gode wille to here þis boke
15 oþer to reden it. Ne ȝeueþ no kepe to þe letter ne to þe speche, bot
vnderstondeþ wel þe reson. God ne [f. 1ᵛ] ȝeueþ no kepe to þe faire
speche, ac to þe spirite he ȝeueþ kepe. Better is for to sei þe soþe
boustouslich þan for to say fals þurtȝh queyntise; for al þat acordeþ wiþ
soþnesse, al is wel said befor God. Haueþ no wunder þeiȝ Y spek as
20 schortlich as I may, for ich it do for to wiþdrawen hem fram greuaunce
þat it here oþer reden. For often longe radinge oþer heringe saddeþ a
mannes hert & makeþ him ful þerof þeiȝe þe þinge liked him ful wele.
Na for þan þeiȝ ich miȝt liuen til domesday & wiþouten ani letteinge
alway writen, & had þe mouþ of iren & þe tonge of stele & had al þe
25 witte þat al men miȝht haue, ȝit ne mihȝt ich nouȝt haluendel write þis
þat falleþ to my mater. Ac better it is to say sumwhat of God þan hold my
mouþe stille; for often þurȝ a litel wele siggeinge turneþ þe hert into
delite. My name ne wil Y nouȝt say for þe enemys þat miȝht heren it &
mihȝt drawen ȝour hertes fram gode þat it had wille to heren. For it is þe
30 maner of þe enemys to ben gruchand & noyouse & wil bleþlich coniecten
þe wordes of holi writte & wil tellen it forþ on her maner & ne letten
nouȝt for to blame oþer. Þe wikked weneþ for to amenden it for to
blamen þe gode & coniecten hem.
　　Þis boke is cleped 'Mirur'. Now hereþ þurȝh what resoun. In þe mirur
35 a man seþ his body, & bi þis writ, body & soule; þe mirur scheweþ þe
fautes wiþouten, & þis þe þoutes & þe vnderstondinge; þe mirur scheweþ

---

6 writen] *partly eras.*　7 an] *alt. to* haue; ne] (.)ne.　15 speche] *ins.*　23 liue]
(.)liue(.).　27 turneþ] it *ins.* turneþ.　36 þoutes] þoutel

Li mirurs mustre les mesprises
E les chosettes mesassises;
E cist mustre en uerite
160 Quanque l'em ad mespris uers De.
Li mirurs mustre adrescement
Del cors, del uis, del uestement,
E cist adresce, co sachez,
Pensers e diz e uolentez.
165 Li mirurs est pur enseigner
Cument hum se deit atiffer;
Cist enseigne ueiraiement /f. 58ʳ
Des uertuz tut l'atiffement.
Li mirurs, quant al secle en uair,
170 Fet les femmes bel pareir
Que plus en seient cuueitees
Quant belement sunt acemees;
E cist demustre la beaute
Que Iesus aime en leaute,
175 E fet les almes adrescer
Que Deu les uoille cuueiter.
Li mirurs sul le cors aturne,
Mais cist e cors e alme aurne;
Pur co est il mirur a dreit
180 Kar tuz mals hoste e tuz biens fait.
Ore pri chescun ki l'ot e uait
Qu'il prie pur celi ki l'ad fait,
Ke Deus li face tel sucurs
Cum il fist a ses prechurs,
185 E pardoint pecche e folie
E met en pardurable uie; Amen
Iesus le doint, le fiz Marie,
A ki trestut li mund se plie. Amen
Li prologes fet ici suiur.
190 Des ore esguardez el mirur:
Tut i uerrez uostre figure,
Vostre nettesce, uostre ordure;
Si bien i guardez, tut i uerrez
Cum en Deu vus atifferez.

195 Deus vus doint issi guarder
K'a lui vus puissez cumfermer. Amen
Saint escripture ad la custume
Del arbre qui port noyz u pume;
Quant est fuillie esspessement
200 Del fruit i pert petit u nient;
Mais si l'em escust l'arbrecel
Li fruit enchet espes e bel,
E la ducur ke fu celee,
Quant l'em en guste, mult li agree.
205 Alsi est de saint escripture:
La lettre pert obscure e dure,
Mais qui i mettrat sun purpens
Pur ueer l'espirital sens,
E si l'escut cum par espundre
210 Le bien ke Deus i uolt respundre
Mult i uerrat pumettes cheres,
Co sunt sentences de maneres;
E mult li sauura bien
La dulcur dunt ainz ne solt rien.
215 Kar lettre de saint escripture
Est ausi cum nue obscure;
La nue i uent obscure e nuble
E les quors des esguardanz truble;
Mais la pluie ke puis s'en ist
220 Tute la terre refreschist,
E fiet les herbes reuerdir,
Oisels chanter e bois flurir.
La nue que tant est obscure
Les dous leis mustre par figure,
225 Dunt nuls ne sauerat la uerrur
Si ne seit par expositur.
Mais les nues la pluie funt
Quant l'esspunur les leis exspunt
E fait entendre vuertement
230 Co que ainz ert dist obscureme[n]t,
Dunt li quors de home est arusez

þe febles & what þat is mismade opon him, & þis boke scheweþ for soþ
what man haþ misdone aȝeines God; þe mirur scheweþ þe dresceinge of
þe body & of þe visage & cloþinge, & þis adresseþ, witȝe wel, þouȝtes
& wordes & willes; þe mirur is made for to teche man & woman how þat
5 hii schul tiffen hem, & þis schew[eþ] for soþe of vertuz al þe tiffeinge; þe
mirur makeþ þes wimmen fair to be sen in þe world þat hii ben þe more
couaited when þat hii ben fair atired, & þis scheweþ þe fairnes þat Ihesus
loueþ in truþe & makeþ þe soules to dresse hem þat God wil couait hem;
þe mirur onlich riȝteþ þe bodi, & þis riȝteþ boþe body and soule.

10 Now beseche ichon þat it seþ & hereþ, bischeþ þat God haue on him
merci þat it haþ made, & þat he ȝeue him swich help & soucors as he haþ
done to his prechours, & forȝeue his sinne & his folie, & bringe him to þe
liif þat euer [sc]hal lasten. Amen.

Þe prolouge endeþ here. Now lokeþ in þe mirur, for al þou schalt se þi
15 figure, þi clennesse & þi filþ; ȝif þou wil lok þerinne, al þou schalt sen
how þou schalt tiffen þe to Goddes worschip & þi note. God send þe his
grace so to lok þerinne þat þou mai be confermed to þe blis þat euer schal
last. Amen.

Holy writ haþ a liknesse vnto tre þat bereþ note oþer appel. Whan it is
20 þicke leued, of þe frout it lest litel oþer nouȝt; ac ȝif men schake þe tre,
þe frout falleþ doun þicke & fair: þan þe swettnesse þat was hidde aforn,
whan man eteþ it, it likeþ him wel. So it fareþ bi holi writ. Þe letter
semeþ derk & hard, ac he þat setteþ his entent to se þe gostlich writ, &
ȝif he schake it as þurȝth vndoinge þe [f. 2ʳ] gode þat God wold don vs,
25 michel gode frout he schal finde þerinne & derworþ, þat ben sentens of
mani maners, & michel þat swettnesse schal turnen him to gode whiche
þat aforn he ne vnderstode nouȝt.

For þe letter of holi writ is, as it wer, a derk cloude. Þe cloud becomeþ
derk & dim, & men þat loken þerto, it trobleþ her hertes; ac þe rayn þat
30 afterward falleþ frescheþ al þe erþe & makeþ þe herbes for to grenen &
foules singen & trewes for to florischen. Þe cloude þat is so derk scheweþ
þe twai lawes þurth figure in whiche noman ne miȝht se þe soþnesse
þerof bot ȝif it were vndon & oponed. Ac þe cloude ȝeueþ þe rayn whan
þe vndoer openeþ holi writ openlicher to mannes vnderstondinge þat
35 afornhond was derke, þurth whiche mannes bodi & womannes is dewed

---

2 dresceinge] dresteinge. 13 euer] eue. 25 ben] *alt. to* beþ. 26 mani] mani(.);
whiche] *alt.* 28 of holi] of (…) holy. 32 twai] *alt.*

E reuerdist tut en buntez,
E l'ame en vrant chante a Crist
E en bons oures flurist.
235    De teles nues Daui dit,
Ki pleins ert del saint espirit:
'Tenebruse ewe est pur ueir
En tutes les nues del air'.
Les nues sunt, que nel vus ceile,
240  La lei antiue e l'ewangeile.
A la lei ke fu Moysant
Sunt li prophetes apendant;
Al ewangeille ensement
Le escrit de cristiens apent.
245  Mais la une e l'autre est si obscur
Qu'entendu n'ert sanz exspunur
Que pluie diz de uerite
E tut desface le obscurte.
Cil alsi cum en nues sunt
250  Ki n'entendent co qu'il funt,
Ne quel seit bien ne quel offens, /f. 58ᵛ
Ne par escriz ne par lur sens.
E dunc n'unt ki lur pluie mie
Quant il n'unt ki assenst lur uie.
255  Dunt Deu uolt ke sainte iglise
De treis ordres fust bien assise,
De guaignurs, de defendurs,
De lettrez, co sunt conseillurs.
Deus ad assis le guaignur

260  Pur pestre tuz de sun labur,
Le cheualer pur tuz defendre,
E les ordenez pur tuz aprendre.
Ki rien encuntre cest mesprent
Deu meimes curuz e offent;
265  Ki Deu ordeinement desdit
Il ad Deu meimes en despit;
A Deu meimes respunderat
Ki sun mester bien ne ferat.
Dunc a l'ordene dur estait,
270  Ki trestuz enseigner deuerait,
Quant il ne uolt ne il n'entent
Sei enseigner ne altre gent,
V il leisse pur amur,
V pur guaigner, u pur pour.
275  Par trestut li estot aprendre
Le bien qu'il deit a tuz despendre,
Qu'il sache tuz conseiller
K'en Deu uoldrat demander.
Mais dire ne pus sanz dolurs
280  Cum il i ad de tels plusurs
K'aiment l'ordre sulement
Sanz faire rien k'a li apent;
Del ordre uolent l'onur aueir
Sanz bien faire u bien saueir;
285  Quantque a l'ordre apent uolent
     prendre,
Mais co qu'il deiuent ne uolent rendre.

& greneþ al in godenes & þe soule singeþ to Crist abouen & florischeþ in
gode werkes. Of swich cloudes Dauid seit þat was ful of þe holi gost:
'Derke waters ben for soþe in al þe cloudes of þe air.' Þe cloudes
bitokene þe old lawe & þe newe, þe old lawe þat þe prophetes spak of, þe
5 newe þat cristen men vsen, þat ben þe godspelles; ac boþe þat on & þat
oþer ben so derk þat men ne miȝht nouȝt vnderstonden hem bot ȝif hii
wer vndon, & þat is þe rain þat fordoþ al þe derkenes. And also, hii ben
as in a cloude þat ne vnderstond nouȝt what þat þei don, ne wote what is
gode, ne what is forboden hem noþer bi holi writ ne bi her wit; & þan hii
10 ne haue no rain whan no man ne techeþ hem. And þerfor God ordeined
þre ordres in holi chirche, of winners, & of defendours, & of asailours.
God haþ sette þe winners for to feden alle wiþ her trauaile, & þat ben þe
commen puple. Þe defendours: þat ben þe kniȝtes þat schul defenden
hem & al þe lond fram iuel. And þe asailours: þat ben men of holi chirche
15 þat schuld techen boþe þat on & þat oþer wiþ fair speche & wiþ reddur.
Ȝif þat hii deden eni sinne & trespast aȝeines God, hii it schuld adresce
hem to God ward; ac as þe world scheppeþ now hii ben þe most dele
rauissours & rauis þe folk fram God ward boþe wiþ her ensaumple
ȝeueinge & wiþ her werkes. Ac þo þat ben gode men & trewe & kepen þe
20 law of God, hii ben of Goddes chesinge, & God himself seit: 'He þat
doþe hem ani harme, hii don it to himself.' Ac al þat ben proude, oþer
coueitouse, oþer licherouse, þes ben Antecristes chesinge & haue þe
toure of holi chirche aȝeines Goddes wille bot þat he suffreþ it. And who
þat mainteneþ swiche men, hii schal gon to helle wiþ hem, bot ȝif hii
25 amenden hem.
    Þan to þe men of ordre it is ful harde whan þat hii schal answeren tofor
God of her office þat hii han taken on hond, & he nil noiþer techen
hemseluen ne oþer men oþer þat he leteþ for loue oþer for winninge oþer
for drede. And þerfor, he þat schuld be riȝtfulliche man of ordre, he ne
30 most drede non of þes, & he most be connand to techen ich man &
conseil him what þat he wold asken him þat fel to God. And þerfor, þer
ne schuld non be [f. 2ᵛ] bot ȝif he couþe boþe þe olde lawe and þe newe.
Ac Y ne may nouȝt say for sorowe on mani þat þer ben now swiche þat
louen þe order; for to han her delices & nouȝt for to don þat falleþ to þe
35 ordre hii wil taken, ac hii nil no þinge don þat falleþ þerto. Of swiche seit

1 florischeþ] *alt.*    15 boþe] (.)boþe.    26 whan] *on eras.*    27 her] *on eras.*

D'itels dit bien Saint Ieremie
Od grant dolurs en sa prophecie:
'Li petit del pain demanderent
290 Mais ki lur depescast ne trouerent'.
　Suuent pain en sainte escripture
La doctrine d'alme figure,
Kar pain sustent la charnale uie
E sainte escripture l'alme uiuifie.
295 Li petit sunt la lai gent
Endreit de co qu'a l'ordre apent;
Il sunt petit, mais en Deu nun,
Mais en umble subiectiun;
Kar par regard est cil petit
300 Qui obeist a altri dit.
　Le pain demandent li petit
Quant li lai funt tut lur delit;
El mund fichent lur espeir
E mettent l'alme a nunchaleir.
305 Kar en cest liu estot demander
Autant cum il en unt mester.
Chescune charnale bosoigne
Demande aie sanz essoigne.
Mais n'i ad ki pain lur fraigne
310 Quant li prouers est baraigne
D'entente de sainte escripture
V de ses subiez ne prent cure.
Kar co est pain depescer
Les Deu paroles bien mustrer,
315 E bien souldre les questiuns
E almes pestre en bon sermuns.
Li prestres pain ne depescoye
Quant par escrit ne mustre uoie
Al lai de leisser sa folie
320 E uenir al pastur de uie.

Cest pain depescerat cument
Ki l'escripture pas n'entent?
Les altres pestre coment pot
Ke sei pestre ne siet ne uolt?
325 Coment pestrat altri u sei
Qui de diuine pagine est lai?
Co dist li prophete uerais:
'Tels est li prestres cum est li lais'.
Tels est li prestre ueraiement
330 Quant sainte escripture n'entent,
V si il est entendant
Ne fait sulum le Deu comant
Mais tut sulum la lai gent.
En terre habite, en terre entent,
335 E dune essample de peccher　/f. 59ʳ
Ki doust altres iustiser.
E quant en terre met sa paine
L'un cius l'altre el fosse amaine.
Dunt Saint Daui dist en dolusant,
340 D'itels ne dist rien en desirant:
'Lur oilz,' fet il, 'seient obscur
Qu'il ne ueient point de luiur,
E lur dos seient tut dis curuez'.
Que co espunt ore entendez.
345 Li oil co sunt li ordene
Ki el frunt de honur sunt pose
Pur guier tute sainte iglise
En amur, bienfait, en iustise,
E pur sa uoye pur guarder
350 E bone essample a tuz duner.
Li dos sunt la lai gent
Ke par lur dotrinement
E par essample de lur faiz

wel Ieremie þe prophete, þat was halwed in his moder wombe wiþ gret
wepinge: *Paruuli petierunt panem & non erant qui frangerent eis &*
*cetera.*

'Þe litel asked bred ac þer nas non funden þat brak it to hem.' Often bi
5  brede in holi writ bitokeneþ þe techeinge of þe soule, for bred susteineþ
þe bodilich liif & holi writ quikeþ þe soule. Þe litel ben þe lewed folk in
þat iche þat þe ordre falleþ. Hii ben litel, bot nouȝt in God, ac in lowe
obedience to her suuerainnes ac for to haue heiȝe mede in þe blis of
heuene. Hii ben litel whan hii fulfillen al her delices in þe world & setten
10 al her hope in þe blis of þe world & forȝeten þe soule. In þis stede it
scheweþ þat hii han nede of brekinge of brede, þat is, vndoinge of holi
writ; ac þer nis non þat brekeþ his brede whan þe prist es barain, þat [is],
naked of gode werkes & of conninge, ne vnderstondeþ nouȝt holi writ,
ne ȝifeþ no kepe to hem þat ben vnder him. Þat is þe brekinge of þe
15 brede, for to schewe wel holi writ & Goddes wordes, & fede þe soules
wiþ gode sermouns. Þe prest ne brekeþ nouȝt þe brede whan he ne vndoþ
nouȝt holi writ as he auȝt for to don vnto þe lewed folk & techen hem
hou þat hii miȝht comen to þe liif þat euer schal last. How schuld he
breke þis brede þat ne vnderstondeþ nouȝt holi writ, & hou schal he fede
20 oþer þat ne can nouȝt ne wil nouȝt fede himseluen, Y ne mai nouȝt wit
hou. As þe prophete seit: *Et erit populus ita sacerdos,* þat is: 'Swiche as
þe lewed folk ben, swiche is þe preste'. And þerfor it schal fallen of hem
as God seit in þe godspelle: 'Whan þe blinde ladeþ þe blinde, boþe fallen
in þe diche'. Swiche mantel-bond, swiche men, swiche prestes hii hiren
25 & susten. And þerfor boþe schul gon oway bot ȝif hii amende her liif, &
þat is in auntre ȝif hii schul haue þat grace. *Si cecus cecum ducat, ambo*
*in foueam cadunt.*

Seynt Dauid sorowand seit of þes: *Obscurentur oculi eorum & dorsum*
*eorum semper in curua:* 'Her eiȝen schul ben blinde þat hii ne schul se
30 nouȝt, & her rigge be euermore croked'. Hou þis owe to be vnderstonden,
hereþ now. Þe eiȝe, he seit, schal be derk. Be þe eiȝen is vnderstonden
men of ordre þat ben sette in Goddes foreheued for to gyen & wissen al
holi cherche, þat ben cristen men. He schuld leden hem in loue & in gode
werkes & in riȝtfulnesse & liue hemseluen in clennesse, þat oþer mai
35 take ensaumple at hem to do wele. And her rigge schal ben alway croked:
þat ben þe lewed folk þat þurth her techinge & þurth ensaumple of her

8 suuerainnes] *alt.*    12 is] *om.*    31 derk] derk(.)    32 gyen] *alt. to* gyed *l.h*

Siure deiuent en bons esplaiz.
355  Mais quant li oil sunt obscuriz
Par pudre de mundein deliz,
Ico espealt, ke li clergiez
Par cuueitise sunt asorbez,
N'est mie merueille si lai gent
360  Sunt acurbez a tel talant;
E cil ad dreite curberie
Ki de terre pense e ciel ublie.
E si auient il mult suuent
Que par les pecchez de la gent
365  Feit Deu les prechurs taisir
E de tuz sermuns enuiir.
Dunt Deus al saint prophete dit
Pur la gent k'il puruerse uit:
'Ta lange,' co dist il, 'frai
370  Aerdre ferm a tun palai;
Kar la gent od ki es manant
Est mult puruerse e tariant'.
Dunt Deus en altre liu manace
Par le prophete plein de grace:
375  'As nues manderai amunt
Qu'il mes nule pluie ne funt
Sur ma uigne pur aruser,
Kar ele ne uolt bon fruit porter'.
Par les nues ki sunt amunt

380  Les prestres a entendre [s]unt
Qui sunt mis amunt sur la gent
Par le Deu establisement
Que deiuent estre repleniz
De la pluie de sainz escriz.
385  La uigne Deu li subiez sunt
Ki fruit de bones oures funt,
Que li clerc deiuent cultiuer
E par bon sermuns aruser.
Mais quant li subiez sunt grucus
390  E enuers Deu en bien percus,
E refusent enseignement
Pur siure lur charnel talant,
Deu mande, co est, il esspire
As nues de clergie par ire
395  Qu'il ne plouent mot de doctrine
A la gent ke de li decline.
Kar co est ire ueiraiment
Quant il sustrait docuement,
Quant il ne uolt endoctriner
400  Pur sa uigne eschiuer;
Kar Deus cel home pas nen aime
Qu'il par doctrine ne reclaime,
Ki il ne uolt endoctriner
Ne par sun flael chastier.

gode werkes schuld folowen hem & don efter hem; ac whan þe eiȝen ben
blinde þurth pouder of worldlich delices, y say, whan þe clergie is
ablinded [f. 3ʳ] þurth couaytise, it nis no wonder þeiȝ þat þe lewed ben
also brouȝt vnto swyche wille. And he mai wele be cleped croked þat
5    setteþ his hert on erþeliche þinges & forȝetteþ þe heuen. And it falleþ
often þat þurth þe synne of þe folk, God doþ þe prechours hold hem
stille, þo þat ben gode men; ac þe oþer þat liuen after delices of þe world,
he mai suffre hem speken ynouȝ, for fewe oþer non schal do þe better for
her speche þeiȝ hii tellen hem al holi writ. And swyche prechours, ich
10   vnderstond, be mani now, & þe folk nis neuer þe better, bot euer lenger
þe wers. Ac þe gode men þat queme God, he wil do hem hold hem stille,
as he seit þurȝt his prophete: *Adherere faciam linguam tuam palato tuo
quia domus exasperans est* – 'For þe folk', he seit, 'þat ben schrewes, Y
schal fasten þi tunge to þi palat of þi mouþe þat þou ne schal nouȝt
15   speken to hem; for þe folk þat þow wonest amonge ben schrewes & al
contrarious aȝeines me'. And also in anoþer stede he manace þe folk
þurth þe prophete: *Nubibus mandabo desuper ne pluant imbrem super
vineam meam* – þat is: 'Y schal sende to þe cloudes abouen þat hii ne rein
no more vp my vine for to dewen it, for it nil bring forþ no gode froute'.
20   Bi þe cloudes þat ben abouen is vnderstonden þe gode men of holi
chirche þat ben Godes chosen, þat ben set abouen þe folk in God stede
for to techen, & ben fulfilled of holi writ. Be þe vine is bitokened þe
lewed folk þat ben vnder hem, þat don frute of gode werkes, þat þe
clerkes schuld tillen & dewen wiþ gode prechinges. Ac whan þe subiettes
25   ben gruchande aȝeines God and wikked, & forsaken techinge for þat hii
wil folow her fleschliche willes & her delices, God sendeþ wratfulliche
vnto þe clerkes apertliche þat hii ne rein no word of techinge vnto þe folk
þat drawen awaywarde fram him. For þat is wratþe for soþe whan he
wiþdraweþ his techinge, þat he nil nouȝt þat his folk ben tauȝt so þat he
30   wiþdroweþ his veniaunce, þat he ne toke nouȝt wreche: & for þat he wil
take wreche, he nil nouȝt þat þe folk be chastist wiþ his ȝerde.

---

3 þeiȝ] *alt. to* þeiȝf *l.h.*  4 brouȝt] broȝuȝt.  9 þeiȝ] *alt. to* þeif *l.h.*  10 nis] *alt. to is.*
12 þuȝt] þurȝt(.).  14 palat] *alt. to* pallat *l.h.;* þou] *alt.;* ne] *canc. l.h.*  16 aȝeines] &
*ins.* aȝeines, *l.h.;* manace] manaceþ.  21 þat (2)] pepyll *ins.* þat, *l.h.*  22 holi writ] of
(…) holi (…..) writ.  25 forsaken] *alt. to* forsakeþ(.).  26 wratfulliche] *partly eras.*
27 rein] & *ins.* rein *l.h.*  28 whan] of good *ins.* whan, *l.h*  30 wiþdroweþ] wilnot *ins.*
wiþdroweþ, *l.h.;* veniaunce] venigaunce *alt. l.h.*

405 Dunt Saint Daui dist el sauter:
    'Deu, tu l'as destruit d'esmunder'.
    D'esmunder destruit est sa uie
    Ki Deus n'en fait n'en dist chastie.
        Dunt io pur tut amonester
410 K'en Deu se uolent chastier
    Enpris ai cest escrit
    V chascun purrat a delit
    Lire e oir vuertement
    Ico qu'en Deu a lui apent:
415 Coment li clerc deit sermuner
    E sei meimes en Deu guarder;
    Coment li lais deit bien oir
    E sun doctur en Deu cherir;
    E cument tuz uiuement   /f. 59ᵛ
420 Ferrunt le Deu comandement;
    E quel merite cil auerunt
    Ke Deu de bon quor seruirunt.
    Les ewangelies des domnees
    Io ai en franceis translatees,
425 E des festes as sainz partie,
    Pur mustrer a chascun sa uie,
    E coment deit essample prendre
    Des sainz pur s'alme a Ihesu rendre.
    Kar enpres chascune lezcun
430 Ki ad del ewangelie nun
    Ai mis del exposiciun
    Vn poi pur mustrer la raisun
    Ke hom le ewangelie puisse entendre
    E li nunlettrez bien aprendre.
435 E chascun ki siet lettrure
    E de franceis la parleure
    Lire i poet pur sei amender
    E pur les autres endoctriner.
    Bien sai tant est grant la matire
440 Que io ne pus a tuz suffire;
    Mais mielz ualt partie tucher
    Pur mei e altres amender,
    Que le tresor Deu enfuir
    En terre par del tut teisir.
445 E ico ai fait tut altresi
    Cum cil ki passe pre fluri;
    De tutes les flurs ad talent
    Mais tutes coillir nes poet nent;

    Tutes aime, tutes espie,
450 E puis en prent une partie.
    Alsi coil io cest escrit
    Co que home poet lire a delit,
    E ke mustre suffisalment
    A chascun co qu'a li apent.
455 Nel faz pas par losengerie,
    Par orgoil ne surquiderie,
    Ne pur mustrer ma clergie,
    Ne pur l'onur de ceste uie;
    Altre luer ne quer prendre
460 Que sul Deu ke tut poet rendre,
    E praeres e uraisu[n]s
    De cels ki orrunt les lescuns.
    Kar co faz pur mei aquiter,
    E cors e alme d'encumbrer
465 De la folie que ai parle,
    E del bien que ai entrelasse.
    Ke cist escrit seit parfesant
    Quanque ai mesfait en mun viuant.
    Si li auturs finist sa uie
470 Bon escrit ne poet finir mie;
    Mais l'escrit par li parlera
    Qu'auant mort e purriz serra;
    E pur coli numeement,
    Ki en ses diz sul Deu entent
475 Escrit pur tuz enseigner
    De faire bien e mal leisser.
    Saint Pol le dist pur uerite:
    'Iammes ne charrat charite'.
    Nun frat oure uieraiement
480 Dunt charite est fundement.
    E li escriz ki serra faiz
    Pur tut tolir de mortels leiz,
    Quant purement est fait en De
    Dun est co droite charite.
485 Pur co ai io cest oure empris
    Kar charite n'ert ia esquis,
    E tut parfrat charite
    Quanque ne poet ma fraellete.
    Bien recunois ma nunsauance,
490 Ma feblesce, ma nunpuissance;
    Mais cil me poet bien assenser
    Qui fist la roche l'ewe ietter,

*Destruxisti eum ab emundacione.* 'Lord, þou hast destrued þe vnclene'.
Vnclene is he þat God nil nouȝt chastise. Þerfor ich amonest alle þat hii
wil chastis hem in God. And þerfor ich made þis boke, þat ich man mai
haue delite for to here & rede openliche what apendeþ to God & to him—
5 how þe clerke schal prechen & kepen himseluen in God, & how þe lewed
schal wele werchen & louen wel his techer, & how al schal wirchen &
don Goddes comaundment, & what meret hii schul han þat seruen God
wiþ god wille. Þe godspelles of sonnendays & a parti of the seyntes þat
ben in heuen, ich haue drawen hem out into englische, first efter þe letter,
10 & þen þe vnderstonding & vndoinge schortliche, þat men may wel
vnderstonden hem, & for to schew ich man his liif & how he schal take
ensaumple of holi [f. 3ᵛ] men how he schal ȝeld God his soule & reden
his boke for to amenden himseluen & for to techen oþer. Wel Y wote þat
al ne mai I nouȝt tellen, ac better it is to tellen a parti for toamend me &
15 oþer þan for to deluen Goddes tresore in þe erþe, & þerfor, a parti ichil
tellen. As he þat passeþ be a medow þat mani fair floures ben inne & to
alle þe floures he haþ gode wille to han, ac al he mai nouȝt gadren &
þerfor he takeþ a parti of þat him likeþ best, also do ich of þis writ. He
þat mai, rede it in delite; it scheweþ suffisauntliche ichon þat falleþ to
20 him. I ne make nouȝt for losangerie, ne for pride, ne for to be praised
þurth clergie, ne for to haue worschip in þis liif; I þenche to anoþer lond
þer better ȝeldinge of mede is þan in þis world, & ich it make for to
aquiten me bodi & soule fram encumberment, & to speke for me þer Y
ne mai ne can. For þeiȝ þe maker ende his liif, holi writ ne mai nouȝt
25 enden. Ac þis writ schal speke for him whan he is ded & roten &
namelich for hem þat set her hert in God & do it to his worschipe, oþer
don it do in þat iche entent þat oþer miȝht be tauȝt þe better þerþurht.
Seynt Paule it seyt for soþe: 'Charite ne schal neuer chaunge'.
*Karitas numquam excidit.* Neuer ne schal charite chaunge, ne þe werke
30 þat is founded vp charite; & þe writ þat is made for to drawe men &
wymmen fram dedlich filþes, whan it is enterliche made in God, þan it is
riȝt charite. For þi ich haue taken þis werk, for charite ne mai neuer al be
soȝt. And al schal charite fulfille þat my frelte ne may nouȝt com to. Wel
ich am knowen myn vnconynge, my febles, & myn vnmiȝht, ac he mai
35 wel techen me þat brouȝt þe water out of þe ston — *Qui eduxit aquam*

---

7 meret] med *alt. l.h.* 12 ensaumple] (.)ensaumple. 13 his] *alt. to* þis. 15 goddes]
& hyde *ins.* goddes, *l.h.* 17 he (1)] but *ins.* he, *l.h.;* &] all *ins.* &, *l.h.* 23 me (1)]
my *on eras.* 24 þeiȝ] *alt. to* þeif *l.h.* 25 roten] roted *alt.*

E ki fit l'asnesse parler
Pur le prophete chastier.
495 Dunc ne me dei pas emaier
De plus sages amonester.
Deus al prophete dist par sei:
'Ta buche oure, io l'emplirai'.
E Saint Daui dist el sauter,
500 Qui saint esperit fist parler:
'Deus a celi uerbe durrat
Qui par grant uertu nuntterat'.
Par ices diz sui esmuz  /f. 60ʳ
Parler de Deu e de ses uertuz,
505 E les autres endoctriner
Que me meimes ne sai guier.
Mais en lur bien faiz partir crei
Qui s'amenderunt par mei;
Ki par mes diz s'amenderunt
510 Lur bien faiz od mei partirunt.
  Nul home ne me deist preiser
Ki de cest oure orra parler:
Si bien i est, de mei n'est mie
Mais del esperit ki tuz guie.
515 Dunt Deus a ses apostles dit,
E par els tuz les autres aprit,
Qu'il ne deiuent enorgoillir,
Ne nul bienfait a lur tenir:
'Vus n'estes pas ki parlez
520 Mais li sainz espiriz, co sachez;
L'espirit, mun pere, par nun,
En vus parole e fait sermun'.
En autre liu redit li sire:
'Espirit, la u uolt, espire'.
525 Quant il espire u li plait,

E la, u il uolt, se retrait,
Dunc n'est pas l'ume a preiser,
Mais celi ki le fait parler,
Nient plus que l'asnesse ki parla
530 E dan Balam chastia.
Mais coli seit mult a preiser
Qui tels merueilles fait ourer.
Dunc nul home ne deit despire
Que sainte escripture deigne dire,
535 N'auiler coli ki parole
Tut seit il de fole escole;
E tut seit il de male uie
Qui les paroles Deu nuncie,
L'em deit mult bien oir sun dit
540 Nient pur li mais pur l'espirit.
L'ewe k'est e pure e clere,
Ki suuent curt par la gutere,
E la gutere n'en beit mie
Mais l'ewe a bone terre guie;
545 Li chanels point de fruit ne fait
Mais la terre ki l'ewe beit.
Tut ausi est del prechur:
Tut ne seit il endreit sei pur,
Purquant bone est la doctrine
550 Que Deus par sa buche destine;
Par li uient mais n'i oure rien
E as entendanz fait grant bien;
A li ne fait fors sul l'issir
E les oanz en Deu flurir.
555 Le palu passe la riuere
Qui mult est bone e bele e clere:
Del palu tres bien vus guardez

*de petra* – & þat made þe asse to speken for to chastis þe prophete.
Wharfor Y ne schal nouȝt desmaien me for to amonesten wiser þan ich
am, for God seid to þe prophete bi him on: *Aperi os tuum & ego implebo*
*illud* – 'Open þi mouþe & i schal fulfillen it,' & Dauid seit in þe sauter
5  þat þe holi gost spake in him.

   *Deus dabit verbum euangelizantibus.* God schal ȝeue to hem word þat
þurth gret vertu he schal be[r]en it forþ. Þurth þes wordes ich am glad for
to speken of God & of his vertuȝ & for to techen oþer þeiȝ Y ne can
rewle me selue; ac ich hope for to haue parte in her gode dedes þat
10  amende hem þurth me. Þai þat þurth þes wordes amenden hem, her gode
dedes hii schal departen wiþ me.

   No man ne schal praysen me for þes sawes þat heren it, for of me nis it
nouȝt, ac of þe spirit þat al wisseþ. For God seit to his apostles þat þurth
hem he tauȝt alle oþer þat hii ne schuld nouȝt wex proude þerþurth, ne no
15  gode dede taken to hemseluen.

   *Non enim vos estis qui loquimini.* 'Ȝe ne be nouȝt þat speken, ac it is þe
holi gost my fader, spirit bi name, spekeþ in ȝou.' In oþer stede seit þe
lord: 'Þe spirit, þer wil, spireþ' [f. 4ʳ] – *Spiritus vbi vult spirat.*

   Whan þe holi gost spireþ þer he wil & draweþ þider þer him likeþ, þan
20  nis nouȝt þe man to praysen (ac þat þinge is to praysen þat doþ him
speken) namore þan þe asse þat spake & chastist þe prophete Balam.
*Ivdas apostolus habuit correpcionem vesame sue brutum animal hominis*
*non loquens.*

   Ac he þat scheweþ swiche wonder, he is muchel to praisen. Whar þurth
25  no man owe to despise þat þe holi gost wil say, ne praise nouȝt him þat
spekeþ, bot God þat holdeþ his scole in him. And þeiȝ al he be of iuel liif
þat bereþ forþ Godes wordes, men owe ful wel here his worde, nouȝt for
[him, ac for] þe spirit þat spekeþ in him. For often men seþ þat þurth þe
goter comeþ þe cler water & fair, & þe goter ne drinkeþ it nouȝt, ac ladeþ
30  þe water to gode erþe. Þe goter bringgeþ forþ no gode frout, ac þe erþe
doþ þat drinkeþ þe water. Also it fareþ be þe sinner; þeiȝ al he ne be
nouȝt clere & pure in himself, ne for þan þe techinge is gode þat God
spekeþ þurth his mouþe. Þurth him it comeþ, ac it ne doþ him no profite,
ac vnto þe vnderstonders it doþ gret gode. In him ne doþ it nouȝt, bot goþ
35  þurth him; & hii þat vnderstonden it, it makeþ hem for to florischen in
gode werkes. Þe riuer passeþ þurth mudde: fro þe mudde kep þe wel &

---

1 asse] alle *alt. to* asse; chastis] chastie *alt.*   7 beren] besen.   16 þat] he *ins.* þat, *l.h.*
28 him ac for] *om.*   31 þeiȝ] *alt. to* þeif *l.h.*

E del ewe clere beuez.
L'em ne deit nuli refuser
560 Mais bonement tuz escuter,
E tuz lur diz de quor iuger,
Le bien tenir, le mal leisser.
Nul n'est ke partut bien die,
E alcun bien dist qui mult crie.
565 E l'em ne deit pas auiler
La persone que l'om ot parler.
De bordel poet produme issir
E de chastel malueis saillir,
E queique la pe[r]sone seit,
570 Cil est pruz ke bien fait.
Nul ne dit mielz pur richete
Ne nul pis pur sa pourete;
Ne cherir un ne altre despire
Quant l'espirit, qui uolt, espire.
575 Ki bien dit ne seit pas repris,
La rose met l'espine en pris:
Ne deit auer la duce rose
Qui l'espine cherir nen ose.
L'em deit cherir le prechur
580 Mult pur li, plus pur Deu amur;
Qui al ciel mustre le ueage,
Quel k'il seit, si est Deu message.
Plus ne poet li riches duner

Que li poures en cest mester;
585 Mais li poures pur Deu plus to[l]t
Quant l'om bien faire ne li uolt;
Kar li riches est asacez   /f. 60ᵛ
E li poures est mesaisez.
E Deu dist que li ourer
590 Est digne d'auer sun luer;
Bien deit auer mundein aie
Ki al manger de ciel enuie;
Bien deit auer chose terrestre
Ki pramet uie celestre.
595 Del ciel ert forsclos a estrus
Ki sun prechur leist busoignus.
Saint Pol commande ueirement
Ke chascun home ki d'altre aprent
Od sun doctur deit comuigner
600 De tuz ses biens sanz demander.
   Ore pri tuz cels que orrunt
Icest escrit e ki le lirrunt
Qu'il prient Deu omnipotent
K'il de tuz mals me defent,
605 E doint cest oure si parfeire
Qu'en dreite fei le puisse plaire,
E puis le curs de ceste uie
Od ses sainz seie en sa baillie.
Kar cest oure faz uerraiement

drink of þe fair water. Noman ne schal noman forsaken þat spekeþ
Goddes worde, ac wiþ gode wille heren him & al her wordes iuggen wel
wiþin her hertes, & leten þe iuel & taken þe gode. No man ne may in al
þinge say wele, for sumtime, þei3 he be ful gode, sum word may passen
5    fram him þat mi3t be ful wel vnseied. And so it dede fram Seynt Petre
whan Ihesus Crist seyd to his deciples, 'Go we to Ierusalem', & Peter
seid, 'Lord, what wiltow do þer? Hii ne loue þe nou3t', & Ihesus seid
a3ein, 'Go awai, deuel'. Lo, þer þe fynde spake in Peter as holi as he was.
Þerfor noman schal take 3eme to him þat spekeþ þe word, for out of
10   bordel may a gode man comen & out of þe castel, a wikked man. What
þat þe persone is, he is gode þat hereþ it & doþ it in dede. No man ne seyt
þe better for his riches, ne þe wers for his pouerte. It nis nou3t for to
despisen whan þe holi gost wil spiren in hem, ac take þe rose & lete þe
þorne. And no man ne owe to haue þe swete rose þat nil nou3t norische
15   þe þorn þat þe rose comeþ of. Men owe to louen þe prechour for him, &
more for þe loue of God, for þat he techeþ vs þe way to heuen. For what
þat he be, 3itte he is Goddes messanger, for þe fendes ben sumtime sent
for to don Godes messages. It telleþ þat þe deuel prechede on a tyme in
mannes likkenes to þe folk, & so he seyd to hem whan he hade preched,
20   þat he was a deuel & was sent þider for to prechen hem for hii had hadde
so mani prechours aforn & weren euer þe lenger þe more schrewes, &
were so harded in her schrewednesse, þat hii ne mi3ht nou3t ben
amended, & þerfor he was sent for to prechen hem. Namor ne may þe
riche don in þat mister þan þe pouer. Our lord seyd þat þe wircher is
25   worþi to han his mede. *Dignus est operarius mercede sua.* [f. 4ᵛ]

Wel he owe to han worldlich mete þat bringgeþ þe mede of heuen; wel
he owe to han worldlich þinges þat behoteþ þe godes of heuen; out of
heuen he schal be put þat leteþ his prechour haue nede. Seynt Poule it
seyt for soþe, þat ich man þat oþer lereþ & techeþ, he schal 3eue him of
30   alle his godes wiþouten askinge. *Communicet autem his qui catezizatur*
*verbo.*

Now ich beseche alle þat heren þis writ & reden it, þat hii besechen to
God almi3ti þat he defende me fram al iuels, & so for to make þis werk
þat it mai plesen him in ri3t bileue, & efter þe passeinge out of þis liif, be
35   wiþ his holi halwen in his compaynie. For þis werk Y do, for soþe, for

---

3 wiþin her hertes] in her hertes wiþ *transp.*   4 þei3] *alt. to* þeif *l.h.*   10 &] (...) &.
14 norische] *alt.*   16 loue] *ins.*   20 hadde] hated *alt.*   24 þat (2)] þt(.); þe (2)] þ(e.).
25 his] *alt.*

610 Pur mei e pur tute gent.
　　Tuz n'aiment mie escripture
　　Ne tuz n'entendent pas lectrure.
　　Tels l'ewangelie ot e lit
　　Ke n'entent pas quantque il dit.
615 E pur tuz faire tut entendre
　　En Deu osai cest oure enprendre.
　　Ki tuz oent uuertement
　　Quoi l'ewangelie lur aprent,
　　E tuz ueient en cest escrit
620 Ke li latins esspealt e dit;
　　Pur nient aillurs trauaillerunt,
　　Suffisaument ici l'orrunt.
　　Io nel di pas as clers lettrez
　　Qui sunt en sainz escriz fundez,
625 Mais as altres meins entendanz
　　Cum io sui memes e asquanz,
　　Ki ne poum tut encercher
　　Mais a peine le fruit parer.
　　Dunt io comunement tuz pri
630 Ki l'orrunt e lirrunt ausi,
　　K'il i mettent amendeisun
　　Si rien i ad de mesprisiun.
　　Deu li doint pardurable uie
　　Qui pur Robert de Grettam prie.Amen.
635 　Ore pri io de quor parfunt
　　Tuz cels ki cest escrit auerunt
　　Qu'il le prestent a deliuere
　　A tuz cels k'il voldrunt escriure.
　　Kar custume est del Deu sermun:
640 Plus est cher cum plus est commun.
　　Qui Deu sermun en celant nie
　　Semble ki il ait de Deu enuie,
　　E as almes fait guere grande
　　Qui lur tout lur iurnel uiande.
645 Dunt tantes rendre li estolt

　　Cum il poet aider, e ne uolt,
　　De tantes rendra raisun
　　Cum sunt periz sanz sun sermun.
　　E pur tantes ert en tirpel
650 Cum sunt periz par sun conseil.
　　Deu uolt ki nul ne seit auer
　　De ses sermuns a tuz mustrer;
　　Ki siet e poet, mustre par diz,
　　Qui ne poet, mustre ses escriz.
655 Certes qui plus les mustra
　　Deus abanduner plus li fra,
　　E en fra trestuz riches
　　Fors cels ki de mustrer sunt chiches,
　　Kar auarice en nule place
660 Ne poet encuntrer la Deu grace.
　　Ki uolenters comunera
　　E Deu uolenters li durra,
　　Kar il le dist en uerite:
　　'Dunez e il vus ert dune'.
665 Dunez al cors nient sulement
　　Mais a l'alme tut ensement:
　　Al cors uiande e dras dunez,
　　L'alme del sermun Deu peissez.
　　Qui sei e altres si peistra,
670 Sa despense Deus acreistra.
　　Le tresor Deu ne faudra mie　/f. 61ʳ
　　Mais al despendant multeplie;
　　Cum del soen plus despenderez
　　A li, sachez, plus guaignerez;
675 Ki le soen despendre ne uolt,
　　Co ki il ad en sei Deu li tolt.
　　E pur co prestez uolenters
　　Kar Ihesu est mult bon renters;
　　Il ne faudra ia a nuli
680 Fors ki primes faldra a li;

me & for al men. Al ne han nouȝt al holi writ, ne al ne vnderstonde nouȝt
letterure; swiche hereþ þe godspelle & redeþ it þat ne vnderstondeþ nouȝt
what he seit. And for to don al vnderstonde it, in God ich dare take þis
werke vnder hond, þat al mai heren openlich, heren what þe godspelle
5   techeþ hem. And al he mai sen in þis writ þat þe Latyn spelleþ & seiþ;
suffisauntliche hii mowen heren here al þat nedeþ to hem. Y ne say nouȝt
for þis clerkes þat ben founden in holi writ, ac vnto hem þat ben lasse
vnderstondinge, as ich am myseluen, þat ne may nouȝt serchen alle, ac
vnneþ pare þe frut. Whareþurth Y beseche hem al comunliche þat it reden
10  oþer heren, þat ȝeue þer be ani defaute in, þat hii amende it, & þat God
ȝif hem þe liue þat euer schal last þat for hem þat it ordeined & made
besechen. Amen.
    Now ich beseche wiþ gode hert to alle þat þis writ han, þat hii lene it
wiþ gode wille to al þat it wil writen. For þe custome is of Goddes word,
15  þe more þat it spredeþ obrode, þe better it is, & more hii quemen God þat
it owen. For he þat heleþ Goddes word, it semeþ þat he haþ enuie to God,
& to soules he doþ gret harme, for he benimmeþ hem her fode. Wharfor
he most ȝeld rekenynge þat may helpen & wil nouȝt; of as mani he schal
ȝeld reckenynge as ben lorn þurth his consel, for þurth his consel it is
20  whan he haþ a þinge þat he mai help soules wiþ & nil nouȝt. God nil
nouȝt þat non wiþdrawe him þat he ne schewe his wordes to alle. He þat
can & mai, schewe hem wiþ word, & he þat [may] nouȝt wiþ word,
schewe forþ his bokes, for certes, þe more þat he scheweþ hem, þe more
grace he geteþ of God & þe better he wil helpen him boþe here &
25  elleswhere. For he schal maken al riche bot hem þat it hold & nil nouȝt
schewen it; for auarice [in] no place ne mai stonde wiþ Goddes grace. Þat
wiþ gode wille ȝeueþ, wiþ gode wille God wil ȝeue him, for he it seit for
soþe: 'ȝif, it schal be ȝeuen to þe'. *Date & dabitur vobis &c.*
    ȝif nouȝt onlich to þi body, ac vnto þi soule also; vnto þe body mete &
30  drink & cloþes ȝeueþ, & þe soule fedeþ wiþ Goddes word. Þat himseluen
& oþer þus feden, his despense God schal multiplie. Þe tresore of God ne
schal neuer faile, ac it multiplieþ vnto him þat largeliche despendeþ. Þe
more þat [f. 5ʳ] þow despendest of his vnto þiseluen, þe more þou schalt
wynnen. He þat nil nouȝt despenden of his, þat he haþ & himself God
35  binymmeþ him. And þerfor, leneþ & ȝeueþ wiþ god wille, for God is a
gode renter. He ne schal neuer fayle to non bot ȝif he faile first to him; &

5 seiþ] *alt.*   7 founden] founded *alt.*   10 & þat god] god & þat *transp.*   12 besechen]
besecheþ *alt.*   22 may] scheweþ, *ins.*   26 in] &.   31 feden] feden *alt. to* fedeþ.

E encore si se repent
Puis sa falture tut li rent,
Kar il ne tent nul a mentur
Qui de sun mal ad fait bon retur,
685 Ne il ne guerpist nuli uie
Qui puis ses pecchez se chastie.
Trestuz tent il a bons amis

Ki del amender sunt penis,
Cum vus en cest mirrur uerrez,
690 Si vus de bon quer i guardez.
Deu nus doint si ses biens despendre
Que tuz biens puissum od li prendre;
Il le uoille par sa pite
Ki maint un Deus en trinite.   Amen.

ȝete, efter, ȝif he repente him, al þat him failed he ȝeldeþ him, for he ne
holdeþ non for leiȝer þat wil amenden him of his iuel, ne he ne forsakeþ
no liif þat efter his synnes chastis him. Alle he holdeþ for his gode
frendes þat ententiliche ben aboute for to amenden hem, as ȝe schul sen
5    in þis mirour. He ȝeue ȝou his grace & me so his godes for to despenden,
þat al godes we may take wiþ him þat is on in Trinite. Amen.

1 he] he(.);  repente] repenteþ *Rev.*   3 chastis] chasteþ *alt.*

# DOMINICA I IN ADUENTU DOMINI

695 Iesus uint pres d'une cite
Ke Ierusalem est apele.
E quant il uint a Bethphage,
K'est el Munt de Oliue,
Dunt ad des soens dous enueie.

700 'Alez', fait il, 'en la cite
El chastel encuntre vus leue;
Vne asnesse i ad lie,
E sun asnun li est al pe.
Quant les auerez bel deslie

705 Tanttost me seient ca mene.
Si nul vus ad rien demande,
Dites qu'il est li sires a gre,
Mester en ad sa uolente;
Cist vus auera tanttost leisse'.

710 Ico fait ad bien auerre
Co que fut ainz prophetize:
La fille Syon seit nuncie:
Ti reis uient en paisiblete;
Sur une asnesse ad fait sun se,

715 E sur le fiz al suziuke.
Li disciple s'en sunt ale,
Fait unt cum lur est comande.
L'asnesse e l'asnun unt mene
E sur els unt lur dras iete.

720 E puis unt Iesum ensun munte;
Ensi sunt la cite entre.
Li sergant a la gent Hebre
Encuntre li en sunt ale;
Lur dras el chemin unt iete.

725 Plusurs unt arbres desrame,
Si en unt le chemin estrame.
De tute parz unt crie,
E cil deuant e cil detre:
'Osanna al fiz Daui de gre,

730 Osanna seit en halte chante,
Bienait ki uient el nun de De'.
Ore auez oi la lescun,
Ore oez l'entrepretaciun,
Ke Deus vus doint sa beneicun

735 E des pecchez vus face pardun.
Cest nun Iesus espealt salueur
Ki nus salua par sa dulcur;
E Ierusalem, icest nun
Espealt de peis la uisiun.

740 Maisun de buche est Beetphage;
Misericorde est Oliue.
Jerusalem Iesus aprocha
Sa salue peis quant nus duna.
Mais primes uint a Beetphage,

745 Kar ainz estoet qu'il seit nuncie
Par sainte predicaciun
E la fei que tenir deuum;
Kar nul ne siet k'il purra craire,
Ne coment purra le bien faire,   /f. 61ᵛ

750 S'il n'en ait oi par raisun,
V par escrit, u par sermun.
Kar par buche de precheisun
Vient buche de confessiun;
Kar si issi auient que hom se recorde

# SERMON 1
## DOMINICA PRIMA ADUENTUS DOMINI

*Secundum Mathium. Cum appropinquasset Ihesus Ierosolimam &c.*
Ihesus come nere a cite þat is cleped Ierusalem. And whan he come to
Bethphage, þat is be þe mount of Oliuete, þan he cleped two of his
deciples. 'Goþ', he seyd, 'into þe cite, into þe castel þat is risen oȝaines
5   ȝou; þerin is an asse bounden, & her fole standeþ be hir. Whan ȝe han
faire & wel vnbounden hem, as son bringgeþ hem hider to me. ȝif ani
man aske ȝou whi þat ȝe do so, seit it is þe lordes wille, þe maister schal
haue his wille, & hii schul leten ȝou gon as swiþe'. Þis dede was wel sen
bi þat was prophecied aforn: 'Þe child Syon be schewed; þat comeþ in
10  pesiblete, vpon an asse haþ made his sete & opon þe fole he sat also'. His
desciples ben gon & þe asse & þe fole hii han brouȝt & layed her cloþes
opon hem & þan set Ihesu þeropon, & so hii entred into þe cite. Þe
ceriauntes & þe men Ebrus comen aȝeines him & spradde her cloþes in
þe strete, & mani brouȝt floures & braunches of þe tres & han strewed þe
15  strete wiþ hem. On al half hii criden, hii biforn & hii behinde, 'Osanna
vnto Dauid sone; osanna be songen on heiȝe; blissed be he þat comeþ in
þe name of God'.
   Now ȝe han herd þe letter, now hereþ what it meneþ so þat God ȝeue
vs his blissingge & of oure sinnes forȝeuenes. Þis name 'Ihesu' is as
20  muchel to say as 'saueour' þat saued vs þurth his godenesse, & þis name
'Ierusalem' is as michel to say as 'siȝt o pes'; 'hous of mouþe' is
Bethphage, & Oliuete is as michel to say as 'merci'. Vnto Ierusalem
Ihesus come whan he ȝaue vs his pes of sauacion. [Ac ferst he com to
Bethphage ffor first hit mot be told þurth holi predicacion] þe faith þat
25  we owe to hold. For no man ne miȝt witen hou he miȝt wel beleuen, ne
hou he schuld do wele, bot ȝif he hadde herd þurth reson, oþer þurth
writ, oþer þurth prechinge. For þurth mouþe of prechinge comeþ mouþe
of schrifte, for whan consciencie biteþ him inwiþ & forþencheþ his sinne,

---

3 þe] *ins.* two] *ins.* 8 sen] sene (.). 14 strewed] *on eras.* 20 as] al *alt. to* as.
23 sauacion] *alt. to* saluacion *l.h.* 24 ac ... predicacion] *om.;* þe] & *ins.* þe.; faith]
*alt. l.h.*

755 Dunc est pres de misericorde.
Kar la uile de Betphage
Munt Oliuete sist al pe,
E nul ne poet en halt munter
Si il ne seit estruit premer;
760 E li prechers bien resache
Par Betphage ki siet en la place,
Partut se deit humilier,
Tut sache il mult bien parler.
Kar Iesus i est areste
765 Qui tut dis aime humilite.
  Ore auez oi de la buche
Ki en dous maners nus tuche,
Co est par predicaciun
E par bone confessiun.
770 Maisun de buche est sainte eglise
V l'em Deu loe en tute guise;
Ele est maisun de uraisun,
Maisun de satisfactiun.
A ceste maisun deit uenir
775 Ki od Iesu uoldra ioir.
  De ceste maisun Betphage
Ad Iesus ses dous enueie
Al chastel encuntre els leue
Pur l'adnesse ki ert lie.
780 Iesus i ad dous enueie
Par les dous reims de charite,
Kar charite est une chose
Mais en dous raims est bien desclose,
Co est, amer Deu sur tute riens
785 E puis sun prosme en tuz biens.
Nuls ne deit estre prechur
S'il nen ad icest amur,
Kar si il preche pur aueir
Deus ad perdu tut pur ueir.
790 E s'il pur Deu leist sermun
Sun prosme met a perdiciun.
Pur co l'estoet si atemprer

Que il ambedous puisse guaigner;
E coli ki l'orrat parler
795 Sun estouer li deit trouer
K'il pur nul charnel bosoing
N'eit de taisir nul assoing.
Kar si li lais co ne fessoit,
A Iesu Crist grant tort ferroit
800 Quant uoid ad leisse sun message
Ke li ad mustre soen curage.
Kar ico n'est pas charite
Quant li pasturs est uoid leisse.
  Li chastels u cil dous uont
805 Co signefie tut le mund
Qui encuntre Deu est aleuez
Par orgoil e par mal pensez.
Kar ore esguardez tut entur,
De rei, de prince, de cuntur,
810 A peine uerrez nule assise
Que aukes n'i ait cuntre eglise.
E li malfe de cels plus hauz
Les plus poueres en fait plus bauz,
Dunt il aueriunt greignur turment
815 Al departir del iugement,
Pur co qu'il memes mesalerent
E les altres ne chastierent,
Mais mal essample lur dunerent
E quant mespristrent le loerent.
820   L'asnesse en cel chastel lie
Sunt cil a ki lur mals agre;
Jl sunt chastel, il sunt asnesse,
Dunc par orgoil, dunc par peresce;
Kar qui uers Deu est orgoillus,
825 De bien faire est mult percus.
Par l'asnun ki fu lie
Sunt cil bien signefie,
Ki pecchent si tres franchement
Ke de Deu ne lur est noent.
830 Mais Iesus par sa grant dulcur

þan he is nere merci; for þe toun of Bethphage stondeþ atte þe fote of þe
mount of Oliuete, & no man ne may climben on heiȝe [f. 5ᵛ] bot he be
ytauȝt. And þe synner wel it wot þurth Bethphage þat sitt in place, in al
þinge he schal lowen him þeiȝ al he can wele speken, for Ihesus is rested
5 þat alway loueþ lownes.

Now ȝe han herd of mouþe, þat ich haue touched ȝou in two maner,
þat is, þurȝ predicacion & þurth schrift. Hous of mouþe is holy chirche
where men herieþ God in al wise, & it is hous of orizoun & hous of ful
ȝildinge. Vnto þis hous he owe come þat wiþ Ihesus wil gladen.

10 Fram þis hous, Bethphage, haþ Ihesus sent his two deciples into þe
castel þat is arisen aȝeines hem for þe asse þat was bounden þerin. Ihesus
haþ sent two disciples for þe two braunches of charite; ac charite is o
þinge, ac in two braunches it is wel opened, þat is, to louen God ouer al
þinge, & efter, his euen cristen as himseluen. No man ne owe to ben
15 prechour bot ȝif þat he haue his loue, for ȝif he preche for to wynne
erþliche gode, God he haþ forlorn for soþe; & ȝif he, for drede of God,
lateþ his prechinge, he forlest his euen cristen. Forþi he most so atempren
him þat he may wynnen hem boþe. And he þat hereþ him speken, his
sustinaunce he owe to fynden him þat he ne be letted for non erþlich
20 werk; for bot ȝif þe lewed dede þis, vnto Ihesus Crist hii deden gret
wronge whan he leteþ his messager gon voide fram him þat haþ schewed
him his hert; for þat nis no charite whan þe prechour is leten go voide
away.

Þe castel þat þe two disciples ȝeden vnto, þat betokeneþ al þe world
25 þat is arisen aȝaines God þurth pride & þurth iuel þouȝtes. Now loke ouer
al of kinge, of prince & of countour; vnneþes ne schaltow sen on asise
þat it ne ariseþ oȝain holi chirche, þat ben gode trewe men. And þe dedes
of þe heiȝest maken þe pouerest lowest, wharþurth he schul han þe
gretter turment atte departinge of þe iugement forþi þat hii gon
30 hemseluen amisse & ne chastis nouȝt þe oþer, ac iuel ensample ȝaf to
hem, & whan hii misdeden, praysed hem.

Þe asse þat is bounden in þis castel ben hii þat han wille to do synne.
Hii ben castel & hii ben asses, now þurth pride & now þurth oþer synnes.
For he þat oȝain God is proude, for to do wele he is ful slowe. Bi þe asse,
35 þat asse þat vnbounden is, ben hii wele betokened þat synnen so freliche
þat hem nis riȝt nouȝt of God. Ac Ihesu, þurth his gret godnesse, of al

---

3 wel] wel(.).    4 þeiȝ] *alt. to* þeif *l.h.*    6 two] *alt.*    7 þurȝ] *on eras.;*  predicacion]
*alt.;*  hous] *canc.*    16 &] *ins.*    19 erþlich] *alt.*    30 chastis] *alt. to* (.)chastiþ.    31
misdeden] (.m)isdede(.).    32 is bounden] bounde(.) is *transp.*    35 is] *ins.*

De tuz peccheurs uolt le retur,
E pur co enueit ses messages
Pur deslier lur fol curages;   /f. 62$^r$
Kar qui ot predicaciun
835 E mettre i uolt sa entenciun,
S'il se repent tant sulement
Desliez est tut ueirement.
   Mais puis estoet qu'il seit menez
A Iesu par les dreit degrez,
840 Primes par dreit gemissement
E puis par bon amendement;
Kar nul ne poet al Deu uenir
Qui espace ad de repentir
S'il ne cunuisse sun pecche
845 E puis l'amende de sun gre;
Kar quicunke issi le fait
Al salueur en uient tut dreit.
Dunc uerra plus parfundement
Des apostles l'enseignement;
850 Co sunt les dras qu'il unt pose
Sur l'asnesse que est amene.
   E dunc i est Iesus munte
Quant uers li s'est humilie;
En sun quor munte ueirement
855 Quant il del tut a li se prent.
   E puis le meine en la cite
Que Ierusalem est apele;
Co est la uisiun de pais
V uerrat ioie sanz relais.
860 Jci le uerrat par espeir,
E ilokis trestut pur ueir.
   E cil ki sunt encuntre uenu
En l'onurance de Iesu,
Quant il uint si cheuauchant
865 Co sunt li angele bienuoillant,

Ki a Iesu funt loement
Quant nul peccheres se repent.
   Cil ki unt lur dras iete
Les martirs unt signefie
870 Qui la uesture de lur char
Mistrent en peine e en eschar.
Cil se ioisent uerraiement
Quant un peccheres se repent.
   Cil qui les arbres desramerent
875 Les confessurs signefierent
Qui par flaels se turmenterent
E de bien faire ne cesserent;
E cil refunt ioie mult grant
De un peccheur bien repentant.
880 E cil qu'enuirun chanterent
Les peccheurs signefierent
Qui ci par penitences dures
Amendent lur forfaitures;
Cil refunt ioie al fiz Marie
885 Quant nus ueient en lur compaignie.
   Tuit distrent a haute uoiz uni:
'Osanna al bon fiz Daui' –
Co est cum l'em desist issi –
'Sauue nus, tu le fiz Daui'.
890 Kar co sachez uerraiement
Quant nul pecchers se repent
Grant ioie en funt trestuz de gre
Tuz cil ke Iesus ad salue.
E nus, seignurs, pur Deu amur
895 Hastum de faire bon retur
Que poissum faire as seinz leesce
Ki dolent sunt pur nostre peresce,
E poissum dire en lur regnee:
'Bienait ki uient el nun de De'.
   Amen.

synnes he wil wiþdrawen hem. And forþi he sendeþ hem his messangers
for to vnbynden þe foule hertes, for who þat hereþ prechinge & wil ȝiue
his hert þerto, ȝif he repente him onliche, þan he is vnbounden for soþe;
ac efter, it bihoueþ þat he be brouȝt to Ihesus bi þe riȝt way, first þurth
5  riȝt schrift & þan þurth amendement, for non ne may comen to God þat
haþ space to repenten him bot ȝif he be aknowen his synne & þan
amende it be his gode wille. For who þat doþ on þat maner, vnto þe
saueour [f. 6ʳ] he goþ ful riȝt. Þan schal he se wele depper þe techinge of
þe apostels þat ben þe cloþes þat hii han layd opon þe asse þat hii han
10 brouȝt: & þan is Ihesus lopen vp whan hii han lowed hem aȝaines him.
Into his hert he comeþ for soþe whan he in al þing repenteþ him, & þan
he ladeþ him into þe cite þat is cleped Ierusalem; þat is þe siȝt of pes þer
he schal se ioye wiþouten ani ende. And here he schal sen it þurth bileue,
& þer he schal sen it verraylich.
15      And hii þat ben comen oȝain Ihesu for to worschipen him whan he
come so ridande, þat ben þe angels ioiand, & to Ihesu hii maken heriinge
whan a sinful man repenteþ him. And hii þat kesten her cloþes, þat
bitokeneþ þe martirs whan hii laden her flesche in pine & in scorninge;
hii herien God also whan a sinful man repenteþ him. And hii þat breken
20 þe bowes & floures bitokeneþ þe confessours þat turmented hem wiþ
scourginge & ne cesed nouȝt to do wele; hii maken gret ioye of a sinful
man þat repenteþ him. And hii þat songen on heiȝe bitokeneþ þe sinful
men & wymmen þat here þurth hard penuance amended her trespasses;
hii maken ioie also vnto Ihesu Marie sone whan on comeþ into her
25 compaynie.
       Al seiden at o voice: 'Osanna vnto Dauid sone þe gode'. Þis is, men
sayd: 'Þus saued haþ vs Dauid sone'. For þat, wite ȝe wele for soþe, al
þat Ihesus haþ saued maken gret ioie whan a synful man repenteþ him.
And þerfor, gode men, for Goddes loue, heiȝe we vs to forsaken oure
30 synnes þat we mai gladen þe seyntes þat ben in heuen þat ben sori for
oure harmes, þat mai sai wiþ hem in her blis, 'Blissed ben hii þat comeþ
in þe name of God'. Amen.

---

6 haþ] haþ(.).   7 þat (2)] *ins.*   9 cloþes] *alt.*   18 laden] *alt. to* ladde; scorninge] *alt.*
*to* scourgynge.   19 breken] *alt.*   20 confessours] *alt.*   26 o] *on eras.*

## DOMINICA II IN ADVENTU DOMINI

900 Une feiz Iesu Crist
A ses dicipiles issi dist:
'Signes erent e granz merueilles
El soleil e en la lune e es esteiles,
E pressure en terre de genz
905 Deuant les confusemenz
Ke mers e fluies ietterunt
E les homes esfreierunt
Pur la pour e pur l'atente
V tut li mund mettra entente,
910 Kar les celestiens uertuz
Serrunt mouanz trestuz,    /f. 62ᵛ
E dunc uerrunt le fiz al home
Venant es nues – co est la sume –
Oue mult grant poeste
915 E od mirable maieste.
Quant cestes choses cumencerent
Guardez, leuez uos chefs amunt,
Kar pres est uostre rancun'.
Puis dist une conparisun.
920 'Le figer', fait il, 'esguardez,
E trestuz les arbres auisez;
Quant il mettent auant lur fruit
Pres est l'este, co sauez tuit.
E issi, vus di, quant co uerrez,
925 Deu rengne est pres, co sachez.
En ueir, vus di, ne tresirra
Iceste generaciun ia
Desque trestut seit auerre
Quantque vus ai ci cunte.

930 E ciel e terre tresirrunt
Mais mes paroles ferm serrunt'.
La lectre par oi auez;
A uostre pru ore escutez.
Li duz Iesus, qui tant nus aime,
935 Tant bel a sei tuz nos reclaime;
Il nus apelle par essamples,
Par diz, par feiz ki mult sunt amples.
Par les baraz ke auendrunt
Tuz nus guarnist, tuz nos sumunt.
940 Si nel uolum en pais duter
Dutum le uels en encumbrer.
Tut pur la nostre garnisun
Dist il as sons icest sermun:
Li mund cum plus esueillira
945 E de sa fin plus pres serra
Plus i auera de males genz,
Plus pestilences, plus turmenz.
Ore est li mund de mult peiurs
Qu'il ne fut a nos ancesurs.
950 Certes encore ert il peiurs
A ces ki erent apres nos iurs.
Deit l'em dunc auer amur grant
Vers chose ki uait enpirant?
Nuls ne purra fors enpeirer
955 Par rien ki ne purrat amender.
Pur co fist Deu conparisun
Al mund ki tant est bricun
Des arbres ke portent fruit,

# SERMON 2
## DOMINICA SECUNDA ADUENTUS DOMINI

*Secundum Luc[am]. In illo tempore, dixit Ihesus discipulis suis: erunt signa in sole & luna &c.*

On time Ihesus Crist seyd þus to his disciples: 'Toknes schul ben & gret wondres in þe sunne & mone & in þe sterres & crudinge in þe erþe of
5  folk er þat þe destruinges schul comen þat sees & raynes schul cessen & þe men schul bicomen drie for þe drede & for þe vnderstondinge. Þer al þe world schal ȝeuen his entent, for þe heuenlich vertuz schullen al ben ystered, seand al men. And þan hii schul sen mannes sone comand in þe cloudes wiþ gret miȝt & wiþ wonderful maieste. Whan swych þinges
10 bigynnen, lokeþ & lifteþ ȝour heued on heiȝe, for nerhond is þan ȝour raunsun'. And þan he seid on ensaumple. 'ȝe childer', he seit, 'lokeþ & ȝiueþ kepe to al þe trewes; whan hii putten forþ her frout, þan is it ner heruest, ȝe mowe wel witen. Y say ȝou, whan ȝe se þis, Goddes kynge-dome is ner, þat wite ȝe wele. Y say ȝou þat it schal nouȝt comen er al
15 þis be don þat ich haue saied vnto ȝou. And heuen & erþe schal pass & myn wordes schal stonden fast.'

    Now ȝe han herd þe letter, now vnderstondeþ þe vndoinge to ȝour profite. Þe swete Ihesu þat loueþ vs alle & so fair clepeþ vs alle vnto his voice, he clepeþ vs be ensaumple, be word, be dedes þat ben so gode;
20 þurth þe trauayles þat schul comen, alle warneþ, al he somun[f. 6ᵛ]deþ vs. ȝif we nil nouȝt douten his mekenesse & his pes, doute we þe gret dredes & þe harmes þat be to comen. Al for oure helþe he sayed to his þis sermoun: þe elder þat þe world wereþ, þe ner he schal be his ende, þe more wicked folk þer schul ben inne, & þe more slauȝ & þe more
25 turmence. Now is þe world wele wers þan it was toforn wiþ oure elders; certes ȝit it schal be wers to hem þat comen efter vs. Owe man, þan, for to haue gret loue vnto þat þinge þat is euer lenger þe wers? No man mai bot enpairen þurth þat þing þat mai nouȝt ben amended. Forþi sette oure lord ensaumple bi þe world þat is fals & fayland be þe trewes þat beren

---

1 Lucam] Luc- *trim.*   5 folk] *ins.;* destruinges] *alt.*   11 ȝe] *alt.*   12 trewes] *alt.;* is it] it is *transp.*   15-16 & myn wordes] *on eras.*   20 schul] *alt. to* schulle.   22 þis] disciples *ins.* þis.   25 turmence] *alt. to* turmente.

Kar mult dure poi lur deduit.
960   Tost flurit l'arbre e tost flestrit
E tost trespasse quanqu'en ist.
Les pestilences, les turmenz
Ferent defors, butent dedeinz.
Si point i pend iesqu'a maurtez
965   Tost ert purri e fors ruez.
Si est de cest boban mundain,
Tut seit beus, tut dis est uain,
Tut dis trait il a defauture.
E que uaut chose ke ne dure,
970   Ia ne seit home tant honurez,
Tant enrichiz, tant bien feffez,
Qu'il ne soffre grant turment,
Paines defors, dolurs dedenz?
Si les homes sunt enrichiz
975   Laruns dutent nis en lur liz.
Si alcuns i poet sa pais auer
Par sei guarder e sun aueir,
Alcune feiz enpouerira
V a la mort trestut larra.
980   Pur Deu, seignurs, kar ueez cler,
Que uaut la rien que poet finer?
Dirrai vus dreite medicine:
Amez celi ki pas ne fine;
Laissez le mund ke vus suduit,
985   Querez la ioie ki ne fuit.
Oez cument cil sunt destruit
Ki del mund aiment le grant bruit,
E cum cil sunt tost aleue
Qui aiment Deu en uerite.
990     Vn curtillers prodome esteit
Qui Deu amout e Deu cremeit.
Quant que il poait esparnier,
Fors sul sun cors a sustener
E ses ustilz a achater,
995   As poures sout trestut duner.   /f. 63ʳ
A une feiz se purpensa:
'Issi', fait il, 'plus n'en irra.
Si io chaisse en langur
Ki me ferreit pur nient suiur?

1000   Si io deuenc uielz e defraiz
Qui me durra pur noent cunraiz?
Mielz me uaut alkes retenir
Dunt io me puisse sustenir;
Queique auenge, queike nun,
1005   Ki rien ne tient mult est bricun.
Tut n'ai femme nes enfanz
Mis auers me serra guaranz'.
Cum l'out pense issi l'ad feit,
Deners acuilt, deners atreit.
1010   Tant en ad fait sicum li plot
Que empli ad un grant pot.
Ne demura pas longement
Que Deus n'en prist le uengement:
Vns maus li est al pe ferruz
1015   Dunt mult est mat e esperduz;
Ne poet ouerer, ne poet aler,
A l'un pe poet a peine ester.
Mires en ad plusurs mande,
De sun auair mult ad dune;
1020   Queique promette, queique dunt,
Cum pur guarir rien ne li funt;
En mires tant despent li sot
Ke trestut est uoid li pot.
Kar cil ki Deu ne uolt aider
1025   Pur nent se fereit medeciner.
A la parfin se purpensa
De un cyrugien qu'il mandera
Saueir si coli le guarreit;
Trestuz ses dras li durreit,
1030   Il n'aueit plus que duner,
Tut out despendu des autrer.
Menez li unt le cyrugier
E il le fait sun pe garder.
Bien li ad dit ke ia n'ert sain
1035   Si il nel coupe a l'endemain.
Sicum celi l'ad deuise
Li curtillers l'ad tut grante.
Celi s'en ua pur ses ustiz
E cil remaint mat e mariz;
1040   De ses mesfeiz mult se repent,

frute, for litel while lasteþ her solas. Sone leueþ þe tre & sone it
florischeþ & sone it passeþ þat comeþ out þerof; pestilens & þe
turmences smiten wiþouten & putten wiþinne. So it fareþ of al þis
worldliche bobaunce; þei3 it seme faire, al it is vain, euer it draweþ to
5  wers & wers. And what is þinge worþ þat ne lasteþ nou3t, be neuer man
so michel worschipped, ne so riche, ne so wil feffed, þat he ne suffreþ
gret turmentes, pines wiþouten & sorowes wiþinne? 3if þe men ben riche,
hii douten þeues ani3t in her beddes. 3if ani may haue his pes, sum tyme
it prikeþ him in þe hert þat he schal deye & forgon al þat [ich]. For
10  Goddes loue, leue lordinges, lokeþ wel befor 3ou & beþincheþ 3ou what
þat þinge is worþ þat schal enden. Y schal say 3ou þe best medecine:
loueþ him þat neuer schal haue ende; leteþ þe world þat haþ ende &
secheþ þe ioie þat naþ non ende & 3eueþ kepe how þat hii ben destrued
þat loueþ þe blisse & þe worschip of þis world, & how þat hii ben sone
15  hei3ed þat louen God in soþenesse.

A gode werkman it was þat loued God & dradde him. Al þat he mi3t
spelen ouer his sustinaunce & for to bigge him tole wiþalle, al he 3af to
pouer men & wymmen. And on a tyme he beþou3t him & seyd, 'Þus ne
schal it no more gon. 3if þat ich fel seke, who schuld for nou3t helpen
20  me, & 3if Y become eld & mi3t nou3t weld me, hou schal ich þan fare?
Better me is for to holden me sumwhat for þinge þat may befalle. He þat
noþinge holdeþ, a gret fole he is. Þei3 Y ne haue wyfe ne child, myn
godes schal helpen me'. And as he þou3t, so he dede, & gadred him
siluer so þat he fulfilled a gret pot. And it nas nou3t long efter þat God ne
25  toke veniaunce on him, & an iuel come into his fote þat he ne mi3t
wirchen ne gon — vnneþ he mi3t stond opon his o fot. He sent efter
leches mani & haþ 3euen hem michel of his gode, & what þat he 3eueþ
& what þat hii hoten him, his fote is euer lenger þe wers. Ac so þe fole
haþ despended in lechecrafte þat al his pot is emtye & he is euer lenger
30  þe wers; for þinge þat God wil haue don, no man ne þar be þera3aines.
On a tyme he beþou3t him & sent efter a leche & seyed vnto him þat he
ne hadde no more to 3euen him [f. 7ʳ] bot his cloþes & beso3t him þat he
schuld say him 3if þat his fot mi3t be heled oþer it ne mi3t. And he sayd
vnto him þat it mi3t nou3t be heled bot smite of þe fote & hele a3eyne þe
35  stumpe. And as he haþ deuised, þe gardiner haþ graunted him. And þe
leche 3ede hom & on þe morwen made his tole redy to smiten of his
legge. And he beleft sori & sorowful & biknewe his misdedes &

---

3 turmences] *alt. to* turmences.   6 wil] wel *alt.*   9 ich] hii haueþ *ins.*   14 blisse] *partly
eras.*   18 men] *partly eras.*   25 his] his *ins.*   28 ac] *eras.*

Merci demande e acordement.
'Sire, merci, Deu de uertu,
Mi bienfeit serrunt il perdu?
Bien le sauez comment le fis,
1045 Tut ai io ore uers vus mespris'.
A ces paroles s'endormit
E un home deuant li uit.
Le pe li ad bel manie
De tutes parz l'ad esguarde.
1050 Puis li ad dist tut en estant:
'Dormez vus, chaitif mescraiant?
V sunt deuenu ti dener
Qui plus ous ke Deu cher?
Pur tei guarir tu les coillis,
1055 Perdu les as e tu peris'.
E cil cumence en sun dormant
Merci crier, pur Deu le grant.
Bien l'ad premis, s'il guarisseit,
Ke tel ouere mes ne ferreit.
1060 E cil l'en ad pris par la main:
'Leuez', fait il, 'le pe as sain'.
Atant s'en est celi turne,
Cil saut e tut sain l'ad troue.
Li cyrugiens uint l'endemain:
1065 'Va t'en', feit il, 'io sui tut sain'.
Sun pe li ad tanttost mustre
Tut ausi sain cum il fu ne.
   Veez, seignurs, quei fait richesce,
L'alme destrut e le cors blesce.
1070 Coment purra il estre sage
Qui rien aime a sun damage?
Certes, mult par est fol amer
Ki de sun gre se leist blescer.
Pur co, guardez a la lescun
1075 Que Iesus dist en sun sermun:
Quant les arbres sunt fructizez,
Dunc sauez que pres est l'estez;
Kar par ceus ke aiment le mund

E par les baraz ke il funt,     /f. 63ᵛ
1080 Poum sauer en uerite
Ke mult est pres le regne De.
   Este par mult bele semblance
Del ceil ad la signefiance,
Kar li solail dunc munte en haut,
1085 Les nues hoste si fait chaut.
E cil ke sunt el regne De
Le chaud auerunt de charite;
N'i auerunt neint de tristur
Ne de pesance tenebrur;
1090 Kar il sunt od le fiz Marie
El iur de pardurable uie.
E co sachez, qu'en enfer
Ad tut dis nuit e fort yuer,
Pour, puur e feu ardant
1095 E tenebrur e freit tres grant.
Ne ia nen ert par la freidur
Del feu d'enfer le chaut menur.
Cil ki la est les ad ensemble
Dedenz tresart, dedefors tremble.
1100 Certes, mult par est l'alme lasse
Ke pur la uie ke trespasse
Se met en la perdiciun
Dunt ia nen auera rancun.
Kar co sachez seurement,
1105 Iesus uendra al iugement;
Es nues, cum il dist, uendra
E tut le mund iugera.
Il est fiz de home, co est, Marie,
Qui tant amenda nostre uie.
1110 Iesus est li fiz de la meschine
Ki cuntre mort nos fist mescine.
Il uendra tut le mund iuger,
E ciel e terre e air e mer.
Il uint ia pur estre iuge
1115 Quant il prist nostre humanite,

repented him & cried God merci wiþ god wille. 'Lord', he sayd, 'schal
myn gode dedes be lorn? Wele wostow hou þat Y dede þeiȝ al ich haue
now misdon'. And wiþ þo wordes he fel on slepe. And a man come &
stode beforn him & hondled his fot & loked it on al half & þan he sayd
5   vnto him: 'Slepestow, wreche misbileuand? Whar ben bicomen þi pans
þatow trusted more to þan to Ihesu Crist for to hele þe? Þou gadred hem;
now þou has lorn hem, & þou nart neuer bot þe wers.' And he began to
crien merci in his slepe for Godes loue, & wel haþ he beheȝt himȝif he
hele him, þat he ne schal neuer do so mor. And he toke him bi þe hond:
10  'Arisse', he seyd, 'þi fot is hole'. And þisman went away, & he wakened
& aros & fond his fot al hole. And omorowen he met þe man þat schuld
haue smiten of his fot. 'Go', he seid to him, 'hom; ich am al hole', &
schewed him his fot as hole as it euer was.
      Lokeþ, lordinges, what riches doþ, destrueþþe soule & hirteþ þe body.
15  Hou may he be wise þat ani þinge loueþ to his harme? Certes, a fole he is
þat hirteþ him be his wille. Forþi, lokeþ to þe lesoun þat Ihesus seyt in his
techinge; whan þe tres ben ful of frut, þan wot ȝe wele þat it is ner
heruest. Bi hem þat louen gretlich þe world, & be þe cuntakes & be þe
sorowes þat ben þerinne, we may wel witen for soþe þat þe kingdome of
20  heuen is nerhond.
      Þe somer is ful wel likened to þe heuen, for þe sunne þan arist on heiȝe
& doþ away þe cloudes & makeþ hete; & hii þat in þe kingdome of heuen
han þe hete of loue & charite, hii ne schul nouȝt haue no sorowe ne
heuinisse ne derkenesse, for hii ben wiþ þe lord of blis þat neuer ne schal
25  haue ende. And þat wite ȝe wele, þat in helle is euermore niȝt & strong
wynter, stink & drede & fure brennand & derkenesse & kold riȝt gret, &
ne schal neuer þe fure of helle for þe cold be þe lasse, ne þe cold for þe
hete. He þat is þer haþ hem boþe togider; wiþinnen he brenneþ &
wiþouten he trembleþ. Certes, iuel he þencheþ bi him þat for þe liif þat
30  schal passe leseþ boþe bodi & soule vnto þe pyne wiþouten ende þer
neuer ne schal be no remedy. For þat wite ȝe to soþe, Ihesus Crist schal
come atte jugement in þe cloudes as he seit, & schal jugen alle þe world.
He þat is Marie sone (þat maiden is & moder) þat so muchel haþe
amended oure liif ȝif we wil, he schal come & jugen al þe world, heuen
35  & erþ, water & wynde. He come hider for ben juged whan þat he toke

---

1 repented] *alt.*   2 dedes be] *ins.;*   al] *canc.*   6 þatow] *alt. to* þattow *l.h.;*   trusted]
(.)trusted.   7 bot] þe better *ins.* neuer, *l.h.;*   began] be(.)gan.   22 in] beþ *ins.* in.
28 þer] *ins.;*   haþ] haþ(.);   wiþinnen] wiþ inne(…).

Dunt nus feimes le saint aduent
Deuant noel al nessement.
Vn altre feiz encore uendra:
Dunc fu iuge, ore iugera.
1120 Dunc uint en feble charnalite;
Ore uendra od grant poeste.
Tut i uendruns, tut i serrums;
Cum il fu penez, tut le uerrums.
Li angele adunc tremblerunt,
1125 Li peccheur idunc, quei frunt?
Quant li saint ne sunt pas cert,
Ke frat ki ci mort desert?
Dunc rendra a chascun sun dreit
Sulum qu'il auera ici fait;
1130 As boens durra uie durable,
As mauueis peine permanable.
  Pur co vus di en bone fei,
De vus memes pernez cunrai,

Kar ici li estuuerat De seruir
1135 Qui a Iesu uoldra uenir
Par repentir de ses mesfeiz
E par bien faire a tut aheiz.
Fouls est ki en autre s'afie:
Qui li remembra quant il se ublie?
1140 Si vus uulez estre seurs,
Par vus memes fetes les curs,
Le curs, di io, de ceste uie,
Chascun pur sei en sa baillie;
Quantque de ben ici ferrez
1145 A cent duble iloec receuerez.
Si vus de co ne me creez,
Le dit Iesu ueals en oez:
'E ciel e terre tresirrunt,
Mes mes paroles ferm serrunt'.
1150 Metez vos en sa fermete
Qu'il vos met en sa clarte.

our kinde, of which we maken mynde in þe aduent oӡain his beringe at
cristenmesse. Anoþer time [f. 7ᵛ] ӡete he schal come. First he was juged,
& þan he schal jugen; þan he com in oure feble kynde, & now he schal
comen wiþ gret miӡt, & al we schul arisen & com toforn him þer & se
5   hou he was pined for vs. Þan þe angels schul tremblen for drede. Þe
sinful þan, what schullen hii whan þe angels ne ben nouӡt siker, what
schullen hii don þat han deserued þe deþ her? Þan he schul ӡeld ich man
riӡt efter þat he haþ don here. Vnto þe gode he schal ӡeuen liif wiþouten
ende, & to þe wiked, pine þat euer schal last. Forþi Y sai ӡou in gode
10   fayþ & rede ӡou þat ӡe take ӡeme to ӡourseluen her, for here he most
nedes seruen God þat þider wil comen to him þurht repentaunce of his
misdedes & efter, þurth werchinge of gode werkes. A gret fole he is þat
afieþ him in oþer whan he forӡeteþ himself. Ӡif þat ӡe wil be siker, do
ӡourseluen sumwhat & trusteþ nouӡt to non oþer, for a wonder þinge it
15   were þat ani oþer man oþer woman schuld better þenche on me whan ich
wer dede þan Y dede myseluen whan þat I liued. And þerfor, ich man
þenche opon himseluen here whiles þat he liueþ; for ich gode dede þat he
doþ her he schal receyue þer an hundredfold mede, & for al þat is ӡeuen
efter his day he ne schal haue no mede in þe blis of heuen þerfor. Ac ӡif
20   he go to pine of purgatorie, he may þe soner be deliuerd out þerof for þat
men doþ her for him efter his deþ, ac more ioie in heuen geteþ he nouӡt
þa[n] þe gode dedes wil amounten þat he dede whil þat he liued her. If
ӡe ne leue me nouӡt herof, troweþ & hereþ þe wordes þat Ihesus Crist
seit: 'Heuen & erþe schal passen and my word schal stond'. Þerfor, binde
25   ӡou fast to him þat sett ӡou in his briӡtnesse. God is graunt ӡou. Amen.

---

2 cristenmesse] *alt. to* cristes messe.    7 han] *alt. to* haueþ;   deserued] *alt.;*   schul]
schal *alt. to* schul.    10 to] to to.    18 doþ] doþ(.).    22 þan] þat.    22-23 if ӡe] ӡe if
*transp.*    24 passen] passe(.).

## DOMINICA III IN ADUENTU DOMINI

Quant Iohan aueit entendu
En ses liens les feiz Iesu,
Ses dous disciples enueia,
1155 E par ces dous li demanda:
'Es tu celi ki deit uenir,
V altre atent nostre desir?'
Iesus mult bel li respundit
E ducement lur ad dit:  /f. 64$^r$
1160 'Alez a Iohan. Renunciez
Co que oi e ueu auez:
Li ciu ueient e li clop vunt
E li leprus bien mundez sunt,
Oent li surd, leuent li mort,
1165 Li poure sunt prechez a confort,
E celi est bonure
Ki n'est en mei scandalize'.
Quant cil s'en esteient alez
Iesus ad la gent araisunez:
1170 'Que alastes vus el desert ueer?
Le rosel od le uent mouer?
Quei alastes ueer nequedent?
Home afuble molement?
Cil ke tant molement se uestent
1175 Es granz maisuns as reis s'arestent.
Alastes vus ueer prophete?
En ueir, vus di, plus que prophete:
Il est cist de qui est escrit:
Es vus mun angle bon eslit
1180 Ke io enuai deuant ta face
Tun chemin aprester par grace'.
La lectre ke oi auums
A nostre pru la conuertums.

Herodes out pris Saint Iohan
1185 Si li fist traire maint ahan.
Cist Herodes qui dunc ere
La femme tint ki fu sun frere;
En sun uiuant l'out toleit
E puis ke mort fu la teneit;
1190 Puis que Filippes esteit mort
Herodias teneit a tort.
Li saint baptistres enparla
Pur quei ele sa mort purchaca.
Ainz le fist lier durement
1195 Dunt il manda cest mandement.
Veez, seignurs, de leccherie,
Coment traist cors e uie.
L'auultre ne uolt cist guerpir;
Pur co fist il Iohan tenir.
1200 E ele dutout estre guerpie,
Pur co tolit a Iohan la u[ie],
Pur co k'il les chastiout
E ambesdous sauuer uout.
Mult i ad des Herodes hui
1205 Qui nus ferraient tut ennui
Si ne fust la crestienete
Ke Iesus ad tant auance.
E si il ne funt ueant la gent
Purquant il le funt priueement.
1210 Quantque l'em dist pur lur grant bien
Trestut dient que ne uaut rien;
Quantque ne pleist a lur curage
Trestut tenent a grant folage.
E pur co qui il sunt afolez
1215 Quident ke nus seium desuez.

# SERMON 3
## DOMINICA TERCIA ADUENTUS DOMINI

*Secundum Mathium. Cum audisset Iohannes in vinculis.*

Whan Seynt Ion vnderstode in his bondes þe werkes þat Ihesu dede,
thway of his desciples he sent vnto him, & þurth þes two asked him,
'Artow þat schal come oþer oþer abiden þi desire?'. Ihesus fair answerd
5 hem & swetliche sayd vnto hem, 'Goþ to Ion & telleþ him þat ȝe han sen
& herd: þe blind sen & þe croked gon & þe mesels ben made clene & þe
def heren & þe dede arisen & þe pouer ben heiȝed wiþ strengþe. He is
blissed þat is sclaundred in me.' And whan hii had herd þes, hii wenten
oȝain. And Ihesus loked to þe folk & aresound hem. 'What', he said,
10 'ȝede ȝe to sen man cloþed softliche? Hii þat ben cloþed softlich, in gret
kinges howses hii ben. ȝede ȝe for to sen a prophete? ȝa, Y say ȝou,
more þan a prophete he is þat of wiche is cried: "Þou art my gode angel
chosen þat Y sende bifor þi face þat schal drescen þi way þurth grace".'

Now ȝe han herd þe letter, [f. 8ʳ] now hereþ þe vnderstondinge.
15 Herodes had taken Seint Ion & dede him mani harmes & scornes. Þat
Herodes þat was heeld his broþeres wife efter þat his broþer was dede, &
seþen þat Philippes was dede, he held Herodia wiþ wrong. And þe holi
baptist spake þerof, þurth whiche he had his deþ, for wiþ bondes he dede
binde him hard. And þan he sent þis sond vnto Ihesu.

20 Lokeþ, lordinges, how lecherie destrueþ boþ bodi & soule. Þe spouse-
breker ne wolde nouȝt forsaken his avouterie & forþi he dede take Ion&
biname him his liif for he castised hem & wold haue saued hem boþe.
Mani þer ben of Herodes kinde þat now don as he dede. Þat miȝt be
vndertaken ne war þat Ihesu haþ auaunced cristendome so heiȝe. And ȝif
25 hii ne do it nouȝt befor þe folk, hii don it priuiliche. And al þat men seyn
for her gode, al hii seyn þat nis nouȝt worþ; ac al þing þat is likeand to
her fole hertes, al hem þenche gode & profite for hem. And for þat hii
ben so afoled, hii wenen þat hii ne mowe nouȝt ben deceyued.

---

4 oþer (1)] *canc.;* þi] an oþer *ins.* þi.    5 sen] seiȝe *alt.*    6 sen] seþ *alt.;*  made] milde
*alt. to* made *by H.*    10 ȝe] *ins.*    21 Ion] seint *ins.* Ion.

Pur Deu amendum nostre uie;
Laissum orgoil e leccherie.
Leccherie fait trestuz maus
E murdre e pecchez criminaus.
1220 Kar cil ki aime leccherie
Part n'auera od le fiz Marie.
Craiez uos femmes mes en bien,
E en mesfeiz nes craiez rien.
Vus dames, amez uos seignurs
1225 En chastete e en honurs,
Pur co estes vus assemble
Que chascun seit par altre amende.
Vus estes en Deu une char;
Gardez ke n'i surde eschar.
1230 Chascune rien prise la fin;
L'em lo al seir le beu matin.
Ore est Iohan en grant honurs
E cil en peine e en tristurs.
  Cist Iohan dunt vus ci oez,
1235 Quant il en chartre fu posez,
Ses dous diciples enueia
E par els dous Iesus demanda
Si il le mund sauuer ueneit
V il autre atendereit.
1240 Il ne duta pas de Iesu
Que pur sauuer ne fust uenu,
Mais une chose enquerreit
S'il e[n en]fern descendereit   /f. 64ᵛ
Pur icels oster de parfunt
1245 Ke puis Adam entrez i sunt,
Ke il le puisse a els nuncier
Cum il le fist al mund premer.
Kar co sachez de ueritez,
En enfern furent tuz entrez,
1250 Adam e quantque de lui fu issu,
Desque a la passiun Iesu.
Mais Iesus, quant il releua,

La mort uenqui e mort robba.
Ces qui ainz furent ses amis
1255 Menat od sei en parais.
  Iesus li mande sanz respit,
Co ke ourent li prophete escrit,
Ke il ne seit mes en aruair,
Que par oir, que par ueair:
1260 Li ciu ueient e li clop uunt,
E li leprus esmunde sunt.
Li ciu beaus oilz e ouerz ad,
Mais ia pur co rien ne uerrad.
Ces sunt cil ki ueent le bien
1265 E puis ne funt nule rien;
Sages sunt mult e entendant
Mais en bienfait ne tant ne cant.
Les maus ueient e funt par lius
Mais en bienfait sunt trestut cius.
1270 Mais cels uint Ihesus pur sauuer
E dreite ueie demustrer.
Cist ki est clop l'un pe ad dreit
E del autre en chaant ueit.
Ces sunt cil ki alcune feiz
1275 Ore funt les torz e ore les dreiz;
Del une part funt charite,
Del autre part iniquite.
Ia lunges en un ne serrunt;
Ore sunt en haut, ore en parfunt.
1280 E cels uint Ihesus a amender
E par sa dulcur a drescer.
  Li leprus sunt li sudiuant
Qui funt le mal par bel semblant
Kar leprus sunt de tele nature,
1285 Blanc unt le quir mais plein de ordure.
Ces sunt li traitre cri[m]inal
Kar bel parolent e funt mal.
E li leprus est chaud dedeinz,

For Godes loue, amende we our liif, lete we pride & licherie, for
licherie doþ mani harmes, manslauȝt and mani oþer. Ne schal neuer he
þat loueþ licherie haue parte in heuen wiþ Ihesus, Marie sone. Beleueþ
nouȝt ȝoure wiues bot in gode; in iuel ne troweþ hem nouȝt. And ȝe
5   wymmen, loueþ ȝour lordes in chastite & in worchipes; forþi ȝe ben
asembled for þat ichon of ȝou schal helpen oþer. ȝe ben in God o flesche
& o blode; lokeþ þat ȝe ne fordo it nouȝt. Ich þinge ow to be praised at þe
endinge. At euen men praysen þe fair day. Now is Ion in gret worchipe
& hii ben in sorowe & woo.
10   Þis Ion þat ȝe her of here, whan he was don in prisoun, his tway
desciples he sent to Ihesu & þurth hem asked him ȝif þat he come to
[sauen þe werlde oiþer hii schulden] abiden anoþer. He ne douted him
nouȝt of Ihesu þat he nas comen to sauen þe world, ac o þing he enquered
of him, ȝif þat he schuld wend adoun into þe fre prisoun of helle, for to
15   bring hem out of þat depenesse þat were þerinne seþþen þat Adam had
sinned, þat he miȝt bring hem word þerof as he dede first to þe world. For
þat wete ȝe for soþe, al hii wenten to helle, Adam & al þat efter him
come, vntil Ihesus Crist died upon þe rode; & þan he toke out al his
chosen þat weren his frendes & brouȝt hem wiþ him into paradis.
20   Ihesu sent word vnto Ion oȝain as þe prophetes hadden seyd toforn, þat
he ne schuld no more be diswarre what þurth heryng, what þurth seinge:
þe blinde sen & þe croked gon & þe mesels ben made clene. Þe blinde
haþ his eiȝen open ac þerfor ne may he neuer þe better sen. Þat ben hii
þat sen þe gode & noþinge don þerefter; wise hii ben & wel vnderstond,
25   ac hii ne do noþing þerefter. Þe iuels hii sen riȝt [f. 8ᵛ] wele, ac for to do
wele hii ben al blinde. Ac swiche come Ihesu to sauen & schewen hem
[riȝt] liȝt.
He þat is halt, þat o fot he haþ riȝt & þat oþer wronge. Þat ben hii þat
now don þe riȝt & now þe wronge; on þat on half hii don charite & on þat
30   oþer half, wikednesse. Hii ne be neuer long while in on; now hii ben an
heiȝe & now lowe. Þes come Ihesu for to amenden & þurth his godenesse
bring hem to be riȝt way.
Hii ben mesels þat don þe iuel þurth fair semblaunt þurth þe iuel wille
þat he haþ. For mesels ben of þis kinde: hii han þe fel white ac it is ful of
35   filþe. Þat ben þes þat speken fair & don þat iuel. Þe mesel is hote wiþinne

---

2 licherie] *alt. to* lecherie.   3 licherie] *alt. to* lecherie.   10 ȝe] *ins.*   12 sauen …
schulden] *om.*   15 of] *ins.*   16 he miȝt] he (…) miȝt.   17 wenten] wente(.).   18 vntil]
or *on eras.*   21 heryng] *alt.*   25 ne] (.)ne.   26 schewen] sethe wen *alt.*   27 riȝt] wiþ
*on eras.;* liȝt] riȝt *alt.*   34 haþ] haþ(.).

E defors est freiz e pulenz.
1290 Si ad li fels le quor ardant
De parfaire tut sun maltalant;
Quant ne poet parfaire ses esspleiz
De anguisse grant deuient tut freiz.
E cels uint Ihesus esmunder
1295 E a sa grace rapeller.
  Cil sunt surd ki oent le bien
Mais ne retenent nule rien,
Ki de lur grant biens parler oent
Frunchent des nes e les oilz cloent;
1300 Ne uolent nule rien oir
Fors co ke lur uient a plaisir.
Tut quident ke seit fanflue
Quantque ne pert a lur ueue;
Mult le tenent a grant folie
1305 Quant oent parler de altre uie.
  De co oir sunt ententifs
Ke uer poent tant cum sunt uifs,
E quant oent le Deu sermun
Surdz sunt sanz nule guarisun.
1310 Mais tels reuint Ihesus guarir
E restorer le droit oir.
  Mort sunt ki gisent en pecche
E en delit de iniquite,
Ki ne pensent de repentir
1315 Fors sulement a lur murir.
De tuz lur maus pernent respit
Desque lur poair lur defit;

'Adunc', dient, 'repentirums
Quant nus peccher mes ne purrums'.
1320 Mais l'escripture dist pur uair:
'Mal ait ke pecche en espair'.
E quant il craient en tel sort,
En char sunt uifs, en alme mort.
Mais tels uint Iesus resusciter
1325 E oue li al ciel mener.
  Oez, seignurs, pur amur De
Que Ihesus a Iohan ad mande;   /f. 65ʳ
Veez l'ordre del mandement
Si l'entendez escordrement.
1330 Cius est li hom quant il ne crait,
Clop quant il le bien ne fait,
Leprus quant pecche plurelment,
Surdz quant despit chastiement;
Partant chet il en cele mort
1335 Dunt ia n'auera par sei confort.
Mais Iesu Crist deigna uenir
Pur nus de tuz ces mals guarir.
Il nus alume par ferme craire
E desenclope par dreit faire;
1340 Lepre cure par fin amer,
Surdesce par bien escuter;
Partant nus iette de male gort,
De fol atente dunt surd la mort.
Kar la craance est baraigne
1345 Ki ne se mustre par oueraigne,

& wiþowten cold & stinkeand: so haþ þe wiked þe hert brennand whan he ne may nouȝt don his wille, & þurth anguische he becomeþ al cold. And þes come Ihesu for to maken clene & ȝif hem his grace.

He is def þat hereþ þe gode & ne doþ noþing þerefter. Whan hii her
5 speken þe gode, hii turnen her visage þenward & schetten her hertes þerfrom, & hii ne wil noþinge heren bot þat hem likeþ. Al hem þenche is fantom bot þat her hertes falleþ to, & holden it for a gret folie whan hii heren speken of anoþer liif. Þat hii ben bisie to heren þat hii mowe sen þe whiles þat hii liuen, & whan hii heren Godes wordes, hii ben def, for it ne
10 profiteþ hem nouȝt. Ac þes come Ihesu for to sauen & ȝeue hem riȝt hereinge.

Ded hii ben þat lien in sinne & in delite of wickednesses, þat ne þenche nouȝt to amenden hem bot onlich whan hii schal deie. Of al her iuels hii taken respit til þat her power faileþ hem: þan, hii seyn, we schul amenden
15 vs. Ac holi writ seit for soþe: 'Iuel is to him þat synnen in hope'. *Maledictus homo qui peccat in spe.*

Þe man is weried þat sinneþ in hope. Whan hii fallen in swich sinne, her bodis liuen & her soules ben ded. Ac swich come Ihesu for to arere & leden hem wiþ him to heuen ȝif þat hii wil bidden him. And nim ȝeme
20 herto: he ne arered non fram deþ to liue bot ȝif men bad him; na more ne wil he swich men ne wymmen bot ȝif he be beden, & þat wiþ gode wille, for he arered þre fram ded to liue & he was bid[den] arere þe ferþ & he nold nouȝt.

Now, lordinges, for þe loue of God ȝeueþ kepe what Ihesu sent vnto
25 Ion, & þe riȝt rewele of sendinge, vnderstondeþ it wele.

Blind is þe man whan he beleueþ nouȝt ariȝt, halt whan he doþ nouȝt þe gode, mesel whan he sinneþ communlich, & þan holi writ biddeþ he schuld ben put out of comune puple. Def he is whan he despiseþ chastisinge; þurth þat he falleþ into swiche deþ þat be himseluen ne geteþ
30 he neuer coumfort. Ac Ihesus Crist wolde comen hider for to deliuer vs of al iuels, ȝif [f. 9ʳ] we wil ourseluen. He liȝteþ vs þurth riȝt bileue & wisseþ vs bi riȝt wirchinge; mesel he heleþ for fine loue & def þurth wele listeninge: in as michel he kesteþ vs fram iuel deþ þer we schuld haue ben wiþouten ende & counfort, for þe bileue is barain þat ne scheweþ
35 him nouȝt in werk. *Fides sine operibus mortua est &c.*

---

1 &] (.)&. 3 clene] clene(.). 6 þerfrom] *alt.;* heren] here(.); þenche] þencheþ *alt.*
8 mowe] hii … mowe; þe] be(.). 10 sauen] saue(.) (…). 13 deie] *alt.* 15 synnen]
*alt.* to synneþ. 18 arere] *alt.* 22 bidden] bede (…); he] he (…..). 30 crist wolde]
*on eras.* 33 kesteþ] (.)kesteþ.

E nul ouere ne poet sauuer
Ki ne se guarde de peccher,
E nul n'ad de pecche guarisun
Ki n'ot de gre le Deu sermun.
1350 E ki sermun bien ot e fait
De mort a uie od Ihesu uait.
　E si pouere hom bien vus dit,
Nel deuez tenir en despit,
Kar Iesus ad a Iohan mande:
1355 Li pouere sunt bien anuncie.
Mult pouerement uint Ihesu Crist,
Poueres ama, poueres eslist.
Par poueres uint les poueres conquere,
Nient par riches, ne par guere.
1360 Pouere furent li saint trestut
Ki uenquirent le mundein brut,
E Ihesu par sa pouerete
Suuent fu esscandalize.
Mais celi est de Deu beneit
1365 Ki esclandre de li ne trait.
Il uint pur nos tuz mals suffrir,
Liens, flaels, e puis murir.
Cum plus se uout humilier
E plus le deussum honurer,
1370 Kar le soen humiliement
Si fu nostre auancement.
Mais il en out esclandre grant
Par co dunt il nus mist auant,
Par co fut charnelment huni
1375 Des mescreanz, e escharni.
Mais cil ki fermement co crait,
Que il e Deu e home sait,
E ke il suffrit mort par charnelte,
E tut dis uit en uerite,
1380 Quant esclandre de li ne trait
Tut dis ert salf, tut dis beneit.
　Puis dist al pople de Iohan

Que el desert prescha maint an:
'Alastes vus ueer le ros
1385 V home de bon dras enclos?'
Saint Iohan pas ros n'esteit,
Kar nule rien nel commoueit,
Ne par uent de peruersete,
Ne par uent de prosperite.
1390 N'enorgoillit par richete
Ne fu defraz par pouerete;
E quant il rien ne cuueita
De nule rien ne s'esmaia.
Pernez essample de Iohan,
1395 Vus ki traiez le mundein boban,
Laissez orgoil e cuueitise,
Amez sul Deu e sainte eglise.
Ne metez pas uostre essperance
En chose ki est en balance.
1400 Laissez la rien ki truble tute
Cum fait li ros ki li uenz bute;
Laissez le mund e quantqu'en est
Qui tut dis est en grant tempest.
Nuls ne poet auer Dampnede
1405 E le mund tut a uolente.
　Iohan pas bien uestu n'esteit
Kar sa char tint en grant destreit.
Souent par riche uesteure
Munte li quors a desmesure
1410 De orgoil e de surquiderie
En est la char de plus hardie,   /f. 65ᵛ
E ne ueit pas la fole cure
Que co est painte pureture.
Es vus, cil ki bien uestu sunt
1415 As riches reis seruise funt.
Veez qu'il dist qu'a Deu ne sert
Ki as terriens reis aert;
Par l'orgoil del bon uestement

No þing ne may sauen man bot ȝif he kepe him fram sinne, & non ne may haue help of sinne bot ȝif he here wiþ gode wille Goddes word. And he þat hereþ wel Goddes word & efter doþ in dede, fram deþ to liue he goþ wiþ Ihesus Crist.

5 And ȝif a pouer man sey wel, ȝe ne schal nouȝt haue him in despite, for Ihesu sent vnto Ion & seid þat þe pouer ware wel heiȝd. Wel pouerlich come Ihesus Crist; pouer he loued & pouer he ches. Þurth pouerte he come to winne þis world & nouȝt þurth riches ne þurth wer. Pouer wer þes holi halwen al þat ouercome þe bost of þis world, & Ihesus

10 þurth his pouert often he was sclaunderd & scorned. Ac he is blissed of God þat is sclaunderd & scorned for his loue. He come for to suffer for vs alle iuels, binding & scourging, & efterward be slain for our loue. Þe more þat he wold lowen him for vs, þe more we auȝt to worschipen him, for þurth his lownes we come to gret auaunscement. Ac he had gret

15 sclaunders & mani þurth whiche he brouȝt vs forþ, & þerfor he was schent & scorned of misbileuand men. Ac hii þat stedfastlich bileue þat he is God & man & þat he sufferd deþ bodilich & alway liueþ in his godhed, who þat is sclaunderd in him alway he schal ben sauf & alway he schal ben blisced.

20 Þan sayd Ihesu to þe puple of Ion, 'ȝede ȝe for to se þe rede oþer man cloþed softlich?'. Seyn Ion nas no rede, for no þing ne miȝt stirren him, noyþer wind of riches, ne winde of pouerte, ne winde of anguis, ne of sorowe. He ne prouded nouȝt þurth riches, no he ne sorowed nouȝt for pouerte, & whan he nouȝt ne couayte, for no þing he ne dismayed him.

25 Takeþ ensaumple of Ion, ȝe þat louen þe bobaunce of þis world, & leteþ pride & couaytise, & loueþ God & holi chirche. Ne sett nouȝt al ȝour hope on þing þat is in were ne þat lasteþ bot a while; leteþ þat þing þat is euer trembland as þe rede þat stirreþ wiþ ech winde; leteþ þe world & þat is þerin, for it is euer in gret tempest. No man ne may haue God almiȝten

30 & þe world at wille.

Ion ne was nouȝt wel cloþed for he held his flesche in gret þraldome. For often þurth fair cloþing & riche þe hert falleþ into out of mesure of pride & makeþ þe flesche þe folehardier & ne seþ nouȝt þat is al stink þat is so paynted. ȝeueþ kepe to þis word þat Ihesus sayþ; hii þat ben

35 richelich cloþed, hii seruen tofor kingges. Loke what he sayþ: God he ne serueþ nouȝt þat draweþ him to erþlich kinges for pride of her riche

6 heiȝd] hieȝd.   8 wer] *alt. to* werr.   9 halwen] halawen *alt. to* halwen.   14 had] hadde.   23 no] ne *alt.*   24 couayte] couayted *alt.*   28 world] word *alt. to* world *by H.* 33 makeþ] ma(.)keþ.   34 sayþ] *alt.*

Les riches homs sert a talent;
1420 Ne siut Iesu ne seint Iohan
Mais de co mund le faus boban.
Mes ki uolt le mund user
Sul pur uiuere, nient pur amer,
Vse les feiz seint Iohan sanz buffai
1425 E Deu aime e dreite fei,
Vmblesce e bons feiz tenir,
A Deu en purrat bien uenir.
  Iohan plus ke prophete esteit
Kar co k'il dist, puis le ueit.
1430 E celi k'il nunciat el desert,
Puis le uit tut en apert.
  Il ert angle, co ert, message,
Kar  il mustrat le Deu curage.
Il fu angle uerraiement
1435 Kar il mustrat le Deu talent.
Le Deu talent est nus sauuer;

Pur co se leissat encharner.
Deu uolt le nostre amendement;
Co fu le Iohan preschement.
1440   E vus repoez angles estre
Si co que oez de uostre prestre,
V en essample, v en sermun,
Recuntez en uostre meisun;
Si vus as autres recuntez
1445 Le bien ke vus oi auez.
Quicunke nume rien de De
En tant est angle de uerite,
E le chemin fet aprester
Par ki puissum a Deu aler.
1450   Pur co, seignurs, partut contez
Le bien ke vus oi auez;
Endreit sei chescun tant en face
Ke tuz ueum la Iesu face.   Amen.

cloþinge. Hii seruen þe riche man to wille & þerfor hii ne mowe noy[f.
9ᵛ]þer folowen God ne Seyn Ion for þe foule bobance of þis world.
Þerfor, non ne may comen to God bot hii þat vsen þe world onlich for to
liuen & nouȝt for to louen it. Vsen it, Y say, a man may wiþouten
5  bobance & pride, & loue God ouer al þinge, & lowenesse, & do gode
werkes; & þan may he wel come vnto God & queme him wel anouȝ.

Ion, he sayd, was more þan a prophete, for of him þat he spake, efter
he seiȝe him; for þat he teld of in þe desert, efter he seiȝe him apertliche.

He was angel, þat is, messager, for he schewed Goddes wille. Goddes
10  wille is for to sauen vs, & þerfor he toke flesche & blode. God wold our
sauacioun & þat was Iones prechinge. And ȝe may ben angels ful wel
also ȝif þat ȝe here of holi chirche oþer in ensaumple oþer in word, ȝif
þat ȝe telle vnto oþer þe god þat ȝe han herd. Who þat bereþ furþ ani þing
of gode þat is to Goddes worchipe & to help of his euen cristen, in þat he
15  is angel, þat is as michel to say as Godes messager in as michel as he
techeþ þe way to Ihesus Crist. Forþi, lordinges, ouer al telleþ þe god þat
ȝe han herd & ich do as michel as in him is, so þat we mowe al sen þe
face of God. Amen.

4 vsen it] vse hit *alt.*   10 our] (.)our.

# DOMINICA IV IN ADUENTU DOMINI

Li Giu ki en cel cuntemple erent
1455 En Ierusalem suiurnerent
E prestres e diaknes enueierent
A Seint Iohan si demanderent:
'Tu, qui es'? E il lur dist:
'En ueir grantant, ne sui pas Crist'.
1460 Il demanderent, 'Ies Helye'?
Il respundit, 'Ne sui nun mie'.
'Es tu prophete'? Il dist: 'Nun'
'Di nus dunc que respundrum
A cels ki nus unt enueie;
1465 De tei, que dis tu, de tun gre'?
Il dist: 'Io sui uoiz al criant
El desert, seez adrescant
La ueie al seignur ki uendra
Cum Ysaie prophetiza'.
1470 Les Iuielz furent des pharisez,
E puis li unt il demandez:
'Quei baptizes quant n'es Crist grant,
Ne Elyes, ne prophetant'?
Iohan respundit umblement:
1475 'Io lief en l'ewe uerreiement.
En mi de vus estant auez
Celi ke vus pas ne sauez;
Il est ki puis mei uenir deit,
Kar deuant mei en bien esteit,
1480 A ki ne sui pas digne deslier
La curaie de sun chaucer'.
En Bethanie utre Iordan

Ert co u baptizat Iohan.
La lectre oi auez retrere,
1485 Ore oez ke vus deuez feire.
Iohan est partut nostre escren
Pur mal leisser e feire bien.
Iohan ert de teles uertuz
Que pur Crist le teneient tuz. /f. 66ʳ
1490 Purquant ne uolt enorgoillir
Mais umble e bas tut dis tenir.
A cels ki uindrent essaier
Pur li mettre en encumbrer
Respondit il si dulcement
1495 E parla tant umblement;
Pur nule rien qu'il sousent dire
Ne mustrat il tencun ne ire.
Pernez en garde, vus seignurs,
Prestres e clers e sermunurs,
1500 Ke vus ne seiez orgoillus,
Ne surquiders, ne ramponus.
S'om vus demande tant ne quant,
Respunez bel par beu semblant.
E quant vus parlez a la gent
1505 Sanz fruis le festes simplement,
Kar co dist bien Seint Pol li ber
Ke li serf Deu ne deit pas tencer,
Ainz deit parler pesiblement
Nient a un mes a tute gent.
1510 Maint prestre pur sun cher uestir
A le gent quide mult pleisir;

# SERMON 4
## DOMINICA QUARTA ADUENTUS DOMINI

*Secundum Iohannem et cetera. Miserunt Iudei ab Ierosolimis &c.*
Þe Iewes þat in þat tyme were in Ierusalem, prestes & dekenes sent þay
vnto Seyn Iohn þe baptist & asked him: 'What artow? Artow Crist?'.
And he answerd & sayd, 'Nay, for soþe, Y ne am nouȝt Crist'. 'What
5   artow þan? Artow Helie'? And he seyd, 'Nay'. 'Ertow þan prophete?'.
'Nay', he sayd. 'Say vs þan what we schul seyn to hem þat sent vs hider;
say vs now what þow art bi þi gode wille'. And he sayd to hem, 'Ich am
voice criand in desert, wite ȝe wel, for to adressen þe way of þe lord þat
schal come as Ysaye prophecied'. Þe messangers wer abayst & asked
10   him, 'Whi baptisettow whan nart Crist, ne Helie, ne prophete?'. Ion
answerd lowelich & mekelich, 'Y cristn in water for soþe; & amiddes
ȝou stondeþ he þat ȝe not nouȝt of, & he is þat efter me schal comen þat
befor me in God is made of which Y ne am nouȝt worþi to vndon þe
þonge of his schone'. In Bethanie beȝond Iordan, þer baptist Seyn Ion.
15   Now ȝe han herd þe letter, hereþ now what is þe vnderstonding so þat
ȝe may leten þe iuel & do þe gode.
Ion liued so holi liif & had swich vertuz wiþ him þat hii held him al for
Crist. Ne for þan he nas nouȝt proude þerof, ac held him alway meke &
lowe. Vnto hem þat come for to asayen him & for to han fordon him ȝif
20   hii had miȝt he spake to hem to swetlich & so mekelich; for nouȝt þat hii
miȝten say ne schewed he no wreþ vnto hem ac alway spake to hem
sobirliche.
Takeþ gode kepe lordinges, prestes & clerkes & prechours, þat ȝe ne
be nouȝt proude ne misanswarand. 3if man ask ȝou ani þing, [f. 10ʳ]
25   answereþ fair & wiþ gode semblant, for þat seyt wel Seynt Poule þat
Goddes seruant ne schal nouȝt chiden, ac schal spek mekelich nouȝt to on
ac to al men.
Mani prest for his fair cloþing weneþ wel to plesen men þerwiþ, ac

8 voice] a *ins.* voice; wel] *alt.*   10 nart] þou *ins.* nart.   11 cristn] cristne *alt.* hym *ins.*,
*l.h.*   14 Ion] crist *ins. after* Ion, *l.h.*   20 swetlich] (.)swetlich.   26 ac] he *on eras.*   28
plesen men] plese (....)men.

Mais quant co ueient, li plusur
Dient ke co est tut de lur.
Mal unt lur bienfeiz enplaiez
1515 Quant il est si desraiez;
Lur bienfeiz perdent a estrus
Quant il est tant orgoillus.
Par sun orgoil, par sun fol gas,
Pas ne li mustrent lur trespas.
1520 Quant il uenent pur confesser
Ne li mustrent fors le leger;
S'orgoil e sa surquiderie
Les feit a li celer lur uie,
E cil ki dust estre pastur
1525 Est pire ke lu rauissur.
Mais co ne doust nul penser;
Quelque seit l'ome, l'ordre est cler.
Seit il de bone u de male bunte
Mult par est grant sa poeste.
1530 Si nuls le set a peccheur
Amer le deit pur Deu amur,
Kar s'il mesprent en nule guise
Cil est Deus k'il sert en eglise.
Par essample sauer poez
1535 Cum prestre est digne, si vus l'oez.
  Vn hermite seint hem esteit
Pur ki Deus granz uertuz feseit.
Vn prestre sout a li uenir
Pur messe dire e Deu servir.
1540 Vn home le prestre ad encuse,
Dist qu'il ert plein de malueiste.
L'ermite en est tresbien craant;
Al prestre dist qu'il laist atant;
Granz grez li set de sun mester
1545 Mais nel uoldra mes trauailler.
La nuit apres est endormiz
Quant out ses ureisuns pardiz.
En sun dormant tel seif ad;
Co li est uis k'il creuad.

1550 Ne troue ewe en tut le mund
Fors un puiz estreit e parfund.
Mult uolenters i trebuchat
Si il soust qu'il releuat;
De beiure aueit si grant desir
1555 Qui de la seif quida murir.
Vn leprus i est lors uenuz,
Laiz e horribles e pres nuz.
De fin or teneit une seille;
L'ermiz l'esguarde a grant merueille.
1560 La chaine de fin or esteit
E a merueille reluseit.
Il treist de l'ewe si en but,
E li hermites arestut
E unkes aprocher n'i uolt
1565 Pur le leprus ki le maniout.
Atant oit une parole:
'Dan mestre, tis pensers est fole.
Dun n'est de fin or cele seille,
E l'ewe clere a grant merueille,
1570 E la chaine de or resplent,
E li puiz trestut ensement.
Est dunkes l'ewe malurez
Pur li ki l'ad amunt leuez?    /f. 66ᵛ
Nun est plus le seruise De
1575 Pur le fol prestre enpire'.
  Pur co di io icest respit
Que n'aiez prestre en despit.
Tel quide l'om ke seit uolage
Ki vers Deu ad mult boen curage.
1580 Quant ueez prestre mesaler
De vus memes deuez penser;
Fols est ki pur autri mesfeit
De sun bienfeire se retreit;
Li sages par autri folie
1585 Set amender la sue uie.
Trestuz nasquimes charnelment;
N'est home ki suuent ne mesprent.

whan sum sen þat it is al of hers þat he is proude of, & for his pride & for
his jolifte hii ne wil nou3t schewe to him her trespasses. Whan hii comen
for to ben schriuen, hii ne schewe him nou3t bot þe li3test. His pride &
his nice bering makeþ þat hii hiden her liif, & he þat schuld ben feder &
5    keper is wers þan a rauisour. Ac þat ne schuld no man þenche, what þat
þe man be. Þe order is clere: 3if he be god oþer qued, his power is gret;
for þei3 he misdo alway, Goddes seruise he seyt, & bi ensample Y may
schewe 3ou.
     It was an holi hermite þat God dede mani vertuz fore. A prest was
10   wont come to him & do him his messe, & anoþer man warned þe hermite
þat he was of wicked liif. Þe ermite was a wel bileueand man & sayd
vnto þe prest & þonked him michel of his seruise, ac he nold no more
charge him. And on þe ni3t efter, as þe hermite lay & slepe, he had
swiche þrest þat he wende þat his hert schuld brest, & in alle þe world ne
15   fonde he bot on welle & þat ri3t depe þe water was fram him. And
bleþlich he wold haue fallen adoun þerto 3if he hadde had ani for to haue
hulpen him vp, for he had so gret þrest þat he wende for to deye. And a
mesel come þer þan, foule & orrible & almest naked, & hadde a cheine in
his hond of fine gold & a coupe of gold & drow vp of þe water & dranke.
20   And þe hermete stode and nold nou3t com nere him for þe mesel þat held
it in his hond. And þan sayd a voice to him, 'Hermite, þou þenchest folie.
Nis nou3t þe coupe of fine gold & þe cheyne also wonderlich bri3t
schinand & þe water clere & fair & þe welle? Is þan þe water wers for
him þat haþ drawen it vp? No more is Goddes seruise þe wers for þe
25   prest þat doþ it.' Þerfor Y say þis, þat 3e ne schal nou3t haue no prestes
in despite, for swiche men may be þat ben volage þat han ful gode wille
to God. Whan we sen ani man misdon, prest oþer any oþer we owe to
þenchen opon ourseluen. A fole he is þat for oþer mannes gilt wiþdraweþ
him fram his gode dedes; þe wise man þurth oþer mennes folie can
30   amenden his liif. Al we ben bi3eten bitwixen man & woman; nis þer non
þat he ne misdoþ sumtime. Vnderstondeþ nou3t þis tale bot for
ensaumple; soþe it may wel be bot holi writt nis it nou3t. And herfor Y
telle now þis efterwarde for sum mi3t heren it & do sinne þerþurth in þis
maner. As bleþliche wold [f. 10ᵛ] a man susteine an iuel man as a gode,
35   & so he mi3t be lorn þerþurth. And þerfor Y schal say 3ou hou 3e schal

9 hermite] *on eras.* 10 wont] wont(...); to him] *on eras.* 12 of his] of (...) his; ac] *eras.* 18 cheine] chine *alt. to* cheine *by H.* 24 wers for] wers (.) for. 26 be] *on eras.* 27 we] *on eras.;* any oþer] *on eras.* 28 wiþdraweþ] wiþ (...) draweþ. 32 -for Y telle] *on eras.*

Pernum essample de Iohan
Ki n'amat terrien boban,
1590 E si nus alcun bien feisums
A Deu les graces en rendums.
Si nul nus loe de bienfeit
En umblesce seit nostre aheit,
Kar cil ki de rien s'enorgoille
1595 En haste cheit cum feit la foille,
Cum feit la pudre ki uent chace
E tolt de terriene face.
  Iohan ki unc n'amat superbe,
Il uint cum uoiz deuant le uerbe.
1600 Iesus Crist est le uerbe De
Par ki sumes aseure;
Kar si Iesus uenuz ne fust
Ia nuls hom Deu ne conust.
La uoiz Iesu Iohan esteit
1605 Kar il de mult pres le nuncieit;
Il le nunciat en desert,

Co est li mundz ke tut se pert.
Desert est terre deguerpie
Ke tut le mund bien signefie.
1610 Guerpiz sumes en desertez
Par noz orgoilz, par noz pecchez;
Guerpi nus ad nostre herbergur,
L'espirit, nostre creatur;
Guerpi nos ad la nostre uie
1615 Iesus, le fiz Sainte Marie;
Del pere e fiz e esspirit
Sumes guerpiz e cuntredit.
Guerpi sumes en saluagine;
N'est guiur ki nus achemine.
1620 N'auum ki nus maine a suiur;
Perdu auum le cheminur.
N'auum d'utre ki nus aie;
Perdu auum la dreite ueie
Par noz pecchez, par noz forfeiz,
1625 Par noz orgoills ki tant sunt leiz.

vnderstonde þis bi holi writ. Ʒe ne schul nouʒt despise no man ne ʒe ne schal nouʒt lett to heren swiche a mannes masse ʒif þat ʒe not nouʒt bi him bot gode, for to ʒou þe masse nis neuer þe wers. Ac if ʒe wist it & miʒt amend him, it wer wers to ʒou; for ʒe dede dedlich sinne for ʒe
5 mainten him in his sinne; for he is confort in his sinne as ʒe bere him as god felawchip as anoþer man. Ʒef he be a gode man þat doþ þe masse, ʒour bedes ben þe better herd for his bidding; & ʒif he be a sinful man, þat is to say, liþ in his sinne, his bede ne profiteþ nouʒt, for God nil nouʒt here him. As Ihesu Crist seyt þurth Ysaye: *si extenderitis manus vestras*
10 *&c* – þat is, þeiʒ ʒe held vp ʒour hondes & make manifold ʒour bones, Y nil ʒou nouʒt heren, for ʒour hondes ben blodi, þat is, ʒour werkes ben ful of sinne. Now Gregorii seyt also: 'As ner as ʒour mouþe is worldlich filþ, as fer it is fram God whan ʒe speke to him'. Dauid also: *iniquitatem si aspexi in corde meo, non exaudiet deus* – ʒif wickednesse be in myn
15 hert, þat is, sinne, God ne hereþ me nouʒt. More hereof Y miʒt telle ʒou michel, for God seyt: 'Drawe ʒou to holi & ʒe schal ben holi: drawe ʒou to schrewes & ʒe schal ben schrewes'. Hereof nil ich telle namore. Fonde we folowe þe wayes of Seyn Ion þat ne loued no þing þe bost of þis world. And ʒif we do ani gode dede, þonk we God ʒern of his swete
20 grace þat we may ani gode dede don to his worschipe, for of him it comeþ & nouʒt of vs self. Þerfor, hold we vs meke & lowe, for who þat haþ ani wele likeing of pride in his hert of his wel doinge, he falleþ fram heiʒ as doþ þe lef, & al his gode werkes faren as who bar pouder in þe winde.
25 Ion þat loued no pride, he come as voice befor þe word. Ihesus Crist is Goddes word þurth which man is made siker & stedfast, for if Ihesu ne had nouʒt comen, neuer ne schuld man haue knowen God. Ion was Ihesus voice, for he tauʒt his cominge nerhond. He tauʒt it in þis wildernesse, þat is, þis world þat draweþ al to forlernisse; for al þis world
30 betokeneþ wele lond þat is forsaken as wildernesse. Forsaken we ben in þis desert for our pride & our sinnes; forsaken vs haþ þe holi gost; forsaken haþ vs our liif, liif þat is Ihesus Crist, Marie sone; of þe fader & þe sone & þe holi gost we ben forsaken & oʒainseyd; forsaken we be in þis wildernesse þer nis no leder þat techeþ vs þe way, for we han lore þe
35 riʒt way þurth oure sinnes & our giltes & þurth oure pride þat is so

---

5 mainten] *alt. to* maintened; confort] *alt. to* conforted. 6 ʒef] *alt.* 8 bede] *alt. to* bedes. 18 bost] bobace *alt.* 20 for] (.)for. 25 voice] a *ins.* voice. 27 haue knowen] knowe(.) haue, *transp.* 32 liif] *alt.* 34 lore] *ins.*

  Prium Iesu le dreiturel
Qu'il nus enseigne la uoie al ciel,
Qu'il nus adresce le dreit chemin
Ki par char nus est frere e ueisin,

1630  Ke par bienfeit clos e apert
      Seium iete de cest desert,
      E en la cit puissum maneir
      Ke ia n'auerat matin ne seir

foule. Take we þan to Ihesu þe riȝtful þat techeþ vs þe riȝt way to heuen,
þat, þurth þat he tok our flesche & our blod, he is becomen our broþer &
our neiȝtbour, þat þurth gode dedes priuy & open þat we mowe ben
brouȝt out of þis desert & þat we may wonen þer þat neuer ne schal be
5    morowe ne euen, bot euer more day. God it vs graunt. Amen.

---

1 we þan] þan we *transp.;* riȝtful] riȝt way ful *alt. to* riȝtful.  2 tok] *alt.*  3 gode]
gode(.); priuy] *alt.*

# IN DIE NATIVITATIS DOMINI

Cesar Auguste out comande
1635 Que tut li mund fust abreue.
Cest escrit fist primes escrire
Cyrin ki prouost ert de Syre.
Tuz en alouent as citez
Dunt il erent nurriz e nez.
1640 E Ioseph uint de Galilee,
De Nazaret desqu'en Iudee,
En Bethleem u fut manant
Li reis David en sun uiuant,
Kar il esteit de sa lignee,
1645 De sa meisun, de sa meisnee.
Marie i ad od sei menee
Qu'il aueit anceis esspusee.
Amdui i uenent sanz recur
Pur estre escrit entre le lur.
1650 Quant il erent en cel pays
A Marie sun uentre est pris,  /f. 67ʳ
De sun fiz s'est bien deliuere;
En drapels l'ad bien enuolupe
E en une creche l'ad culche
1655 Kar ele n'out autre desturne.
E pasturs erent en cel pays
Ki ueillouent sur lur berbiz.
Vn angle Deu lur aparout
E deiuste els pres arestout.
1660 Quant il uirent si grant clarte
Mult grantment sunt espunte.
Li angle lur dit en oant:
'Ne vus dutez tant ne quant;
Io vus annunce ioye grant
1665 Dunt tut li poples ert ioiant.
Hui nus est nez li sires Crist
En la cite u Dauid mist:
Il est salueur de tuz pecchez,
E par cest signe le uerrez:

1670 L'enfant trouerez en dras uolse
E en la creche recline'.
Quant co out dit, demaintenant
D'angels i uint un tropel grant
Ki Deu loerent en disant:
1675 'En haut seit glorie a Deu le grant
E en terre as homes peis
Ki unt boen uuleir sanz releis'.
Ci nus estoet un poi targer
E del estoire alkes tucher.
1680 Cesar Auguste ert fort guerrere,
Prince de Rome e emperere;
De tut le mund se out feit seignur.
Que par guere, que par pour,
Trestuz li rendaient treuage
1685 Pur eschure greignur damage.
Pur co k'il uout trestut sauer
Cumbien dust pur tut auer,
Trestut li mund fist enbreuer,
Mais les regnes chescun par ser.
1690 Custume ert dunc en Iudee
Chescun uint a sa lignee,
A la gent dunt eissuz esteit
Quant nule rien lur aueneit.
Ioseph ki ert de Daui lin
1695 A Bethleem tint sun chemin
Od Marie k'il pris aueit
E sulum la lei la teneit,
Kar de la lei ourent l'entente
Que chescuns perneit sa parente.
1700 Partant poum estre fiz
Qu'il erent del lin li rei Dauiz,
Dunt Iesus est suuent numez
Le fiz Daui pur ses buntez.
Ioseph reuint a sa cite

# SERMON 5
## IN NOCTE NATIUITATIS DOMINI
## AD PRIMAM MISSAM

*Secundum Lucam. Exiit edictum a Cesare Augusto. &c.*

Cesar August had comaunded þat al þe world schuld ben breued. Þis writ
dede first writ Cirin þat was prest of Sire, þat al men schuld wend to þe
cites þer þat hii were born & norist. And Ioseph come out of Galile fro
5    Nazareth þer he dwelled & come to Iude, in Bedlem þer Dauid woned in
his liue, for he was of his kinde & of his hous & of his meyne þat had
wedded þe mayden Marie. Boþe hii comen wiþouten ani duellinge for to
ben writen amongges her kinde. Whan hii comen into þat cuntre, Marie
trauayled & was deliuerd of her sone & in cloutes haþ wonden him & haþ
10   layd him in a crache, for sche ne had no better wane. And hirdmen were
in þat cuntre þat woken her schepe, & goddes angel come to hem & stod
beside hem, & whan hii seiȝen þe angel hii weren adradde of þe briȝtnesse. And þe angel sayd to hem, 'Ne dout ȝou nouȝt; Y bringe ȝou
typinges of gret ioie þat al folk schul ben glad of. Born is þe lord Crist in
15   þe cite þer Dauid duelled: he is helþ & medicine of al þingges & sinnes.
And bi þis tokene ȝe schul sen him: ȝe schal finde þe childe wounden in
cloutes & layd in a crache.' And whan þis angel had sayd þus, of angels
come a gret compaynie þat heried God & sayden, 'Heiȝed be glorie to
God þe gret & in erþ, pes to men þat ben of gode wille'.
20   Now ich mot a while leten of þis & tellen of þe storie. Cesar August
was a gret werreour, prince of Rome & emperour; of al þe world he was
made lord. What þurth werr & what þurth drede, al hii ȝeld him truage
for to flen þe more harme. Forþi þat he wold witen hou michel he had of
men vnder him, he dede abreuen al þe world.
25   Custome it was þan in Iude þat ich on come to his kinde. Ioseph, þat
was of Dauid kinde, come vnto Bedlem wiþ Marie þat he had taken to his
wiife in þe maner of her lawe þat ich on schuld wedde in his kinde. In þat
may we ben cleped Dauid childer & of his kinde þurth whiche Ihesus was
often cleped Dauid sone for his godnesse. And Ioseph come to þat cite

---

7 wiþouten] wiþ oute(.) *ins.* 8 þat cuntre] cuntre þat *transp.* 11 come] come(.).
15 þer] *alt.* 25 þan] *alt.* 29 Ioseph] on *eras., by H.*

1705 Pur estre ilokes enbreue;
Ioseph reuint a sun lignage
Pur rendre ilokes le truage.
El chemin defors la cite
Vindrent la gent de cel regne;
1710 La nuit i unt tuz demurrez
Pur estre le matin enbreuez.
Icele nuit a sun dreit terme
Sanz doel, sanz peine, e sanz lerme,
Iesum Marie genuit
1715 Cum la lezcun auant nus dit.
 Dit est l'estoire en la lezcun;
A nostre pru ore entendum.
Saueir poum ke peis esteit
Quant uns hom tut le mund enbreueit,
1720 E dreit fust ke dunc nasquesist
Cil ki trestut guuerne e fist,
Kar il est peis pardurable
A tuz ki uers li sunt estable.
Li mundz ert dunkes enbreuez
1725 Quant Iesus ert en terre nez,
Kar il enbreue ses amis
En la ioie de parais.
Cuntre co dit Dauid li reis
De cels ke n'aiment Deu ne peis:
1730 'Del liuere Deu seient desdit;
Ne seient od les boens escrit'.
 En Bethlem uolt Deu nestre
Pur tutes bones almes pestre,
Kar Bethlem meisun de pain
1735 Esspealt adreit e nient en uain. /f. 67ᵛ
Kar iloc nasqui Ihesu Crist
Qui tuz nus pest, reint e fist.
Il est li pains dunt Daui dit
El salter par seint essperit:
1740 'Le pain des angles home manga;
Viande a plente lur duna'.
Il peist les angles sanz faillir
E homes ki le seuent merir.

Il est le pain ke demandums
1745 La Pater Noster quant disums:
'Nostre pain chescuniurnel
Nus dune a hui, li sire del ciel'.
Chescuniurnel est ueirement
Kar ia ne prendra finement;
1750 Trestut nus peist, tuz nos furmat,
Ne ia pur co fin ne ferat.
Icest pain nus dunat Marie
Ke tut peist e ne fine mie.
Il peist les angles par amur
1755 E homes par sa grant dulcur.
Ki de co pain ne prent ne creit,
De ceste uie a mort se treit.
Ki prent e creit le fiz Marie
De ceste mort s'en ua a uie.
1760  De pucele neistre deignat
Ki sa char en pain nus turnat.
Veez, seignurs, de pucellage
Cum est cheri de Deu curage.
Quant Deus humanite uolt prendre
1765 Sul en pucele uolt descendre.
Mais la pucele espuse esteit.
Veez, seignurs, ke Deus ad feit
Par espusaille e pucellage:
Vout restorer nostre damage.
1770 Ki pucele est, guarde ben sa uie,
Si est cumpainz al fiz Marie.
Ki espus est, guard ben sa lei,
Si auerat Deus tut dis od sei.
E si il cheit en ueduete,
1775 Guard sei bien en nettete.
Sul ices treis estages sunt
Par ki les genz al ciel uendrunt.
Ki de gre pert sun pucellage
Iames n'ert seins de cel damage.
1780 Le mesfeit poet il espener,
Mais ia le cors n'aurat enter.

for to ben enbreued þer; Ioseph come vnto his kinde for to ȝeld þer his
truage. And out of al þe kingdome comen þe folk into þe cite & duelled
þer al þat niȝt for to ben writen in on þe morowe. In þat niȝt it was
Maries time for to han child wiþouten sorwe, wiþouten pine, wiþouten
5    wepeinge. Ihesus was þat niȝt born of Marie as þe lesoun seit vs biforn.
     Now is seyd þe storie & þe lesoun, now vnderstonde we to our profite.
Wil may we wete þat it was pes whan o man enbreued al þe world, & it
semed wel þan þat he þat was wel of wisdome were þat iche time born in
þis world; he þat was pes & brouȝt pes, it semed wel þat it schuld ben pes
10   in his cominge, for he kepeþ al & saueþ þat schal ben ysaued. Þe world
was þan writen whan Ihesus was born, for he witeþ his frendes in þe ioie
of paradis. Oȝain þes spekeþ þis kinges [f. 11ᵛ] of hem þat ne loue not
God ne pes; out of Goddes boke hii schullen be put & nouȝt writen wiþ
þe gode.
15   In Bedlem wold Ihesu be born for to feden al gode soules, for Bedlem
is as michel to say as hous of brede. Þer was Ihesus Crist born þat al
fedeþ & al fourmed & made. Þis is þat brede þat Dauid seyþ of in þe
souter, þat spake þurth þe holi gost: 'Þe bred of angel man ete & gret
plenteþ of mete he ȝaue hem'. He fedeþ þe angels & þe men þat cunnen
20   seruen him wel. He is þe brede þat we asken whan we sayen our pater
noster: 'Our bred of ich day ȝif vs lord of heuene'. Ich day he is for soþe;
he ne schal neuer haue ende. Al he fedeþ vs & al he made vs to lasten
wiþouten ende. Þis brede haþ ȝeuen vs Marie þat al fedeþ & ne ceseþ
nouȝt: he fedeþ þe angels wiþ his loue & men þurth his gret swetenesse.
25   He þat þis brede ne takeþ nouȝt ne bileueþ it nouȝt, fram þis liif he goþ to
þe deþ; he þat takeþ it and bileueþ þe brede of Marie, fram þis deþ he goþ
to liif.
     Of þe mayden he wold be born þat his flesche in fourme of brede
ȝeueþ vs. Lokeþ, lordinges, of maydenhode what it is priue to Godes
30   hert. Whan God wold taken our kinde, he wold onlich come into a
mayden, ac þe maden was wedded. Lokeþ, lordinges, what God haþ don
þurth maydenhode & wedloke; he wold astoren oȝain our harmes. Þat
mayden is, kepe wel her liif & hii schul ben felawes to Ihesu, Marie sone;
þat wedded is, kepe wel his lawe, for he schal euer haue God wiþ him;
35   and ȝif hii falle in widuhede, kepe him wele in her clennesse; for be þes
ilke þre stages men & wimmen schul comen to heuen & þurth non oþer.
Þat wiþ will lest her maydenhode, neuer more ne schul hii keuer þat
harm; amenden hii mow wel þe misgilt, ac neuer ne schal hii comen

---

7 wil] *alt. to* wel.   8 wel] *alt. to* well;   born] bore *alt.*   32 our] (.)our.   36 ilke] *alt.*

Perdu en ad la compaignie
Des uirgines ki sunt entur Marie.
Mais cil qui est en espusaille,
1785 Guard sei bien de rien n'i ait faille,
Kar s'il de rien mesperneit
A grant peine l'amendereit,
Kar Deu en auerat curuce
Qui l'espuser ad comande.
1790 En sun cors ad mult mesfeit
Quant de sa femme se retreit,
Kar par la force d'espusaille
Vne char sunt il dous sanz faille.
E Seint Pol dit sanz ubliance:
1795 'L'espus n'at de sun cors puissance;
Li hom est tut a sa muiler
E la femme tut a sun ber'.
Ensi sunt il entrelace
Que nuls n'ad de sei poeste;
1800 Pur co est li pecchez mult grant
E al amender trespesant.
Amendums, seignurs, nostre uie,
Ke seiums od le fiz Marie;
Vne des riens qu'il plus deffie
1805 Co est le charnel leccherie;
Il nus en fist mustrance bele
Kant il prist char de la pucele.
El chemin neistre se leissat,
E par ico bien nus mustrat
1810 Que ceste uie est tut chemin
Parunt passum seir e matin.
Ici estut en ben aler
Ki uolt od Deu el ciel regner.
Ci n'auum pas manantie;
1815 Quere l'estoet en autre uie.
El chemin neist Crist nostre ueie
Qui par ses diz si nus aueie:
'Io sui ueie, io sui ueritez,
Io sui uie, bien le sachez'. /f. 68ʳ

1820 Par ceste ueie en ueir alum
Si ses preceps del quor feisum;
Alum a sun comandement
Kar il est ueritez ki ia ne ment.
Si nus sulum ses diz alums
1825 La uie pardurable auerums,
Kar le luer ke as soens rent
Est uie tut dis sanz finement.
Pur nus atreire a cele uie
De nuiz nasqui le fiz Marie.
1830 Quantque nos uiuerums en cest mund,
Nuit est e tenebrur parfund;
Kar ia ne seit tant clers cest iur
Que kant al ciel ne seit obscur,
Ne cist secle tant delitus
1835 Vers celi ne seit perillus.
E cist secles ua definant;
Cist maint sanz fin en ioie grant.
Mult par deuum li aioir
Ki ceste nuit nus uint tolir.
1840 Amer deuum la sue umblesce
Ki co nos tout ke trop nos blesce.
Il nos uint tolir del treuage
V nus mist Adam par sa rage;
Co espelt le treu ke fu escrit
1845 A la seisun quant il nasquit;
Tut le son humiliement
Fist il pur nostre auancement.
Il fu uestu de drapelez
Pur nus duner oueraignes nez;
1850 Cuuerir se fist de uiels drapels
Pur nos cuuerir de biens nouels;
Nus esteimes tut enveilliz
E en pecchez tut enordiz.
Li nouels hom nos uint garir
1855 E de ses noueltez uestir;
Il duna nofs comandemenz
Pur eslauer nos quors sullenz.

oȝain to þat degre; lorn hii han þe felaweschip of virgines þat ben wiþ
Marie. And hii þat ben wedded, kepe hem wel wiþouten trespassing, for
ȝif hii trespasse, wiþ gret pine hii schullen amenden it, for hii han
wreþþed God þat made þe weddinge. And gret trespas he doþ his wiif
5    oþer sche to him, for þurth strengþe of wedloke hii ben of flesche
wiþouten doute. And Seynt Poule it seiþ for soþe: 'Þe spouse ne haþ
nouȝt his body at wille for he is al ȝeuen to his wif & þe wiif al to þe
husbond'. And so hii ben ybounden togider þat non ne haþ pouste of
himseluen; forþi is þe trespas ful gret, & strong for to amende.
10    Amende we, lordinges, our liif þat may be in compaynie wiþ Ihesus,
Marie sone. It is on of þe sinnes þat he hateþ most, þat is, licherie, & þat
he schewed vs wel whan he toke flesche & blod of a mayden & in way he
wold be born. And in þat he schewed vs wel þat al þis liif nis bot a way
þat we schul passen in, oþer to gode oþer to qued. [f. 12ʳ] And he þat
15    wille regne in þe blis of heuen wiþ our lord, he most nedes take her þe
way in gode. For her ne haue we no certeyne wonieing stede; anoþer we
mote sechen in þe way Crist was born. Þat is our way þat þurth his
wordes we ben ytauȝt. He seiþ himseluen: 'Ich am way & soþnesse; ich
am liif'. Wite ȝe wel, be þis way we gon ȝif þat we don his
20    comaundement, þat is soþenesse, þat neuer ne schal liȝen. Ȝif we gon
efter his wordes, we schal haue þe lif þat euer schal last. For to drawe vs
fram þis liif Ihesus Crist was born of his moder o niȝt, for as long as we
ben in þis world, in niȝt we ben & in depe derkenesse. For be þis dayes
neuer so liȝt, as vnto heuen to se to it is al derkenesse; ne be þis world
25    neuer so delicius, as aȝaines þat it is perelous; & þis world haþ ende, &
þat duelleþ euer more in gret blis. Gretlich we owe to þonken him þat
com for to bring vs fram þis niȝt; loue we owe his gret lowenesse þat
binemeþ vs þe þing þat hirteþ vs gretlich. He come for to benim vs out of
truage & þraldome þat Adam sett vs inne; þat iche time þat he was born
30    he schewed him forþ for to pay truage for vs, for al his lownesse he dede
for to heiȝen vs.
    He was cloþed in cloutes for to cloþen vs in clen werkes; couerd he
was in cloutes for to couer vs wiþ newe godes, for we wer al elded & wiþ
sinne al filed. Þe newe man come for to helen vs & for to cloþe vs in
35    newe cloþinge. He ȝaf vs his comaundmence for to wasche wiþ our

---

7 he] *on eras.*   11 on] wiþ on; licherie] *alt. to* lecherie.   12 blod] blod(.).   17 in] *on
eras.*   21 lif þat] *ins.*   30 forþ] forþ forþ *eras.*   34 helen] *alt.*   35 comaundmence]
*alt. to* comaundmente

E en la creche se fit poser
Pur noz bestialtez oster.
1860 Creche est mangure a celes bestes
Ki tudis enbrunchent de lur testes,
Ki ne pensent fors sul de terre
Coment puissunt lur uiuers quere.
Dun ne sunt cil ben bestial
1865 Ki rien ne pensent fors le mal,
Ki unt le quor en terre mis,
Ne pensent rien de parais.
Enbrunche sunt uers lur aueir
Cil ke ne uulent Deu saueir.
1870 Mais Iesus iust en uils drapels
Pur nus oster de tels auels;
En la creche se uolt cucher
Pur nus tolir de icel penser,
Pur tolir a nus auertez
1875 Vilement uestuz fut la posez.
La cunuit l'asne sun seignur
E li bouez sun creatur.
  E nus cheitifs, ke purrum dire
Quant il uendra od sa grant ire,
1880 Ki ore ne uulum en li creire
Ne ses comandemenz parfeire?
Quant il fera el ciel sa feste
Plus serrum uil ke nule beste.
Certis cum home en creche iust,
1885 Mais as pasturs cum Deu parut;
Cum emfes iust en uils drapels,
Cum Deu parut as pasturels.
L'angle od clarte celi nuncieit
Cum en or[d]e creche giseit.

1890 Quant il fu tels en sa enfance
Quels ert quant uendra en puissance?
Pensez ao[re cume] par uus
Ke [ne] seez adunc c[onfus];
Pensez en p[arfite] creance
1895 E [veil]lez en bone [fesance].
Li pasturel ki ueilles firent
Les angles od lumere uirent.
Cil ueille bien uerreiment
Ki ne dort en nul maltalent;
1900 Cil ueille bien ke mal ne feit
Ne n'ad d'altri pecche aheit,
Ki ne feit uers sei pecche,
Ne uers sun prosme, ne uers De.
  Mais mult ualt poi de mal retreire
1905 Qui poet e ne uolt le bien feire.
Kar li pastur ki l'angle uirent
Sur lur bestes ueilles firent.  /f. 68ᵛ
Tuz sumes bestes par charnage
E quant al cors tut d'un parage;
1910 De terre sunt comunment
Homes e bestes ensement.
Mais Deus les uolt si ordeiner:
Les uns feit les autres garder.
Des gardeins tels en sunt seignur
1915 Des cors, tels des almes doctur.
Mais tut estoet issi garder,
Si seignurer, si enseigner,
Que li poples se tenge en bien
E il ne mesfacent de rien;
1920 Kar si els issi le funt,
Li angle Deu ouec els sunt

hertes þat wer filed. In þe crache he lete liggen him for to don away our
bestlich likeinges. Crache is maniure vnto bestes þat euer more put doun
þe heued, þat ne þenche bot onlich of erþe, hou þat hii mowe geten her
mete. And ben hii nouȝt wel bestes þat noþinge ne þenche þot þe iuel, þat
5    han sett her heuedes in erþ & þenche nouȝt of paradis? Hii sett so her
hertes opon her godes þat hii nil nouȝt knowen God. Ac Ihesus was layd
in vile cloutes for to do fram vs swiche chaimmcchipes; in þe crache he
wold lien for to benimen vs swiche þouȝtes, for to benimen vs fram
coueytise in foule cloutes he was layd þer. Þer knewe þe asse his lord &
10   þe ox his maker.
   And we wretches, what may we say whan þat he schal comen wiþ his
gret wreþþe þat now ne wil we nouȝt beleuen in him ne don his comand-
mence. Whan he makeþ in heuen his fest, more we schul be viler þan ani
best. Certes, as man he lay in þe crache, ac as God he schewed him to þe
15   schepeherdes; as child he lay in vile cloutes & foule, & as God he
schewed him to þe herdmen. Þe angel wiþ gret briȝtnesse brouȝt þe
schepherdes tiþinges of him þat lay in foule crache. Whan he was swich
in his childehode, what schal he be whan he becomeþ in his miȝt. Þenche
we now so opon him here þat we ne be nouȝt þan confounded; þenche we
20   in stedfast bileue & woni in gode werkes. Þe hirdmen þat wer wakeand
seiȝen þe angels in gret liȝt. [f. 12ᵛ] He wakeþ wel for soþe þat ne slepeþ
nouȝt in no wikked wille. He wakeþ wel þat ne doþ non iuel ne haþ no
gladdenes of oþer men sinnes, þat ne doþ no sinne himseluen, ne oȝaines
God ne his neiȝebour.
25   Ac litel it is worþ for to wiþdrawen men fram iuel bot ȝif men do þe
gode; for ȝif he do iuel, he brekeþ Godes comaundement, for God haþ
forboden iuel þat he ne schal nouȝt don it, & he haþ comaund him to do
þe gode. And ȝif he do nouȝt þe gode, he brekeþ Godes comaundment &
goþ to helle þerþurth bot ȝif he amende him. For þe schepeherdes þat
30   seiȝen þe angels woken her bestes. Al we ben bestes in as muchel as we
han flesche & blode, for of erþe ben comunliche men & bestes. Ac God
wold so ordeyn hem þat he made þat on schuld kepen anoþer. Of kepers,
swyiche ben lordes ouer þe oþer bodiis, & þat ben þes lordes ouer þe
comune puple; & sum ben lordes of soules, & þat ben þes doctours. Ac al
35   hii moten so kepen, þe lord & þe techer, þat þe folk hold hem in þe gode
& þat hii ne misdon in noþing. And ȝif hii don so, Goddes angels ben wiþ

---

2 maniure] maniute.     7 chaimmcchipes] *alt. to* chaimmschipes.     12-13
comandmence] *alt. to* comandmente.     16 briȝtnesse] liȝtnesse *canc.* briȝtnesse.     20
in] *ins.*     32 ordeyn] *alt.;* schuld] *alt.*     33 bodiis] *alt.*

Ki les alument en poeir;
Tant cum il funt le Deu uuleir
Tut facent il bien lur mester.
1925 Purquant se deiuent il duter:
Quant l'angle uirent li pastur,
Mult en aueient grant pour.
E Salamon a co s'acute:
'Bien eit', feit il, 'ki tut dis dute'.
1930 As dutanz dist l'angle bien:
'Ne vus tamez, ne dutez rien,
Bone nuuele io vus cunt:
Hui est nez li sauuers del mund'.
Ico espelt: ne dutez mie,
1935 Vus ki amez le fiz Marie.
Mais il se poent bien duter
Ki n'unt le fiz Marie cher,
Kar ses duturs il sauuera
E des autres se uengera
1940 Il sauuera les bienuoillianz
E destrura les mals dormanz.
Li angles ki puis sunt uenuz
Pur co l'unt feit ke seient creuz;
Kar celi tient l'om a ueir
1945 Ki testmonie uolt aueir.
Le chant qu'il unt chante
A nostre bien est turne.

Nus deuum Deu en haut loer,
Nient en bassesce de peccher;
1950 E nus li faimes glorie grant
Quant en li sumes bien creiant,
E demustrum nostre creance
En amur e en bone fesance.
Co est la bone uolente
1955 Ki tut dis auerat peis en De.
Entendez iceste parole
Que dist li angeliel esscole:
'Homes de bone uolente
Auerunt en terre peis de De'.
1960 Sul la uolente parfeit
De nos oueraignes tut l'espleit;
Ne uaut rien si n'es bienuoillant,
Ia n'ert li feiz si bels, si grant;
Bone uolente sulement
1965 Suffist ki ne poet autrement.
Tenum, seignurs, bone uoillance;
Fichum en Deu nostre creance;
Amum Iesu le fiz Marie
Ki hui nasquit en ceste uie.
1970 Il vint en ceste uie mortel
Pur nus amener a sun ciel.
Seruum le si en ceste uie
K'il nus grante sa compaignie.

hem þat liȝteþ hem in miȝt as long as hii don Goddes wille & þen al don
hii wel her mister. Ȝete hii owen alway to ben in doute, for whan þe
hirdmen seiȝen þe angel hii were in gret drede, & Salemon sayþ also:
'Wel he haþ don þat alway douteþ him'. Vnto hem þat douten hem seyþ
5   þe angel wel: 'Ne douteþ ȝou noþing, for gode tydynges Y telle ȝou, for
today is bore þe saueour of þe world'. Þat is to say, ne doute ȝou nouȝt,
ȝe þat louen Ihesus Crist, Marie sone. Ac hii mowe michel douten hem
þat ne loue him nouȝt, for hii þat douten him, hem he schal sauen, & hii
þat ne doute him nouȝt, he schal vengen him opon hem. He schal sauen
10  hem þat ben of god wille & he schal destruen hem þat ben of wicked will.
Þe angels þat comen efterward, forþi hii comen for þat hii ben wel leued;
for men seyþ: he þat bringgeþ gode wittnes, he is to leuen. Þe song þat hii
han songen is al turned to our god: we schal herien God on heyȝe &
nouȝt in lowenes of sinne. And we make to him gret blis whan we
15  bileuen in him & schewe our bileue in loue & in gode werkes. Þat is þe
gode wille þat euer schal haue pes in Gode.

Vnderstondeþ wel þis worde þat þe angel seyþ: 'To men of god wille
be pes in erþe'. Onlich our god wille fulfilleþ al þe strengþe of our
werkes. Þe dede ne is nouȝt worþ, ne be it neuer so gret, bot ȝif it be don
20  wiþ gode wille, for gode wille suffiseþ anouȝ þat ne may non oþer don.
Þerfor, lordinges, haue we gode wille & sett our bileue fast in God. Loue
Ihesus Crist þat liif brouȝt vnto vs in þis liif. He come into þis dedlich liif
for to bring vs to heuen. Þerfor, serue we him so her þat we may com to
him & be wiþ him in his felaweschipe. Amen.

3 angel] angel(.).   6 bore þe] *on eras.*   13 on heyȝe &] *on eras.*   19 be it] be þe it *alt.*
*to* be it.   20 suffiseþ] *alt.*   23 vs] *ins.;*   com] *alt.*

# IN DIE EPIPHANIE

Quant ert nez en Iudee
1975 Iesus, en Bethlem la bonure,
Es iurs Herodes ki regneit
E de Iudee reis esteit,
D'orient i sunt uenuz reis,
A Ierusalem en uont tut treis.
1980 Ilokes unt bien demande:
'Li reis des Gius, u est il ne?
Vou', funt il, 'auum s'esteile
En orient, pas ne se ceile;
Venuz sumes li aurer,
1985 E de nos beals duns honurer'.  /f. 69ʳ
Quant Herodes out co oiz,
Trublez iert e mult mariz,
E le pays en ert truble,
E Ierusalem la cite.
1990 Herodes ad dunc asemble
Les sages si ad demande
V Crist nestreit. Il li unt dit,
En Beetlem la Iude cit,
Kar li prophetes si nuncia:
1995 'Tu Beetlem, terre Iuda,
Es princes Iude n'es menur,
De tai istrat des ducs la flur
Ki mun pople guuernerat
De Israel, quant il uendrat'.
2000 Herodes dunc priuement
Des reis aprist ententiuement
Cum bien out qu'il orent ueu
L'esteile ke ert aparceu.
En Beetlem les enueia,
2005 E ducementes les preia
Quant il ousent troue l'enfant

Qu'il le mandassent meitenant.
Co dist k'il uoldra uenir
Pur le aurrer e pur cherir.
2010 Quant il de Herode sunt turne
L'esteile unt tanttost retroue;
Dreit les menat a la maisun
A l'enfant, si estut en sum.
Les reis quant l'esteile uirent
2015 De grant leesce s'esioirent.
En la maisun tantost entrerent,
Marie e l'enfant i trouerent.
Aual chairent e aurerent
E de lur tresor li dunerent,
2020 Or, e encens, e mirre offrirent,
Co sunt les duns ki li firent.
En dormant sunt sumuns tut treis
Qu'il a Herode n'augent meis;
Par altre ueie sunt alez
2025 E en lur regnes repairez.
  Icest iur ad Tiphayne a nun;
Entendez i, seignur, barun.
Co est diuin apariciun,
De Deu meimes la mustreisun;
2030 Hui se mustra Deu uerraiment
En treis maneres a la gent,
Cum vus auez oi brefment:
Primes as treis reis d'orient,
E de cel iur al trentime an
2035 Fu il baptize de Iohan.
De cel iur a un an enterin
Fist il as noces de l'ewe uin.
En tuz ces treis feiz s'est mustre
Que Iesus est e home e De.

## SERMON 6
## IN DIE EPYPHANIE DOMINI

*Secundum Matheum. Cvm natus esset Ihesus in Bethlem.*
Whan Ihesu was born in Iude & in Bedleem þe blisced in þe time þat
Herode regned & was king of Iude, out of þe est come þre kinges vnto
Ierusalem, & þer hii asked where þe king of Iues was born. 'We han
5  sen', hii seiden, 'þe sterr in þe est, & we be comen to worschipen him'.
Whan Herodes herd þis, he was al trubled in his hert & sori, & al þe lond
so was ytrubled for her wordes. Herodes dede þan come togider al þe
wise men of þe cite of Ierusalem & asked hem where þat Crist schuld ben
yborn. And hii seiden him, in Bedlem Iude; for þe prophete so seid: 'Þou
10  lond of Iude, in þe schal be born þe flour of princes þat my folk schul
gouernen & kepen of Israel'. Whan Herodes herd þis, he held it stille in
his hert & seyd to þe kinges & besouȝt hem ententilich hou long it was
agon þat hii had sen þe sterre. He sent hem into Bedlem & besouȝt hem
þat whan hii had founden þe child, þat hii schuld wite him to say, & sayd
15  he wold comen þan to anoure him & do him worschip. And whan hii wer
departed fram Herodes, þan hii founden þe sterr þat lad hem þer þe child
was, riȝt vnto þe hous. Þe kinges, whan hii seiȝen þe sterr, hii maden gret
ioie, & alson hii wenten into þe hous, hii founden Marie & her child. Hii
fellen doun on kenewes & toke out her tresor & offerd him gold & mirre
20  & encens — þo were þe ȝiftes þat hii offerd him. In her slepe hii ben
warned of þe angel þat hii ne schuld nouȝt gon by Herodes. By anoþer
way hii ben went hom into her cuntre.
   Þis day is cleped Epiphanie, þat is as muchel as scheweing of diuine,
þat is, þe schewing of God himseluen. Today schewed God him soþe-
25  liche in þre maners to þe folk, & first vnto þre kinges of þe est, as ȝe han
herd schortlich. And on þat day þritti ȝer he was baptist of Seyn Ion, &
on þat day a ȝer after he made of water wyne. And in al þes þre dedes he
schewed him þat Ihesus is boþ God & man.

7 so] al *ins.* so.   10 schul] *alt. to* sc(.)hal, *l.h.*   11 of] my folk *ins.* of.   14 wite] do
*ins.* wite.   15 anoure] anour(e..).   19 kenewes] her *ins.* kenewes.   21 by (1)] *alt.;*
by (2)] *alt.*   27 in] (.)in; þre] þre(.).   28 schewed] *alt.*

2040 Ore oum la premere fesance.
Del iur trezime de sa enfance
Treis reis d'orient sunt uenuz
Par un esteile k'il unt uouz.
Icest esteile ferm n'esteit
2045 Mais pres d'els en l'eir les guieit.
L'esteile ert clere de grant fin,
Sa grandure les mist al chemin.
Mais del esteile riens ne uirent
Kant uers Herodes descendirent;
2050 E quant de Herode partiz sunt
L'esteile lors retroue unt.
Ces reis, seignurs, sages esteient
E des esteiles mult saueient.
Par cest esteile, ki grant ere
2055 E ietout si tres grant lumere,
Pur co ke n'orent tele ueu,
Pensent ke grant ert sa uertu.
E Balaam out prophetize,
Ki en lur terre out conuerse:
2060 'De Iacob une esteile nestra
E de Israel un hom leuera;
Les aliens ducs defreindra,
De tutes teres reis serra'.
Quant cele esteile ert esclarzie
2065 Suiunt lur de la prophecie.
De l'esteile funt lur guiur,
Tut dis la ueient nuit e iur;
L'esteile en l'eir pendeit errant
E il la uunt de pres siuant. /f. 69ᵛ
2070 Par co se mustrat Iesu Crist
K'il home e ciel e le mund fist.
Kar tut seit il en furme de home,
Deus est, quant il l'esteile alume.
Cum emfes en maisun maneit,
2075 Cum Deu l'esteile feit aueit;
Cum emfes en sun berz giseit,

Cum Deus l'esteile cunduieit.
Dunc est la ueritez aemplie
Ki ainz out dist la prophecie:
2080 'La gent ki ert en tenebrur
Del ciel uit raier grant luiur;
As mananz en umbre de mort
Est nee clarte de confort'.
Par ces treis reis sunt mustre bien
2085 Li sarazin e li paen
Ki n'urent unc lei ne doctur
Pur co furent en tenebrur.
Mais Iesu Crist les aluma
E les alumez auogla.
2090 Li alumez li Giu esteient
Ki la lei Deu receu aueient;
Dunt il distrent en uerite
K'en Beetlem serreit Crist nee.
Mais auogles del tut esteient
2095 Quant co ke distrent ne creaient.
E quant uirent Ihesu parlant,
Miracles e uertuz fesant,
Quant dunc ne crurent k'il ert De
Ne furent il del tut auogle?
2100 Pur co les ad Deu leissez
E les paens enluminez.
Nus eimes la gent paenur
Ki Deus ad dune sa luiur:
La luiur de la cristienete
2105 Par sa grace nus ad dune.
Ici l'auum par esperance,
El ciel l'auerum sanz dutance.
Co est l'esteile ki nus duit,
C'a Iesu tut dreit conduit.
2110 Pur nent se dirra cristien
Ki ci n'espeire autre bien;
Pur nient auera cristienie

Now here we þe first dede. In his childhode, opon þe þrittenþe day
efter þat he was bore of his moder, þre kinges ben comen out of þe est
þurth a sterr þat hii han sen. Þis sterre ne stod nouȝt omong þe oþer
sterres, ac bineþen in þe aier it was & lad hem. Þe sterr was gret & clere,
5 & þe grettnesse þerof made hem for to sechen it. Ac of þe sterr ne seiȝ hii
nouȝt whan hii comen toward Herodes; & whan hii war departed fram
Herodes, þan þe sterr schewed him to hem. Þes þre kinges wer wise men
& muchel couþe of þe sterres; bi þis sterr þat was so gret & kest so gret
liȝt, & þan for hii ne had neuer ȝete aforn sen non swiche, þerfor hii
10 þouȝten þat his vertu was gret. And Balam had prophecide þat had
duelled in her lond: 'Of [f. 13ᵛ] þe schal a sterr be born & of Israel a man
schal arisen; þe straunge dukes he schal fordon & of alle londes he schal
ben king'. And whan þis sterr schone so briȝt, þan hii beþouȝt hem of þe
prophecie, & of þat sterre hii maden her giour. And alway hii seiȝen it
15 niȝt & day; þe sterr hong in þe air & hii folowed it. Be þat schewed him
Ihesus Crist þat he made man & witt & al þe world; for þeiȝ al he be in
fourme of man, God he is whan þat he liȝteþ þe sterr. As child he lay in
his cradel & as God he lad þe ster. Þan was þe soþe fulfilled þat aforn
had said þe prophecie: 'Þe folk þat ben in derkenesse, fram heuen come
20 gret liȝt; to hem þat were in schadue of deþ is born clerete of confort'. Be
þes þre kinges is wel schewed þe sarrain & þe payen þat ne had no liȝt no
swettnesse forþi hii weren in derknesse; ac Ihesus Crist liȝted hem, & hii
þat wer liȝted he made hem blinde. Hii þat wer liȝtted wer þe Iues þat
had receyued þe lawe of God. Þan hii sayden þat Crist schuld ben born in
25 Bedlem, ac blinde hii were al whan þat ne bileued nouȝt þat hii sayden.
As child he lay in þe hous & as God he made þe ster. And whan hii
seiȝen Ihesu spekeand & doand mani wonders, whan þat hii ne leued
nouȝt þan þat he was God, weren hii nouȝt þan blind anouȝ? Þer God
almiȝti left hem & haþ aliȝted þe paynes. We ben comen of þe sarraines
30 þat God haþ ȝeuen his liȝt; liȝt of cristendome þurth his grace he haþ
ȝeuen vs. Here we han it þurth bileue; in heuen we schal haue it openlich.
Þis is þe ster þat ledeþ vs & to Ihesu bringeþ vs riȝt. For nouȝt he is
cleped cristen man þat he ne hopeþ efter oþer godes; for nouȝt he haþ

---

1 opon] *alt.;* þrittenþe] *on eras.*   2 bore] *ins.*   8 kest so gret] & kest so gret *canc.* &
kest so gret.   9 swiche] swiche(.).   11 þe] *on eras.*   14 giour] *alt. to* gidur.
19 prophecie] *alt. to* prophet(...);   þe] to *ins.* þe.   20 is] (.)is.   21 sarrain] *alt. to*
sarraines;   payen] *alt. to* payenmes;   no (2)] ne *alt.*   25 al] *alt. to* all;   ne] hii *ins.* ne.
29 paynes] paynemes *alt.*   30 grace] grace(.).   31 haue] *alt.*   32 ledeþ] *alt.*

Qui ne quert la durable uie.
En esperance e en ferm creire
2115 Est trestut nostre luminaire,
Kar ki de ces dous se decline
Lors perd la lumere diuine
Cum les reis l'esteile perdirent
Quant uers Herode se guenchirent.
2120 Kar Herodes est li malfeiz
Ki tut asorbet par pecchez;
Kar la lumere de fiance
Feit obscurir par mescreance,
E par cest amur terrien
2125 Nus tout l'espeir celestien.
A Ierusalem Herodes esteit;
Iloec le trouerent tut dreit.
Veez, seignurs, cum li malfez
Par seinz lius ad mult enginez;
2130 Pur co k'il del ciel chait
En seinz lius mustre sun delit.
Ierusalem co est muster
V nus alum Deu aurrer.
A peine i serrum nus entrez
2135 Ki ne surdent les mals pensez,
V pur co ke nus iunum,
V pur quiete ke auum.
Tels pense de husbonderie,
Tels de meignee, tels d'amie,
2140 Tels de sa terre guaigner,
Tels de sun ueisin enginer.
Tels pense de sun enemi
E met Iesu tut en ubli;
Tels pense de grant uanitez

2145 Entant l'engine li malfez.
Cum plus nus peinum del urer
E il plus peine del encumbrer,
Kar il est trublez de nos odes
Cum fu de la nouele Herodes;
2150 Il est dolenz e si sergant
Quant nul se repent en urant.
  Herodes dist par bel semblant:
'Alez', feit il, 'quere l'enfant'.   /f. 70ʳ
E les sons soffre li malfez
2155 Qu'il facent bien od lur pecche,
Kar s'il leissassent tuz bienfeiz
Tost parceiuereient lur agueiz.
Semblant lur feit k'il uendra
Quant de sun nestre cert serra.
2160 Li malfez pur plus enginier
Grant semblant feit de Deu amer.
Vunt s'en li rei, trouent l'esteile,
E as conuers Deu ne se ceile;
Tanttost cum leissum le pecche
2165 Deu nus alume de sun gre;
Quant entrum en dreite preere
E Deu nus mustre sa lumere.
Mais l'esteile uait auant
E les reis le uont suiant.
2170 Ke par doctrine e repentir
Deuum le dreit chemin tenir;
En oure bone aler sanz feindre
Si nus a Deu uolum ateindre;
Par boen oueraigne e uraisun
2175 Vendrum a la Iesu maisun.

taken cristendome þat ne hopeþ nouȝt vnto anoþer liif. In hope & in
stedfast bileue is al euerildel our liȝt; for he þat draweþ him from þes
two, he leseþ þe syȝt of God as þe kinges whan hii wenten toward
Herodes — þe cloudes did hide þe ster. For Herodes is þe fende þat
5  ablindeþ al þurth sinne, þat þe liȝt of stedfast bileue he makeþ it derk
þurth misbileue & þurth þis erþlich loue þat he putteþ in our hertes. He
binimmeþ vs þe heuenlich hope þat we schuld haue to God.
    In Ierusalem Herodes was þat time & þer þes þre kinges founden him.
Loke, lordinges, þat þe fende may tempte men in holy stede & duelleþ
10 þer. For þat he fel fram heuen, he scheweþ in holy stede his delites. By
Ierusalem is schewed þe stede þat we gon to to worschipe God. Þerfor,
vnneþ we schul come into Ierusalem, þat is, vnneþ schal we bid ani bede
þat þer ne schal come iuel þouȝtes vnto vs, oþerfor þat we sen oþer for
þat we han. Sum þenche of [f. 14ʳ] husbandrie, sum on loue, sum hou hii
15 schul gouernen hir lond, sum hou hii schul wynnen lond & riches, sum
þat hii mowe bigilen her neiȝebour; & swich þouȝtes comeþ of þe wicked
gost & makeþ a man al forȝeten God. Sum þenchen of wicked vanites, &
al þis is gile of þe fende; þe more þat we þenchen for to bidden our
bedes, þe mor he is aboute for to acumbren vs. For he is trubled of our
20 gode dedes, as of þe newe tidinges, Herodes; he is sori, & his seruantes,
whan ani repenten ham in her liue.
    Herodes sayd wiþ fair semblaunt, 'Goþ', he sayd, '& secheþ þe child'.
So þe fende soffreþ wel þat men do gode dedes whiles þat hii ben in her
synnes, for ȝif hii leften al her gode dedes, sone hii schulden aperceyuen
25 her werkes. And he made semblaunt as he wold come & offer to him
whan þat he wer siker wher þat þe child was; þe fende, for to bigilen
more a man, he makeþ gret semblaunt to louen God. Þe kinges wenten
forþ & fond þe ster; þat is, to hem þat repenten hem God ne hideþ him
nouȝt, for al sone as we lete our sinnes, God aliȝteþ vs wiþ his grace
30 þurth his gode wille þat he haþ to vs; whan we entren into riȝt bileue,
God scheweþ vs his liȝt, þat is, his grace. Bot þe ster went forþ & þe
kinges folowed; þat is, þurth techeing & þurth repentance we owe to hold
þe riȝt way & go in gode werkes wiþouten fayntise ȝif þat we wil comen
to God, for þurth gode werkes & þurth bisecheing schul we comen to
35 Godes hous.

---

2 stedfast bileue] stedfast (.....) bileue; from] fro.   3 þe syȝt] *ins.*   4 fende] *alt.*
10 by] *alt.*   15 hir] *alt.*   28 hem] *alt. to* them *l.h.*   29 al] *alt. to* also; lete] *canc.,* for
sake *ins., l.h.*   32 þat] hym *ins.* þat; owe] owegt *alt., l.h.*

L'esteile estut sur la maisun;
Entrez sunt, trouent Iesum.
La maisun signe seinte iglise
Ki Deus alume en tute guise.
2180 Iloec estet l'esteile clere,
Co est creance dreiture[r]e.
Fols est ki creire plus demande
Qui seinte eglise ne comande.
Mais nuls ne sauera la creiance
2185 Qui n'entret par bone fesance.
La creance unt li rei mustre;
Veient l'enfant, aurent De.
De la creiance est la sume
Ke Iesus est e Deus e home;
2190 Il est ueirs hom en deite,
E ueirs Deus en humanite;
Deus n'est par l'ume enpeire
Mais l'ume est par Deu amende.
Les treis duns unt co demustre
2195 Que les treis reis li unt dune;
Chescun li dunat les treis duns
Par grant significaciuns,
Kar il est un en trinite
E si est treis en vnite.
2200 Or li presentent cum a rei,
Encens cum a Deu uerrei;
Mirre dunent a mortel home,
De lur treis duns co est la sume.
Or est plus cher de tuz metals
2205 E signefie les reials.
Encens ard l'um el Deu seruise
E mustre Deu en tute guise.
Mirre est un oygnement amer
Ki le cors garde d'enpeirer;
2210 Le cors ke est oynt de ceste oynture
Iames ne uerrat pureture;
E pur co ke tant amortist
La mortel char mustre de Crist.
Creium co ki crurent li rei

2215 K'il seit Deus e home uerrei;
Offrum des duns la demustrance
Ke nus eium ferme creiance.
Creium k'il seit omnipotent
E or li durrums uerraiement;
2220 Creium k'il seit Deus a tut tens
Si offrum uerrai encens.
En ueritez mirre offrum
Qu'il mortels seit si bien creium .
Les duns unt autre mustrement
2225 Ki turne a nostre amendement.
Or est cler e bien resplendie
E charite bien signefie;
Encens demustre ureisuns,
Kar al urer encens ardums;
2230 Mirre ke la char amortie
La penitence signefie.
E nus offrum l'or bien lusant
Quant nus en Deu sumes amant;
Encens offrums par ureisuns,
2235 Mirre par nos espeneisuns.
Co est l'offrande ke Deus uolt
E par ki il les sons assolt.
Primes estoet il amer De /f. 70ᵛ
E tutes genz en uerite,
2240 E puis urer pur tutes genz
E puis amortir mals talenz.
Quant home ad talent de peccher,
V poi u nient ualt sun urer;
E ki sanz amur uolt urer
2245 Vers Deu ne poet riens espleiter.
Tut treis estoet ensemble offrir
Ki uers Deu uoldra rien merir;
Ki si le feit tut surement
Grant guerdun de Deu atent.
2250 En dormant sunt guarni les reis
Qu'il n'aulgent a Herode meis.
Cil ki la char ad endormie
Ne pense rien de ceste uie;

Þe ster stode abouen þe hous & hii wenten in & fond Ihesus Crist: þe
hous betokene holi chirche þat God aliȝteþ in al maner. Þer stode þe ster
cler & briȝt: þat is riȝtful bileue; fole he is þat bileueþ more þan holi
chirche biddeþ him. Bot noman ne may wite þe bileue bot ȝif he entre
5   wiþ god werkes doinge. Þe bileue þe kinges scheweden; hii seiȝ þe child
& worschiped God. Of þe bileue is þis, þat Ihesus is God & man. He is
soþefast God in manhode & soþfast man in godhod. God nis nouȝt
empayred þurth þe manhod, ac þe manhod is amended þurth þe godhod.
    Þe þre ȝiftes schewen þis þat þe þre kinges offerd him. Ichon ȝaf him
10  þes þre ȝiftes þurth gret significacion, for he is on in þre & he is þre in
on. Gold hii present him as to king, & encens as to soþfast God. Mirre hii
offerd him in tokene þat he was man dedlich. Þis bitokeneþ her þre
ȝiftes. Gold is derworþiest of al metels & bitokeneþ þe realtes þat man
schal haue in Goddes seruise & bitokeneþ God in al maner. Mirre is an
15  ognement þat is bitter & kepeþ þe bodis fram rotinge. Þe body þat is
anoynt wiþ þat ognement neuer ne schal it roten; & þat bitokeneþ þe
dedliche flesche of Crist. As þe kinges bileueden þat he was God & man,
offre we him so [f. 14ᵛ] þe ȝiftes, þe betokening, þat is, þat we have
stedfast bileue. Bileue we þat he is almiȝtiful & þan offre we him gold.
20  Byleue we þat he is God wiþouten ende & þan offre we him ensens. And
we offre him mirre ȝif we bileue soþefastlich þat he is stedfast man.
    Þes ȝiftes han oþer scheweing & vndoing þat falleþ to our amende-
ment. Gold is clere & schineþ briȝt & bitokeneþ wel charite; & we offre
gold briȝt schinand cler whan we loue God ouer al þing. And ensens we
25  offre whan we bid our bedes vnto him. Mirre offre we him whan we pine
our bodis for our sinnes. Þat is þe offerand þat God wil haue þurth which
he asoileþ al his; first he most loue God in al þing & his euen cristen in
soþenesse & þan sle wicked willes þat ben in him. Whan man haþ wille
to sinne, litel oþer nouȝt is worþ his prayer, tofor God ne may he noþing
30  spede. And þerfor, he þat wil spede & ben herd of God, he most offren al
þre; & he þat doþ so, gret mede he receyueþ of God.
    In slepe ben warned þes þre kinges þat hii ne wende nouȝt by Herodes
homward. He þat haþ þe flesche slepeand, he ne þencheþ nouȝt o þis liif;

2 in] & *ins*. in.  5 þe (2)] that *ins*. þe, *l.h.*  6 þe] þt *alt., l.h.*  8 þe manhod] manhod þe
*transp.*  11 encens] *on* eras.  13 gold] *alt.*  15 bodis] bodiis *alt.*  16 þat (1)] *ins.*  18
þe (1)] þe(.).  19 stedfast] stedstast *eras. and alt.*  20 byleue] *alt.;* is] *ins.*  26 bodis]
bodiis *alt.*  29 is] *ins.*  30 al] *alt.* all.  31 doþ] *ins.*  32 ne] *eras.;* by] *alt.*  33 þe]
cyth *ins.*þe, *l.h.;*  slepeand] & *ins.* slepeand *alt.;*  he (1)] *eras.;* o] *alt. to* own.

E si nus uulum tut guerpir
2255 L'amur del mund e le desir,
Od les treis reis serrum guarniz
Qu'al malfe n'algum de reiz.
  E il Herode tut leisserent
E altre ueie repeirerent;
2260 A lur realme sunt alez
Par altre ueie tut de grez.
Grant essample nos unt mustre
Li rei ki si sunt repeire.
Nostre realme est paradis
2265 V Adam esteit primes mis.
Perdu l'auum par gulusie,
Par orgoil e par leccherie;

Par nostre grant iniquite
Perdu auum nostre dreit fe;
2270 Par altre ueie estoet aler
Si nus le uulum recuuerer.
Par iune e par humilite,
Par almone e par charite,
Par nettete, par uraisun,
2275 Par bienfeit, par confessiun,
Par tuz mesfeiz amender
Estoet il la repeirer.
Certis ki si ne se penist
Iames ne regnerat od Crist.
2280 Pensum, seignurs, del amender
Qu'al regne Deu puissum aler.

## DE BAPTISMO IOHANIS; EODEM DIE

Oi auez l'aurement,
Ore oez le baptizement.
A icel iur al trentime an
2285 Vint Iesu Crist al flum Iordan.
Iohan iert dunc le baptiste
Sicum nus dist l'ewangeliste.
A li en uint Iesus li sire
Pur prendre de li baptire,
2290 Nient pur ses pecchez oster
Mais pur l'ewe seintefier
Que puissance eust d'esmunder
E cors e alme d'encumbrer.
Ainz ne laueit fors sul dehors,
2295 Ore leue tut, e alme e cors,
Puis ke Iesus fu baptize
E de sun cors l'out seintefie.
  Ore escutez grant e petit
Co ke l'ewangeliste dit.
2300 Iesus, co dist, uint a Iohan
V baptizout al flum Iordan.
Tanttost cum Seint Iohan le uit
Amunt se treist si li ad dit:

'De tei dei estre baptize,
2305 E tu uens a mei de tun gre?'
Iesus li dit: 'Ore del suffrir
Tute iustise estoet emplir'.
Atant l'ad Iohan si leisse
E si ad Iesum baptize.
2310 Puis uint de l'ewe tost amunt
E li ciel sur li uuert sunt
E cum columb descendit
E s'asist sur li seint esperit,
E une uoiz del ciel li dit:
2315 Cist est mun fiz, u me delit.
  Iesus se leissa baptizer
De sun serf pur nus demustrer
Ke ne deuum pas refuser
De un bas home le mester;
2320 Kar kike seit le seruitur,
Deu memes est baptizur.    /f. 71ʳ
Iordan espealt discensiun,
Le flums est del mund le cursun.
E li mund est tut trespassant
2325 Cum est li flum tut dis currant

& ȝif we wil so forsaken al þe loue of þis world & þe desire, we schul ben warned as þe þre kinges were, þat we ne schal nouȝt com to fende bot we schul leten him altogider & taken anoþer way; we schul turnen hom into our owen lond, þat is, þe blis of heuen, as þe þre kinges dede.

5 Gret emsample þes kinges han schewed vs þat went by anoþer way hom into her cuntre. Our kingdome is paradis þer Adam was first sett; lorn we it han þurth glotonie, pride, coueytise & lecherie & oþer sinnes. Þurth our gret wickednesse we han lorn our riȝt heritage, & þerfor by anoþer way we moten gon ȝif þat we wil keuern it oȝain— þurth fastinge
10 & þurth lowenesse, þurth almesȝeuinge & þurth charite, þurth clennes & þurth orisoun & þurth oþer godes, & þurth schrift & repentaunce and haue in wille to amenden al our trespas: and on þis maner we mowe come þider oȝain. Certes, he þat ne peyneþ him nouȝt þus to do ne schal he neuer regne wiþ Crist. Þenche we, lordinges, to amenden vs þat we may
15 come to þe kingdome of heuene.

Now ȝe han herd þe offering to Ihesu Crist, now hereþ þe baptisinge.

On þat ilke day þretti ȝer efter come Ihesu Crist to þe flumme Iordan vnto Iohannes þe baptist, as þe godspelle telleþ vs. Vnto him com Ihesu Crist for to take cristendome, nouȝt for to do away his sinnes (for he ne
20 had neuer non), ac for to halowe þe water þat it schuld haue miȝt for to make clene þe bodi & soule & schild vs fram encombringe. Beforn it ne wesche bot onlich þe bodi, & now it wascheþ boþe bodi & soule siþen þat Ihesu Crist was baptized & halowed it wiþ his blisful body.

Now hereþ litel and muchel þat þe godspelle seiþ. Ihesu, it seiþ, come
25 to Iohannes þe baptist [f. 15ʳ] at þe flumme Iordane. And also sone as Seyn Iohannes seiȝ him, he come vp & seid to him: 'Of þe Lord ich wold be baptized, & þou comest to me wiþ þi gode wille'. Ihesus seid: 'Þus it mot be to fulfille alle riȝtwisnesse'. And þan Iohannes ne spak no more bot baptised Ihesu Crist. Þan Ihesus com vp of þe water, þe heuen oponed
30 abouen & whit coluer com adoun and þe holi gost liȝt opon him, and a voice sayd out of heuen: 'Þis is my sone þat Y loue muchel'.

Ihesu let cristenen him of his seruaunt for to schewe vs ensample þat we ne schul forsaken þe seruise of a symple man, for who so is þe seruaunt, God is þe baptizer. Iordan is michel to say as departing, and be
35 þe flode is betokened þe world, for þe world is passand als a flode

---

1 wil] w(.)il.    2 fende] þe *ins.* fende.    3 leten] *alt.*    6 þer] (.)þer.    9 keuern] *alt. to* rekeuern.    11 godes] gode(.),dedes *ins.*    13 to do ne] *eras.*    20 to (1)] *ins.*    21 þe] *alt. to* boþe.    22 wesche] wescheþ *alt.;*    siþen] (...)siþen.    32 let] *ins.*    35 flode] *alt.;* world (1)] *alt.*

En cest decurs Deus descendist
Pur nus eshaucer en sa cit;
Pur nus se fist il baptizer
Pur l'ewe a nostre os seintifier.
2330 Li ciels ki sur li furent uuert
Co nus mustre tut en apert
Ke li ciels est tut aprestez
A cels ke ci sunt baptizez;
Sauer poez, n'i enterunt
2335 Qui en Crist baptize ne sunt.
   Li columbs sur Crist descendit,
E il dune sun esperit
As trestuz ki sunt baptizez
E en sun nun regenerez.
2340   La uoiz al pere li ad dist:
'Cist est mun fiz u me delit'.
Co mustre ke tuz sunt fiz De
Ki sunt de funz regenere
Par Iesu nostre charnal frere
2345 E par iglise, nostre mere,

E par l'esperit ke receiuums
Quant nus crestiens deuenums.
Li Deu del ciel est nostre pere
Si nus siuum la sue manere,
2350 Kar ki en Iesu creire uolt
Il deit aler sicum il solt;
Si deit aler cum il ala
V sa creiance li faudra.
Iesus ala partut en bien
2355 E ne mesprit de nule rien.
Ausi deit li cristien feire
Si de Crist uolt dreit nun treire;
Cil se deceit, cil se traist
Quant sanz bienfeit ad nun de Crist.
2360 De Crist sumes nus crestiens
Pur mals leisser e fere biens;
Guardum, seignurs, cristienete
Par boen uueraigne en charite.
Deu la nus doint issi guarder
2365 Qu'od li puissum el ciel regner.

## DE NUPTIIS FACTIS IN CHANA GALILEE; EODEM DIE

   Del baptisteire un an tut dreit
Sicum a cel iur aueneit.
En une uile en Galilee,
Chana esteit adunc numee,
2370 Vnes noces i furent feit.
La mere Iesu i esteit,
E Iesus i est apeled,
Ses diciples i ad mened.
E quant li uins lur defaillit
2375 La mere Iesu li ad dit:
'N'unt point de uin'. Dunc dist Iesus:
'Muiller, que apent ico a nus?'
Marie dist as ministranz:
'Feitis trestuz les soens cumanz'.
2380 Sis poz de pere i esteient
Sulum ke li Iu se l'aueient;
Chascuns perneit sulum les cures
V dous u treis de lur mesures.
Iesus lur dist: 'Emplez les poz'
2385 E il unt feit sulum ses moz.
De l'ewe sulum ses diz

En boen uin est conuertiz.
Dunc dist Iesus: 'Ore espuchez
E a Architriclin enportez'.
2390 Quant out guste Architriclin
De l'ewe ke fut feit le uin
E ne saueit dunt co ueneit
L'espus apella si disait:
'Primes prent l'em le uin meillur,
2395 E quant l'om est yueres le peiur;
Mais tu as tun boen uin guarde
Endesqu'a ore de tun gre'.
Ses diciples cest signe uirent
E puis le crurent e siuirent.
2400   Galilee espealt trespas;
Chana amur en nostre glas.
E en amur cum pur passer
Deit l'um cest secle bel user.
Kar iloec aime l'um les punz   /f. 71ᵛ
2405 V les guez sunt mals e parfunz.
Ki n'at le gue de pucelage

is euermore ernand. In þis erninge Ihesu ȝede adoun for to heiȝen vs into
his cite; for vs he lete him cristen for to halowen þe water to our bihoue.
Þe heuen þat opened abouen him, þat scheweþ vs apertliche þat þe heuen
is al redy to hem þat so ben baptised.

5    And wel may ȝe wite þat þay ne schul nouȝt come in heuen þat ne be
nouȝt baptised in Crist. Þe coluer com adoun to him, and þat is betokened, þat he ȝiueþ þe holi gost to alle þat ben baptised, & in his name
þay schul regnen. Þe voice of þe fader þat saiþ, 'Þis is my sone þat Y
delite me inne' — þat scheweþ þat we ben alle Goddes sones þat ben
10   bizeten aȝein þurth bapteme, þurth Ihesu Crist our fleschelich broþer &
þurth holi chirche our moder & for þe holi gost þat we receyue whan we
become Cristen. God of heuen is our fader ȝif we folowe his maner, for
hii þat in Ihesu wil bileue, þay owe to don as he dede, þay owen to gon in
his wayes or his bileue schal faylen him. Ihesus ȝede alway in gode, he
15   ne misdede in no þing; & also owen cristen men to do ȝif we wil drawe
his name of Crist; ac wrongfulliche he bereþ his name þat liueþ in wicked
liif. Of Crist be we cristned for to leten þe iuel and do þe gode. Kepe we,
lordinges, cristendome þurth gode werkes in charite; God it vs graunt so
to kepen þat we may regnen wiþ him in heuen. Amen.

20   Fram þis baptisinge a ȝer riȝt als in þat day, fel in a cite of Galile
(Chane, it was þan cleped) a bridale was maked. And Ihesus & his moder
wer bode þider and he brouȝt his deciples wiþ him. And whan hem
fayled wyne, Ihesus moder sayd to him: 'Þai ne haue no wyne'. Þan sayd
Ihesu: 'Woman, what is þat to vs'. Marie said to þe seruantes: 'Doþ al þat
25   my sone biddiþ ȝou'. Sex pottes of stone þar weren þat þe Iewes hadden,
& echon held two oþer þre of her mesures. Ihesu said to hem: 'Filleþ þe
pottes'. And þai dede also he bad hem, filled hem ful of water. And whan
þai had filled þe pottes, 'Now', said Ihesu, 'filleþ out & bereþ to
Archetrecline'. Whan Archetreclin [f. 15ᵛ] had tasted of þe water þat was
30   turned into wyne and ne wist nouȝt whannes it com, he cleped þe spouse
and seid: 'First men takeþ þe gode wyn, & when men be dronken, þe
wers; ac þou hast kept þi god wyne vntil now'. His decyples seiȝen þis
wonder and trowed him & folowed him.

    Galile spelleþ passynge, and Galile is as muchel to saien as loue & þe
35   loue is for passinge. Men owen for to vsen þis world for þer louen men
þe bregges þar þat riuers ben iuel and depe. He þat ne haþ þe riuer of

---

2 cristen] to be *ins.* cristen, *l.h.*   10 biȝeten] bigoten, *alt. l.h.*   13 hii] *alt.;* þat] þ(.)t
*ins.*  14 faylen] falylen *alt.*   20 a ȝer] a(...)ȝer; als] *after ins.* als.  22 he] his *alt.*  24
to (1)] þe *canc.*  26 two] *alt.*  32 ac] wyne ys best *ins.* and *alt., l.h.*  35 þer] þat *alt.*

Par punt d'espus guart sei de rage;
Kar pucellage est li guez
Ki par passant nest malfez.
2410 Ki en co ne se poet tenir
Vn punt i ad dunt poet guarir;
Co est li dreit punz de espusaille
Ke par leccherie ne messaille.
Chascun se deit bien guarder
2415 Que pucelle uenge a l'espuser;
Kar pucellage e espusaille
Quant sunt en bien e sanz contraille,
Deu les cherit, Deu les auance,
E od li erent sanz dutance.
2420 De pucellage uout Deu neistre,
Les noceans uisiter e peistre;
De la pucelle nostre char prist
E as espusailles de ewe uin fist.
Mais vus ne orrez ia dire mie
2425 Qu'il feist bien a leccherie;
Iames a fornicaciun
Ne ferrat Deus se tuz mals nun.
Cum plus atent e meins engruce,
Pis uengera quant il s'esbruce;
2430 Cum plus le soffre e plus atent,
Plus se uengera durement.
Li apostles Seint Pol le dit
En plusurs lius en sun escrit:
'Fornicatur ne auultrant
2435 Del ciel n'auerunt tant ne quant'.
E li prophetes dist Osee:
'Pute ert cum fens defulee'.

Ne trouerez seint ne prophecie
Ki n'escomenge puterie.
2440 Mais n'ert ti pecchez tant leiz
Ne si orribles li mesfeiz
Dunt ne pusse auer amendement.
Quant en sante se repent,
Par espusaille e par bien feire,
2445 Poet l'um cest mal a bien retreire.
Mult grant essample dunat Crist
Quant uin de ewe as noces fist.
As noces uint nient pur manger
Mais pur beneistre e cumfermer;
2450 Co qu'out feit al commencement
Ore conferma presentement.
Adam e Eue il les furma
E par sun comant espusa
Pur co k'il doussent a bien treire
2455 E seint engendrure feire.
Dunt Moyses li seint hom dit
Quant il lur furmaisun escrit:
'Pere e mere home guerpira
E a sa mulier aerdera
2460 E erent dous en une char'.
Fols est ki de co feit eschar;
Que Deus iuint home ne deit seuerer.
Gua[r]d sei chascun de folaier.
Sicum Deus en Adam out feit
2465 E par Moysen l'out retreit,
E il uint tut confermer
E par miracles demustrer.
As noces uint ki noces fist,

mayden þurth bregge of wedloke, kepe him fro harm; for maydenhede is
þe riuer þat non iuel þing may passen bi. He þat ne may nouȝt helden him
in þis, a bregge þar is þat may kepen him in — þat is þe riȝt wedlok —
þat he ne go wrong þurth lecherie. And echon owen to kepen hem þat þay
5   com mayden to wedlok, for maidenhede & wedlok, whan þay ben wel
ikepte als þai auȝte for to ben, God loueþ hem & auaunceþ hem and wiþ
hem he holdeþ wiþouten doute. Of mayden wold Ihesu be born and
sposaile visiten & feden. Of maydenhede he toke our flesche & atte
sposaile made wyn of water. And we ne herd neuer telle þat Ihesus dede
10  gode to lecherie. Neuer vnto lecherie schal gode be don, bot iuel. Þe
lenger þat he habitt to take wreche, þe more it greueþ him; and þe lenger
abideþ him, þe gretter schal ben þe veniaunce. Þe apostil Seyn Poule seiþ
in mani stede in his writing: 'Lechour ne spousbrecher schul neuer
comen into heuen'. And þe prophete Osee seiþ: 'Hores schul ben de-
15  fouled in helle as donge'. Ȝe ne schul fynde holi man ne prophete þat he
ne curseþ hordom. Ac be þe sinne neuer so foule ne so orrible ne so oft
don, þat he ne may amenden him whan he repenteþ him, and þe betir he
may amenden him ȝif he repenteþ him whiles he is in gode hele. Þurth
wedlok & þurth gode dedes þat he doþ may men amenden him of þis iuel
20  & drawe it to gode. Gret ensample ȝaue vs Crist whan he turned þe water
into wyn at þe brudale. Vnto þe bridale he ne com nouȝt þider for to eten
ac for to blissen it and to conferme it. Þat he made at þe gynnynge þan
be confermed it þar in present. Adam & Eue, he made hem and þurth his
comaundement he wedded hem togider for þat þai schul[d] drawe hem to
25  gode & bring furþ holi engendrur. Þe holi Moyses seid whan he wrot her
makeinge: 'Fader & moder he schal forsaken & take to his wiif & þay
becomen boþe o flesche & o blode'. A gret fole he is þat makeþ
departinge þat God makeþ on; þat God made on þer oweþ noman
departen hit. Kepe ich man him from þat foli. As God in Adam hadde
30  made it, and þan Moyses bar wittenesse þarto, & him com to confermen
it þurth [f. 16ʳ] miracles doyng. Vnto weddyng com þat weddyng made,

---

8 visiten] *alt.*    8-9 & atte sposaile] *on eras.*    11 habitt] habittyth *alt., l.h.;* wreche]
þat *ins.* wreched *alt., l.h.;* þe (1)] lyf *ins.* þe, *l.h.*    12 abideþ] he *ins.* abideþ, *l.h.;* þe
(1)] þer in *ins.* þe, *l.h.;* þe (3)] a pon hem *ins.,* þe *l.h.*    16 ac] *alt. to* and, *l.h.;* orrible]
occible *alt. to* orrible, *l.h.*    17 þat] but *ins.* þat, *l.h.;* ne] *partly eras.*    20 gret] þat *ins.*
gret, *l.h.*    21 brudale] *alt. to* brydale, *l.h.*    22 and] *canc.,* but *ins., l.h.;* it] *partly*
*eras.;* gynnynge] *alt. to* bigynnynge, *l.h.*    24 schuld] schul.    26 & (2)] & *alt. to* to;
& (3)] & e contra *ins., l.h.*    28 on (1)] *partly eras.;* þat god made on] *canc.*    30 þan]
*alt.*    31 weddyng (1)] þat *ins.* weddyng, *l.h.;* þat] he *ins.* þat, *l.h.*

Ki espusaillies benesquit.
2470 Il est espus de seinte iglise,
Kar il la guard e iustise.
Tut cil ki espusailles funt
Ses compaignuns e ses fiz sunt.
  As espusailles fu Marie
2475 E Iesus e sa compaignie.
Sachez, grant est li sacremenz
V tant sunt de si seinte genz.
E vus deuez tenir cher
La rien ki Deus uout tant amer;
2480 Kar tut n'i seit il charnelment
Vncore est il en present;
Kar quantqu'en seinte iglise est feit
En sa presence tut esteit.
E ki k'en seit le seruitur
2485 Sue est la force e le uigur.
Tut ausi cum est de baptistire
E de espusaille est il sire.
As espusailles uin faillit   /f. 72ʳ
Kar la uielz lei n'ert pas parfit;
2490 D'espuser n'est perfectiun
Ki n'est feit si pur faute nun;
Ki ne se poet pucelle guarder
Saluer se poet par espuser.
Pur saluer charnel corrupture
2495 Fist Deus iceste seinte cure;
E l'ewe bien co signefie
Ke en uin i fut conuertie.
Kar ewe est chose esculuriable
E ia par sei nen ert estable;
2500 Nun est la char kar ia ne fine
Mais tut dis en pis se decline.
  Iesus fist l'ewe mettre en pere
Quant il estrainst tele manere,
Quant il estrainst nos charneltez,
2505 Que ne seium trop deslaiz,
Ke dur seium contre le mal
E ne seium trop comunal.
  Mais nuls nen auerat guarisun
S'en part feit bien e en part nun.

2510 Pur co fist Deus de l'ewe uin
Pur demustrer le dreit chemin.
Li uin eschaufe si enyuere,
E de cures le quor deliuere.
Si feit la lei de l'espuser,
2515 Les quors eschauffe par amer,
E enyure pur mals leisser,
E cures tolt de fol penser.
E Deus de l'ewe le uin furma,
Nos uolentez quant amenda,
2520 Quant li floz de noz charneltez
Par espuser sunt amendez.
Co mustre bien Architriclin
Quant out guste l'ewe feit uin;
Quant uin de l'ewe feit gusta
2525 Sur tuz les autres le preisa.
Kar n'est manere en cest eage
Ki tant uaille fors pucellage,
Kar pucellage est cum flur
E espusaille cum tur.
2530 Ki enz en un ne poet flurir
En l'autre se purra guarir.
Co est la premere de meruailles
Ke Iesus fist as espusailles,
Kar co est miracle mult parfunt
2535 Que dous homes une char sunt.
Vne char sunt pur la fesance
Dunt par noces unt la lyance;
Il resunt un en charitez
Par amur ki les ad lyez.
2540 Vne char feit charnel leissur,
Vn esperit le Deu amur.
Pur co feit il trop grant pecche
Ki desfeit itel unite.
Ces sunt les treis feiz Ihesu Crist
2545 Qu'il a ceste feste fist.
A treis reis a hui se mustra
E cum a hui se baptiza;
A hui le uin de l'ewe furma
E en chascun Deu se pruua.
2550 Deu fu quant l'esteile furma;

and he þat blessed spousale, he himself is spouse of holi chirche, þat is, cristen man and woman, for he kepeþ hem in riȝtfulnesse. Alle þat mak spousailes his felawes and his children þai ben. At þe spousaile was Marie & Ihesus and his compaynie: wite ȝe wel þat gret is þe sacrament
5  þer is so muchel holi folke. And we owen to holden wel derworþi þe þinge þat God wil so muchel louen, for þouȝ he be nouȝt seiȝen þer bodylich, ȝit he is þer in present; for alle þat is don in holi cherche, al is in his present, and who þat þer be seruant, he is þe strengþe of al þat þer is. As he is at þe bapteme, of spousaile he is lord, for at weddeing he
10  turned water to wyn for þe old lawe was nouȝt parfit. Weddyng is nouȝt bot to sauacioun, for þay þat may nouȝt kepen hem madenes, saued he mai be þurth wedloke. For to sauen flescheli corrupcioun made God þis holi werk, and þe water wel betokeneþ þat was turned into wyn, for water is alwei ernynge and neuer in himself ne schal it be stable. Swich is þe
15  flesche þat neuer ne fineþ bot euer draweþ to wors and wors. Ihesus bad þe water in ston whan þat he changed it. In þat maner he doþ whan he wiþdrawiþ our flescheliche likinges þat we be nouȝt ouercomen & þat we be hard aȝein þe iuel. For noman ne may haue helpe bote he wiþstonde his fleschliche likinges for to schewe þe riȝt way. Þe wyn heteþ and
20  makeþ þe hert clere and deliuer; so doþ þe lawe of spousailes— heteþ þe hert þurth loue and liȝt for to lete þe euel and drawe þe hert fram iuel þouȝtes. And God makeþ of water wyn whan amendeþ our willes, whan þe flode[s] of flescheliche liking ben amended þurth wedlok. Þat scheweþ wel Architrecline whan he had dronk þe wyn þat was made of
25  water; ouer al oþer wyn he praised it, for þar nis no degre in þis world þat is so muchel worþ as þat saue maidenhode. For maidenhode so is as flour & wedlok is as þe tour, for ȝif þat on may nouȝt florische, in þat oþer he may sauen him. Þis is þe first of þe wonders þat Ihesus Crist made — wedlok; for þat is wonderful gret þat two men maken o flesche; he makeþ
30  þurth þe making of God in þe wedlok. Þay beþ on als in charite þurth loue þat haþ bounden hem. O flesche & o blode makeþ flesche fondinges & o gost þurth loue of God. Forþi he doþ ful gret sinne þat fordoþ þis onyng. Þes ben þe þre werkes of Ihesu Crist þat he made at þis feste: vnto þe þre kinges he schewed him; þis day he was baptised; and on þis day he
35  turned þe water into wyn. In al þes þre þinges he schewed þat he was God: [God he schewed him whan he made þe sterre & in þat he

---

Deu fu quant li ciels le nuncia;                    Cil ki se deignat si mustrer,
Deu fu quant de l'ewe uin fist.          2555   Nos mals nus doint tuz amender.
Veez que Deus est Iesu Crist:

schewed þat he was God] whan þe heuen opened & þe voice seid: [f. 16ᵛ]
þis is my sone; and also he schewed þat he was God whan he turned
water into wyn. Lokeþ þan wel þat Ihesu Crist is god; he þat wold so
schewen him, he forȝeue vs al our synnes & amende vs ȝif it be his
5   wille. Amen.

---

3-4 wold so schewen him] so schewen him wold *transp.,* wold *eras.*

# DOMINICA I POST EPIPHANIAM

Quant Iesus de duze anz esteit,
A la feste qui dunc ueneit
En Ierusalem la cite.
Li paisant i sunt ale.
2560 Ioseph e Marie i alerent
E Iesus ouec els amenerent,
Kar la custume itele esteit
Qui tut li poples i ueneit.
E quant li iurs erent passe
2565 E chescun al son est repeire,
Iesus remist si coiement   /f. 72ᵛ
Ke pas ne sorent si parent;
Ainz quiderent uerraiement
K'il s'en uenist entre la gent.
2570 Pur co l'unt il lugment quis
Entre cunuz e entre amis,
E quant il pas nel unt troue
En Ierusalem sunt repeire.
Tant le quistrent e demanderent
2575 K'empres le tierz iur le trouerent
Entre les docturs u seait
E demandout e escutait;
N'i out nuls ke ne fut esbaiz
De sun saueir e de ses diz.
2580 Marie e Ioseph quant co uirent
A grant merueille s'esbairent.
Sa mere li dist entresait:
'Bel fiz, pur quei nus as si fait?
Io e ti peres t'auum quis
2585 Dolenz e murnes e mariz'.
Iesus li dist cume senez:

'Ke deit ke vus me querez?
Ne sauez ke les riens me tenent
Ki a mun pere apartenent?'
2590 E il nen unt pas entendu
Ico ke lur ad dit Iesu.
Dunc uint od els a Nazareth,
Si lur ert umbles e suef.
Sa mere tuz ses moz guardout
2595 E en sun quor les recordout.
E Iesus espleitout en uair
De age, de sens e de sauair,
E de grace tut ensement
Enuers Deu e enuers la gent.
2600    Veez, seignurs, ceste lescun
Si i metez entenciun;
Mult i purrez granz biens aprendre
Si de quor i uolez entendre.
Deus ki est sanz comencement
2605 E ki meint sanz definement
Pur nus se deignat encharner
E sulunc la char cumencer,
Sulunc la char de nostre humage
Out iurz e meis e anz e age.
2610 Quantke deignat u dire u fere
Tut fist pur nus a sei atrere;
Quant k'il deignat faire u parler
Tut fist pur nus endoctriner.
Kar ses seinz faiz paroles sunt
2615 A cels ki bien l'entenderunt.
Veez cum il a feste alat
Ki temple e feste e lei donat.

## SERMON 7
## DOMINICA PRIMA POST OCTAUAS EPYPHANIE

*Secundum Lucam. Cum factus esset Ihesus annorum duodecim.*
Whan Ihesus was twelf ʒer olde he com to fest, into Ierusalem. Whan
men of þe cuntre comen þider, Ioseph and Marie went þider & toke Ihesu
wiþ hem, for it was þe custome þan þat alle folk schuld come þider to þe
5    feste. And whan had don & went hom aʒein, Ihesu belefte so priuilich þat
his kinde ne wist it nouʒt, ac vnderstonde for soþe þat he come wiþ þe
folk; forþi þai souʒt him a gret while among her frendes & among her
kinde and þai ne founden him nouʒt. Þai com to Ierusalem aʒein and so
souʒten him & asked after him þat opon þe þridde day þai founden him
10   in þe temple among þe techers. Þer he sate and herd hem & asked hem;
þar nas non þat nas abaist of his witt and of his wordes. Marie and
Ioseph, whan þai seiʒen þis, for gret wonder þai wer abaisched. His
moder said to him þan: 'Sone, whi hastow þus don? Ich & þi fader haue
souʒt þe sori & sorowful.' Ihesu seid þan to hem: 'Whi han ʒe souʒt me?
15   Ne wist ʒe wel þat y mot do my faders wille?'. And þai ne vnderstode
nouʒt þat Ihesus had said. Þan he com wiþ hem vnto Nazareth and was to
hem bouxsum & meke. His moder kept al his wordes & in her herte
recorded hem wel. And Ihesu wex for soþe of eld and witt and of wisdom
and of grace also aʒeines God & aʒeines þe folk.
20       Now vnderstondeþ, lordinges, þe lessoun & ʒeueþ god kepe þerto;
muchel god ʒe may lern in ʒif ʒe wil vnderstonden it in ʒour hert. God
þat is wiþouten bigynnyng and dwelleþ wiþoute endeing, he wold take
our kinde & after þe flesch wex in dais, in monþes, and ʒeres & in eld
for to amende our harmes. Al þat he wolde don & say, al was for he
25   wolde drawe vs vnto him, and in our kinde he schewed be is dedes þat he
was wise, for his holi werkes wer wordes vnto hem þat vnderstode hem.
Lokeþ: now he ʒed to þe fest þat fest made & temple and ʒaue þe lawe;

5 had] hii *ins.* had; belefte] *canc.*, hyd *ins.*, *l.h.*    6 kinde] kin(..); ac] þat *on eras.*, hyt
schold be he but *ins.*, *l.h.*    7 forþi] *partly eras.*    8 kinde] kin(..).    11 þat] *canc.*, but
*ins.;* nas] nas *alt. to* was, *l.h.*    12 þis] him *canc.* þis.    18 witt] of *ins.* wyt *alt.*, *l.h.*
21 lern] lerne *alt.;* in] þer *ins.* in; vnderstonden] *alt. to* vnderstondeþ.    22 wiþoute]
wiþ *alt. to* wiþoute.    24 amende] *ins.* 25 is] *alt. to* his.    26 for his] for (…) his;
vnderstode] wel *ins.* vnderstode.    27 &] *ins.*

As festes alat pur urer
E par co uolt demustrer
2620 Ke nus deuum hanter eglise
E festes tenir en Deu seruise.
Si ne poum a sursemeine
As festes ueals e al dimaine
Tuz deuerium hanter eglise
2625 Chescun iur a Deu seruise.
Mais par co poum saueir bien
Ke cil nen aiment Deu de rien
Ki nis as festes ni acurent
Ne Deu ne eglise adunc ne honurent.
2630 Deu uint al temple pur urer
E pur les docturs escuter,
E nus muster hanter deuum
Pur urer e pur oir sermun;
Kar cil ki ure en uerite
2635 Buche a buche parole od De,
E ki de quor ot sermuner,
Sachez de fi, Deu ot parler.
Kar il dist: 'Vus ne parlez mie
Mais l'esperit ki en vus crie'.
2640 Par les sages u il se trait
Iesus entendre bien nus fait
Ke as sages deuum aqueinter
E lur paroles tenir cher.
Kar de fols surd mortel folie
2645 E honur de sage cumpaignie;
Ne nuls ne ert ia bien senez
Ki des sages nen est priuez.
Vuel i fait bien a entendre
Ke chescun home deit aprendre
2650 E en sa iuuente e demander   /f. 73ʳ
K'il en age puisse parler.
Quant Iesus la Deu sapience
Tant bel escute e point ne tence,
Tant bel demande, ot, e respunt,
2655 Mult par sunt fols ki si ne funt.
Kar li iofne deiuent oir

Dunt il puissent empres ioir,
E demander mult dulcement
E aprendre mult humblement;
2660 Kar dunc est tart a demander
Quant l'um deit altres enseigner.
Pur co deiuent li iofne aprendre
K'il sachent puis par tens rendre;
Kar tut se sente alcuns mult sage,
2665 Si deit il atendre sun eage,
E ne deit pas sei trop haster
Mais as einez honur porter
Quant cil ki fiz est al altisme
Ne uolt as einez faire cysme;
2670 Einz lur demanda bonement
E escutat mult dulcement.
Mais cument ert co entendu
Ke Marie dist a Iesu:
'Bel fiz, en dolur nus as mis;
2675 Io e tis peres t'auum quis'?
Cument esteit Ioseph sun pere
Ki unkes ne cunuit sa mere?
Sis peres ert de nureture
E ne mie d'engendrure;
2680 Sis peres ert quant il le put,
Mais unc sa mere ne cunut;
Kar ele ert uirgine al engendrer
E al nestre e al porter.
Mais Ioseph Iesu pere esteit
2685 En co k'il le nurriseit;
Sis peres ert il par quidance,
Nient par charnel cunisance.
Kar il aueit en terre mere
Sanz ouere de charnel pere,
2690 E il aueit sun pere el ciel
Sanz ouere de mere charnel.
Pur co respundit a sa mere;
'Ne sauez k'es oures mun pere
M'estot il estre entendant?' –
2695 Kar sis peres est Deu le grant.

to þe fest he ʒede for to beseche, for to schewen vs þat we schuld vsen on
holiday to gon to holi chirche & hold þe holi daies in Godes seruise. ʒif
we may nouʒt in al þe weke, hold we þe holi daies & þe sonedaies. Al we
owen to com to holi chirche, and ech dai, to her God seruise; ac þarbi we
5     may wite wel þat þay ne louen nouʒt God þat ne holden nouʒt þe fest
dayes ne holi chirche ne God ne wirschipen nouʒt. God com to þe temple
for to make his praiere and for to her þe techers of þe lawe, & ʒaue vs
ensample to biseche [f. 17ʳ] to him and for to her sermoun; for he þat
besecheþ in soþnesse, mouþe wiþ mouþ he spekeþ wiþ God; and þat wiþ
10    gode wille hereþ sermoun, wite ʒe for soþe þat he hereþ God speken, for
it seiþ: ʒe ne speke nouʒt, ac þe spirit spekeþ in ʒou. Be þe wise men þat
he ʒede vnto, so ʒeueþ vs ensaumple þat we schul aquinten vs wiþ wise
men and kepe we her wordes; for of foles comeþ dedlich folie, &
wirschipe of wise companie; for non ne schal be wel norisched þat nis
15    priue wiþ wise men. And also he schewed vs þat ich man schuld lere in
his ʒougþe þat he miʒt speke wiselich in his eld. Whan he þat was
wisdome of God so mildeliche listned wiþouten chiding and so sweteliche answerd and asked, a fole he is þat nil nouʒt do so. For þe ʒonge
man oweþ to leren so þat he may afterwardes gladen, and aske wel
20    swetlich & lerne wel mekeliche; for þan is to late for to asken whan a
man schal techen oþer. And þerfor, þe ʒong owen for to lere while þat þai
ben ʒonge, & ʒif þat ani fel þat he be wise, he owen for to abiden his elde
and ne owen nouʒt to hiʒen hem to sone, ac vnto old ʒeue reuerence
whan he þat was Goddes sone ne wold nouʒt do non dishonour toþe old
25    þouʒ he wer wiser þan þai, ac he asked hem ful sweteliche and listned
hem ful mekelich. Ac hou schal þis ben vnderstonden þat Marie said to
Ihesu, Goddes sone: 'In sorowe Y and þi fader han souʒt þe?'. Hou was
Ioseph his fader þat neuer knew his moder flescheliche? His fader he was
þurth þat he norischet him & nouʒt þurth beʒetyng; his fader he was
30    whan þat he fedde him. Ac neuer he ne knew his moder for ʒhe was
maiden at þe beʒeting and at þe bering. Ac Ioseph was his fader in þat þat
he norischet him; his fader he was þurth wenynge and nouʒt þurth
fleschliche knowing. For he had in þis world a moder wiþouten knowinge
of bodiliche fader, forþi he answerd to his moder: 'Ne wostow nouʒt wel
35    þat Y mot do my faderes wille' — for his fader was God almiʒten.

1 fest] *alt. to* festes.   2 to gon] (..) go(.).   4 god] *alt. to* godes.   5 þat] *ins.*   6 ne (3)]
*eras.;* wirschipen] wirschipeþ *alt. and eras.;* nouʒt] hii *ins. and eras.,* nouʒt.
9 mouþe] of *ins.* mouþe; þat] he *ins.* þat.   11 it] he *ins.* it.   12 vs] he *ins.* vs; wiþ] *on
eras.*   13 we] wel *alt.*   14 ne] *eras.*   15 wise] *on eras.*   17 chiding] (.)chiding.
19 and] tech *ins.* and, *l.h.*   22 he (2)] *on eras.*   23 vnto] (.bot.) to.   28 flescheliche]
fleschcliche.   29 his] h(.)is.   35 almiʒten] *partly eras.*

Puis uint od els a Nazareth
Si lur ert humbles e suef.
Pernez en guarde bon enfant,
E iuuencel e enueillant,
2700  Cument Iesus umbles esteit,
A ses parenz obeiseit.
Faire l'estot si cum il fist,
Si vus uolez regner od Crist.
A ses parenz il obeit
2705  Sanz contenciun e cuntredit
Cil ki est Deus trestut puissant
Ia seit k'il fut pur nus enfant,
Cil ki est Deus en trinite
E tut dis maint en maieste,
2710  Que ert de nostre chaitif hvmesce.
Ki pere e mere fuit e blesce
Certis, Deu dist, ke de mort murrat;
Ki pere u mere maldirat,
Ki de ses parenz ne prent cure,
2715  Deus ki est pere deshonure;
Pur co murrat de male mort,
Co est, en cel enfernal gort.
L'um deit ses parenz honurer
En trestuz sens e tenir cher
2720  Nient sulementis en parler
Mais en tuz biens quant est mester,
En pestre, en uestir, en seruise,
E en tut altre bone guise.
Quant busuing est, ki si nel fait,
2725  Sachez de fi k'il se deceit.
E li parent deiuent guarder
Lur enfanz tut dis d'encumbrer

E nient de sur els chacier
Mais belementes chastier.
2730  Kar sis parenz quistrent Iesu
Quant il fu si de gre perdu.
E Seint Pol dist entre ses diz:
'Peres ne curecez uos fiz'.
Kar quant les peres irus grucent
/f. 73$^v$
2735  E li fiz uers els se curucent,
Tost purrunt Dampnedeu offendre
Par mesaler e par mesprendre.
Al pere apent le chastier,
Al fiz oir e escuter;
2740  Al pere faire sanz rancur,
Al fiz endurer par amur.
Kar Seint Pol redit as enfanz
K'a lur parenz seient suffranz.
Ki as sons ne uolt obeir
2745  Cument deuerat altres suffrir;
Sul pur suffrir en dreit amur
Est paie nostre creatur.
Sens e saueir nurist suffrance,
E grace dune obediance,
2750  E obedience alunge uie
E dune grace e tolt folie.
Pur co dist Seint Luc de Iesu,
Puis k'a ses parenz subiet fu,
D'age, de grace, de ensensement
2755  Cresseit a Deu e a la gent.
E nus si uolum crestre en grace
Siure deuum la sue trace.

Þan he come wiþ hem to Nazereth and was to hem meke & milde. Takeþ god ȝeme ȝe ȝonge children, ȝonge men & eld men, how Ihesu was meke & buxsum to his kinde. Do we most als he dede ȝif we wil regne wiþ Crist. Vnto his kinde he was buxsum wiþouten anoyȝing and
5 aȝeinsayinge, he þat is God almiȝti þouȝ al he become a child for vs, he þat o God is in þre and alwai dwelleþ in maieste. Vnderstondeþ wel, he þat hertteþ his fader oþer his moder or smiteþ, certes God seiþ hit: 'On iuel deþ he schal deye þat misdoþe fader oþer moder'. He þat ne ȝeueþ no kepe to hi[s] kinde, God of heuen he dishonoureþ; forþi he schal deye
10 an iuel deþ, þat is, he schal go to helle. Man oweþ to wirschipen his kynde and in al þing louen hem wel, nouȝt onlich in speking, ac in al þing loue hem wel þat þai han mister, [f. 17ᵛ] in feding, in cloþing and in seruise, & in al oþer gode maner whan mister is. And ȝif þat he ne do nouȝt, he deseiueþ himseluen. And þe faderes and þe moderes owen to
15 kepen þe children fram encombrynge of alle harmes & nouȝt put hem away fram hem, & mekeliche chastis hem, for his frendes souȝten Ihesu whan he was bi his wille fram hem hid.

And Seyn Poul seiþ in his sawe: 'Fadres wreþth nouȝt ȝour children'. For whan þe faders wraþfulliche grutcheþ toward her sones & her
20 childern wraþþen to hem warde, sone þai mowen þan greuen God þurth misdede, þat on aȝen þat oþer. [T]o þe fader falleþ to chastise þe child & to þe child it falleþ to heren & vnderstonde þe fader teching wiþouten groching and þe fader to don it wiþouten wraþe & to þe child it falleþ to doute þe fader þurth loue. Seyn Poul seiþ ȝit after to þe children and
25 biddiþ hem þat þai ben suffreable to her kinde onlich for to suffre in gode loue þat payeþ our lord in al þinge. Witt & wisdom norischeþ suffraunce & ȝeueþ grace to hem þat ben buxsum. Buxsumnesse haþ long liif & ȝeueþ grace & doþ awai folie. For þi seiþ Seyn Luc of Ihesu, whan þat he was buxsum to his kinde, he wex in age & in grace also & in witte wex
30 and to God and to þe folk. And we schul so wex in grace ȝif þat we folowe his weis. Ihesus it vs graunt. Amen.

3 kinde] kin(..); do] so *ins. on eras.* we; als] do *ins.* als; wil] wiþ *canc.* willeþ *alt.*
4 kinde] kin(..). 5 al] *partly eras.* 7 hit on] hi(t on). 8 misdoþe] *alt.* 9 no kepe to hi-] *ins. by H, trim.;* kinde] kende, *alt. to* kinde *by H;* þi] *eras.* 10 go] (.) go.
11 kynde] kyn(..). 12 þat] in *ins.* þat; in] to *ins.* in. 13 ne] *eras.* 14 faderes] *alt.*
18 seyn] *alt.;* fadres wreþth] *alt. on eras., l.h.* 19 faders] fader *alt. to* faders; wraþfulliche] wraþ fulliche. 20 wraþþen] wrath *ins.* wraþþen, *l.h.;* hem warde] hem (.) warde. 21 þat] þt, *l.h.;* oþer] oþer *on eras.* 21-22 to ... & to] *ins., partly on eras., trim.* 22 fader] *alt. to* faders. 25 kinde] kin(..). 26 payeþ] *alt. to* payeth, *l.h.* 27 hem] *alt. to* them, *l.h.* 28 þi] *eras.* 29 kinde] kin(..). 29-30 wex and ... folk] wex and to þe folk and to god *transp.*

# DOMINICA III POST EPIPHANIAM

Quant Iesus del munt descendit
Grant genz par tropels li siuit.
2760 Este vus un leprus uenant
Si l'auroit ensi disant:
'Sire, si uols, munder me poes'.
Iesus ses braz estendit lors,
Tuchat le si li dit de but:
2765 'Io le uoil: net seez' – e il fut.
E Iesus li dit entresait:
'Gard ke ne diez icest fait
A nul home pur remembrer;
Mais ua t'en tost as prestres mustrer
2770 E fai l'offrende e le present
Ke lur cumande Moysent'.
Puis uint il a Capharnaum
Si uint a li centuriun.
Mult li priout si li dist:
2775 'Sire, mi serf malade gist
De paralise tut greuez
En ma maisun mal turmentez'.
Iesus li dist: 'Io uendrai
E ignelepas le sauerai'.
2780 Dunc respundi centuriun
E si ad dist a Iesum:
'Sire, ne sui pas dignes hom
Ke tu entres en ma maisun;
Mais sulement di le ton dit
2785 E mis serfs ert sains sanz respit.
Kar io sui hom desuz mun rei
E cheualers ai desuz mei;

Al un di ua, e il s'en ua,
Al altre uen, e il uent ca.
2790 A mun serf di: "Ico me fai" –
E il le feit sanz nul delai'.
Quant co out oi Iesu Crist
Par merueille as sons dist:
'En ueir, un ki tant est fedel
2795 N'ai pas troue en Israel.
E si vus di ke d'orient
Mult en uendrunt e d'occident
E od Abraam reposerunt,
Od Ysaac e Iacob u sunt,
2800 Co est, el ciel ueirement,
El regne ki n'ad finement.
E li fiz del regne erent mis
Es foreins obscurtez tut dis;
Ilokes ert li pluremenz
2805 E tres horibles fruis de denz'. /f. 74ʳ
Dunc dist Iesus a centuriun:
'Va t'en arere a ta maisun,
Si cum creis, seit fait sanz demure'.
E li sers fut saue cel ure.
2810 Ore escutez, seignurs, de grez,
Ke Deus vus pardunt vos pecchez
Si ueir cum le leprus mundat
E le sergant centoir sanat.
Signifiance i ad mult grant
2815 A tuz ki sunt el mund pecchant,
Cument Deus pur nos mals guarir
Del ciel deignat el mund uenir.

# SERMON 8
## DOMINICA TERCIA POST EPYPHANIAM

*Secundum Matheum. Cum descendisset Ihesus de monte.*

Whan Ihesus com doun of þe mount, muchel folk sewed him. And þer
com a mesel & honoured him and seid þus to him: 'Lord, ʒif þou wilt,
þou miʒt make me clene'. Ihesus put out his hond and touched him &
5  said: 'Y wil; be þou clene'. And he was so. And Ihesu said vnto him:
'Loke þou telle nouʒt þis dede to noman, bot go & schewe þe to þe prest
& do offerende and þe present þat Moyses bad hem don'. Þan com Ihesus
to Capharnaim. And þar com centurion to him and besouʒt him & seid:
'Sir, my seruant liþ seke in palsie. Wiltow com into my hous and helen
10  him?'. Ihesu answerd & seid to him: 'Y schal come & hele him'. 'Nay',
seid centurion, and answerd to Ihesu: 'Lord', he seid, 'Y ne am nouʒt
worþi þat þou com into my hous; ac onlich say þi worde and my seruant
schal be hole wiþouten ani lett. For ich am man vnder my lord king &
haue kniʒttes vnder me; vnto þat on Y say "go", and he goþ, & to anoþer
15  "com", & he comeþ; vnto my seruant Y say "do þat", & he it doþ as
swiþe'. Whan Ihesu Crist herd þis, for wonder he seid to hem o loude þat
folowed him: 'And Y say ʒou for soþe, so muchel beleue Y fonde nouʒt
in al Israel. And Y sai ʒou for soþe, mani schal com out of þe est & fram
þe west & schal rest wiþ Abraham and Ysaac and Iacob þat þat þai ben,
20  þat is, in heuen, for soþe, in kingdome þat haþ non ende, and þe childer
of þe kingdom schullen be brouʒt in forþer derknes. Alwai þer schal be
weping and gnaystyng of teþe.' Þan seid Ihesu [f. 18ʳ] to centurion: 'Go
aʒen into þi hous and as þou bileuest so be don wiþouten letting'. And his
seruant was hole maked in þat ilke our.

25     Now hereþ þe vndoyng of þis lessoun so þat God forʒeue vs our trespas as wislich als made clene þe mesel and held þe seruant of centurion.
Tokne it is ful gret vnto alle þat beþ synnand in þe world þat God of
heuen wold com fro heuen adoun into þis world for to helen vs of al

5 said] (.)said; be þou] þou be *transp.*  6 nouʒt] *eras.*  7 offerende] *alt. to* offerenge.
8 centurion] centurio *alt.*  9 palsie] þe *ins.* palsie.  11 centurion] centurio *alt.*  13
am] *ins.;* king] *ins. by H.*  17 and] *eras.*  18 mani] þat *ins.* mani.  21 forþer] þe *ins.*
forþer.  22 centurion] *alt.*  25 God] *on eras.*  26 made] he *ins.* made.  27 beþ] *ins.*

Kar li munt ki en halt se tent
Le ciel demustre ueirement;
2820 E Iesus le munt aualat
Quant pur nos saluer s'encharnat,
Quant Deus nature humaine prist
E uertuz e miracles fist.
Grant gent adunkes li siueit
2825 Ki unkes ainz nel cunusseit;
S'il se fut en sei tenuz
E il ne fust en char uenuz
Iameis ne fust de tant seuz,
Ne honurez, ne cunuz.
2830 Purquant pur sei ne uint il pas,
Mais pur guarir les nos trespas,
Kar queu mester ad il de nus
A ki del ciel sert la uertuz,
Angles, archangles e cherubin,
2835 Princes, puissances e seraphin?
Tut est a sun cumandement
E ciel e terre e mer e uent.
Quel mester ad il dunc de nus
Cheitifs, neimcels e peccheurs?
2840 Pur son busoigne ne uint il mie
Mais pur de mort nos traire a uie;
Pur nus od sei mener al ciel
Prist il la nostre char mortel;
Pur nus garir de nos pecchez
2845 Deuint il home de ses grez.
   Co signefie le leprus
K'il guarit par ses uertuz,
Kar lepre pecche signefie
Ki tuz nus tient en sa baillie,
2850 Kar si cum lepre la char runt
E li pecche l'alme confunt,
La lepre le cors desfait
E li pecchez l'alme a mort trait.
Mais cil ki se cunust leprus,
2855 Co est, de pecchez langurus,
A Deu l'estot de quor crier:
'Si uols, sire, me poez munder'.

Veez del leprus la creiance
Ki sul de Crist quert la uoillance,
2860 En sul la Deu uolente
Mist sun espeir e sa sante.
Kar co est ueir, Daui le dist:
'Quantkunkes Deu uolt, il si fist
En ciel, en terre, en abysmes'.
2865 Pur co dist li leprus de primes:
'Sire, si uols'. Veez fiance
Cum poet quant ele est sanz dutance.
Il dist: 'Si uols, saner me poes'.
Deus dist: 'Iol uoil' – si est sain lors.
2870 Kar sachez ke ferme creiance
Poet quantke uolt sanz dutance.
Crist deignat le leprus tucher,
E par co nus uolt chastier
Ke nus ne deuum nul despire
2875 Quant co fist Iesu, nostre sire;
Quant cil ki est tut suuerein
Le leprus tuche de sa main,
Qe en ert de nus ki les fuium
E sul de ueer aucun haium?
2880 Nostre char est il de naisance
E nostre frere de creiance;
Vne char sumes par nature,
Freres par crestiene cure.
Si nostre frere despisum
2885 Vels nostre char kar receuum;
Si nus despisum nostre frere
Vels nostre char kar tenum chere.
E nepurquant Ihesu despit
Ki l'un u l'altre cuntredit.   /f. 74ᵛ
2890 Mais kikunkes le leprus ueit
De sei memes duter se deit
K'il ne seit leprus par peccher
E deit a Deu merci crier.
De cest leprus deit prendre essample
2895 Del Deu poair ke tant est ample,
Ke par uolair e par tucher

iuels. For þe hil þat stondeþ on heiȝe bitokneþ þe heuen for soþe, and
Ihesu com adoun fro þe hil for to sauen vs whan he wold take our kinde
& dede vertues & mani wonders. Muchel folc þan folowed him þat neuer
bifor ne knewe him; ȝif he ne had nouȝt comen into our kinde, neuer ne
5   schuld he haue ben knowen of so mani ne worschiped. Nouȝt for himself
ne com he nouȝt ac for to amenden our trespas. Þan what mister haþ he to
vs, þat to whom al þe vertues of heuen seruen, angels, archangels,
cherubin, princes, potestates and seraphin? Al is at his comaundement,
heuen and erþe, see and wynd. What mister haþ he þan to vs þat ben
10   wreches and synners? For his nede ne com he nouȝt, bot for to drawe vs
fro deþ to liue, for to lede vs wiþ him into heuen. He toke our dedliche
kynde for to helen vs of al our trespas; he become man be his owen wille.
Þat is bitokned bi þe mesel þat he heled þurth his vertu, for meselrie
betokneþ synne þat holdeþ vs alle in his bailie; for as meselrye makeþ þe
15   flesche knotty and rotiþ it, so synne confoundeþ þe soule. Meselrie
fordoþ þe liknes of þe body & so synne draweþ þe soule to deþ; ac he þat
wot him mesel, þat is, he þat wot him in synne, vnto God he most crie
wiþ gode hert & sai: 'ȝif þou wilt, lord, þou miȝt hele me'. Lokeþ wel to
þe criynge of þe mesel, þat onlich he asked þe wille of Crist, onlich in
20   Godes wille he sett his hope & al his helþ. For þat is soþ— Dauid it seiþ:
'What þat God wil do, he doþ in heuen and in erþe and in alle stedes'.
Þerfor saiþ þe mesel first: 'Lord ȝif þou wilt'.
    Lokeþ what bileue mai do, lordynges, whan it is wiþouten doute. He
said: 'ȝif þou wilt þou mai hele me' — & God said he wold and he was
25   hole also swiþe. For wite ȝe wel þat stedfast bileue mai do what he wil
wiþouten any doute. Crist wold touch þe mesel and be þat he wold
chastise vs þat we ne schuld dispisen noman. Whan þat dede Ihesu our
lord, whan he þat is lord ouer al þing wold touche þe mesel wiþ his hond,
what schal ben of vs þat flen hem & haueþ desdayn for to sen hem? Our
30   flesche he is þurth kynde & our broþer þurth bileue; ȝif we despisen our
broþer, hou schul we sai þan þat we louen our flesche? And Ihesu
despiseþ hem þat han despite of her broþer. Ac who þat seþ þe mesel, of
himseluen [f. 18ᵛ] he owe to douten him þat he ne be nouȝt mesel þurth
sinne; and ȝif he be, he oweþ to crien to God merci. Of þis mesel he owe
35   to take ensaumple of Goddes miȝt þat is so muchel, þat þurth wille

---

3 & (2)] *on eras.*   5 haue] *ins.;* ben] *alt.*   10 nede] nede(.).   12 man] *ins.;* owen] *on
eras.*   16 liknes] *alt. on eras.*   23 wiþouten] *alt. by H.*   28 he þat] *transp.*   31 broþer]
*ins. by H.*   33 him] hem *alt. to* him.   34 he (1)] *partly on eras.;* be] ben *alt. to* be; he
(2)] *on eras.;* oweþ] owen *alt. to* oweþ; of þis] *on eras.;* he owe] he...owe *on eras.*
35 ensaumple] emsaumple *alt. to* ensaumple.

Poet cors saner, almes saluer.
Mais co fait bien a remembrer
K'il le roue al prestre aler
2900 Pur sei al prestre demustrer
E pur s'offrande aquiter.
Kar en la lei ert cumande
Ki li leprus fussent iete
Hors de comune de la gent
2905 Desk'il oussent sanement.
E si nuls en poust guarir
Al prestre deust tost uenir
S'offrende faire e sei mustrer
E par li en comune entrer.
2910 Veez ke Deus en nule guise
Ne uolt desfaire sun assise;
Co qu'en la lei out cumande,
Quant home fu, tut ad grante.
Il uolt les prestres honurer
2915 E nul despire ne blastenger.
Certis il dist en la uielz lei:
Qui par orgoil u par bufai
Le prestre ne deignet oir
Od sun pople ne poet ioir.
2920 Bien le mustrat quant il al prestre
Transmet le leprus mustrer sun estre.
Li leprus, cum ainz ai dit,
Sunt cil ki pecchent par delit.
Quant il pecchent vuertement
2925 E ne redutent Deu ne gent,
Dunc deit lur char estre forsmise
De comune de sainte eglise

Ke par lur male cumpaignie
Ne seit la bone gent hunie.
2930 E tant deiuent dehors gisir
Desk'il se uoillent repentir;
Dunc deuient il al prestre uenir
Lur pecche e lur estre mustir;
Kar repentance uent par De
2935 Dunt li pecchez est pardune.
Mais, sachez, li pecchez recoure
Ki al prestre ne se descoure;
E tut seit li mals pardune
Si deit li hom estre pene
2940 Pur ses grant mesfaiz remenbrer
E pur en auant chastier.
Kar chascun serreit deslaez
S'il ne fust unkes chastiez,
E chastiez ne poet nuls estre
2945 Fors par le conseil de sun prestre.
Li prestres nel poet conseiller
Si il de quei nel uolt mustrer.
Primes deit l'em ses mals granter,
E la manere del hanter,
2950 E cum lung tens il l'ad cele
E quanz il ad trait a pecche;
E puis par le conseil de sun prestre,
Ki desuz Deu de l'alme est mestre,
Tut amender par ureisuns,
2955 Par iunes, par afflictiuns,
Par almosnes, par bienfaiz,
E par sei tenir mes delaiz.

and þurth touching mai hele þe bodies & saue þe soules. Ac þat is gode
for to haue in remembraunce þat he bad him go to þe prest for to schewen
himseluen to þe prest and for to offre þe offerende. For in þe lawe it was
comaund þat þe mesels schuld be put out of þe comune of þe folk or þat
5    þai wer heled, and ʒif ani miʒt haue amendement, vnto þe prest he schuld
comen for to make his offerende and schewen himseluen and þurth þe
prest entren to þe comune peple. Loke þat God in no maner nold fordon
his ordinaunce þat in þe lawe was comaund, whan man was al brouʒt
adoun. He wolde honoure þe prestes and nouʒt despisen hem. Certes he
10   seiþ in þe old lawe: þat þurth pride oþer þurth enuie misdoþ þe prest, wiþ
his folk he ne mai nouʒt ioysen. Wel he schewed it whan he bad þe mesel
schewe him to þe prest. Þe mesel þat Y spak of beforn ben þai þat sinnen
þurth delite. Whan þai sinnen openlich þat þai ne douteþ God ne man,
þan þai schul be put out of þe comune of holi cherche þat þurth here
15   wicked felawschipe þe gode folk ne be nouʒt filed; and also long þai
schul liggen out of compaynye of holi chirche or þat þai wil repenten
hem and leten her sinnes. Þan þai schul com to þe prest for to schewen
her synnes and her liif; for þe repentaunce comeþ fram God þurth which
þe synnes be forʒeue. Ac wite ʒe wel þat he þat mai schewe him to þe
20   prest and nil nouʒt, his synnes beþ nouʒt forʒeuen him; & ʒif God
forʒeueþ him his synne, he mot make amendes of his trespases be consail
of þe prest and lerne at þe prest hou he schal wiþstonde synne. For boþ
owe þe prest to do — ʒeue him penaunce for his synne and teche him hou
he schal kepe Godes lawe — for þes falleþ to þe prest. And þerfor schuld
25   non take þe ordre bot he couþe boþ þe old lawe and þe newe and kepe
himseluen out of synne.

He ne schal neuer wel teche anoþer þat liþ in dedly synne; himseluen is
a rauischour and no kepere. Now, þe prest mai nouʒt chastise him ne
techen him bot he wit of what. First oweþ man tellen his synnes and
30   þanne þe maner hou he haþ vsed hem and hou long he haþ lie þerin and
hid it & hou many he haþ drawe to synne; and bi consail of þe prest þat
vnder God of þe soule is maister, he schal eniune him for to amende it
wiþ praiers & wiþ fastinges and god deuociouns in God wiþ wis almes-
ʒeuyng & wiþ god dedes doyng and wiþdrawe him fram his synne. For

---

1 ac] *eras.* 2 him] *ins.* 3 himseluen] *alt. to* himself. 4 or] *on eras.* 6 comen] sone
*ins.* comen; himseluen] *alt. to* himself. 9 despisen] despicen *alt. to* despisen *by H.*
10 þat] oþer *canc.,* þat *ins.* 13 þat] *on eras.* 14 of holi] *transp.* 16 or þat þai] *on*
*eras.* 18 which] *ins. probably by H.* 19 ac] bote *on eras.;* him] *ins.* 22 lerne]
(…)ler(ne), *alt.* 23 owe] *alt. to* oweþ. 26 himseluen] him *alt.* self(..); synne] dedli
*ins.* synne. 32 amende] amende (.)it.

Kar poi u nient ualt le bienfait
A li ki le pecche ne lait;
2960 Ne almosne n'iert a Deu priuee
Tant cum li mals a home agree.
Ki bien fait e en mal repose
Sei dune al diable, a Deu sa chose!
Mais pur co ne deit nuls laisser
2965 De faire bien e praier,
Kar kant li home s'amenderat
Tut si bienfaiz repeirerat;
E mult suuent par lur bienfait
Sunt plusurs de lur pecche retrait;
2970 Kar nul bien n'ert sanz guerdun
Ne nul mal sanz espenisun.
Co mustrat cist centuriun
Ki ruuat saner sun garcun.    /f. 75ʳ
Ceturiun grant bien feseit
2975 Mais la paene lei teneit,
E tut le deffendist sa lei
Pur ses bienfaiz e pur sa fei
Li dist Iesus: 'A tei uendrai
E tun sergant te sanerai'.
2980    Sachez ke cist centuriun
Ne uint pas memes a Iesum;
Ainz li mandat par ses amis
K'il guarisist sun paralis.
Ne se tint digne a li parler,
2985 Pur co parla par messager.
Les princes de la Iuerie
Enueit pur auer aie,
Pur co k'erent priue de De

Kar il lur aueit la lei dune,
2990 E il distrent bonement:
'Sire, il aime nostre gent;
Sinagoge nus ad il fait.
Oez le, sire, co est dreit'.
Veez, seignurs, tuz bienfaiz
2995 Deuant Deu mesmes sunt retraiz.
Tut fust paien centuriun
De sun bienfait out guerdun.
Co k'il out fait par bon entente,
Quant demanda, si out la rente.
3000 Pur co ne deit nuls crestiens,
Tut seit il orde, leisser ses biens;
Tanttost cum il s'amenderat
E si bienfaiz reuiuerat.
Quant bienfait ualt al paen
3005 Mult uauldrat plus al crestien.
Iesu lur dist: 'Io i uendrai
E sun garcun li sanerai'.
Veez, seignurs, cum Deus est prez
A tuz ki uolent estre nez;
3010 Ki par sei uient cum li leprus
Ia ne se partira confus.
Qui par messager cum centuriun
Quant k'il uolt li ert a bandun.
Ore poez saueir certeinement
3015 K'altri preiere ualt suuent;
Pur co fait celi grant folie
Ki en sei mesmes trop s'afie.
Nus deuum quere de praianz,

litel oþer nouȝt is worþ þe gode dede to him þat nil nouȝt leten his synne
as for to haue þe mede of heuene. Þerfor, as long as þe man haþ wille to
his synne and doþ gode dedes and resteþ him in euel, he ȝeueþ him to þe
fende and [f. 19ʳ] doþ God fram him. And þerfor schal no man let to do
5   þe gode, for ȝif he do gode dedes he mai þe soner haue grace for to
repenten him and þanne al þe gode dedes þat he dede whiles he was out
of dedly synne schal arisen wiþ him to liue aȝen. For whan he fel into
synne, alle his gode dedes deyde wiþ him. For no gode dede schal ben
vnȝulden þat he ne schal haue mede þarfor oþer her oþer in heuen, ne non
10  euel dede schal ben vnpunisched þat he ne schal be pined her þarfor oþer
in purgatorie oþer in helle. Þat schewed Crist to centirion þat [b]esouȝt of
Crist þe helþ of his seruant.

    Centurion dede gret god, ac he held þe payne lawe; and ȝet, þouȝ þat
he held þat lawe, for his god dedes and for his stedfast bileue þat he had
15  to Crist, Ihesu seid þat he wold comen and helen his seruant.

    Wite ȝe wel, þat centurion ne come nouȝt first himseluen to Ihesu ac
besouȝt him þurth his frendes þat he schuld helen his seruant and he held
him nouȝt worþi to speke to him. And he spake be mesangers, for þe
princes of þe Ieweri, he besouȝt hem for to speke for him. Forþi þai
20  besouȝt for him to God, þo þat God had ȝeuen his lawe, and þai said to
Ihesu: 'Sire', þai seiden, 'he loueþ our folk; he haþ made vs a synagoge.
Her him lord: it is riȝt.' Lokeþ, lordinges, þat alle gode befor God be put
forþe; þeiȝ alle wer centurion payen, ȝit he hadde mede of his gode dede
þat he hadde don wiþ his gode wille whan he asked help. Forþi ne schal
25  no cristen man, alþouȝ he be foule, leten for to do gode dedes. Whan his
gode dedes halpe so þe payen, muchel better it is worþ to a cristen man.
Ihesu saiþ: 'Y schal come & hele his seruant'.

    Lokeþ, lordinges, what God is nere vnto alle þat wil be clene in him;
þat comeþ be him one as þe mesel dede, he ne schal nouȝt fayle þat he ne
30  schal haue help; oþer þat comeþ to him þourȝ oþer as centurion dede, al
þat þai wil han & asken schal comen to hem.

    Now mai ȝe wite for soþe þat oþer menes praier ofte helpeþ. Forþi he
doþ a gret folye þat afieþ him to gretlich in himseluen. We schul beseche

---

1 worþ þe] worþ (............) þe; nil] *ins. by H.* 4 let] let(.). 7 synne] synne(.).
8 dede] *ins. on eras.* 10 schal (1)] (.)schal. 11 to centirion] *ins. probably by H.* 12
þe helþ of] *ins. probably by H.* 13 centurion] *on eras.;* payne] payne(.) *alt. to*
paynemes. 20 for] first *ins.* for; god (2)] *on eras.* 22 befor] dede *ins.* befor. 23
payen] *alt. to* payene; mede] Y *eras.* mede *alt.* 24 help] *alt.* 25 al] ȝef *ins.* al;
leten] *alt. to* letten. 26 payen] *alt. to* payenem. 29 one] *partly eras.* 30 þourȝ] on
*canc.* þourȝ. 31 hem] *alt.* 33 schul] *alt. to* schulleþ.

Prestres, clers e mendianz,
3020 Ki en bienfaiz seient pur nus
Quant nus entendre n'i poums
V dignes n'eimes d'aprocher
Pur nos mesfaiz a seint alter.
E deuum duner largement,
3025 Dras e uitaille, or e argent,
Cum fist icist centuriuns
Dunt Deus oit ses ureisuns.
   Mais ore oez k'il remandat
Quant Iesus dist k'a li uendrat:
3030 'Sire, ne sui pas dignes hum
Ke tu entres en ma maisun'.
Quant si respundit li paens
Ke deit penser li crestiens
Quant en sei deit Deu herberger
3035 E sun seintisme cors user?
Mult se deit enceis purpenser
E tuz ses pecchez esmunder
En plurs, en iunes, en humblesces,
E en tutes altres pruesces.
3040 Tut n'ait il de rien mespris
Si se deit il duter tut dis;
Tut se sache il u pur u cler
A neint digne se deit iuger
De cel seintisme cors manger
3045 Ki ciel guuerne e terre e mer,
De herberger en sa baillie
Le Deu ki guarde e mort e uie.
Kar co sachez, ki dignement
E en humblesce sa char prent
3050 De ceste mort s'en ua a uie
Tut dis en la Deu cumpaignie.
Cil ki la prendrunt folement
En pecche sanz repentement
Il pernent lur dampnaciun
3055 Cum dist Saint Pol en sun sermun.

Oez plus ke centurie dist:
'Io sui home e tu es Crist;    /f. 75ᵛ
Io sui suz altri poeste
E tu es Deus de maieste.
3060 Cheualers ai a mun cumant
E li angle sunt ti seruant.
Mis serf fait mun cumandement
E tut li mundz fait tun talent;
Mi cheualer funt mes aueols
3065 E tut li munde co ke tu uols.
Pur co ne sui pas dignes hom
Ke tu entres en ma maisun,
Mais sulement di le ton dit
E mis garz ert sains sanz respit'.
3070 Creium cum fist cist paens
Si uers Deu uulum merir riens,
E co k'il quist a sun sergant
Querum as almes meintenant.
   Li garz ki languist en maisun
3075 Demustre l'alme par raisun
Ki de pecche trait dur flael
El cors ki ci est sun ostel.
Paralisie est un langur
Ki tolt force e uigur;
3080 Bel sunt li membre k'il tient
Mais ne poent aider de nient,
Kar li membre endormi sunt
Pur la chalur ke perdu unt.
Itele est l'alme en uerite
3085 Quant perd chalur de charite;
Dunc est pesante e amortie
E de pecche tut entumie,
E dunkes gist en grant langur
Quant par pecche perd Deu amur.
3090 Mais dunc estoet merci crier
Par repentance e par urer;
Bien repentir est fort crier

to beseche for vs prestes and clerkes and men þat biddiþ here mete þat
þai bidde for vs whan we ne mai nouȝt entent þerto, þat þai beseche for
vs at þe holi auter þat God schal sende vs his grace. And we schul
largeliche ȝeue hem mete and drinke, seluer and gold as dede centurion
5   of which God herd his biddyng.

Ac now vnderstondeþ what he seide aȝen whan Ihesu seid he wold
come: 'Lord', he seid, 'Y am nout worþi þat þou com into myn hous'.
Whan swich a worde seid þe payen, what owe þan a cristen man say
whan he schal take God inwiþ him and schal vsen his holi body. Gretlich
10   he owe to biþenche him before and make him clene wiþ wepyng and wiþ
fastinge and in lownes and [f. 19ᵛ] in alle oþer gode dedes. 3ef þouȝ he
dede neuer non euel, ȝit he oweþ alway to douten him; þouȝ alle he se
him pur and clere, he oweþ to holden himseluen vnworþi for to receyuen
him þat kepeþ boþ heuen and erþe and al þat is in þis world, for to
15   heberwe him in his bayly, þat God þat ȝeueþ liif and deþ. For þat wite
ȝe wel, who þat worþilich receyueþ his body here and in lowenesse, out
of þis deþ he schal go to lyue and alway be in Goddes companye; and þo
þat takeþ it folilich and in dedly synne wiþouten repentaunce, þai taken
her dampnacioun, and Seyn Poul seiþ and techeþ. Hereþ more what
20   centurion said: 'Ich am man & þou art Crist; & ich am vnder oþer in
mennes pouste and þou art God almiȝtful; knyȝtes ich haue to my
comaundement and aungels ben to þe seruantes; my seruant doþ my
comaundement and al þe world is at þi wille; myn knyȝtes don my
biddynges and al þe world doþe þi wille; for Y nam nouȝt worþi þat þou
25   come into myn hous, ac onlich sai þi word & my seruant schal ben hole
as swiþe'. Beleue we as dede þe payne ȝif þat we wil queme God and
serue him; þat he asked to his seruaunt aske we to our soules.

Þe seruant þat lay seke in þe hous bitokneþ wel þe soule be skil þat
þurth synne haþ many pyny[n]ges and his body, is ostele. Palasie is an
30   euel þat binimeþ a man his strengþe. Fair beþ his membres ac þai mowe
nouȝt helpen him, for his lemes ben al aslepe þourȝ þe hete þat þai han
forlorn. Þat is þe soule, for soþe; whan it haþ forlorn þe hete of charite,
þan it is ded & þouȝtful and slepeþ in synne. Þan it lieþ in gret siknesse
whan þurth synne he leseþ þe loue of God, ac þan he mot cry mercy þurth
35   repentaunce and þurth biddi[n]g. God repentaunce is a stronge criynge

---

2 entent] ent(.)ent *alt.*   7 nout] nouȝt *alt.*   8 say] to *ins.* say.   9 he] *on eras.;* god] his
*ins.* god *on eras.*   17 be] *ins.*   19 seyn] þt *ins.* seyn.   24 doþe] *partly eras.*   26
payne] *alt. to* paynem.   27 his seruaunt] *ins. probably by H;* our] to *ins.* our.   28
wel] (.)wel; skil] skil(.).   29 pynynges] pynyges.   32 hete] *ins., probably by H.*   34
loue of god] of god loue *transp.*   35 bidding] biddig.

V raisun est boen messager.
Si il unt od sei ferme creance
3095 Tost uenent a la Deu oiance,
E tost respunt li pius Iesus
Ki sanez seit li langurus,
Cum il dist a centuriun
E sein li rendit sun garcun.
3100  Mais de centuriun ore esguardez,
Cum il ert humbles e senez.
Quant il n'osat a Deu aler
Mais les seinz homes enueier
Quant pur sun serf deignat preier,
3105 Quant il n'osat Deu herberger.
Tant cum il plus s'umiliat
E Iesu Crist plus le loat.
La riche gent ke ore sunt,
A Deu coment respunderunt
3110 Cum plus mesfunt en tute guise
Plustost entrent en seinte eglise,
Plustost pernent comuignement,
Si ne lur est de Deu nient.
Si un lur tenant malades gist
3115 Tart lur semble k'il ne perist
Pur l'aueir k'il desirent tant
E point ne dutent Deu le grant.
Si garcun languist u sergant
De lur n'auerat tant ne quant;
3120 Ne pensent pas k'il languirunt
Kar lur richesce les confunt.
E pur co ke ualt crestien
Ki fait pis ke le paen?
Pur Deu ke ualt cristienisme
3125 Ke peiur est ke paienisme?
Pur Deu, pensez en, riche gent;
Turnez uers Deu uostre talent;
Faites tant en uostre sante
Ke uos mals seient alegge.
3130 Kar ki de altre auerat merci

E Deus auerat de li alsi;
Ki d'altre auerat misericorde
S'alme e sun cors a Deu acorde.
Ki d'altre n'auerat cumpassiun
3135 De Deu n'auerat ia pardun.
Si uos auez home u sergant
E vus e li fist Deu le grant.
Si li uns sert, l'altre cumande,
Sa creature Deus demande;
3140 En co k'il est Deu creature
Vostre per est il par nature.    /f. 76ʳ
Si Deu vus ad sur li pose,
Guardez ne seiez trop ose,
Kar quant ke vus li mesferez
3145 Deu uengerat, bien le sachez.
  Oez cum Deus est ioissant
Quant troue un riche bien fesant,
Quant troue un riche de creance,
Vmble e de bone fesance.
3150 Cum il en ad ioie e delit
Cum il de centuriun dist:
'Amen, vus di k'en Israel
Ne trouai un tant fedel.
Pur co vus di ke mult uendrunt
3155 E el ciel od Abraam serrunt'.
Kar quant la riche gent funt bien
E se tenent cum cristien,
Ke pur essample, ke pur dute,
Tut li poples en bien s'arute.
3160 Si li riche funt malement
E li poples fait ensement.
E sachez k'il respunderunt
Pur cels k'il a mal trarrunt,
E grant guerdun auerunt
3165 Pur cels k'il chastierunt.
Cil ki pernent chastiement
Co sunt la peccheresse gent

and besechyng is gode mesager. ȝif þai han wiþ hem stedfast bileue, sone
it comeþ in Godes ere and sone answereþ him Ihesu þanne and seiþ þat
saued is þe seke als he said to centurion and ȝald him his seruant hole
and sounde.

5  Ac beholdeþ now to centurion how þat he was meke and milde whan
he ne dorst nouȝt comen to Crist; ac he sent his holy men to him first
what þat he wold beseche for his seruant and ne dorst nouȝt lete Ihesus
com into his hous. Þe more þat he loued him, þe more Ihesus Crist
praised him. Þe riche folk þat now ben, how schul answer to God þat þe
10  more þat misdon þe soner þai comen to holi chirche, for hem nis nouȝt of
God. ȝif on of her tenaunce leggen seke, hem longeþ sore of þat he be
dede for þe [f. 20ʳ] godes þat þai wold han, ȝif he haþ any, and ne douteþ
noþing God. And ȝif her tenaunt oþer her seruant lyen seke, of hem ne
schul þai han noþing; þai ne þenchen nouȝt þat þai schul anguischen for
15  her riches ablindeþ hem and confundeþ hem. And þarfor, what is worþe
to cristen man þat doþ wors þan þe sarazin? For Godes loue, þencheþ
heropon ȝe riche, turneþ to God ward ȝour hertes, doþ so muchel þarwhiles þat ȝe beþ in god poynt, þat ȝour soules mowe be saued. For he
þat haþ of oþer mercy, God schal haue on him also, and he þat haþ no
20  mercy of oþer, he geteþ no mercy of God. ȝif he haue man oþer seruant,
boþ ȝou & hem mad God almyȝt. ȝif þat on be ȝeuen to ben vnder þat
oþer, God wil asken his creature; and in þat þat he is Godes creature, þi
broþer he is þurth kynde. ȝif God þe haþ sett ouer him, loke þat þou be
nouȝt so hardy for to misdon him; and ȝif þou do, God wil vengen him,
25  siker þou be.

Hereþ hou God is gladde whan he fyndeþ a riche man wel doand, whan
he fyndeþ a riche man wel bileueand, meke and milde & wel doand. Als
he said of centurion, he turned aboute & said aloude: 'For soþe', he said,
'so muchel faiþ ne fond y nouȝt in Israel; forþi Y sai ȝou þat many schal
30  comen out of þe est and out of þe west þat schal ben wiþ Abraham in
heuen'. For whan þe riche man doþ wel and holdeþ him as cristen men
owe to don, what þurth ensample of hem and what for doute, alle folk
kepe hem in gode. And ȝif þe riche don euel, þe comune puple doþ also.
And wite ȝe wel, þai schul answer for al þat þai drawe to ille, and gret
35  mede þai schul han for hem þat þai chastisen. Þo ben þe synful men þat

1 gode] a ins. gode; mesager] alt. to mesanger.   8 loued] lowed alt.   9 answer] þai
ins. answer.   10 misdon] þai ins. misdon.   11 tenaunce] alt. to tenauntes; hem] alt.
by H.   21 on] on (.) be.   22 þat (1)] partly eras.   28 for soþe] for (.) soþe.   30 wiþ]
ins., probably by H.   31 men] (.)men.   34 þai (1)] on eras.; ille] euel ins. ille.

Ki uenent loinz del orient
E loinz de uers l'occident.
3170 De loinz uenent kar Deus est loing
A cels ki pecchent sanz bosoign.
Dauid le dist en ueritez:
'De peccheurs loinz est santez'.
Purquant, quant il s'amenderunt
3175 E de quor a Deu se tenderunt,
El regne del ciel regnerunt
V Abraham e Ysaac sunt.
Li fiz del regne sunt li Giu
Ki pires sunt ki chen u lu;
3180 E cil ki sivent lur manere
Si serrunt iete la derere

En la foreine tenebrur,
Kar ne cunurent lur salueur;
Il ne cunussent pas creance,
3185 Ne par bienfait, ne par penance;
Kar ki en mal est endurcis
A tut dis ert de Deu maldiz.
La plurrunt malaitement
Ki trop siuirent lur talent;
3190 Par fruis de denz eschiuerunt
Pur lur mesfaiz ki ci fait unt.
De tut ico fussent guariz
Si par tens fussent repentiz.
Iesus nus doinst issi repentir
3195 K'alme e cors puissum guarir.   Amen.

comen fro fer out of þe west and out of þe est; fro fer þai comen for God
is fer fro hem þat synne nedeles, þat han no nede to synne.

Dauid saiþ it for soþe: 'Fro þe synner, helþ is fer fro hem'. Nouȝt for
þanne, whan þai amenden hem & take hem to God wiþ gode wille, in þe
5    kingdom of heuen þai schul regnen wiþ Abraham and wiþ Ysaac and wiþ
Iacob. Þe children of þe kyngdom ben þai þat worse ben þan þe Cananes,
& þai þat folowen her maner, þai schul ben cast into þe forþermoste
derkenes, for þai ne knew nouȝt her saueour noyþer in bileue no in wel
doyng ne þurth penaunce. For þai þat beþ lastend in euel, for euer þai
10   schul be waried of God; þer þai schul wepe stron[g]liche and siþe in her
owen teres for þat þai folowed to muchel þe lustes of her flesche. And
gnaystyng of teþ þer schal be, þat is, brennynge of fur þat euer schal
laste. [f. 20ᵛ] And of þis þai miȝt ben hulpen ȝif þat þai hadde repented
hem bitymes her in þis world whiles þat þai wer þerinne. Ihesus sende vs
15   his grace of swich repentaunce þat we mot come to þat sauacioun, body
and soule.

---

3 fro (1)] *alt. to* from; helþ] *alt.*   4 god] god(.).   8 no] ne *alt.*   10 strongliche]
stronliche; siþe] siþe *canc.,* seþen *ins.*   13 þis] al *ins.* þis; miȝt] m(.)iȝt; hulpen] *alt.*
*to* holpen.

# DOMINICA IV POST EPIPHANIAM

En une nef muntat Iesu
E si disciple i sunt uenu.
E la mer lors se comoueit
Si ki la nef l'ewe couereit,
3200 Kar li uenz encuntre els esteit.
E Iesus en la nef dormeit,
E il a li sunt aproche,
E en dissant l'unt esueille:
'Salue nus, sire Iesu Crist,
3205 Nus perissum'. E il lur dist:
'Purquei este uos tant dutus?
Petite fei parad en vus'.
Dunc cumandat, tut en leuant,
As mers, as uenz, e pais fut grant.
3210 Les homes grant merueille prist,
E si diseient: 'Quels est cist,
Kar li uenz e la mer ruant
Obeissent a sun cumant?'
En ceste lescun, ki l'entent,
3215 Mustra Iesu uerraiement
K'il est ueirs Deus e ueirs home;
De nostre lei co est la sume.
Cum home par nef entra en mer,
Cum Deus fist la mer trubler;   /f. 76ᵛ
3220 Cum home en la nef sumillat,
Cum Deus les tempestes apeisat.
Quel mester out de nef munter
Ki Piers fist sur la mer aler
E sec pez fist la Ruge Mer
3225 Les fiz Israel trespasser?
Mais quant il ert pur nus uenuz
Mult atemprat ses grant uertuz;

Si il oust ses uertuz mustre
Iames ne fust crucifie.
3230 E nus ne fussum iamais reins
Si il ne fust mort par altri mains.
Si nus redune essample grant.
Tut seit un home mult puissant
Par tut se deit humillier
3235 E nient sun poair tut mustrer.
E ceste nascele en une guise
Bien signefie seinte eglise
V Iesus entrat pur passer,
Co est, pur le mund laisser.
3240 La mer signefie cest munde
Ki dunc retrait e dunc surunde.
Ia lunges n'auerat pais ensemble
Plus ke la mer est k[e] tut dis tremble.
En ceste mer est seinte eglise,
3245 Mult turmente e dur assise.
Eglise n'est pas sule maisun
Mais tut cil qui craient en Ihesum.
Dunt li disciple en la nef erent
Ki tuz fedels signefierent;
3250 Kar nuls ne poet creire Iesum
Ki ne soffre temptaciun.
Co mustre bien li tempestez
Ki sur la nef est aleuez;
Li uenz bute, l'unde la fert,
3255 Ore est parfund e ore pert;
La mer ne cesse de ferir
E cil dedeinz quident murir.
Tut est alsi de seinte eglise
Ki entre mundeins est asise.

## [D]OMINICA QUARTA [P]OST EPYPHANIAM

*Secundum Matheum. Ascendente Ihesu in nauiculam.*

Into a schippe went Ihesu and his deciples comen to him. And þe see
began to stiren fast and wawes to risen and þe wynde put on þat on halfe
and þe stormes wexen gret so þat þe water keuerd þe schippe and þai wer
5    in poynt to drenchen. And Ihesu slep in þe schip, and þai com to him and
bad him arisen; þai weren in poynt to drenchen: 'Saue vs lord Ihesu
Crist'. And he seid to hem: 'Whi be ȝe so sore adrade? Litel faiþ is in
ȝou.' Þan he bad þe wynde & þe water be stille, and it was in pes. And þe
men awonderd þeroffen and said: 'What man is þis þat þe wynd and þe
10   see beþ at his comaundement?'.

    In þis leson, whoso vnderstondeþ it ariȝt, schewed Ihesu þat he was
soþefast God and man, and þis is al þe stryngþe of our lawe. As man he
entred into þe schippe and as God he made þe stormes to arise; and as
man he slep in þe schip and as God he deposed þe tempest. What nede
15   had he for to gon into þe schip þat made Petre for to gon o þe see and
made þe rede see drye so þat þe childer of Israel ȝed ouer drie fot? Ac
whan he com hider to sauen vs, muchel he tempred his gret vertues, for
ȝif he had schewed his gret vertues, neuer ne hadde he bi don on þe rode,
and we ne had neuer ben bouȝt bot ȝif he had be don vpon þe rode þurth
20   oþer.

    And he ȝaf gret ensaumple to men þat ben of gret power; ȝit he owe
muchel to lowen him and nouȝt schewen him alle his miȝt. Þis schip in o
maner betokeneþ wel holi chirche þat Ihesus entred in for to pasen, þat is,
for to leten þis world þat now ebbeþ & now floweþ— it haþ neuer rest
25   ne pes, ne stondeþ stille in o stede namore þan þe see þat allewai stereþ.
In þis see is holi chirche gretliche turmented and hard be sett. Þe chirche
is nouȝt onlich þe hous bot alle þat leuen on Ihesu Crist þat hii ne mot
suffre gret anguische and temptaciouns. And vpon þis schip þe wawes
arisen, þe wynde putteþ, þe wawes smyten; now is it lowe and in depnes,
30   and now it is sen. Þe see ne cesseþ nouȝt for to smyten and þai þat beþ
þerinne wenen for to deien. Also it is bi holi chirche þat is sett among

---

2 wynde] wyndn *alt. to* wynde, *probably by H.*   19 ben] ben(.).   22 schewen] *alt.*
25 wai] *ins.*   29 lowe] law *canc.* lowe.

3260  Les undes sunt la riche gent;
      Male parole, co est li uent.
      Li riche asaillent seinte eglise
      E turmentent en tute guise,
      Dunc par ses honurs abeisser,
3265  Dunc par ses dreiz amenuser,
      Dunc par les ordres anentir,
      Dunc par les dimes retenir.
      Quant li riches ne set purquei
      La gent uolage trait a sei;
3270  Par les diz a la male gent,
      Quant li riches a els se prent,
      La wage fiert, bute li uent,
      Es vus, eglise en grant turment.
      Tut quident ke Iesus se dort
3275  Quant ne li fait point de confort;
      Tut quident ki li seit a nient
      Quant il ne prent lores uengement.
      Mais il le fait tut pur taster
      Les malueis e les bons pruuer;
3280  Il se dort par bone suffrance
      Pur uer des mals la uoillance
      E pur esprouer la suffrance
      De cels ki unt en li bone fiance.
      Pur co deiuent la seinte gent,
3285  Quant il sunt en tel turment,
      Crier a Deu par uraisuns:
      'Leuez, Iesu, nus perissums'.
      Kar co sachez tut finement,
      Qui Iesus prie escordrement,
3290  Par dreit e bone entenciun,
      Tut li parfrat sa uraisun.
      Co mustrat il bien en la mer
      Quant li son quiderent neer;
      Dunt il dist: 'Dunt estes dutus;

3295  Petite fei parad en vus'.
      Veirs est, mult par ourent poi de fei
      Ki ourent le salueur od sei
      E iloc duterent turment
      V lur uie fut en present.
3300  Par co chastie il tuz les sons
      Ki sunt el munde, tuz les bons,
      K'il ne seient desesperant
      Tut ne face il tanttost lur grant,   /f. 77ʳ
      Mais ke ferm seient en creance,
3305  En uraisuns, en atendance.
      Kar tut face il alcun delai
      Ne oblie pas la bone fei;
      Kar il dist ki endurerat
      Desk'en la fin, cil salf serrat.
3310  Dunc cumandat Iesus as uenz,
      E a la mer, e as turmenz;
      Lores fu fait grant paisiblete
      Kar tut ueint ki ad endure.
         La mer demustre en altre guise
3315  La croiz ke tut le munde iustise.
      En la nascele Crist muntat
      Quant en la croiz sa char peina.
      Ilokes s'endormit en la mort,
      Dunt as sons surt tempeste fort
3320  Des reis, de princes, de Iuels,
      Des publicans, de pharisels;
      Tuz le buterent e dechacerent
      E encuserent e turmenterent.
      Mais la nef de lur unite
3325  Ne poet unkes estre quasse,
      La nascele de lur creance
      Ne fu unc mis en balance,
      K'il ne crusent la Deu mort

worldliche men. Þe wawes ben þe riche men; wicked word, þat is þe
wynde. Þe riche asailen holi cherche þat ben gode cristen men, now for to
abaten her honour, now for to fordo þe gode men of ordre, and now for to
wiþdrawe her riȝtes. And whan þe riche mai haue no encheson, he
5 draweþ þe wild men to him; & þurth wordes of wicked men þat he haþ
wiþ him, and whan he leueþ her wordes, þan bigynneþ þe wawes to
smyten and þe wynde to blowen & setteþ al holi cherche in [f. 21ʳ] gret
tourment. And þan whan þai ben in gret anguische, þai wenen þat Ihesu
slepeþ and haþ forȝeten hem for þat he sendeþ hem non confort. And alle
10 hem þencheþ þanne þat it is lorn þat þai gon aboute for þat he ne takeþ
nouȝt sone vengance. Ac he it doþ for to loke what þe wicked wil do and
for to proue þe gode; he slepeþ þurth god suffraunce to se þe euel wil of
þe wicked & for to proue þe suffraunce of hem þat affien hem in him.
Forþi schal þis holi men, whan þai ben in swiche tempeste, crien to God
15 þurth bisechynges and sai to him, 'Ihesu, arisse; we perischen'. For þat
wite ȝe wel soþelich and riȝtfulich wiþ riȝt gode vnderstondyng, al he
schal fulfille his biddynge, and þat he schewed wel in þe see whan his
deciples wende to drenchen, whan he aros up & seide: 'Whi bi   ȝe
adrede: Litel faiþ is in ȝou.'
20   For soþe, litel faiþ þai hadden whan þai weren in doute and hadde her
saueour wiþ hem & douted þer any turment þar her liif was in present.
And wiþ þat worde he chastised alle his þat ben in þe worlde, in tourment
and in anguische, þat þai ne falle nouȝt in misbileue þouȝ þat he ne do
nouȝt her wille also sone, ac þat þai be stedfast in bileue and abiden his
25 wille in gode besechynges and wiseliche. For ȝif al he make delay, ne
forȝet nouȝt þou þe riȝt bileue. For he saiþ, who þat doþ and holdeþ his
bileue stedefast vnto last ende of his liif, þouȝ þat him come neuer so
muchel anguische her, it schal be for his gode. Þan bad Ihesu to þe wynde
and to þe see: 'Beþ in pes' — & þan wer þai in pes. For sone he schal
30 ouercome and wel þat abideþ his tyme.
   Þe see betokeneþ in þe oþer maner þe croys þat riȝteþ and wisseþ alle
þe world; into þe schip God went vp also þo he pyned so his flesche
þaron. Þer he slep on his deþ, þurth whiche deþ gret tempest aros to him
þat him loued. Princes and kynges and of þe Iewes of þe comune and þe
35 phariseues, alle þai putted him and chased him and acused him and
tourmented him; ac þe schip of her onhed ne miȝt neuer be tobroken, þe
vessel of her riȝt bileue ne was nouȝt sett in wer, for þat þurth Ihesu is

---

1 men wicked] men (.) wicked.   6 her] *partly on eras.*   9 slepeþ] slepleþ.   12 se] þe
*eras.* se; wil] *alt. to* will.   14 forþi] *with* þi *ins.*   22 worlde] *alt. by H.*   24 ac] *ins.,*
*probably by H.*   27 come] *ins., probably by H.*   37 ne] *eras;* wer] werr *alt.*

Parunt il uindrent a dreit port;
3330 E par li en ki creirent
Trestuz lur enemis uenquirent
Tanttost cum Iesus s'esueillat
E de la mort releuat,
A ses apostles se mustrat
3335 E sa pais ferme lur dunat.
Lores furent tant confortez,
Tant hardiz, tant confermez
K'il ne duterent nule gent,
Rei ne tirant, mer ne uent.
3340 Ne deiuent cil ki ore sunt,
Ki a Deu tenir se uoldrunt,
Ne deiuent nuli duter
Mais en Deu auer quor enter.
Certes tuz ad uenge Iesus
3345 Ki lealment se sunt tenuz.
Ke sunt deuenu li tirant,
Li orguillus, li mesfesant,
Li occisurs des crestiens
E ki lur tolirent lur biens?
3350 Certes tuz sunt a deables alez
E Iesus ad lei sons feffez.
Veez alsi des rauisurs
E de eglise les turmenturs:
Vncore regne seinte eglise
3355 E il sunt en male iuise.
    Seint Gregoire cunte d'un home,
Estefne out nun si mist en Rome;
A mesmes del muster maneit
Ki de Seinte Cecilie esteit.
3360 E pur alaisser sun purpris
Vn poi del cymiter aueit pris.
Li pruuers li dist suuent
K'il en feist amendement;
Riches hom ert e mult poant
3365 Nel uoet oir ne tant ne quant.
Mais il resolt grantment cherir
Seint Preiect, un seint martir.
A sun iur grant feste feseit
E poures e mendifs peisseit;

3370 Dras e uiande lur donout
E ses ueisins puis apellout.
Ne demurat grantment mie
K'il ne chait en maladie,
E apres lung languissement
3375 Rauiz en fut al iugement;
Deuant le iuge est amenez
Mult pourus e esmaiez,
Kar mult i uit des malmenez
Qui a dampner erent iugez.
3380 E mult i uit sainz en lur flurs,
Martirs, uirgines e confessurs.
Entre els uit Sainte Cecilie,
Plus blanche ke n'est flur de lilie.
Mais ele li fist malueis semblant
3385 E mult alout uers li grucant;
Mult paresguardout ferement
E manacout mult durement.    /f. 77ᵛ
E li iuges ert entendant
A iuger altres entretant.
3390 Dunc dut Seinte Cecilie aler
E par Estefne trespasser;
En passant par le braz l'ad pris
E pince l'ad, coli ert uis;
Mais tant li dolait cel pincer
3395 Ke mielz uoldrat le braz colper.
Atant fut al iuge apellez
E a dampner i fut iugez
Pur co ke mesfait out grantment
Enuers Cecilie memement.
3400 Li sergant adunc le pristrent,
Mais li seinz ki pres erent distrent:
'Cument, Estefne, es esbai?
Dun as tu Seint Preiect serui?
Va tost demander sa aie;
3405 Nel deis amer si ore te ublie'.
Estefne aueit tant a penser,
N'ose mot dire fors esguarder.
E Preiect, quant l'out esguarde,
Deuant le iuge s'est encline;
3410 Mult le preiat en tute guise

ded þai scholde come to liue þat euer schal last, and þurth him in whom
þat þai bileuen þai ouercome alle her enemys also sone as Ihesu aros fro
deþ to liue and ȝaf hem stedfast pes and made hem so hardy and coun-
forted hem þat þai ne douted noman, kyng ne prince, see ne wynde. No
5   more ne schuld þai þat now ben, þat wil stedfast bileue on Ihesu Crist;
þai ne schuld no man douten bot sett her hert onlich in God. For certes,
God himseluen haþ venged alle þat truliche helden to him. Whar beþ
bicome þes tirauntes, þis proude and þes eueldoers and þai þat dede
cristen folk to deþ and þat [f. 21ᵛ] benam her godes? Certes, þai ben gon
10   to þe deuel and Ihesu haþ auaunced his in þe blisse of heuen. Se also þes
rauissours and þes robbours of holi chirche, [& þat dide hit so gret
turment; ȝete lasteþ holi chirche,] and þai ben in pyne and in wo.
     Seynt Gregori telleþ of a man þat hiȝt Steuen þat wonede in Rome and
had his [stede] fast bi þe chirche þat was of Seynt Cecilie. And for to
15   make his hous þe larger, he toke in a litel of þe auter. And þe prest seid to
him often þat he schuld make amendes; and for he was a riche man and
of gret power, he nolde nouȝt heren him. Ac he was wont to make gret
solennite of an holi martir, and on his day he made gret feste and fedde
þe pouer and þe feble. And it nas nouȝt longe after þat he fel seke in gret
20   sekenesse. And als he lay in anguisch, he was rauisched to þe jugement
and before þe juge he was brouȝt sorowful & sory, for he was juged to
damnacioun. And he seiȝ many seyntes in her floures, martires, confessours & virgines, and amonges hem he seiȝ Seyn Cecile whitter þan snow
oþer lilie. Ac ȝche made him euel semblaunt and com to him ward &
25   manaced him riȝt gretlich. And þe juge was entendaunt for to jugen oþer.
Þan come Seyn Cecile bi Steuen, and as sche ȝede bi him, sche toke him
be þe arme and pynched him þarbi, and so gretlich it greued him þat him
hadde bi leuer, him þouȝt, þat his arme hadde be smyten of. And þan he
was cleped befor þe juge and he was juged to pyne him þouȝt wiþouten
30   ende for þat he hadde trespased aȝenes Cecile. And þe seriaunt þan toke
him for tourmenten him, and þe holy seyntes þat weren bisides him seide
to him: 'What, Steuen, artow abascht? Ne hastow serued Seynt Proiecte?
Go swiþe and bidde him help þe. Þow ne owest nomore to seruen himȝif
he forȝete þe now.' And Steuen was in a gret þouȝt þat he ne dorst speke
35   o word bot loked vpon him. And Seynt Proiecte, whan he seiȝ he loked
vpon him, he went him as swiþe befor þe juge and bisouȝt him þat he

4 ne (1)] *partly eras.*   7 truliche] trulihche, *alt.*   14 stede] hows *on eras, l.h.*   19 nas]
was *alt., l.h.*   22 damnacioun] dmnacioun *alt. to* damnacioun.   32 ne] *eras.,* & þu-
ins., *l.h;*   hastow] *partly eras.*   33 nomore] nomare *alt. to* nomore.

Ke Estefne rendist sun seruise;
Les seinz enprie, par amur,
K'il enprient lur seignur.
E il si funt escordrement,
3415 E li iuges a els s'asent;
Pur Seint Proiect le releisat
E a sun cors le remenat
Par si k'amendast uers la gent
E uers Cecilie numeement.
3420 Quant Estefne ert reuenuz
E de la mort ert reuescuz,
A Sainte Cecilie manais
Rendit le son od grant acrais,
E puis uesqui bien lungement
3425 Si s'aquita uers tute gent.
Mais li pincers tut dis parait

Ke Seinte Cecilie li out fait.
Par cest essample est parisant
Ke Deus est de eglise garant,
3430 E l'um ne deit pas pur un seint
Estre uers altres faus ne feint,
E ke li seint grucent grantment
Quant nuls mortels uers els mesprent,
E k'il poent estre sour
3435 Ki en cest mund lur fait honur,
E ki li seint se uengerunt
De cels ki musters mesferunt.
Deus nus doint ses seinz si seruir
E sainte eglise meintenir
3440 Ke nus puissum a li uenir
E od ses seinz sanz fin ioir.   Amen

schuld ȝelde him his seruise þat he hadde serued him and bisouȝt þe holi
halwen þat þai schuld beseche her lord. And þai dede so wiþ gode wille
and þe juge acente to hem; for þe loue of Seynt Proiecte, he forȝaf it him
& sent þe soule aȝen to þe body in þat maner þat he amended him aȝenes
5    alle men and aȝen Cecile also. Whan Steuen was comen aȝen to liue, he
amended þat he had don aȝen Seynt Cecile and aȝenes alle men and liued
þarafter longe. And þe pynchyng þat Seynt Cecile hadde pynched him
greued him alway.

Be þis ensaumple it semeþ þat God is warant of holi chirche. And
10   þarfor ne schuld noman, þouȝ he serue o seynt, trespas aȝenes anoþer. [f.
22ʳ] And þerbi may men wite þat þe seyntes be wroþe whan þat man
trespas aȝeines hem, and þat þai mowe bi siker, þat who þat doþe hem
worschipe in þis world, þat þe seyntes wil ȝelde it hem. God graunte vs
so þe seyntes for to serue and mayntenen holi cherche þat we may comen
15   to þe blisse of heuen and dwelle wiþ his seyntes wiþouten ende. Amen.

1 ȝelde] *alt. by H.*   2 þai] þat, *partly eras;*  wiþ] wo *eras.* wiþ.

# DOMINICA V POST EPIPHANIAM

En cest contemple Iesu Crist
As sons ceste semblance dist,
As apostles dist ceste parable.
3445 Li regnes del ciel est semblable
Al home ki sun champ semat
E bon semail i getat.
E quant dormirent li guardein
Sis enemis i mist sa main,
3450 Es furmenz naele semat
E malueis grein si s'en alat.
Quant l'erbe crut e fructiza
E la naele se mustra
Dunc uindrent li serf al seignur
3455 Si li distrent tut par amur:
'Ne semas tu semaille bele?
E dunt ad ele dunc naele?'
Cil lur dist tost entreshait:
'Mis enemis ad co fait'.
3460 E li sergant li distrent lores:
'Volez que nus le cuillum hors?'
E il lur dist: 'Nun frez, cheles!
Kar si vus cuillez les naeles
Par auenture esracirez
3465 Ensemblementes od els les blez.
    /f. 78ʳ
Leissez les crestre ensemblement

E al messun dirrai ma gent:
"La naele primes cuillez
E en fesselez les liez;
3470 La naele lie ardez,
Le ble en ma grange assemblez."'
    Entendez a ceste lescun
Vus ki amez Deu e raisun.
Sachez ki bien l'entenderat
3475 E bien la siut, bor le uerrat;
Kar poi u nient ualt l'escuter
A li ki bien ne uolt ouerer.
Parable est signifiance
V l'um deit mettre entendance,
3480 Kar ia parole n'ert apert
Si ele ne seit par bel vuert.
Plus ke li nuels ert ueuz
Dunt li teste n'est primes frussuz.
Deus deignat mesmes cest espundre
3485 Pur nus aider e els confundre
Ki ne se uolent entremettre
De rien entendre fors la lettre.
Le semeur est Iesu Crist;
Sa semence, les biens k'il fist.
3490 Sun champ est tute seinte eglise
Ki par tut le mund est assise.

# SERMON 10
## DOMINICA QUINTA POST EPYPHANIAM

*Secundum Matheum. Simile est regnum celorum.*

Ihesus Crist saied to his deciples: 'Þe kyngdom of heuen is likened to aman þat sewe his sede in þe feld and sewe þer on gode whete. Whan þe keper slepe, his enemy comeþ & soweþ þeron kokel abouen his whete
5 and went þennes. And whan þe corn wex, þanne come vp among þe whete kokel. Þan come þe lordes seruaunt and seid to him: "Ne sewe þou nouȝt god whete? How is it þat þar comeþ vp kokel?". And he seid to hem also sone: "Myn enemy haþ do þat". And his seruauntes seid þan vnto þe lord: "Wil ȝe þat we gader it out?". And he seid vnto hem: "Ȝe ne
10 schul nouȝt; for ȝif ȝe pulled vp þe kokel, so miȝt falle ȝe schuld pulle vp þe corne. Lete hem waxe togiders, and at heruest Y schal say to my men þat þai schul gader ferst þe kokel and bynden it on knottes and kast it in to fur to brennen, and bryng hom þe whete into my berne."'

Understondeþ now to þis my lessoun, ȝe þat louen God & skil &
15 resoun, what þat it is to menen. For wite ȝe wel, he þat vnderstondeþ it wel & doþ þerafter, it wil profite him gretliche, for litel oþer nouȝt is it worþe to heren it þat nel nouȝt werchen þarafter. For wordes beþ ordined for þat men schul ȝeuen vnderstondyng þerto & vnderstondyng ne comeþ no gode of bot ȝif it be don in werk to Godes werschipe. Ne men may
20 neuer se þe kernel of þe note bot ȝif þe schelle be broken first; na more may Godes word ben vnderstonden bote it be openlich opened to mennes vnderstondyng. And þerfor Ihesus Cris[t him] seluen wold vn[do] þis & open it a[riȝt] to our vnder[ston]dinge for to helpen vs & confounden his enemys and our þat ne wil noþing ȝeue hem to bote to vnderstonde þe
25 letter. Þe sede is Ihesu Crist and his wordes and his werkes þat he spak & dede; & his feld is holi chirche þat ben alle gode cristen men, þat is sett

---

3 sewe (1)] *alt.;* sewe (2)] *alt.;* þer] *alt.;* whete] sede *canc.* whete. 4 comeþ] *alt. to* came; &] yn to hes fyld of whet, *ins.* &, *l.h.* 12 þai] *alt.;* kokel] corn *canc.* kokel; kast it] *ins. by H.* 13 to] and *canc.* to *ins. by H.* 14 þis] *ins. by H, then eras.;* god] gode, *alt.;* & (1)] *ins.* 15 menen] *alt. to* mene, *l.h.;* he] ȝe *canc.* he *ins., both eras.* 16 &] *ins. by H;* doþ] *alt. to* doþ, *probably by H;* him] *alt.* 17 werchen] -en *eras.* 18 ne] *eras.* 20 note] notte *alt.* 22 and] *eras.* 22-23 þerfor ... vnderstondinge] *ins. by H; trim.* 23 his] *on eras.* 24 ne] *eras.* 26 feld] *on eras.*

Sis enemis est li malfez,
E sa semaille, iniquitez.
Li Deu sergant e li messur
3495 Li angle sunt e li doctur.
Li messuns est ueraiement
De cest mund le definement.
Li feus u la naele est mise
Demustre l'enfernale iuise.
3500 La grange u li furment est mis
Mustre le celestien pays.
Pur co trop par est desue
Ki siut diable e guerpist De.
Deus est al home cum a destre
3505 E li malfez cum a senestre.
Li home estet cum entre dous;
Chascuns li dist ses auols.
Deus li cumande tus biens faire
E de tuz mals sun quor retraire;
3510 Par sei e par ses menestrals
Li cumande laisser tuz mals,
Viuere en almone, en charite,
En iunes, en humilite,
En uraisuns, en chastete,
3515 En suffrance, en lealte,
En bien uoleir, en uerite,
En pais, en bienfaiz, en bunte,
En tuz les biens ke Iesus dist,

Co est le grein k'en nus mist;
3520 La semence est quant k'il fist
Kar unkes de rien ne mesprist.
  Mais quant li home ad co oi,
Mult tost l'ad mis en ubli;
Tost l'ublie quant est turnez
3525 E sis doctur est aloignez.
Si li doctur dort en peeresce,
Ke par sermun les mals n'adresce,
Dunc est li malfez a senestre
Ki desfait tut k'out fait li prestre;
3530 Ke par sei, ke par mal cunseil,
Tost ad tresturne le fedel.
Kar chascun home ki mal fait
E altre entice al mal u trait,
Sachez de fi, sanz mot de fable,
3535 K'il est menbre al uif diable.
E quant ne pot par sei ouerer
Par altres fait le mal semer,
Par les puruers, par les ypocritis,
E par les sudiuanz herites,
3540 Par baciners, par enchanturs,
Par les feluns nigromancurs.
Quant par cels ne fait sun esplait
Les suns les rotuenges fait;
Des estoires fait les chancuns
3545 Pur anentir les Deu sermuns.

þurth alle þe world; is enemys is þe fend & al þat folowen his lore; and
his sede is wykkednes þat is þe kokel.

Goddes seruauntes ben þe angels and þe techers of þe lawe. Be þe
heruest is bitokened þe endyng of þe world. Þe fur þar þe kokel is laide
5  betokeneþ þe pyne of helle, and þe berne þer þe whete is laid betokeneþ
þe blisse of heuen. Þarfor he is vilich desceyued þat foloweþ þe fende
and forsakeþ God. God is vnto ma[n] als a[t] [f. 22ᵛ] riȝt half, and þe fend
at þe left half; þe man & þe woman betwexen þis to ben sett, & aiþer of
hem saiþ her avis. God biddeþ him do alle god dedes and wiþdrawe his
10  herte fram euels. Þus he biddeþ and alle his and liue in almus and in
charite & in fastyng and in lowenesse and in besechynges and in chastite
and in suffraunce and in treweþ and in god wille and in soþnesse & in pes
and in godenesse. And alle þe godes þat God biddeþ vs don is his sede;
þat is bitokened bi þe whete and biddeþ þat we schal folowen him, for he
15  ne mysdede neuer.

Ac whan man oþer woman haþ herd þis and vnderstondeþ it wel, sone
he forȝeteþ it whan he is turned away fro his techer. And ȝif þe techer
slepe in sleweþ þat he ne dresse nouȝt þe euel þourȝ techyng, þan is þe
fend at þe left half and fordoþ alle þat þe prest dede. What þurth
20  himseluen & what þurth euel counsail of þe fend oþer of his lemes, he
chaungeþ alle þe gode sede into euel. For ich man þat euel doþ oþer
entiseþ oþer and draweþ hem to euel, wite ȝe for soþe, wiþouten any
fable he is on of þe fendes lemes. For whan þe fend ne may nouȝt com
wiþinne a man for to sowen his sede, he soweþ þurth oþer þat liuen in
25  wicked liif aȝenes Godes lawe, and þurth ypocrites þat doþ gode dedes as
ȝif it semed gode to þe world, ac her hertes ar sett in euel. And he ne may
nouȝt comen to fulfille his euel bot þurth coloryng of gode dedes. And
God seiþ: 'For her hertes arne euel ysett, al her gode dedes ben euel', for
as muchel as þai don her euel dedes priuilich þurth hideyng of her gode
30  dedes and also þurth priuy heretikes.

Þe fend wercheþ, þurth baudestrotes and þurth charmers and þurth þe
wicked nigramaunciens. And he may nouȝt [þurth] hem; he doþ it þurth
trowauntes þat maken songes of stories for to lett Goddes werkes, and

---

2 his sede is] *ins. by H;* þat] *ins. by H;* þe] *ins. by H.*  4 þe (3)] & *ins.* þe, *l.h.;* fur]
fyr *alt., l.h.*  5 þe (2)] *eras. and alt.*  6 he] it *canc.* he *ins. by H;* vilich] *partly eras.*
7 is ... at] is lyknyd to stand yn þe *on eras., l.h.;* and] of men & wemen *ins. and l.h.*
8 betwexen] *partly eras.*  9 saiþ] *alt.;* him] hem *alt. to* him.  13 don] *partly eras.;*
is] *ins.;* his] *alt.*  14 is] *ins., then eras.;* bitokened] *alt.;* bi] *ins.*  18 dresse] adresse,
*alt.*  23 com] *ins. probably by H.*  24 inne] *ins. probably by H.*  29 muchel as] *ins.*
*by H.*  31 charmers] *final* -r *ins.*

Par tant entrent en fol delit
La genz enpernent fol respit
De lur uolentez paremplir
E de parfaire lur desir.    /f. 78ᵛ
3550   Dunc surdent pecchez e enuies,
Cuuerties e tricheries,
Orguilz, ranchurs e pensers leiz,
Homicides e buffeiz,
Auoltries e leccheries,
3555   Larcines, murdres, felunies,
E pariures e feimenties,
E trestutes altres diablies.
Co est la semence al malfe
Ki uolt destrure les blez De.
3560   Li enemis seimet itels greins
Pur les bons furme[n]z faire ueins.
Kar co ke nus diums naele
Ke l'euangelie zizanie apelle.
Plusurs dient de zizanie
3565   Que co est uesce u gargerie.
Ne pe chaler le quel co seit
Kar chascun les furmenz defeit.
Kar la naele en lee s'espant
E les furmenz aoche atant;
3570   La uesce trait ius le furment,
La gargerie ensement.
La naele ki en halt munte
Est li peccheurs ki n'ad hunte,
E quant il pecche par delit
3575   Trestuz les bons praue e despit.
La gargerie e la uesce
Ki les blez trait ius e blesce
Sunt cil ki pecchent en requei

E les altres traient od sei.
3580   Kar li furmenz co sunt li seint
E li mal herbe co sunt li feint.
Li furmenz est le grein Iesu;
Li mal grein a Belzebu.
Mais li un al altre tant resemble
3585   Tant cum il sunt creissant ensemble
Ke nul ne poet bien aparceueir
Ki est li faus, ki est le ueir.
Mais tant cum il ert en peis
E plus se mustre li malueis;
3590   Quant dort li prestres en taisant
E li malueis plus sunt nuisant.
Quant li mal n'unt chastiement
Ne li bon n'unt guarnissement
Tost unt li fel les bons atrait
3595   Par le malfe ki tut deceit.
Pur co deit li doctur ueiller
Par uraisuns, par sermuner,
Kar si il par peresce dort
Sei e les sons met a la mort.
3600   E tant cum meins poet entercer,
Plus deit le sermun rehercer.
Kar nul n'en ad discreciun
Ki seit produm ne ki felun,
Nul fors Deu ki trestut ueit
3605   E tut cunust quantk'il ad feit.
Pur co dist a ses serfs: 'Lassez
La male herbe, pas n'enracerez;
Kar trop freiez grant ennui
Al furmenz qui creist iuste lui'.
3610      Ici poum nus bien aprendre
Cument deuum le ciel entendre

þurth þat folk fallen into foule delite, and þurth þat men setteþ her willes
in folies to fulfille her desire. Þan wexen synnes and gret vices, couaites
and lecherie, and many maner of trecheries and giles, pride and þefte and
manslauȝt and foule þouȝtes and auoutries, ȝelpyngges and lesynges and
5    many oþer diuers deuelries.

Þis is þe sede of þe fende þat wil destrue Godes sede, and þe fend
soweþ swiche sedes for to fordo gode whete. Þat Y clepe kokel, þe
godesspelle clepeþ zizannie & sum meysters saiþ þat it is veches oþer
lentils. It is no force þerof whiche it is, for echon of þes fordoþ þe whete.
10   For þe kokel riseþ on heiȝe and fordoþ þe whete and þe feches & þe
lentiles drawen adoun þe corn. Þe kokel þat wexeþ on heiȝ is þe synner
and ne haþ no schame of his synne. Whan he deliteþ him in synne, he
leteþ nouȝt be þe gode, bot he haþ despit of hem. Be þe feches and þe
lentiles ben þai [f. 23ʳ] [vnderstonden] þat synne in pryuyte and draweþ
15   oþer to hem. For bi þe whete is bitokened þe holi men, and þe wycked
sede, þat is þe wicked man. Þe whete is Ihesu Crist is sede and þe kokel
is Belsabub is sede. Ac þat on and þat oþer wexen togider, and ȝif men
pulled þat on fram þat oþer man miȝt distriue þat on wiþ þat oþer. So doþ
þe gode man and þe wicked; & ȝif God toke awai þe wicked fro þe gode,
20   þe gode miȝt falle liȝtlich into synne þurth wel late of hemseluen & þan
miȝt þai nouȝt erne bot litel mede for to haue any blisse in heuen. Þe
more þat a gode man wold ben in pes, þe more is þe wycked aboute to
greuen him, and þe more þat a prest heldeþ him stille, þe more is þe fend
doand harme. Whan þe wikke haþ no chastisynge ne þe gode no
25   techynge, sone þan han þe wicked drawen doun þe gode vnto hem þurth
þe fend þat alle deceyueþ. Forþi schuld þe prest waken þurth orisouns
and þurth prechynges, for ȝif he slepe þurth slouþ of himseluen and þai
þat ben vnder him he slepe. And þe more þat þe wickednesse is, þe mor
þe prest schal prechen. For noman ne mai riȝt soþelich wite which schal
30   be chosen ne which schal be damned, non bote God þat alle seȝþe & al
knows þat he haþ made. Forþi he seid to his seruauntes: 'Letteþ be and ne
pulle nouȝt vp þe wycked ere for ȝe may don harme to þe whete þat
waxeþ þerbi'. Þurth þis lessoun we mai vnderstonde how we schul abide

---

4 auoutries] *ins. by H.*   5 deuelries] *ins. by H.*   7 þat … kokel] þat (..) y clepe(.)
kokel.   8 zizannie] *on eras.;* saiþ] *ins. by H.*   9 þerof] þer *ins. probably by H.*   12
his] -is *on eras.;* deliteþ] *alt., probably by H.*   16 crist is] cristes *alt.*   17 belsabub is]
belsabubes *alt.*   18 on] on *ins.;* wiþ] wiþ *on eras.*   19 þe (3)] *ins., probably by H.*
21 erne] (.)erne; in] þurth *eras.* in.   24 doand] *canc.* redi to do *ins. l.h.*   26 þi] *ins.,
probably by H.*   29 ne] *canc.;* riȝt] not *ins.* riȝt, *probably by H.*   31 þi] þo *alt.;*
letteþ] *partly eras.*   31 ne] *canc.*   32 ere] sede *ins.* ere, *l.h.*

Dunt Iesus dist iceste parable;
Co est eglise, tut sanz fable,
Kar el regne del ciel amunt
3615 N'ad nul fors cil ki beneit sunt.
Mais en cest ciel ci aual,
Co est eglise comunal,
Sunt li malueis, sunt li beneit,
Mais lur afferes sul Deu ueit.
3620 Il ne uolt pas ke home esrace
Les malueis k'as bons mal ne face,
Kar si li fel sunt fors gete
Cument serrunt li bon proue?
Pur co dist bien Dan Salomun
3625 En une prouerbe de raisun:
'Bon or s'esproue en la furneise
E les seinz homes la malaise'.
Ne poet la grace Crist merir
Ki les malueis ne poet suffrir;
3630 Kar cil ke est hui peccheur
Demain purrat estre meillur.
E si li fel sunt hors bute
Li bon en serrunt moleste     /f. 79ʳ
Pur cumpaignie u parente,
3635 Pur seruise u pur amiste.
Kar li seint pleint mult tendrement
Le fel e sur tut sun parent,
E tost purra par tel tendrur
Li seinz hom entrer en folur
3640 Si auerat perdu la racine
De charite ke tant est fine.
Icest essample n'est pas dit
De cels ki pecchent par delit,
Ki pecchent tut vuertement
3645 E ne redutent Deu ne gent.
Cil deiuent estre esrace

E del regne d'eglise chace
Desque il facent amendement
E repe[n]tent sei vuertement.
3650 Kar cil ki pecchent en requei,
Tut traient il altres od sei,
Ne deiuent estre fors bute
Ne de comune desrute
Ke li bon ne seient malmis
3655 Quant il perdent lur amis;
Kar quant li fel plus espurune
Li biensuffrant plus se curune.
Ensemble les uolt Deus auer
Deske lur fruit puisse parer,
3660 Deske paruenge li messun,
Co est del mund la fineisun.
Kar li fruiz signefie l'oure
Ke chascun home uers Deu se
     descoure,
Kar chascun home auerat le fruit
3665 Sulum l'oueraigne u s'est deduit.
Ki diable siut e sa semaille
El feu d'enfern irrat sanz faille.
Ki fait ke Ihesus seme ad
En la grange del ciel irrat.
3670 Siuez seignurs les diz al prestre
K'en cele grange puissez estre;
Tenez vus a la destre main
V Iesus est ami certein.
De la senestre vus turnez
3675 V vus aguaite li malfez.
L'amur del mund est la senestre
Ki tuz les sons trait a mal estre;
La destre est la Deu amur
V il nus mette sanz clamur.

to comen into heuen, wharbi Ihesu seid þis ensaumple þat is holi chirche
wiþouten fable. For in þe kyngdom of heuen aboue ne beþ non bot gode,
ac in þis heuene her bineþe þer beþ comunelich boþe wike and gode, ac
her werkes, onlich God seþ. He ne wil nouȝt þat men don awai þe euel
5    for þat men schuld nouȝt don harme to þe gode. For ȝif þe wicked were
casten out, how schuld þe gode ben proued? For so saiþ Salemon: 'Þe
ouen proueþ þe gold and þe holi suffreþ þe myseis'. He ne mai nouȝt
haue þe grace of God þat ne mai nouȝt suffre þe wicked men & wymmen
bi him, for he þat is todai synful, to morowe mai ben amended. And ȝif
10   wik wer put out, þe gode had harme for felauschip or þurth kynrede oþer
þurth seruise oþer þurth loue; for þe holi men pleynen ful tenderlich þe
wicked and alle his kynde, and sone miȝt an holi man þurth swiche a
tendrour miȝt falle into harme and into hertynge of soule and lese
þarþurth þe rote of charite þat is so gode. Þis is nouȝt said to hem þat
15   synnen þurth delite, þat synnen openlich so þat þai ne douten God ne
man; for þis schuld be don out of þe comune puple of holi cherche vntil
þai had made amendment and repenten hem openliche. Ac hii þat synnen
priuiliche, þeiȝ al þai drawe oþer vnto hem, þai ne schul nouȝt ben put
out of þe [f. 23ᵛ] comune þat þe gode ne be nouȝt harmed þarþurth whan
20   þat þai lesen her fole frendes; for þe more harme þat þe synful man doþ
to þe gode, þe ofter he gildeþ his croune, ȝif þat he it take in paciencie.
And þerfor, God wil haue hem togider til þat her frut mai be sen of her
werkes, boþe gode and euel, vntil þat heruest come, þat is, þe endyng of
þis world. His frut bitokeneþ his werkes þat euerich man schal bryng forþ
25   tofore God, for ech man schal haue his werkes redy þat he haþ don here.
Þo þat folowen þe deuel and his sede, þai schul go to þe fur of helle wiþ
þe fend, and þo þat han folowed Ihesu Crist and his sede, he schal entre
into þe blisse þat is in heuene. Kepeþ, lordynges, þe wordes of þe prest
þat ȝe mai be in þat goyng; holdeþ ȝou on þe riȝt side þar Ihesus is our
30   certayn frende, and kepeþ ȝou from þe left half þar þat þe fende wayteþ
ȝou. Þe loue of þis world al is at þe left half þat draweþ alle his to euel
endyng; þe riȝt half, þat is, loue of God, þat he vs graunt ȝif it be his
wille. Amen.

---

2 þe] *ins., probably by H;* ne] *eras.*   3 heuene] *canc.* warryll *ins. l.h.*   8 ne] *eras.*   10
wik] *alt. to* wiked, *l.h.;* gode] *ins., probably by H.*   16 cherche] *partly on eras.*   18
al] *eras.*   19 þat] *canc.,* people for *ins. l.h.*   19-20 whan … frendes] *canc.*

# DOMINICA IN SEPTUAGESIMA

3680  En cel contemple Iesu Crist
      As sons icest parable dist:
      'Le regne del ciel semblant trait
      De un riche home ki estait,
      Ki issit par matin luer
3685  Vuerurs en sa uigne a vuerer.
      Al iur dener lur couenancat;
      En sa uigne les enueiat.
      Al ure de terce puis issit
      E altres usdifs ester i uit
3690  Einz el marche. Dist lur li ber:
      "Alez vus en ma uigne vuerer
      E co ke dreiz est io vus durrai."
      Il i alerent sanz delai.
      Entur midi e nune issi
3695  E dunc refist il altresi.
      Entur l'unzime ure alat
      E altres estanz i trouat.
      Il lur dist: "Que esteez vus
      Ici trestut cest iur oisus?" /f. 79$^v$
3700  Il dient: "Nul ne nus ad luez."
      Il respunt: "En ma uigne alez."
      E quant li uespres uint auant
      Li sires dist a sun sergant:
      "Apellez tuz ces ouerers
3705  Si lur rendez tost lur luers;
      Mais comencez tut as dereins
      Si finerez as premereins."
      Cil ki uindrent al vnzime ure
      Pristrent lur dener sanz demure.
3710  Li premer uindrent tut ioius

      Kar bien quiderent prendre plus;
      Mais ne recurent tant ne quant
      Fors sul le dener del cuuenant.
      E grundillouent en pernant
3715  Vers le riche home ensi disant:
      "Cil derein unt un ure fait
      E pers a nus les auez fait
      Ki portames le fes del iur
      E vue[ra]mes en la chalur."
3720  E il a un d'els respundi:
      "Io ne te faz nul tort ami;
      Dun n'est un dener tun couenant?
      Pren co k'est ton si ua auant;
      Io uoil duner a cest derein
3725  Sicum a tut le premerein.
      Ne me leist faire co ke io uoil?
      Pur ma bunte fel est tun oil.
      Si serrunt premer li derein
      E li derein tut premerein.
3730  Mult sunt apellez, poi eslu'.
      Craiez le bien; co dist Iesu.
        Cist husbonde est Iesu Crist
      Ki tut guuerne quanque il fist.
      Il guuerne terre e ciel
3735  Cum fait li prudum sun ostel.
      Il ad sa uigne, seinte eglise,
      Qui par tut le mund est assise,
      Ki de Seint Abel cumencat
      E vnkes de creistre ne cessat;
3740  Ne iames ne purrat finir
      Desque al derein k'il deit uenir;

# SERMON 11
## DOMINICA IN SEPTUAGESIME

*Secundum Matheum. Dixit Ihesus discipulis suis: simile est regnum celorum.*

'Þe kyngdom of heuen is liche to a man þat arose vp in þe morowenwhile and hired men for to werchen in his vineʒerde & made kouenont wiþ hem
5 of o peny on þe day and sent hem into his vinʒerde. And at þe vnderne he went out and also he hired men and sent [hem] into his ʒerd, and saiþ: "Þat riʒt is Y schal ʒif ʒou". And at midday and at non he dede also, and at þe eleuenþe hour of þe day, þat is, euesong time, he dede also; he fonde men stondyng idel and said vnto hem, "Whi stonde ʒe her alday
10 ydel?", And þei said: "Noman ne hered vs". And he bad hem go into his vinʒerd. And whan it was euen, þe lord seid to his seruant: "Clepe al þe werchers and ʒif hem her seruise; ac bigynne at þe last and ende at þe ferst". And þai þat comen at þe eleuenþe hour toke her peny and wente forþ. Þe ferst weren glade, for þay þouʒten wel þat þai schuld han mor;
15 and þai ne toke noyþer more ne lasse, bot þe peny þat was her couenaunt. And þai grochedhen & toke it aʒen & said to þe riche man: "Þes þat come last han as muchel as we þat han trauailed alday and wrouʒt in þe hete". And þe lord answerd to hem: "Y ne do þe no wrong my frend. Nis a peny þi couenaunt? Take þat þyn is & go forþ, for Y wil
20 ʒif to þes last als muchel as to þe first. And whi ne mai Y nouʒt do als Y wil? For my godenesse ich it wil ʒeuen. Þus schal þe last be þe ferst and þe ferst þe last; many ben ycleped and few ben ychosen."' Leueþ þis wel for þus saiþ Ihesu.

Ihesus Crist is þe housbonde þat gouerneþ and kepeþ alle þat he made,
25 þat gouerneþ heuen [f. 24ʳ] and þe erþe also þe gode housbonde doþ his hous. He haþ his vyn, holi cherche, þat is sprad ouer al þe world, þat began at Abel for to wexen and euer siþe haþ don, more and more. And it ne schal neuer ende or þe laste man þat schal ben saued, þat is, þe laste

---

3 morowenwhile] *partly eras.*  6 hem] *om.;*  ʒerd] *alt. to* vinʒerde.  7 at (1)] *ins.*  8 eleuenþe] euenþe *alt. to* eleuenþe.  10 bad] b(.)ad.  13 eleuenþe] euenþe *alt. to* eleuenþe.  18 ne] *eras.*  19 frend] *ins.* H;  nis] nis *alt. to* is;  a] noʒt *ins.* a;  þyn] ys *ins.* þyn, *l.h.;*  is] *canc.*  20 ne] *eras.*  21 þus] as me list *ins.* þus, *l.h.*  25 doþ] *canc.* 28 or þe] *on eras.*

Desque al derein seint ki uendrat
Seinte eglise ne finerat;
Mais tant cum ele seinz auerat
3745  Alsi cum tant rains geterat.
Pur ceste uigne cultiuer
Ne cesse il luiz enueier;
Par diuers tens les enueiat,
A chascun un dener donat.
3750  Li matins de Adam comencat
E deske al tens Noe durat.
Co fut matin ueiraiement
Kar del mund ert cumencement.
E terce fu de Dan Noe
3755  Desque Abraam, le fiz Thare.
Li midis de Abraam s'estent
Desqu'al prophete Moysent.
La nune, seignurs, se estent
Iesqu'al Iesu aduenement.
3760  E l'ure unzime se destent
De cest mund desk'al finement.
En chascun tens Deus enueiat
Alcun ki en sa uigne vuerat,
Les patriarches e lur peres,
3765  Les seinz prophetes e lur freres,
Les ducs, les reis k'il meintint,
E enpres els il mesmes uint.
E les apostles i enueiat
E par els sa uigne mundat,
3770  Par ki il getat meint bon raim,
Co sunt li seint de grace plain.
Mais cil ki plus tart i vuererent
Plus tost lur luer receurent.
Kar plus tost uint li lere a De
3775  Ke ne fist Abel u Noe;
Li leres ki pendit en croiz,
Quant il oit la Iesu uoiz:

'Hui ers od mei en parais'.
Vncore fust Abel esquis
3780  Kar puis le mesfait Dan Adam,
Ki tut le munde mist en han,
Vnkes nul home el ciel entrat
Desque Iesu de mort leuat.  /f. 80$^r$
Dunc entrerent od li si dru
3785  Ki depres l'orent cunu,
E apres els la seinte gent,
Tut cil des le comencement.
Co est li deners k'il pristrent
Ke tut en glorie od li mistrent;
3790  Tuz sunt en une glorie uif,
Li nuuel seint e li antif.
Mais co qu'espealt k'il grucerent
Quant pristrent meins ke ne quiderent?
Kar el ciel n'auerat iammes gruz,
3795  Ne nul grundille, ne nul curuz.
Trestut ico grundillement
Demustre lur tres grant talent,
Le grant desir de uer Crist
K'il orent ainz k'il uenist.
3800  Dunt il diseient mult suuent
En lur preieres tendrement:
'Enuei nus, Deus, le salueur
Ki nus iette de tenebrur
E nus mette en sa luiur
3805  Hors de cest exil e de cest plur
Si ueirs cum vus l'auez pramis.
Visez vos freres e uos amis'.
Itel esteit lur grundiller,
Nient d'altri honur grucer;
3810  Kar chascun ki el ciel uendrat
D'altri honur s'esioirat.
E co ke respunt li sire

holi man þat schal be saued. Ne schal neuer holi cherche enden, and þe
mo holi men þat þer wexen, þe mo braunches þe vyn kesteþ. For to tilen
þis vyne, Ihesus ne leteþ nouȝt to senden þider in werkmen in eche diuers
time, and echon he ȝeueþ a peny.

5    Þe morowenynge began at Adam and þat lasted or þe tyme of Noe. Þat
was þe morowenynge for soþe, for it was þe gynnynge of þe world. And
þan fro Noe vnto Abraham, fro Abraham to Moyses, þat is cleped þe
midday. And fro Moyses to Ihesu Crist, þat is þe elleuenþe oure of þe
day, þat is, euensonge tyme. Þan comeþ Ihesu in þe laste ende þe juge of
10   þe world. And in echon of þes tymes Ihesu sent summe into his vinȝerd
to tilie his vynye — þat were þe patriarckes & here fadres, and þe
prophetes & here breþeren — to hold vp þe lawe of God vnder him, and
tauȝt hem hov þai schuld tilie þe vynye. And þan after hem com Ihesu
Crist himseluen and tauȝt men hov þai schuld tilie þe vyne and sent his
15   apostels for to techen hem hov þat þai schuld tilye þis vyne, þat is,
mannes soule, þurth whiche techeynge his vyne is diȝt and made clene so
þat it kesteþ many gode braunche þat ben þes holi men ful of grace. Ac
þai þat laste comen taken sonnest her hure.

For soner com þe þef to God þan dede Abel oþer Noe, þe þef þat heng
20   bi Ihesu Crist and herd his voice þat said: 'Today þou schalt be wiþ me
in paradis'. For neuer seþ þat Adam had synned ne come non to þe blisse
of heuen or þat tyme þat Ihesu Crist sofferd deþ vpon þe rode and aros
fro deþ to liue. Þan entred alle wiþ him þat wer his frendes, þat had
knowen him biforn þurth riȝt bileue.

25   Þat is þe peny þat hii taken, þat þai wenten alle to blisse wiþ him. Alle
ben in o blisse, þe newe seyntes and þe olde.

Ac þat þai grocheden for þai token lasse þan þai wend to ha taken, how
mai þis be? For in heuen schal be non grochynge ne no wraþ. Al þis iche
grochynge was þe gret desir and þe gret wille for to sen Ihesu Crist þat
30   þai herden [of] or þat he come. Forþi þai seiden oft ful tenderliche in her
praiers: lord God, send vs þe saueour þat schal kast vs out of derkenes
and þat schal sett vs in þe liȝt out of þis valey of wepeynge als wislich as
þou hast beheȝt vs; visite þi seruauntes and þi frendes. Þis was her
grochynge; oþer grochynge had þai non. For echon þat schal com to
35   heuen [f. 24$^v$] of oþers ioy schal joisen and gladen. And þat þe lord

2 mo (2)] mo *ins.;* kesteþ for] *on eras.*   3 vyne] *alt.*   5 þat] and (.) þat; or] *on eras.*
7 fro (1)] *alt. to* from; fro (2)] *alt. to* from.   8 fro] *alt. to* from.   11 tilie] *alt.*   13
tilie] *alt.*   14 tilie] *alt.*   16 whiche techeynge] *transp.*   19 þan] þat hong on þe rygt
hond of þe cros *ins.* þan *l.h.*   23 fro] *alt. to* from.   27 þat þai] þai þat *alt.;* lasse] litel
*canc.* lasse; wend] *alt.;* ha] haue *alt.*   30 of] *om.*   35 schal] hii *ins.* schal; joisen]
rejoisen *alt., l.h.;* gladen] be *ins.* gladen *l.h.*

Si durementes cum par ire,
Co ne fut pas curucement,
3815  Einz fud tres bon chastiement
Ke nul ne se uante de rien
Tut ait il lunges serui bien.
En poi de tens, par raisun,
Prent bon seruise guerdun.
3820  Suuent auent ke li dereins
Fait mielz ke tut li primereins;
E sul Iesu, ki les quors ueit,
Set ki ad mielz e ki meins fait.
E l'em redit k'en poi d'ure,
3825  Sicum li plaist, Deu labure.
Pur co finat issi Iesu:
'Mult sunt apellez, poi eslu'.
Mais ore entendum cument
Icest essample a nus apent.
3830  Par cinc ures ki sunt numez
Sunt nos cinc eages mustrez.
Li matin mustre l'enfantage
E terce signefie ualetage;
Midi demustre la iuuente;
3835  Nune home parfit presente;
L'unzime ure ueillesce fait
Ki al uespre de mort se trait.
En chascun point de ces eages
Ad Deus alcun gete de rages;
3840  En chascun ad sa grace mise
Pur la uigne de sainte eglise.
Kar cil ki est en boen enfance
En seinte eglise Deu l'auance,
E ki en enfance riens mesprent
3845  Si en uallettage uels s'ament,

A Deu se purrat amender
E seinte eglise enluminer.
E ki en ces dous mesfait
Si en sa iuuente se retrait,
3850  Vers Deu se purrat amender
E sainte eglise auancer.
E ki en ces treis mesprent
En sa homesce uels s'amend,
Kar cum plus ert sains e forz
3855  Plus tost poet amender ses torz,
E par force e par saueir
Poet a eglise mult ualeir.
Qui en ces quatre fait peresce
Ament sei uels en sa ueillesce;
3860  Vncore adunc pot il aider
E sainte eglise consailler.
E s'il le fait de uolente
Tost auerat sun labur fine;
E ainz auerat il sun dener
3865  Ke li iofnes ki uint premer.
Kar Deus n'esguarde pas le tens
Mais le uoleir e le purpens;   /f. 80ᵛ
Ne prise pas tant lunge penance
Cum quor truble par esperance.
3870  Kar Seint Daui de Deu le dit:
'Quor truble e humble ne despit'.
E Deus par le prophete dist:
'Quel ure ke li fel gemist,
Si il gemist de quor uerrai,
3875  Tuz sez pecchez ublierai'.
Pur Deu, seignurs, faites ke sage,
N'afiez trop en vostre eage,

answerd als it wer þurth wraþþe, ac it was no wraþþe, ac it was a gode
chastisyng þat noman schal auaunten him þouȝ he haue long serued wel.
For in litel tyme, þurth reson, takeþ god seruise ȝeldynge. For ofte it
falleþ þat þe laste doþ better þan þe ferst. And namelich Ihesus, þat wote
5  alle hertes, wot who doþ best & moste and who lest. And men sayen also:
'In litel tyme God wercheþ'. Forþi ended Ihesu in þis maner in þis
lessoun: many ben cleped and fewe ben chosen.

Ac vnderstonde we how þis lesson is said by vs. By þe fyue oures ben
oure fyue eldes schewed. Þe morowenynge scheweþ our childhode and
10  þe þridde oure betokeneþ þe eld fram childhede vntil he come to state of
ȝonge man; midday betokeneþ mannes state, euesong tyme bitokeneþ þe
eld fro manhed to endynge of þe liif. In ech of þes eldes haþ God cast out
sum of his synnes, and in echon he sent his grace for to tilie þe vyne, þat
is, holi cherche. For he þat is gode in his childhede, in holi cherche God
15  auaunceþ him; and þat misdoþ in his childhode, in þat oþer eld he may
amenden him and acorden wiþ God and aliȝten holi cherche. And who
þat in þes two misdoþ, in þredde eld he mai amenden him and auauncen
holi cherche; and he þat in þes þre misdoþ, in his manhede he mai
amenden him and sauȝtel wiþ God. For þe strengere and þe better þat he
20  haþ his hele, þe soner he mai amende þe trespas þat he haþ do, and þurth
strengþe and þurth witt, muchel he mai help holi cherche. And he þat in
þes foure misdoþ, in his elde he mai amenden him, and he mai þanne
help to holi cherche for to counsail it wel. And ȝif he amendeþ him wiþ
gode wille, sone he schal haue ended his werk and þan he schal haue his
25  peny sonner þan þe ȝonge child. For God ne lokeþ nouȝt þe tyme, bote þe
wille & þe forþenchynge of þe synne; for God takeþ nouȝt ȝeme to þe
penaunce as he doþ to þe herte þat is trubled and sory for his synne and in
gode bileue. For Seynt Dauid saiþ in þe souter: 'God ne despiseþ nouȝt
þe herte þat is trubled and sory, and meke and milde'. And God saiþ also
30  þurth his prophete: 'What tyme þat þe synful man repenteþ him, ȝif þat
he repenteþ him soþefastliche and wiþ gode wille, alle his synnes he
schal forȝeten'.

For Godes loue, lordynges, affieþ ȝou nouȝt muchel in ȝour eld, comeþ

---

3 takeþ] men *ins.* takeþ *alt.*    8 by (1)] *alt.;*   by (2)] *alt.*    9 eldes schewed] wittes
vnder stonded *canc.* eldes schewed.    10 state] *alt.*    11 state] *alt., possibly H.*    13 þat]
*on eras., possibly by H.*    14 gode] goode *alt.*    15 þat (1)] he *ins.* þat *possibly by H;*
may] many *alt. to* mayy.    17 misdoþ] *alt.;*  þredde] þe *ins.* þredde; mai] may *alt.*
20 þe (2)] (…) þe.    21 he þat] *transp.*    23 amendeþ] amenden *alt.*    26 takeþ] ne *ins.*
takeþ, *possibly by H;*  þe (3)] *alt. to* þer.    31 repenteþ] repenten *alt.*    33 affieþ] *canc.*
be *ins. l.h;*  muchel] obstinat *ins.* muchel *l.h.*

Venez a celi sanz demore
Ki tut receit en chascun ure;
3880 Venez a li en quor uerrai
Ki tuz receit sanz nul delai.
Ici deseruez le dener
Ke vus el ciel prendrez enter;
Deseruez le par uos bienfaiz,
3885 Par amender les trespas laiz.
Li secles est alsi cum en balance,
Fols est ki en li ad fiance,
Fols est ki trop espeire en uie,
Ore est li home, ore n'est il mie.
3890 Li deners ki est tut runt
A bon entente nus sumunt.
Rundesce n'ad definement;
Nul auerat ki a Deu se prent.
Li deners ad furme le rei
3895 E Deus nus furmerat en sei;
En sa furme uerraiement
Si nus fesuns amendement,
En furme de durable glorie
Ki ia nen auerat del mal memorie,
3900 Si laissum la furme del malfe

Ki par mals nus ad desfurme.
De ceste lescun la finaille
Fait a reduter, mult sanz faille.
Mult sunt apellez en cest mund
3905 Mais mult poi rescu en sunt.
Li munz est plains de cristiens
Mais poi en ad ki facent biens.
Apelle sunt en uerite
Tut par nun de cristienete;
3910 Il hunissent le nun de Crist
Quant il ne funt cum Iesu fist.
Iesu ne fist vnkes fors bien
E il ne ferunt nun ia rien.
Gardent ne seient deceu,
3915 Sul apellez, nient ellu.
Pur co nus dist Sein Pol mult bel:
'Guarde', fait il, 'le vostre apel'.
Nostre apel est en charite,
En almone e en uerite,
3920 En tuz bienfaiz, en bon pensers,
Ki rien n'i ait li aduersers.
Deus nus doinst issi guarder
K'il nus deinst rendre sun dener

wiþouten delay to him þat wil receyuen alle þat wil com in ech tyme and
ech our, þat ȝe mai take þe peny, þat is, þat we mai come to þe blisse [f.
25ʳ] of heuen. And deserue we it her þurth gode dedes so þat we mai
amenden our trespas. Þis world is sett as in a weye; a fole he is þat affieþ
5   him þerinne; a fole he is þat trusteþ to muchel to þis liif. Now he is man;
now he nis nouȝt. Þe peny, þat is al rounde, be gode vnderstondynge it
somoneþ vs, for roundehed ne haþ non ende; na more schal he haue ende
þat takeþ him to God. Þe peny haþ þe prent of þe kynge, and God prenteþ
vs after himself, and in his likenes we schul be for soþe ȝif þat we
10  amenden vs her. Þan schul we ben in þe joie þat euer schal last ȝif þat we
lete þe likynges of þe fend þat þurth synne haþ made vs vnliche to Ihesu
and liche to him.

Of þis lessoun þe endynge is muchel to doute. I sai ȝou for soþe,
many, he saiþ, ben cleped of þis world and riȝt fewe ben chosen. Þe
15  world is ful of cristen men and wymmen ac fewe þar beþ þat doþ þe
gode. Þai be cleped cristen men, ac þai schenden Cristes name whan þai
beren it and don nouȝt so as he dede. Ihesus ne dede neuer bote wel, and
þai ne do nouȝt wel. Loke þarfore ech man in himseluen þat he ne be
nouȝt onliche cleped and nouȝt chosen. Forþi seiþ Seynt Poule and
20  warneþ vs ful wel: 'Kepeþ', he saiþ, 'ȝour clepeyng'. Our clepyng is þat
we be in charite to alle men and in soþnesse and in gode dedes and in
þouȝtes, þat þe fend ne come nouȝt wiþinne vs. God graunte vs grace so
for to do þat we mai take our peny, þat is, þe blisse of heuen. Amen.

---

1 ech] *on eras.*   4 affieþ] *canc.* trustyth *ins. l.h.*   5 muchel] muchel (… / ……..).   6
be] ys mane *ins. l.h.*   7 haþ] (…) haþ,   8 haþ] haþ(.).   17 as he dede] *canc.*   18 ne
(2)] he (..) be.   21 gode] gode(.).

# DOMINICA IN SEXAGESIMA

Quant grant turbe fud assemble
3925 E de citez se fust haste,
Il uindrent a Iesu Crist.
Ceste semblance il lur dist:
'Celi s'en issit ki semat
E sa semence bien ietat.
3930 Partie de co k'il sema
Deiuste le chemin ieta
E fut des erranz defule;
Li oiseil del ciel l'unt mange.
Partie sur perre chait
3935 E quant fut nez lores flestrit;
Pur co flestrit ke n'out humur
Pur le caillou ke trop ert dur.
Partie es espines chait
Mais unkes nul bien n'en issit,
3940 Kar l'espine crust od le ble
Si le aueit tanttost aoche.
Partie en bon terrail chait
E cent duble sun fruit rendit'.
Quant Iesus out dist cest respit
3945 Lores escriat en haut petit: /f. 81ʳ
'Ki ad oreilles pur oir
Oid mun dist par grant desir'.
Si diciple demande unt
Cest essample ke espunt.
3950 Il dist: 'A vus est il dune
Sauer le bien del regne De;

As altres en signefiances
K'en oiant aient entendances,
Ke il ueant ne ueient rens
3955 Ne escutant n'entendent biens.
Ceste essample dunt dit vus ai
Issi espealt cum io dirrai.
La semence est la Deu parole,
Li semur est Deus e s'escole.
3960 Lung la ueie co ke chai
Co sunt cil ki unt oi;
Dunc uent li diables ki tost uole
E de lur quor tolt la parole,
Del uerbe Deu tolt remenbrance
3965 K'il ne guarissent par creance.
Co ke sur la perre chait
Sunt cil ki oient par delit;
Quant l'unt oi, grant ioie en funt
Mais ices pas racines n'unt,
3970 Kar il par tens creient en De
E faillent quant il sunt tempte.
Co ke chait en l'espinei
Sunt cil ki oient la Deu lei
E puis si sunt tant curius
3975 E riches e delicius
De ceste uie meintenir
K'il ne poent en Deu teir,
Par tant sunt il si aoche

# SERMON 12
## DOMINICA LX

*Secundum Lucam. Cum turba plurima conuenirent ad Ihesum &cet.*
Whan þe folk wer gaderd togiders and faste hasted out of þe cites and þai
comen to Ihesu Crist and þis ensample he seid to hem: 'On went out and
sewe his sede. And a party of þe sede þat he sewe fel in þe weye & was
5    defoiled vnder mennes fete, & þe briddes comen & eten it. And a party
fel vpon þe ston, & whan it gan to sprynge, it driede as swiþe, for it had
no moystur for þe flynt was so hard. And a party fel amonge þe þornes,
bot no gode come þerof, for þe þorn þat wexeþ amonge þe corn had sone
slokened it. And a party fel in gode erþe, and þat ȝelde an hondredfolde
10   his frut'.
     Whan our lord had said þis word, he cried on heiȝ: 'Listeneþ þat han
eres for to heren þerwiþ, hereþ my word wiþ gret desire'. And whan his
deciples come hom, þai asked him what þis was to say. And he said:
'Vnto ȝou it is ȝeuen for to knowen þe godes of þe kyngdom of heuen.
15   Vnto hem þat heren and vnderstonden nouȝt, [wenen] þat þai sen and ne
se nouȝt, ne lest, ne vnderstondeþ nouȝt, þis ensaumple þat ich haue said
vnto [f. 25ᵛ] ȝou, þus it is vndon.'
     Þe sede is Godes word, and þe sower is God. And his sed þat falleþ in
þe wai, þat ben þai þat han herd it. Whan þai be gon þennes, þan comeþ
20   þe fend and eggeþ hem to lustes and to likynges & binymeþ Godes worde
fram her hertes þat þai ne haue non remembraunce þerof, þat þai ne be
nouȝt saued þurth bileue. Þe sed þat falleþ on þe ston, þat ben þai þat
heren it þurth delite. Whan þai han herd it, þai maken gret joie in hert, ac
it ne haþ no rote, for þai bileuen sumtyme in God and fallen whan þai ben
25   tempted, forþi þai fallen sone. Þe sede þat falleþ in þe þornes ben þai þat
heren wel Godes wordes bot afterward, whan þai comen hom, þai ben so
corious and riche and delicious in þis liif here in þis world þat þai ne
mowe nouȝt holden hem in gode, & þurth þat, þai maken hem so bisy þat

---

9 ȝelde] ȝelde(.).   10 his frut] *on eras.*   12 hereþ] *partly eras.*   14 is] *ins.;* to] *ins.;*
of þe kyngdom] of þe kyngdom *canc.* of þe kyngdom.   15 vnto] in ensample *ins.*
vnto; wenen] *om.*   16 vnderstondeþ] *alt.*   19 han herd] han herd *canc.* no list in *ins.*
*l.h.*   25 þai (1)] þat *alt.;* þe (1)] ys *ins.* þe, *l.h.;* ben] *eras.*   26 bot] *eras.* & *ins.*
27 ne] *eras.*

Ke pur els n'ert ia fruit gete.
3980  Co que chait en bon terral
Co sunt li saint, li bon fedel
Ki uolenters Deu sermun oient
E en bon quor tenent e cloent.
E quant unt oi la sentence
3985  Dunc portent fruit en pacience'.
Deus deignat mesmes cest espundre,
Par co nus uolt il sumundre
Ke nus nus deuum entremetre
D'entendre plus ke dist la lettre.
3990  E si alcuns poet bien espundre
Il ne deit pas sun sens repundre,
Ainz deit tut dire humblement
Pur sei estruire e altre gent.
Mais guard sei chascun de mesprendre
3995  Kar de tut estut raisun rendre.
Mais ki de gloser met sa cure
Laist sun sens pur l'escripture,
Kar si sun sens uoldrat mustrer
Mult i purrat tost mesaler.
4000  Mult estout oir e ueer
Home ki dreit uolt sermuner.
Veez les deciples Iesu
Ki de saueir erent enbu,
Nurri erent de cel saueir
4005  Ki lur mustrat tut pur ueir;
Purquant ne uoldrunt il rien dire
Del sermun ke out dist li sire,
Einz demanderent humblement
E il respunt mult dulcement.
4010  Il respunt pur nus enseigner
Que nus deuum mult tenir cher
Des seinz les exposiciuns
E lur traitiz e lur sermuns.
Kar ki porrat unkes oser
4015  D'espundre riens u de gloser
Si Deus n'oust glose nule riens
Ki set tuz saueirs e tuz bens?
E ki crerrat home mortel

Ki diable semble oisel del ciel,
4020  E k'espine richesce semble
Si Deus n'oust dist tut ensemble?
Purquant si sunt il ueirement
Sicum orrez procheinement.
Mais ore oiez del semeur
4025  Ki tut semat par sa dulcur.
Li semers est Iesu Crist
Ki par dulcur nostre char prist
E semat la nuuele lei
Pur nus renuueler en sei.  /f. 81ᵛ
4030  Kar nus fumes tuz enueilliz
En la uielz lei e en ses diz,
Kar la uielz lei les mals mustrat
Mais unkes nul mal n'amendat
Dekes cil uint ki done l'out
4035  E ki la vueri mot a mot
E mustrat espiritalment
Co ke tenums charnelment,
E trestut paremplit en sei
Quantke faillit en la uielz lei.
4040  Co fut semence e bone e bele
Ki cors e alme renuuele,
La semence de ses diz,
Ses essamples e ses respiz.
Mais tute sa bone parole
4045  Ne chait pas en bon escole.
Partie chait lung l'estree
E par erranz fut defulee.
L'estree mustre ceste uie
Ki est des pensers paremplie;
4050  E ki mult pense uanite
Ne poet tenir la uerbe De,
Kar partant uenent li oisel,
Co sunt li malfe tres ignel,
E tolent la parole De
4055  Par acrestre la uanite.
Les malfez mustrent li oisel
Kar mult sunt leger e ignel,
E li oisel maint en uoid air

þurth hem ne mai come no frut forþ. Þe sede þat falleþ in þe gode erþe,
þat ben þes holi men and wymmen þat setten alle her hertes in God &
wiþ gode wille holden it and bryngeþ furþ frut in paciencie.

God himseluen wold expounden þis for to amonesten vs þat weschul
more vnderstonde þan þe letter saiþ. [And] ech man þat wil expounden
holi writt, mekeliche he owe to ordeyne his speche for to leren himseluen
and techen oþer. Bote eche man kepe him wel þat he ne go nouȝt out of
þe way, for of al he mote ȝeld rekynnynge. And ȝif al he can holi writt
for to schewen his witt, sone he mai mysgon, for euer, wite he, muchel he
mote heren and sen þe man þat schal wel prechen. Lokeþ now to Ihesu
Crist decyples þat wer ful of wysdom, for þai wer norisched of þat
wisdom þat schewed hem alle maner soþenesse. Nouȝt for þanne þai ne
wold noþinge say of þe wordes þat þe lord had said, ac asked mekelich,
and he expounded for to techen vs þat we schuld kepen it derworþilich
þat holi men telle, þe draweynge of holi writt and her sermounes. For
who wolde ben aboute to han expouned any þynge bot ȝif God had
expounded himseluen þe wordes þat he said þat alle wisdom couþe?
What man leuand wold haue trowed þat þe fend wer liche to þe briddes
of heuen, oþer þat oþer, þat þornes wer liche to riches? Nouȝt for þan þa
þouȝ it ben so for soþe, as ȝe schul her afterwarde.

Ac now, hereþ of þe sower. Þe sower is Ihesu Crist þat þurth his grete
godnesse toke our kynde, þat sewe þe newe lawe for to make vs newe in
him. For we wer alle eld in þe eld lawe and in his wordes, for þe old lawe
schewed þe harmes and þe wreche of God. Ac he ne amended non of þe
har[f. 26ʳ]mes or þat he come þat had ȝeuen þe lawe and opened word for
word and schewed it gostlich þat afornhond was schewed bodilich. And
al he fulfilled in himseluen, al þat failed of þe old lawe. Þat was sed fair
and gode þat made body and soule newe aȝen, þe sede of his wordes and
his gode ensaumples. Ac al his gode wordes ne fel nouȝt alle in gode
londe.

A party fel in þe way & was yfouled wiþ goynge. Þe way betokeneþ
þis liif þat is fulfilled of þornes. And who þat muchel þencheþ vanite ne
may nouȝt hold Godes worde, for þurth hem come þe euel þouȝtes þat
ben þe fendes þat ben riȝt swift and don away Godes worde þurth þe
wexeynge of idel wordes and þouȝtes. Bi þe briddes ben bitokened þe
fendes, for þai ben liȝt and swift; & briddes haue her playnge in þe air,

---

3 furþ] furþ (…). 5 and] In. 7 bote eche] *on eras.* 8 al (1)] alle *alt.;* al (2)] *ins.* 11
Crist] Cristes *alt.* 18 liche] likhe *alt.* 20 so] not *ins.* so, *l.h.* 23 eld] old *alt.* 24 ne]
*eras.* 25 or] *on eras.;* had] hadde *alt.* 26 bodilich] *alt.* 28 his] *on eras.* 29 ne]
*eras.* 31 yfouled] *alt.* 32 ne] *eras.*

E li malfe la uolt manair
4060  V il troue le quor uoide
De bienfaiz e de charite;
V il troue le quor uolage
Iloc fait il le son manage.
Pur co, seignurs, vus cristien,
4065  Pur Deu des sermuns pernez le bien,
Ke nes vus toille li maufez
Par pensers de uolagetez.
  La pere sunt li durendal
Kar tant sunt endurci el mal
4070  Ke nul humur de charite
Nes poet amolir enuers De.
Mes quant il oent sermuner
Bel semblant funt de l'amender,
Mais tanttost cum il sunt partiz,
4075  E il reueient lur deliz,
Tut ublient la Deu parole
E reuertent a mal escole.
Atant unt perdu la racine
De la charite diuine.
4080    Les espines co sunt li riches
Ki de bien sunt tenant e chiches.
L'espine la char point e runpt
E richesce l'alme cunfunt.
Richesce point ueir malement
4085  L'alme k'ele tient e susprent
Par cuueitise de amasser,
Par dol de perdre e de laisser,
Ke tut aoche les Deu blez
Par enuie e par auertez.
4090  Quant li riches ot sermuner
E les paroles Deu semer

Il les resceit par bon semblant
Cum fait li blez en sun creissant.
Mais dunc surdent cuueities
4095  E les espines de triccheries,
Les granz orguilz e les rauines.
Co sunt en ueir males espines
Ensemble od els le mal delit
Ki les blez Deu tut descunfit.
4100  Amdui creissent ensemblement,
E l'espinei e le furment,
Kar li riches fait un semblant,
Tut seit il mals, k'il est uaillant.
Mais fin ki proue tute riens
4105  Mustre ses mals, abate ses biens,
E quant sis mals sun bien surmunte
Aochez ert a male hunte.
  La terre bone sunt li seint
Ki unc uer Deu ne furent feint,
4110  Ki oent sermun bonement
E retenent escordrement
E sulum lur bone entendance
Seruent Iesu Crist en suffrance,   /f. 82ʳ
En la suffrance k'il fist
4115  Quant il a mort pur nus se mist.
Kar kikunkes iustise leit
Pur estre murdriz u detreit,
Sachez, bon terrail n'est il mie
Ne sis fruiz ne ualt un alie.
4120  Nel di pas del mundein iustise
Mais de celi ke Iesu prise,
Kar sachez iustise mundein
Deuant Iesu est fals e uein.

and þer is þe wonyng of fendes; þer þat þai fynde þe hert volaious, þar hii
maken her dwellynge. Forþi, lordynges þat ben cristened, holdeþ wel bi
Godes word and kepeþ it derworþilich þat þe fend ne bineme it ȝow
nouȝt þurth þouȝtes & þurth wildnes.

5      Þe stones bitokenen þe dorndales þat ben so harded in þe euel þat no
moystur of charite ne mai neschen her hertes toward God. Ac whan þat
þai heren prechynge, þai maken fair semblaunt as þai wolden amenden
hem, ac as sone as þai ben departed þennes, þai fallen aȝen to her delices
and al forȝeten Godes worde & turnen hem to þe deueles scole, & þurth
10    þat þai lesen þe rote of charite.

      By þes þornes ben bitokened þe riche men and wymmen þat ben
nygardes, þat mai nouȝt dispenden no þinge of her godes bi her liue so
þai ben adrade þat þe world schal failen hem. Þe þorn hirtteþ þe flesche
and tobrekeþ it, and riches confounden þe soule, what þurth couaitise and
15    þurth sorowe in þe gadrynge, what þurth drede in þe holdyng and in þe
lettyng, what þurth enuie þat he seþ oþer han more þan he, so þat in many
maner he slokeneþ Godes sede þat it ne mai brynge forþ no frut. Whan þe
riche hereþ þe prechyng and sowynge of Godes word, he receyueþ hem
wiþ glad semblaunt as doþ þe corn whan it gynneþ to wexen. Ac þan
20    ariseþ couaitise and þe þornes of trecheries and of giles, þe gret prides
and þe ȝiftes, & þes ben for soþe wicked þornes and wiþ [euel delit] þat
þai han wiþ also þat it confoundeþ alle Godes sede. Ac boþ wexen
togider, þe þornes and þe whete, for þe riche makeþ semblaunt of gode
þouȝ al he be euel of wille. Ac þe ende þat scheweþ alle þynges putteþ
25    forþ his euels and doþ away his godes. And whan his euels ben alle
openliche schewed, þan he [f. 26ᵛ] schal be confounded wiþ his owen
turne. Þe gode erþe, þat ben þe holi men & wymmen þat neuer wer feynt
in Godes seruise, þat heren prechyng wiþ gode wille and ben ententiflich
aboute to holden it and do it in werk and wiþ gode suffraunce and
30    þolemodnes seruen God as Ihesu Crist dede þat lete him be don to þe deþ
for vs. Wite ȝe wel, gode erþ is he nouȝt þat loueþ to fordon oþer þurth
destresse for to don riȝt; and for to say þe soþe, wite ȝe wel þat his frut is
litel worþe oþer nouȝt. I ne say nouȝt of worldes riȝtfulnes ne of worldlich wisdom, for al þis is fals and a vanyte þat is idel als afor God. Ac he

---

2 for þi] but ye *on eras.;* bi] *eras.* 3 ne] *eras.;* it] *partly eras.* 6 ne] *eras.* 10 þat]
*on eras.;* þe rote] *ins. H.* 11 by] *alt.* 12 nouȝt] nouȝt (......); so] so (.). 13 failen]
*partly eras.* 14 tobrekeþ] *partly eras.* 17 godes] or dystroyth *ins.* godes, *l.h.* 21
euel delit] medlet. 23 riche] *ins. H.* 24 þouȝ] *alt.* 30 þolemodnes] *partly eras.;*
him] *alt. to* himsylf *l.h.* 31 fordon] hurt or *ins.* fordon *l.h.* 33 ne (1)] *eras.*

Mais ki tut poet pur Deu suffrir
4125 Grant fruit en auerat sanz mentir;
Co est li fruiz ki ia ne fine
El ciel ke Deus as sons destine.

Iesus le conquist par suffrance,
E les suffranz od sei auance;
4130 Il nus doint si bien suffrir
K'a li puissum par li uenir. Amen.

þat mai al suffre for Godes loue, he schal bryng forþ muchel frut
wiþowten any faile. Þat is þe frute þat neuer schal haue ende, þat God
haþ diȝt vnto his chosen. Ihesu it wan þurth þolemodnes and suffraunce,
& alle þat suffre in þolemodnes, sorowes and tenes, he auaunceþ hem
5    wiþ himseluen. And he send vs his grace so for to suffren þat we mai
come to him. Amen.

1 al] *alt.*   3 wan] w(.)an.   4 þolemodnes] *canc.*

# COMMENTARY

The Commentary deals with several areas. Emendations to the text of H are noted and explained. As required in the discussion of textual and linguistic matters, variant readings from the other English manuscripts are recorded along with *Miroir* variants from manuscripts other than $W^2$ where these appear more representative of the readings of the translator's exemplar. In citing readings common to several manuscripts, the spellings of the lemma are those of the first manuscript listed. The word 'lack(s)' indicates that a portion of the text is lacking for mechanical reasons (e.g. the loss of one or more folios), and 'om', that an omission is due to scribal error or to intentional re-writing. Words of particular interest or difficulty are glossed and discussed as necessary, with reference to *MED, AND,* and other relevant works. Pertinent information concerning context and background is also given, and an attempt is made to identify any sources to the text. Biblical references to the Vulgate text are to *Biblia Sacra Iuxta Vulgatam Clementinam*, eds., A Colunga and L. Turrado, 7th edition (Madrid, 1985).

**3/1** Robert de Gretham offered his work to Lady Aline specifically to counteract her predisposition for *chancon de geste e d'estoire* (2/5); this rejection of secular matter is a frequent Anglo-Norman prologue topos in other texts such as saints' lives. The English translator removes all references to Aline, but retains the notion that the work is an alternative to *romaunce and gestes*, indicating that the latter still enjoyed great popularity in the fourteenth century.

**3/5–8** This is the general sentiment expressed in Ecclesiastes.

**3/5–6** The upper of the two tears across the first folio disturbs several readings, causing the loss of [d] from *listned* 3/5, and in *þan* 3/6 the final two letters may just be deciphered; see also the disruption to readings in the second column at 3/29 below. The most recent repairs to the manuscript, particularly those which affect the first leaf, have obscured some readings which were previously visible and which were observed by one of the present editors on an earlier examination of the manuscript; the commentary records the fuller readings visible on that occasion.

**3/9 drawn out** 'write', or perhaps 'translate', if the *litel tretice of diuinite* (3/9) refers to the source, the AN *Miroir*; there is no equivalent in the French. See also note 5/12–13 below.

**3/10** A hole in the manuscript has caused the loss of some letters from *turnen* and *þing*.

**3/11 his** So PBRHa, C lacks.

**3/13–14 & hii gabben** So PBRHa, C lacks. Though the English does not follow the French closely in this sentence, insofar as *& hii gabben* may be taken as a rendering of 2/19: *E co n'est pas chose creiable*, the *&* which gives loose syntax here may be due to *E* in the French. Cf. note 7/23–24 below.

**3/15** Note the translator's addition of the term 'old english' in rendering 2/25–6.

**3/16** By citing Guy of Warwick instead of Mainet and Sansunnet the translator both updates the reference to the typical romance hero and reinforces the English character of the translation.

**3/17 þer nis mani lesinges** Cf. 2/34: *trop n'i ment*; AN *n'i* suggests that *þer* is here to be taken as 'therein' rather than as a formal subject.

**3/18 drawen out of holi writ** 'taken from Scripture'; cf. 2/35: *forstrait d'escripture.*

**3/19 ne for þan** 'nevertheless'; cf. 2/38: *purquant.* See *MED* for-than *adv. & conj.* 3. *Ne for þan* and *na for þan* (5/23) are weakened forms of *nought-*, *not-*, and *no-for-than* quoted by MED.

**3/24 turned to him** Cf. 2/47: *a li turne.* AN *turner* can mean 'to turn, apply' and 'to return, give back' (see *AND* turner[2]). Accordingly, *turned to him* here may mean 'directed towards, devoted to his (God's) purposes', or 'returned, given back to him'.

**3/25 sen & heren, wit & hereing** So B, *siȝth & herynge wyt & speche* P, *eghen eres witte & heryng* R, *seing & hering speking & spelling* Ha, C lacks, cf. 2/50: *Veer, parler, sens e oie* UO; *sens* is omitted in W[2]. The repetition *heren … hereing* seems to derive from the archetype with independent alterations in PRHa.

**3/25–26 for to kepe þe** So B, *forto kepen vs* PR, *for to kepe his comaundementes* Ha, C lacks, cf. 2/52: *pur nus guarder.* The faulty concord of number and person in *vs … þe* (3/24–6) was probably in the archetype and, accordingly, *vs* (3/24) in PR is by independent alteration.

**3/26 of his ofices** Cf. 2/54: *de ces mesters.*

**3/29 on in God ichil fonde to** The upper tear in the manuscript has been badly mended with semi-transparent tape which obscures this reading; it can only be deciphered with the aid of the other manuscripts.

**5/4–7** Note the basic structure of the sermons which is outlined here, and see also the further explanation at 15/8–10; the translator, like Robert de Gretham before him, is concerned to state his fidelity to the authoritative sources of the Bible and the works of the Fathers.

**5/7–11** At this point the English translator follows Robert de Gretham in condemning the folly of using Latin in a work addressed to lay people; however, the translator often cites scriptural texts in Latin before giving a vernacular translation. This practice seems somewhat contradictory, but it may be that the translator's intention was to censure not the use of Latin *per se*, but the gratuitous display of learning by citing Latin with no accompanying translation. See also his further comment at 21/5–6. Robert de Gretham may have decided to omit Latin texts from the *Miroir* partly because it would have been difficult, if not impossible, to accommodate them within his choice of medium (rhyming Anglo-Norman verse).

**5/8 a pride** 'a kind of arrogance'; see *MED* prid(e *n.*(2) 1a (f) for ME *pride* with an indefinite article.

**5/8–10** The lower of the two tears across the first folio, and the attempts to repair it, have caused some disruption at this point. Many of the words in these lines are difficult to read but can be made out by reference to the other manuscripts.

**5/9–10 he entermetteþ him of a fole mester** 'he engages in a foolish undertaking'. See p. xl.

**5/12–13 so to draw & write** Cf. 4/93: *De si traiter e de si dire,* and U: *De si traire e de si escriuere.* Clearly *write* is from the AN variant *escriuere* in U or *escrire* in O for $W^2$ *dire.* The OF verb *treter* could mean 'treat, write, compose' (see AND), and *traire,* 'translate' (see Godefroy and Tobler-Lommatzsch), senses transferred to ME *drawen* (see *MED* drauen v.4.(c) and 2e.(b)). In *draw & write* here, *draw* could mean 'translate' or 'compose'.

**5/14–15** The prologue is peppered with such references to hearing and reading (see also 5/21, 15/4, 19/32, 21/2, 21/9–10). Frequently, as at 15/4, this is a direct rendering of the AN verbs 'oir' and 'lire'; elsewhere, as here, the English translator uses both terms where there is no equivalent in the AN. References to hearing seem to suggest the context for sermons with which we are now most familiar, that is, preaching in church, and, as Spencer (1993:36) notes, the work's organisation as a series of gospel readings in the order in which they would be heard in church seems to indicate its convenience for a preacher. On the other hand, references to reading seem to indicate that the sermons might also be used as part of a private programme of devotional improvement, and it is clear that both Robert de Gretham and the English translator envisaged a lay reading public. Not only did Robert overtly address his work to a female lay reader, 'dame Aline', but his use of the formulation 'seignurs' indicates that he also sought a wider lay audience; similarly the English translator frequently refers to the readers of his text as including both men and women. Clearly both Robert de Gretham and the English translator imagined that their work might be used or received in different contexts, but references to 'hearing' and 'reading' do not *necessarily* indicate different audiences, as Coleman (1996) has shown. Although her survey concentrated on 'secular court-orientated literature' and specifically excluded religious reading, her conclusions that 'from the twelfth through the mid fourteenth century readers in Latin, French/Anglo-Norman, and English show a consistent affinity for public reading' (p. 84) and that 'the hearing of books continued to be a favored mode of reading' (p. 221) are worth noting. It is quite possible that the sermons of the *Mirror* (and the *Miroir*) were read aloud in household groups for edification, in much the same way that romances were read publicly for entertainment.

**5/15 speche** So PBRHa, C lacks.

**5/21 saddeþ** 'wearies (through satiation)'. No instance of the transitive use of this verb in this sense is given under MED *saden* v. One such use (dated 1440) is quoted by OED (see *Sade,* v.2).

**5/27–28 for often þurȝ a litel wele siggeinge turneþ þe hert into delite** Cf. 4/135–36: *Kar suuent ... en grant delit.* The *it* interlined after *siggeinge* in H, in ink and form identical with the hand of the scribe, is not in PBRHa; C lacks. The H scribe appears to have misunderstood the syntax of *turneþ þe hert* (with its inversion of subject and verb) and has added *it* as a subject (referring to *sumwhat of God* 5/26), to make *turneþ* into a transitive verb followed by *þe hert* as object. This addition is, accordingly, excluded from the text.

**5/28–29** Robert de Gretham, anticipating a hostile reception for his work, withholds his name *encore,* 'as yet', in the prologue, eventually identifying himself later in the introduction (20/634) and at the very end of the sermon cycle; the English translator, on the other hand, withholds his name without qualification, and never discards his anonymity. It is clear from this that opposition to popular exposition based on scriptural translation was nothing new, but it also seems that the English translator feared even greater hostility than Robert had anticipated.

**5/30 *coniecten*, 5/33 *coniecten*** *coniecten, coniecten* PBHa, *coniecten, lacke* R, C lacks. *Coniecten* (5/30) translates 4/144: *puruertent*. The phrase *for to blamen þe gode & coniecten hem* (5/33) translates 4/150: *Par le prudome deprauer*. If *tellen it forþ on her maner* (5/31) is taken as an amplification of *coniecten þe wordes of holi writte* (5/30–31), the sense of *coniecten* in this context (i.e. referring to Scripture) is 'misrepresent', that is, 'subject them (the words of Scripture) to their own (false) conjectures'. This is the meaning of *puruertent*: see *AND* purvertir, where the sense is given as 'to distort (the meaning of)' with a quotation including the phrase *purverterent les bons escriz*. The OF verb *depraver* (*AND* depraver 'to decry, disparage') confirms for ME *coniecten* (referring to people) the sense 'misrepresent' or 'disparage'. Significantly, despite the tendency to alteration and rewriting, especially in R and Ha, in only one instance is *coniecten* replaced by another word in the other MSS: for *coniecten* at 5/33 R reads *lacke*, 'disparage, blame', see *MED* lakken *v.*2.(a). This argues acceptability for *coniecten* as used here in senses at some remove from the usual ME senses 'suppose', 'plot', 'contrive', as recorded under *MED* conjecten *v.*

**5/34** The translator follows Robert de Gretham closely in his explanation of why the work is entitled 'Mirror'. The idea that a text might reflect its readers' spiritual faults and failings as clearly as a mirror could demonstrate the physical state of the body was a popular one, and many medieval works of religious and philosophical instruction make use of this trope; see for example the French texts *Miroir du Monde* and *Mirour de l'Omne*, and their English derivatives, and *Miroure of Wysdome, Mirror of Holy Church, Mirror of Simple Souls*, to name but a few, and also Grabes (1982).

**7/5 scheweþ** A hole in the manuscript has caused the loss of the final three letters; the reading has been reconstructed by reference to the other manuscripts.

**7/10 Now beseche ichon þat it seþ & hereþ, bischeþ þat God** *Now bysecheþ echon … bische* [ins.] *þat god* B, *Now I biseche 3ou vchon … þat 3e bischeche god* P, *Now bysekes ilkon þat hit ses or heres þat god* R, *Nou ich* [ins.] *bische ichon þat it saiþ & hereþ þat hii bische to god* Ha, C lacks, cf. 6/181–82: *Ore pri … Qu'il prie …*, i.e. 'Now I pray ….. that he pray etc.' The H reading *Now beseche* ('Now [I] pray') appears to follow the Anglo-Norman in omitting the personal pronoun. The shift from singular to plural (i.e. *bischeþ*, imperative plural here) is unexceptional after *ichon* – cf. *ichon … hii* in Ha and cf. 19/2–3, note. The variants in the other manuscripts have the appearance of independent 'improvements'.

**7/13 euer schal** The 'r' is missing from *euer* by scribal omission. Before the most recent re-binding of H (see p. 136) *eue* (the second 'e' now covered by binding-tape) and a trace of the initial 's' of the following word *schal* (of which the 'sc', mostly lost on account of a tear in the manuscript, came at the end of the line) were plainly visible.

**7/14** The first part of the prologue, *li prologes* (6/189), ends here.

**7/23–24 þe gostlich writ, & 3if** *þe gostliche wit and 3if* CPB, *þe gostliche vnderstanding & 3if* Ha, R lacks, cf. 6/208–9: *l'espirital sens / E si*. *Writ* for *wit* in H is a mistake easily made in collocation with the adjective *gostlich*. The loose syntax with & derives from the French.

**7/25–26 michel gode frout … þat ben sentens of mani maners** Cf. 6/211–12: *Mult i … de maneres*. The awkward concord in *gode frout … þat ben* arises from the translation of the plural *pumettes* by *frout* (singular). Here *sentens* means 'precepts' – see *MED* sentence *n.*2.(b); *of mani maners*, 'of many kinds', correctly renders OF *de maneres* – see Tobler-Lommatzsch, v, cols. 1068–1069. The alteration of *ben* to *beþ*, with *þ* on an erasure, differs from the Reviser's usual change of 'n' to 'þ' made by altering only the second minim of the 'n' (see p. lxi).

**7/26 whiche**  Although occasional *w*- beside *wh*- forms of 'which' are found in London and east midland texts (see Morsbach 1888:101 and Jordan 1934:293), the interlined 'h' here is accepted as a correction by the H scribe to give his usual form.

**7/32 twai**  Here *twai* is formed by the addition of 't' before 'wai' which stands at the beginning of a line. Under an erasure at the end of the previous line, 'th' may perhaps just be made out.

**9/1 florischeþ**  So CBHa, *floureþ* P, R lacks. The *þ* has been added here not to give a plural ending in *þ* (the Reviser's usual change) but a *3 pres. indic.* as in the other manuscripts.

**9/3**  cf. Psalms 18. 11, but there are similar references in other psalms, such as nos. 77 and 97.

**9/11 asailours and 9/14 asailours**  H shares these readings with CPB; Ha has *assoillours*; R lacks. Cf. 8/257–58: *De guaignurs ... sunt conseillurs*. It is tempting to see in *asailours* here a misreading of an abbreviated form of *conseillurs*, with the abbreviation for *con-* misread as 'a'. However, *MED* records *assailour* in the sense 'chastiser'. The only quotation given in this sense is from the late fourteenth-century text, *The Recluse*. The reading in Ha, *assoillours* (twice), unless a repeated error, which is unlikely, suggests that the scribe, or a scribe in the Ha tradition, did not recognize the use of *assailour* in this (recent) sense or, conceivably, that he did not care for this harsh view of the role of the clergy, preferring the notion of 'one who assoils' to 'one who assails'. The agent noun *assoilour* is not recorded in *MED;* it is evidently a formation here from the common ME verb *assoilen*, 'to absolve someone from sin'; see *MED* assoilen *v*. 1.(a.).

**9/16–17 hii it schuld adresce hem to God ward**  *hii it schuld adresce hem to ward* C, *hii it schulden adressen & turnen hem to god ward* P, *þey schulde redrescen hem to godward* B, *hii schuld dressen hem to godward* Ha, R lacks. *God ward* (HPBHa) must be from the archetype. The *it* in HCP appears to be an error in their tradition though, conceivably, the error could have been present in the archetype and subsequently removed independently in BHa, or at some earlier point in their tradition. A scribe, at whatever point, could mistakenly have written *it* as an object (with *eni sinne* (9/16) in mind) before coming to the object *hem*. The versions of C (omitting *God*) and P (adding *& turnen*) appear to be independent alterations to accommodate *it* of HCP. No equivalent in AN.

**9/20–21**  Perhaps referring to Revelations xi.5–6 where it is stated that terrible things will befall the man who seeks to harm God's two witnesses.

**9/21 himself**  i.e. God. Cf. 8/263–64: *Ki rien ... e offent*.

**9/27–28 he (twice)**  'they'; cf. 17/6–7, note.

**11/2–3**  Lamentations iv.4.

**11/4–5 Often bi brede in holi writ bitokeneþ þe techeinge**  *Ofte bi bred in holi writ bitokneþ teching* CB, *often bi bred in holi writ is vnderstonden teching* Ha, om. P, R lacks, cf. 10/291–92: *Suuent pain ... d'alme figure*. The loose syntax in the English with *bi* (*bi brede ... bitokeneþ*), not derived from the *Miroir*, represents the archetype. Ha 'improves'.

**11/6–7 in þat iche þat þe ordre falleþ**  So B, *in þat iche þat to þe ordre falleþ* CPHa, R lacks. The sense is: 'in respect of that which appertains to the order', i.e. 'religious order' or 'order of priesthood', see *MED* ordre *n.* 9.(a) and 10.(a). Cf. 10/295–96: *Li petit … ordre apent.* In this sense *fallen,* without *to,* does occur in ME, see *MED* fallen *v.* 38.(b), though the construction with the preposition *to* (possibly independent additions in CPHa), is much more common.

**11/7 bot nouȝt in God** 'but not in regard to God'. Cf. 10/297: *mais en Deu nun.*

**11/8 ac for to haue** So CP, *ay for to haue* B, *forto haue* Ha, R lacks. Not in AN. Ha, in fact, omits *ac … ac* (11/7–8). The sense, with *ac* as 'and' (see *MED* ac *conj.* 4) may be: 'and (through humility) to have etc.'

**11/12 his brede** *þis bred* CPBHa, R lacks.

**11/12–13 prist es barain þat is naked** PB, *prest is baraine & naked* Ha, *prist is barain þat naked* C. The *is* in *þat is naked* lacking in HC is supplied from P. In H, *prist es* is written as one word.

**11/21** Isaiah xxiv.2.

**11/24–25 Swiche mantel-bond, swiche men, swiche prestes hii hiren & susten** So CP, *suche prestes suche men suche ben þey þat susteyn hem* B, Ha rewrites, R lacks. Not in AN. Both *mantel*, 'sleeveless overgarment worn … over a kirtle or tunic' (*MED* mantel *n.* 1.(a)), and *bond,* 'something used for tying, binding … fastening' (*MED* bond *n.* 1.a.), are common in ME. *MED* (under mantel *n.*) gives the compounds *mantel-cloth, mantel-lap* and *mantel-nok,* and *OED* (see mantle, *sb.,* 11) adds later compounds including *mantel-knot* (first for 1896), 'an ornament in the form of a clasp, composed of a number of precious stones', but neither records *mantel-bond.* In this context, it is perhaps a kind of ornamental fastening or clasp worn as a device by the retainers of a lord – see *OED sb.* 2 for clothing or items of clothing (e.g. collars of silver or hoods) worn by retaine livery,rs or servants as a distinctive badge. The phrase *swiche mantel-bond, swiche men* is of the common 'Such master, such man' type (see *OED* such, 6.a.) and thus 'such livery (*mantel-bond*), such men' here. The whole sentence may therefore be understood as follows: just as the men wearing his livery are typical of the lord who hires them, so priests will reflect the character of those who hire and sustain them. The rather elliptical mode of this proverbial expression may have caused confusion and so have given rise to the alterations in B (where the sense is rather: 'as the priests are so are the people who sustain them'), and the rewriting of the passage in Ha.

**11/26–27** Matthew xv.14.

**11/28–29** Psalms lxviii.24.

**11/32 sette in Goddes foreheued** *set in godes stede for heuede* CPBR, *sette in holi churche* Ha, cf. 10/346: *Ki el frunt de honur sunt pose.* Sense can be made of the H reading as 'set in God's vanguard to guide' – see *MED* forhed *n.5.* for the sense 'the van of an army', which is also one of the senses of AN *frunt* (see *AND*). The agreement of CPBR supports *set in godes stede for heuede* as the reading of the archetype. The H reading, *sette in goddes foreheued,* could have arisen from the omission of *stede.* Yet, in view of the word *frunt* in the AN text and its principal sense 'forehead' (see *AND*), it is difficult to discount *foreheued* in H as a mere accident of scribal error. Perhaps the translator's AN exemplar read *frunt deu* (with *deu* as a misreading of *den',* an abbreviation of *denur* – see Godefroy *Honor* for the variant form *enor* and the reading *donur* in O for W[2] *de honur*) or *frunt de* (with *honur* omitted). This would account for *goddes foreheued* in H and, indeed, the word 'God' which is absent from the AN text as it stands. However, this would require that scribes in the CP and BR traditions independently took *sette in goddes foreheued* as 'set in God's ... as head' and supplied *stede* to give 'set in God's place as head'. This possibility seems less remote in view of *God stede* in *þat ben set abouen þe folk in God stede for to techen* (13/21–22). See 13/21 note.

**11/32 gyen** The alteration *gyed* (with *ed* on erasure) is rejected in the text; *gyen* is restored, as in CPBR. *Gien* and *giden* (see *MED*) were both fourteenth-century French borrowings, the former early in the century, the latter first in Chaucer and Gower.

**11/34–35 þat oþer mai take ensaumple at hem** 'that others may take them as an example', see *MED* at *prep.* 11(b), *taken ensaumple at* (sth.), quoted from c.1425 (? c.1400). Here *take ensaumple at hem* (referring to persons) certainly pre-dates 1400.

**13/12–13** Ezekiel iii.26.

**13/13 for ... þat** 'because'; cf. 12/368: *Pur la gent k'il puruerse uit.*

**13/14 to þi palat** So B, *to þe palat* CPRHa, cf. 12/370: *a tun palai.* HB *þi* has been carried over from *tun* in the AN, despite the translator's addition of *of þi mouþe* in the English.

**13/16 manace** A 'þ' has been added in H. B *mannas* and R *manasse* (beside *manaceþ* CP, not in Ha, where the text has been rewritten) support the original H reading.

**13/17–18** Isaiah v.6.

**13/21 God stede** *godes stede* CPBRHa. The H reading could be an endlingless genitive before a word beginning with 's'; cf. *God seruise* (87/4).

**13/28–31 For þat is wratþe ... wiþ his ȝerde** 'For that is anger indeed when he withdraws his teaching, when (*þat*, 12/399: *Quant*) he does not wish the people to be taught so that he withdraws his vengeance, so that he should not take revenge; and because he wishes to take revenge, he does not want the people to be chastised with his rod.' The translator's exemplar must have read *Pur sa veniance eschiuer* (with *veniance* as in UO rather than *uigne* as W²) at 12/400. The translator rendered 12/397–400 fairly closely, but with *þat he ne toke nouȝt wreche* (13/30), virtually repeated his translation of 12/400 (presumably for emphasis), and then, caught up in the theme of God's vengeance, departed from the milder sense of 12/401–4.

**13/30 wiþdroweþ** The readings in the other MSS vary in tense and mood: *withdrawe* C, *withdrowȝe* P, *wyþdroue* B, *withdrawes* R, om. Ha. The anomolous *wiþdroweþ* (rather than *wiþdraweþ*) in H may reflect an incomplete change from past subjunctive to present indicative.

**15/1** Psalms lxxxviii.45.

**15/8–10** The form of sermon construction outlined here, involving the exposition of an entire gospel reading, may be defined as the 'ancient' method; the 'modern' method, by contrast, involved the exposition of a short scriptural phrase which was divided into heads. For a lucid explanation of the two methods, see Spencer 1993:231–47.

**15/15 to deluen Goddes tresore** A later hand has emended this to read *to deluen & hyde Goddes tresore*. The words *& hyde* are first added in the centre margin, then erased, then added by the same hand in the left-hand margin. A caret on the erased final 'n' of *deluen* marks the position for insertion.

**15/23 me** So CPHa, *my* BR. H *my* on erasure may have been an alteration by the Reviser since it partly covers the erased final 'n' of *aquiten*; *me* is restored in the text.

**15/25 & roten** So CPBR, om. Ha, cf. 14/472: *mort e purriz*. In H *roted*, the 'd', an alteration in lighter ink, though signs of erasure are slight, has replaced an original 'n', restored here in the text.

**15/28** I Corinthians xiii.8.

**15/32 taken** So CPBR, *taken on hond* Ha. For *taken* in the sense 'undertaken', see *MED* taken *v.* 37b.(a).

**15/33 soȝt** So CP, *ended* B, om. RHa, cf. 14/486: *esquis*, pp. of *esquerre* (see *AND* enquerre²). In *for charite ne mai neuer al be soȝt* here, the sense seems to be that charity, being limitless, can never be wholly 'sought out' (i.e. to the point of exhaustion).

**15/35–17/1** Numbers xx.8. and also Psalms lxxvii.16.

**17/1 chastis** *chastise* PBRHa, *chaste* C, cf. *chastis* (23/3). In H *chastie*, the 'e' on erasure has replaced an original 's', restored here in the text. See *MED* chasten, chastien and chastisen, variant ME forms of the verb derived from OF *chastier*.

**17/3–4** Psalms lxxx.11.

**17/6** Psalms lxvii.12.

**17/6–7 God schal ȝeue to hem word þat þurth gret vertu he schal beren it forþ** Cf. 16/501–2: *Deus a celi ... nuntterat*. The pronouns *hem* and *he* are also in PR; CBHa have *him* and *he*. For occasional instances of *he* ('they') in H, cf. 9/27–28, note.

**17/7 beren** H *besen*, with a long 's' instead of 'r', is emended to *beren* in the text. Cf. *beren* CPB, *tell* R, Ha differs.

**17/12 No man ne schal praysen me for þes sawes þat heren it** *No man / þat heren* CBRHa, *noman / þat hereþ* P. For ME *man* with singular and plural, see Mustanoja 1960:221. Also: *þes sawes / it* CPR, *þys speche / it* B, *þes wordes / þis boke* Ha. The faulty concord of HCPR may represent the archetype and derive from loose translation.

**17/13–14 þat þurth hem** So CPBRHa, cf. 16/516: *E par els*. The conjunction *þat* gives the wrong sense here. Perhaps the archetype read *þat* for & (some forms of & are easily confusable with abbreviations of *þat*); again the translator's exemplar may have read *Ke* for *E*.

**17/16** Matthew x.20.

**17/18 þer wil and 17/19 þer he wil** Cf. 16/524: *la u uolt*, and 16/526: *la u il uolt*.

**17/18** John iii.8.

**17/22–23** II Peter ii.15–16. The story of Balaam's ass is recorded in Numbers xxii.22–35.

**17/26 bot God þat holdeþ his scole in him** Cf. 16/536: *Mes dieus qi en lui tient escole* (U) and *Mes deus en celui qui tient escole* (O). For *tenir escoles* meaning 'teach', see Tobler-Lommatzsch *escole*. s.f.

**17/27–28 for him, ac for** An obvious error of eyeskip after the first 'for' is emended in accordance with *for him ac for* CPBHa, *for hym but for* R.

**17/31 sinner** In 16/547 the translator's exemplar mistakenly read *peccheur* (as UO) instead of *prechur* (as W²).

**19/2–3 heren him & al her wordes iuggen wel wiþin her hertes** The pronoun *him* here (also B) in the sequence *him ... her ... her* may be taken as a plural form, cf. *hem* CPRHa. For the shift from singular (*noman*) at the beginning of the sentence to subsequent plurals, cf. 18/559–61: *L'em ... nuli ... tuz ... tuz lur diz.*

**19/3–8** Note that this passage about the Devil speaking through Peter and the passage concerning the Devil preaching (19/16–23) are interpolations in the English text.

**19/5–8** Referring to Matthew xvi.21–23.

**19/10 bordel** 'cottage'. See *AND* bordel where both the senses 'cottage, hut' and 'brothel' are given. *MED* bordel *n*. records the sense 'brothel' only. It seems unlikely, however, that the ME translator envisaged a 'good man' emerging from a 'brothel' here. For *of bordel* (without article), cf. 18/567: *De bordel*, but *of þe bordel* CPBRHa.

**19/10 may a gode man comen (...)** The word erased was probably *out*, removed, for whatever reason, possibly by the scribe. Cf. *may come a good man* CP, *mai a gode man come* Ha, *may a gode man com out* B, *may come a gode mon oute* R.

**19/13–14 ac take þe rose & lete þe þorne** So BHa, *but take to rose & leue þe thorne* R, *ac take þe rote and let þe þorn* CP. 'But take the rose and leave the thorn' conflicts with the meaning of the next sentence (i.e. that no one should have the rose without the thorn), and is at variance with the sense of 18/576: *La rose met l'espine en pris*, 'the rose (i.e. the beautiful message) gives value to the thorn (the preacher, however unattractively thorn-like)'.

**19/16 loue** So CPBRHa.

**19/20 to prechen hem** For ME *prechen* as 'to preach to (sb.); to exhort (sb.)', see *MED* prechen *v*.1.(e).

**19/20 had hadde** So CPR, *had han* B, *had* Ha. H has *hated*, with *ted* on erasure; *hadde* is restored in the text.

**19/25** I Timothy v.18. On f. 4$^r$ a later hand has added the words *qui laborat manducat* in the bottom margin beneath the second column of text.

**19/29–30 þat ich man ... askinge** 'that each man whom another instructs and teaches, that he (each man) ought to give him (the teacher) from all his goods without asking.' Cf. 18/598–600 (with variants from U):

| Ke chascun home ki d'altre aprent | qe autri U |
| Od sun doctur deit comuigner | A sun U |
| De tuz ses biens sanz demander. | |

**19/30 his (2)** i.e. *is*. See Galatians vi.6: *communicet autem is qui catechizatur* etc.

**19/32–21/1** A plea by the author, and also in this instance, the translator, to the audience for their prayers, was conventional, as was the request that they should correct and forgive any errors in the text, see below 21/9–10.

**19/33 & so for to make þis werk** The awkward syntax here arises from the lack of any equivalent to *doint* of 18/605: *E doint cest oure si parfeire.*

**19/35 þis werk** 'This work' continues as subject to the end of the sentence owing to a misunderstanding of the French arising from the non-expression of pronouns of the first person in 18/606: *le puisse plaire* and 18/608: *seie*.

**21/3 he**  i.e. *þe godspelle* (21/2); the pronoun *he* is perhaps due to *il* in 20/613–14: *Tels l'ewangelie ... il dit.*

**21/7 founden**  All other MSS read *founded*, but in H the final 'd' is on an erasure with the head of the first minim of an erased 'n' still visible. While *founded* was the usual pp. of *founden* (< OF *fonder*), the form *founden* occurred for the pp. of this verb by confusion with the pp. of *founden* (< OE *findan*).

**21/10–11 & þat God ʒif**  *and god ʒef* CP, *god ʒeue* B, *now god giue* R, *so þat god ʒif* Ha. The original word order in H, *god & þat*, makes nonsense. The transposition to *& þat god* as indicated in the manuscript still leaves a dubious reading and loose syntax.

**21/12 besechen**  H has *besecheþ* with 'þ' on an erasure – not the usual 'n' to 'þ' alteration. Cf. 7/25–26, note.

**21/14 of Goddes word**  Cf. 20/639: *Kar custume est del Deu sermun* (*de deu sermoun* U).

**21/22 may**  The added *scheweþ* in H was a bad guess; the omitted word (supplied in the text here) was *may*, cf. *may* CPBR, om. Ha. The distinction here appears to be between those who can preach (i.e. *schewe ... wiþ word*) and those who cannot but who can make available manuscripts for copying (cf. 21/13–14).

**21/26 in**  The H scribe wrote *&*, probably misreading an abbreviated form of *in*; in some medieval hands these forms were much alike. Cf. 21/34, note, 99/29, note, and 131/5, note. The emendation follows the reading in CPR; there is a lacuna in B, and Ha rewrites; cf. 20/659: *en nule place.*

**21/28**  Matthew vii.7.

**21/31 feden**  *fede* CP, *feden* BR, *fedeþ* Ha (with 'þ' by alteration from 'n'). The Reviser's alteration to *fedeþ* here in H was possibly a 'correction' to a singular rather than his usual alteration of plural 'n' to 'þ'. The plural *feden* may have arisen by association with the preceding *oþer.*

**21/33 his**  i.e. 'God's'; so also, *his* (21/34).

**21/34 & himself**  *and him siluen* CBHa, *hymself* P, *in hym selue* R. The archetype read *&* either from a confusion of *in* (abbreviated) and *&* (see 21/26, note) or, as more likely here, from *e sei* instead of *en sei* in line 676 of the translator's AN exemplar – cf. the corrupt reading *& say* in Hm. P and R 'emend', R correctly, to judge from *en sei* in W²UO.

**21/36 renter**  'landlord', here in a figurative sense, *MED* renter(e *n.*(b).

**21/36 fayle to non ... faile ... to him**  Cf. 20/679–80: *faudra ... a nuli ... faldra a li.*

**23/1 repente**  The 'þ' added by the Reviser to *repente* was doubtless intended to give an indicative instead of a subjunctive here.

**23/3 chastis**  H has *chasteþ* ('e' formed by alteration of a minim, 'þ' on erasure), replacing the original form *chastis* which is here restored in the text. Cf. 17/1, note, and the other manuscript readings: *chastys* BRHa, *chastyes* P, *chastizeþ* C.

**25/1–17**  1st Sunday in Advent. Matthew xxi.1–9. Readings from Ha are not recorded for the gospel passages since those in Ha do not derive from the AN version in the *Miroir.*

**25/3 þe mount** So CPBR, cf. 24/698: *el munt*. The *þe* added here is to be distinguished from the many instances of articles added in H at points where the absence of the article in the ME text is paralleled in the AN.

**25/3 two** So CPBR.

**25/4 castel** 'village, small town', especially a walled town; see *MED* castel *n.* 5.(b).

**25/4–5 þat is risen oȝaines ȝou** cf. 24/701: *cuntre vus leue*.

**25/8 was wel sen** So CPB, *was wel sone* R, cf. 24/710: *Ico fait ad bien auerre* i.e. 'this event well fulfilled'. The rendering *was wel sen* may have arisen from confusion of the pp. of AN *averer*, 'to fulfil', and the infinitive of AN *vere*, 'to see' (see *AND* veer¹). The translator's exemplar may have read: *fut bien a vere*; Hm reads *fut* for *ad* W²UO.

**25/9–10** Zechariah ix.9.

**25/9 þe child Syon be schewed** A word-for-word rendering of 24/712: *La fille Syon seit nuncie*; for 'show' as a sense of AN *nuncier*, see *AND* nuncier.

**25/9 þat** 'he that'. Despite 24/713: *Ti reis*, the reading *þi kynge* in R (and only there) must derive from re-writing, probably with *rex tuus* of the Vulgate text in mind.

**25/11** The English follows the AN in the perfect tenses *ben gon* (24/716: *sunt ale*) and *han brouȝt* (24/718: *unt mene*). So also in *han strewed* (24/726: *unt ... estrame*) in 25/14. See Introduction, p. xli.

**25/13 men Ebrus** 'Hebrew people, Hebrews', cf. 24/722: *gent Hebre*.

**25/16 on heiȝe** Cf. 24/730: *en halte*, and Matt. xxi.9: *hosanne in altissimis* (Vulgate), 'Hosanna in the highest' (AV).

**25/23–4 ac ferst he com to Bethphage ffor first hit mot be told þurth holi predicacion** The omission in H is due to mechanical error: the scribe's eye has returned to his exemplar at *predicacion* instead of *sauacion*. The lacuna is supplied from C; PBR have similar readings.

**25/24 þe faith** So CPBRHa. Despite 24/747: *E la fei*, the *&* added before *þe faith* in H is a scribal 'improvement' to the text made in ignorance of the lacuna at this point.

**25/28 inwiþ** Carets added before and after *in* indicate transposition to *wiþin* as in C. However PBRHa have *inwiþ*.

**25/28 forþencheþ** 'repents'. The pronoun *he* is understood. The non-expression of the pronoun here (also in CPBRHa) in the English does not derive from the AN text.

**27/3 synner** Cf. 26/760: *prechers* W²HmO, *pecchers* U. The translator's exemplar presumably had the corrupt reading as in U. Cf. 17/31, note.

**27/3 þat sitt in place** So CPBHa, *þat hynges in lowe place* R, cf. 26/761: *Par Betphage ki siet en la place*, *Par betfage qui set en place* O, *Par bethfage qe seit basse* U, *Par bephage qi est en basse* Hm. In Hm *est* and *basse* are alterations. As read from a microfilm, an erased initial 's' is visible before altered *est* and an initial 'p' before *basse*. The initial 'b' of *basse* is by alteration from 'l'. The original Hm reading, like that of O, was likely to have been *qi set en place* and this seems to have been the reading of the translator's exemplar which, despite its lack of sense, has been carried over word for word into the English. R represents an intelligent guess at emendation guided by the sense of the context.

**27/4 is rested** So CPBHa, *hit rested* R, cf. 26/764: *Kar Iesus i est areste* W²HmO, *Qe ihesus est areste* U. The U reading was clearly that of the translator's exemplar transferred into English word for word without regard to sense. Cf. 27/3, note. For ME *resten* (from OF *rester* / *arester*) meaning 'to stop', see *MED* resten *v*.(3)(c) and aresten *v*.1.(b).

**27/6 þat ich haue touched ȝou** So CHa, *þat ich haue touched to ȝou* PB, *þat y haue tolde ȝow* R, cf. 26/767: *Ki en dous maners nus tuche*, but note the variant reading *vos* in Hm. The sense of the AN is: 'which touches, applies to us' – see *AND* tucher. The translator has taken his exemplar (with *vos* as in Hm) to mean 'which I have interpreted for you', mistakenly assuming a non-expressed first personal pronoun in the AN.

**27/7 þurȝ predicacion** So CPBRHa. A contemporary hand, possibly the Reviser, has supplied the missing preposition in H by writing *þurȝ* (not *þurth*, the usual form in H) over an erased *pre* at the end of the line and by adding *pre* before *dicacion* at the beginning of the next line.

**27/8–9 ful ȝildinge** Cf. AN 773: *satisfactiun*.

**27/15 his loue** *þis loue* CPBHa, *loue* R, cf. 26/787: *icest amur*. The same mistake (*his* for *þis*) is found at 11/12. In H, *his loue* could be taken as an objective genitive, i.e. 'unless he has love for him (God)'.

**27/16 & ȝif he** So CPBRHa. Though not strictly essential for the sense, the & interlined here is supported by the other manuscripts.

**27/17 forlest** 'damn', *MED* forlesen *v*.3.(a). Cf. 26/791: *met a perdiciun*.

**27/17 euen cristen** 'fellow christian', *MED* even *adj*. 16.(c).

**27/19–20 erþlich werk** i.e. 'worldly activity' as against spiritual activity.

**27/20–22 hii deden … he leteþ … fram him … him** *hy deden … he letteþ … fro hym … hym* B, *þai diden … he sendes … fro hym … him* R, *hii deden … hii leten … fram hem … hem* CP, *hii deden … hii laten … fram hem* Ha, cf. 26/798–801. In some ME dialects *he* and *him* can be both singular and plural, cf. 17/6–7, note, and 27/28, note. However if the pronouns and verbs in this passage were originally singular as in the French, *hii* of *hii deden* (plural in all manuscripts) may have arisen from the mistaking of a singular *he* as 'they' at an early stage in transmission. The other plurals in CP and Ha would then have been subsequent independent changes.

**27/26 countour** In association with *kinge* and *prince*, *countour* here must mean 'nobleman' or 'count' as does 26/809: *cuntur* (see *AND* cuntur²). This meaning is not recorded in *MED* under countour *n*.(1) where only the senses 'accountant', 'lawyer', etc. are given.

**27/26 asise** 'court', one mainly concerned with civil actions concerning land-tenure or imprisonment; see *MED* assise *n*. 1a.(a).

**27/28 he** 'they'.

**27/30 chastis** The original form in H has been altered to *chastiþ*; cf. *chastisen* PBRHa, *chastiþ* C. See also 17/1, note, and 23/3, note.

**27/32 is bounden** The transposition of *bounden is*, indicated by double ticks added before the erasure of the final *n* of *bounden* (and therefore probably by the scribe, and not by the Reviser), is supported by the evidence of the other manuscripts.

**27/35 vnbounden is**  *is vnbounden* CPBRHa. The *is* added at the end of the line in H makes good an obvious omission; as it is written partly over an erased *n* this addition may have been the work of the Reviser.

**29/7 þat (3)**  So CPBRHa.

**29/9 cloþes**  So CPBRHa.

**29/10 & þan is Ihesus lopen vp**  Cf. 28/852: *E dunc i est Iesus munte*.

**29/11**  The first *he* is Jesus, the second is the sinner.

**29/18 laden**  'put', *MED* leien *v.*(1) 1a.(a), and cf. 28/871: *mistrent*. The alteration in H, *ladde*, with *–de* on erasure, has been restored to *laden* in the text; cf. *leiden* CPBHa, *ladden* R. The H alteration and R *ladden* suggest that the Essex form *laden* (i.e. *lāden* < *lāēden* < *lægdon*, past plural of OE *lecgan*) has been mistaken for a past plural of *leden* (OE *lædan*).

**29/18 scorninge**  So CPBHa, om. R; cf. 28/871: *eschar*. In H, *scourgynge* must have been an alteration of *scorninge*, which is restored in the text.

**29/19 breken**  *braken* CPBRHa. The original form in H must have been *braken* unless, conceivably, it was *broken*.

**29/24 Marie sone and 29/26, 29/27 Dauid sone**  For the s-less genitive with proper names, see Mustanoja 1960:72 and Sauer 1992: 96–8. Cf. 28/884: *fiz Marie* and 28/887: *fiz Daui*.

**29/31 þat mai**  'that we may', with *we* understood from *we* in *þat we mai gladen* (29/30).

**31/1–16**  2nd Sunday in Advent. Luke xxi.25–33.

**31/8 seand al men**  Cf. AN 911: *veant trestuz* UHm, *veant* om. W²O. For this absolute construction in ME, see Mustanoja 1960:559 and 114–16.

**31/15–16 & myn wordes**  These words are written in a cramped manner over an erasure as *& myn word*, with *word* ending in a flourish. Though *word* could stand, perhaps as an endingless plural, the flourish here has been taken as an abbreviation for *-es*. Cf. *wordes* PCB, *word* R.

**31/20 somundeþ**  'exhorts'; a Northern dialect word, see *OED* summond *v*.

**31/22 he sayed to his**  H and C follow 30/943: *Dist il as sons*. The addition of *disciples*, interlined after *his* in H, is a scribal 'improvement'. B and R also make independent changes: B alters *his* to *us*, and R omits *to his*. Ha omits *Al ... sermoun*. P inverts *his þis* to *þis his*.

**31/23 þe elder þat þe world wereþ**  The use of the verb 'to wear' with a predicative extension is first recorded in the *OED* (under wear, *v*. 1. 14.c.) for the seventeenth century. The verb ought to be *wexeþ* as in CPBRHa; 'x' and 'r' were readily confusable in textura script.

**31/23 he**  i.e. the world.

**31/24 slauȝ**  *slauȝtre* C, *slaw* (*w* on eras.) P, *slouþe* (*ouþe* on eras.) B, *& þe more slauȝ* om. Ha, *slouth* R. The HCP readings suggest MED *slagh* n.(a) 'slaughter, murder'; the BR readings, *MED* slouth(e *n*. (a) 'indolence, slothfulness'. By virtue of variant forms (see *MED*) and other potential ME spelling variations, these words could easily have been confused, and the MS variants, alterations, and possibly the very omission in Ha, point to considerable scribal uncertainty here. Neither word translates 30/947: *pestilences*. 30/962: *pestilences* is translated as *pestilens* in 33/2.

**33/2 florischeþ** Not 32/960: *flestrit* 'withers' W², but *flurist* UHmO.

**33/3 So it fareþ of** 'So it goes as regards'. For *it fareþ of*, see *MED* faren v. 12.(a).

**33/5–7 And what ... wiþinne** Cf. 32/969–73. The somewhat anacoluthic syntax of the English here follows the AN text which appears to mean: 'What is something perishable worth, however honoured a man be, however wealthy, however much land he has [to prevent him] suffering etc.'

**33/9 þat ich** *þat ilche* PB, *þat* C, *þat ryches* RHa. H has *hii* on the erasure of what must originally have been *ich*, and *haueþ* is added in the margin. If, as is likely, this is the work of the Reviser, he has here preferred to clarify the sense than simply to make his usual alteration of *ich* to *ilke*.

**33/16–35/13** Aitken (1922:28) notes that the *Vitae Patrum* is the source of this *exemplum*: Narraverunt senes de quodam hortulano quia laboraret, et omnem laborem suum expenderet in eleemosynam. Et tantum sibi retinebat, quantum ad victum ipsius sufficeret. Postea vero Satanas immisit in corde ejus, dicens: Collige tibi aliquantam pecuniam, ne cum senueris aut ægrotaveris, op us habeas ad expensas. Et collegit et implevit lagenam de nummis. Contigit autem eum infirmari, et putrefieri pedem ejus; et expendit quod collegerat in medicos, et nihil ei prodesse potuit. Postea vero venit quidam de expertis medicis, et dicit ei: Nisi incideris pedem tuum, putrefiet. Et constituerunt diem ut inciderent ejus pedem. Illa autem nocte rediens in semetipsum, et pœnitentiam agens de his quæ gessit, ingemuit et flevit, dicens: Memor esto, Domine, operum meorum priorum quæ faciebam, cum laborarem in horto meo, ex quo pauperibus ministrabam. Et cum hoc dixisset, stetit angelus Domini, et dixit ei: Ubi sunt nummi quos collegisti? et ubi est spes de qua tractasti? Tunc intelligens, dixit: Peccavi, Domine; ignosce mihi, et amodo ulterius hoc non faciam. Tunc angelus tetigit pedem ejus, et sanatus est statim. Et exsurgens mane, abiit in agrum operari. Venit ergo medicus secundum constitutum cum ferramentis, ut secaret pedem ejus; et dicunt ei: Exiit a mane operari in agro. Tunc admiratus medicus perrexit in agrum, ubi operabatur ille. Et videns eum fodientem terram, glorificavit Deum, qui reddiderat ei sanitem. (*PL* 73.892).

Aitken also notes a number of other thirteenth-century instances where this story is cited in collections of sermons or books of instruction: Odo of Cheriton, *Sermons*; Perauld, *Summa de Virtutibus ac Vitiis*, Lib. II; and Vincent de Beauvais, *Speculum Morale*, Lib. III, Dist. 18, Pars VII. Odo of Cheriton included the story of the gardener who ceases alms-giving in his sermon for Epiphany (no. 14); see BL Arundel 231, i, f. 82, noted by Ward and Herbert 1883–1910:iii.61. See also Hervieux 1896:iv.272, 370.

**33/16** A line has been left blank at this point in H, presumably to accommodate a rubricated heading (never supplied), for the following tale.

**33/24–37** This passage reflects the inefficacy of the remedies prescribed by medieval physicians and the ruinous nature of the fees; amputation was typically the last resort. Note that whereas the AN distinguishes between *mires*, *AND* mire 'doctor, physician' (1018) and *cyrugien*, *AND* cirurgian 'surgeon' (1027), in ME the general term *leche* serves for both.

**33/24–5 þat God ne toke veniaunce** Cf. 32/1013: *Que Deus n'en prist le uengement*. The *ne* here has been taken over from the French. See p. xl. It also occurs in C and P, but has been omitted in the other MSS.

**33/25 his** So CPBRHa. This word is interlined, then deleted, and then written twice in the margin, once in a later hand.

**33/27 leches mani** cf. 32/1018: *mires ... plusurs*.

**33/27–28 what þat ... & what þat** For the correlatives, cf. 32/1020: *Queique promette, queique dunt*.

**33/28 Ac** The erased word was doubtless *ac* – cf. *ac* CPBHa, *and* R. The Reviser's usual change to *bot* has not been made possibly because *bot* did not have the weak conjunctive force of *ac* (see *MED* ac *conj.* 4) required here, or because a conjunction was judged to be unnecessary.

**33/30 þar** 'dare'. For confusion in form and meaning of ME *þar* and *dar* (OE *þearf* and *dear*), see *MED* thurven *v.* and durren *v.*

**33/34–5 ... bot smite of þe fote & hele aȝeyne þe stumpe** 'other than by striking off the foot and healing again the stump'. See *MED* but *conj.* 1a.(d).

**35/14** The term *lordinges*, translating AN *seignurs*, is a style of address more appropriate to storytelling than preaching. On this point see Spencer 1993:112–13.

**37/11 þurht** Possibly a mistake for *þurth*, the H scribe's usual form, but there is great variety in the spelling of this word in Middle English.

**37/14–17 for a wonder ... liueþ** and **37/18–22 & for al ... liued her** are interpolations in the English. Emphasis is placed on the need to win salvation by one's own efforts. A man cannot trust in others to think of him after he is dead. In any case the efforts of others can only shorten his stay in purgatory; his reward in heaven will depend solely on his own good deeds while alive. See also 43/19–23 note. However, it is to be noted that later, in sermon 8, the stress placed by Robert de Gretham on the folly of trusting too greatly in ourselves and on the value of prayers offered by others on our behalf (96/3014–98/3023) is carried over without reservation into the English text.

**37/22 þan** So CPBR, om. Ha. In H *þat* is obviously a mistake for *þan*; accordingly the text is emended in line with *þan* in CPBR.

**37/24 passen** Usually only final *n* is erased; possibly *e* was accidentally erased and then re-written.

**39/1–13** 3rd Sunday in Advent. Matthew xi.2–10.

**39/1–43/24 ... þe loue of** lacking in C.

**39/4 oþer oþer abiden þi desire** Cf. 38/1157: *V altre atent nostre desir*, but note the corrupt reading *uostre* in U. As a word-for-word rendering of a corrupt AN text with *uostre* for *nostre* as in U, the H reading appears to represent the original English text. The alteration in H (made before the erasure of final 'n' in *abiden*), to *oþer abiden an oþer þi desire*, and *oiþer we abide þi desire* P, *oþer abyde þy desire* B, *other we abyde other* R and *oþer we abide anoþer* Ha, have the appearance of independent changes, those of R and Ha in the light of the gospel reading, Matthew xi.3: *an alium espectamus?*

**39/5 sen** In MS *seiʒe* the letters *iʒe* are compressed on a single letter-space erasure and the interverbal space, presumably replacing an original 'n' which is restored in the text.

**39/7 þe pouer ben heiʒed wiþ strengþe** So PBR, cf. 38/1165: *Li poure sunt prechez a confort*, but note the variant line-ending *a forz* in U. For AN *prechez a forz* (doubtless the reading of the translator's exemplar) as *heiʒed wiþ strengþe*, see *AND* precher[1] 'exhort, admonish', *MED* hien *v*.3.(a) 'urge', and *a fort* 'strongly' under *AND* fort (3) *adv*.

**39/12 cried** So BPR; cf. 38/1178: *escrit* 'written'. ME *cried* 'declared', see *MED* crien *v*. 7.(f) 'make known (orally or in writing); declare', may have arisen from a confusion of the past participle forms of AN *escrier* 'to proclaim' and *escrivre* 'to write' (see *AND* escrier[1] and escrivre).

**39/12–13 þou art my gode angel chosen** cf. 38/1179: *Es vus mun angle bon eslit*. ME *þou art* is a mistranslation of AN *es vus* 'behold', see *AND* es[3].

**39/26 al hii seyn þat nis nouʒt worþ** cf. 38/1211: *Trestut dient que ne uaut rien*.

**39/27 al hem þenche** A confusion of personal and impersonal constructions.

**41/5 worchipes** Cf. 40/1224–5: *Vus dames, amez uos seignurs / En chastete e en honurs*. Plural *worchipes* here may echo AN *honurs*, in which the 's', possibly to match the rhyme-word *seignurs*, may represent the often indiscriminate use of the '-s' inflection (which was generally silent) in later Anglo-Norman; see Pope 1952:1246.

**41/12 sauen ... schulden** Emendation of lacuna in H from PRHa, cf. 40/1238–9: *Si il le mund sauuer ueneit / V il autre atendereit*. For *þe werlde* B reads *þys world*.

**41/12–13 He ne douted him nouʒt of Ihesu þat he nas comen to sauen þe world** Cf. 40/1240–41: *Il ne duta pas de Iesu / Que pur sauuer ne fust uenu*. See *MED* douten *v*. for the reflexive use of this verb.

**41/14 þe fre prisoun of helle** So PRHa; B omits *fre*. This phrase occurs elsewhere in Middle English sermons, e.g. Ross 1940:4, 8–10: *And also he fowʒthe so in ys passion þat he slowʒ dethe and browthe fro dethe all þat were in þe free prisone of hell vn-to þe ioy of Paradise*. Ross quotes from the *Catholic Encyclopaedia* under 'Limbo': 'Meanwhile they (the righteous who died before the coming of Christ) were 'in prison', as St. Peter says (I *Pet*. iii.19); but, as in Christ's own words to the penitent thief (*Luke* xxiii.43) and the parable of Lazarus (*Luke* xvi.22ff.) clearly imply, their condition was one of happiness, notwithstanding the postponement of the higher bliss to which they looked forward' (p. 338). Thus the 'prison of hell' is 'free' in so far as for the righteous it is a prison without torture. See *MED* fre *adj*. 4c.(k): fre prisoun, 'custody without torture'.

**41/18 vntil** In addition to other evidence of the likely erasure of *vntil*, see p. lxii, faint traces of an initial 'v', possibly also of final 'l', and the size of the erasure, support *vntil* as the erased reading restored here.

**41/21 diswarre** 'unaware'; see *MED* disware *adj*. (a), where the word is first quoted from the fifteenth century.

**41/27 riʒt liʒt** For the restoration of the H reading, cf. *riʒth liʒth* PRHa, *ryʒt syʒt* B.

**41/34 hii han þe fel white** See p. xl.

**43/1 so haþ þe wiked þe hert brennand** See p. xl.

**43/6 Al hem þenche** Cf. 39/27 note. The *þ* inserted after *þenche* may have been intended to complete the impersonal construction.

**43/13–14 hii taken respit** Cf. 42/1316: *pernent respit*. For ME *respit* 'extension of time for action', see *MED* respit(e *n*.1.(a).

**43/15** Perhaps referring to Proverbs x.28.

**43/19–23 ȝif þat ... nold nouȝt** An interpolation in the English stressing the importance of individual responsibility in seeking salvation. See also 37/14–17 note, and 37/18–22 note.

**43/22 ded** 'death'; also 109/1. According to *MED*, under 'deth' (*n.*), the 'confusion with *ded* adj. is chiefly Northern and East Midland'.

**43/22 bidden** The H reading *bede* was formed by alteration of an original *bid*. The oblique stroke after the *d* of *bid* at the end of the line indicates that the word continued in the erased space at the beginning of the next line; [*den*] is supplied as the likely original ending.

**43/22–23 & he nold** Despite the erasure of five letter spaces after *he*, the H text is complete; cf. *and he nolde* PB, *and he wolde* R, om. Ha.

**45/9 holi halwen al** The H reading is *halawen*, with the second 'a' expuncted.

**45/23 no** Possibly a mistake for *ne* as the alteration here suggests (a tail has been added in light ink to 'o' to form 'e'); but for *no* as a conjunction, 'nor', see *MED* no *conj.* (1) 1.

**45/32–33 into out of mesure of pride** See p. xl.

**47/1 to wille** 'willingly'; cf. 46/1419: *a talent* and *OED* will *sb.*[1] 20.

**47/7–8** The sense of this sentence is: John, he (Christ) said, was more than a prophet, for he (John) afterwards saw him (Christ) of whom he had spoken; for he (John) afterwards saw him in person of whom he had spoken in the desert.

**47/12–13 word, ȝif þat ȝe telle** So CPBR, om. Ha. The first half of this sentence is incomplete since a clause equivalent to 46/1443: *Recuntez en uostre meisun* is lacking after *word*.

**49/1–14** 4th Sunday in Advent. John i.19–28

**49/10 Whi baptisettow whan nart Crist** See p. xli.

**49/11 cristn** *lift* CP, *leue* B, *baptize* R, cf. AN 1475: *lief* W[2], *lef* HmOLW[1], *leue* U. AN *lever* 'lift, raise' (*1 sg. pres.* lief) and AN *laver* 'wash' (*1 sg. pres.* lef, leve *analogically from 3 sg. pres.*) were readily confusable. The translator seems to have taken the verb in his exemplar as 'lift' as in CP and probably, originally, in H. The alteration to *cristn* in H and the reading *baptize* in R are revisions perhaps made with the Vulgate: *ego baptizo in aqua* (John i.26) in mind.

**49/12–13 þat befor me in God is made** So CPBR, cf. 48/1479. The English is a word-for-word rendering of the AN text as in HmOL: *Qui deuant moy en bien est fait*.

**49/19 to han fordon** For the ME use of the perfect infinitive to express purpose, see Mustanoja 1960:517.

**49/25–27** II Timothy ii.24

**49/26 ac** *ac* CPBHa, *but* R, cf. AN 1508 *ainz*. Instead of his usual change to *bot*, the Reviser has here altered *ac* to *he*.

**51/1–2 & for his pride & for his jolifte** 'both on account of his pride and on account of his levity'; see *MED* and *conj*. 1c. (a).

**51/9–25** Aitken (1922:28–29) identifies the Latin source of this *exemplum* as the *Vitae Patrum:*

Ad quemdam solitarium venit presbyter cujusdam basilicæ, ut consecraret ei oblationem ad communicandum. Veniens autem quidam ad illum solitarium, accusavit apud ipsum eumdeum presbyterum. Qui cum ex consuetudine iterum venisset ad eum, ut consecraret oblationem, scandalizatus ille solitarius non aperuit ei. Presbyter autem hoc viso discessit. Et ecce vox facta est ad solitarium, dicens: Tulerunt sibi homines judicium meum. Et factus est velut in excessu mentis, et videbat quasi puteum aureum, et situlam auream, et funem aureum, et aquam bonam valde. Videbat autem et quemdam leprosum haurientem et refundentem in vase, et cupiebat bibere, et non poterat propter quod leprosus esset ille qui hauriebat. Et ecce iterum vox ad eum, dicens: Cur non bibis ex aqua hac? quam causam habet qui implet? implet enim solummodo et effundit in vase. In se autem reversus solitarius, et considerans virtutem visionis, vocavit presbyterum, et fecit eum sicut et prius sanctificare sibi oblationem. (*PL* 73.911)

She also notes that the story occurs amongst the *Exempla* of Jacques de Vitry; see Crane 1890:68, 198 (no. 155).

**51/9 þat God dede mani vertuz fore** Cf. 50/1537: *Pur ki Deus granz uertuz feseit.* For *vertuz*, 'mighty works, miracles', see *MED* vertu *n.*9.(c).

**51/11 wel bileueand** Cf. 50/1542: *tresbien craant.*

**51/12 ac** *ac* CPBHa, *and* R, cf. 50/1545: *mais*. Here *ac* has been erased without the usual *bot* being replaced. Cf. 49/27 note.

**51/17–21** The incidence of leprosy in England reached its peak during the twelfth century, when more leper hospitals were founded than at any other time. These were often built near springs for it was thought that medicinal or holy waters might offer a possible cure. Since leprosy was believed to be highly contagious, segregation was the general principle which governed the management of the disease; on this point see also 43/27–28 and 95/3–7. The order of service which might be used when a leper was diagnosed records various prohibitions which may be relevant here, for example, a leper was forbidden to wash himself or his clothes in the local stream, and when he wished to drink he must use his own cup. See Rubin 1974.

**51/20 him** So CPBR, Ha differs. The inappropriate *him* here may have derived from the reading *nel vout* (as Hm) in line 1564 of the translator's AN text rather than *n'i uolt* of W²OLW¹ or *ne vout* of U.

**51/31–53/17 Vnderstondeþ nou3t þis tale ... nil ich telle namore** This is an interpolation in the English emphasising that the tale of the hermit does not have the authority of Holy Writ and that knowingly to support an evil priest is a deadly sin.

**53/9–10** Isaiah i.15–16.

**53/12–13** The source of this quotation from St. Gregory has not been located.

**53/13–14** Psalms lxvi.18.

**53/16–17** Unidentified biblical quotation.

**55/1ff. Take we þan … etc.** A complicated sentence. The sense is: 'Let us then betake ourselves to Jesus the just who teaches us the right way to heaven, who, because he took our flesh and blood, has become our brother and neighbour, so that through good deeds, secret and open, we may be brought etc.'. *Take we* in the ME here suggests that the translator's AN text may have had, or have been read (perhaps in abbreviation) as having a form of OF *prendre* (e.g. *pernum* 'let us take') rather than *prium* 'let us pray' in 54/1626.

**57/1–19** Christmas Eve. Luke ii.1–14. This sermon is absent from R where, midway down f. 44ᵛ, sermon 6 begins immediately after sermon 4.

**57/3 prest** So CPB. The different gospel translation of Ha has *keper*. 56/1637: *prouost* 'governor' may have been confused (as in the O spelling *pruuoz*, with possible mistaking of the letter 'z' for a 2-shaped 'r') with a form of AN *pruueire*, *provoir* 'priest' (see *AND* pruueire); or, conceivably, *prest* here may have been a rendering of AN *primat* 'primate', the reading in W¹.

**57/11 come** If the original H reading was *comen*, the erasure of *n* may have been made as a correction to the required singular form, rather than as part of the common erasure of plural *n*.

**59/3 writen in** Cf. 58/1711: *enbreuez*. See also *OED* write, *v.* 14 where the first instance of *writen in* is quoted from Wyclif *Rev.* xxi 12 (1382), translating Lat. *inscripta*.

**59/8 born** Cf. 58/1720: *nasquesist*. The H scribe mistakenly wrote *lorn*. The Reviser made the obvious correction of 'l' to 'b' when he replaced the 'n' with 'e'.

**59/11 witeþ** An error shared by C for *writeþ* PBHa; cf. 58/1726: *enbreue*.

**59/12 þis kinges** So CP, *þis kynge* B, *Oȝain … gode* (59/11–14) om. Ha. The name *David* (cf. 58/1728: *David li reis*) is lacking from all English manuscripts.

**59/17–19** Psalms lxxviii.25.

**59/18 bred of angel** *bred of angeles* CPBHa, cf. 58/1740: *pain des angles*. For possible H syntax here with the singular *of angel* as a ME genitive of description, see Mustanoja 1960:80.

**61/6–8** I Corinthians vii.4.

**61/11 on** *on* BHa, *wiþ on* HCP, cf. 60/1804: *Vne*. Here *wiþ* is omitted from the text as an apparent HCP error.

**61/12 blod** The tail of an erased 'y' remains below the line; the scribe first wrote *blody*, perhaps confusing *blod* and *body*.

**61/18–19** John xiv.6.

**61/29 truage** 'obligation to pay tribute' or 'servitude'; see *MED* treuage *n.*1.(b) and (d).

**61/33 to couer vs wiþ newe godes** Cf. 60/1851: *Pur nos cuuerir de biens nouels.*

**63/2 maniure vnto bestes** Cf. 62/1860: *mangure a celes bestes.*

**63/4 wel bestes** Cf. 62/1864: *ben bestial.*

**63/7 chaimmcchipes** *chanschipes* C, *schenschepes* B, *schames* P, Ha rewrites. *MED* first records this suffix-formation from the fifteenth century; see *MED* shamshippe *n.* ME *shame* and *shende* sometimes appeared as variant readings and commonly occurred together in the phrases *shame and shende* and *shame and shen(d)shipe* – see *MED* shende *n.* and shame *n.*3.(a). Doubtless the suffix-formation *shamshippe* was formed after ME *shen(d)shipe*.

**63/12 þat now ne wil we nouȝt beleuen** So CP, *þat ne wol noȝt byleuen* B, *þat nou ne wil* [eras.] *nouȝt don* Ha. For the Middle English relative construction with 'that' followed by a personal pronoun (as in *þat ... we* in HCP here), see Mustanoja 1960:202. The pronoun *we* may have been intended to distinguish the relative *þat* from *he*, the subject of the immediately preceding clause.

**63/13–14 more we schul be viler þan ani best** So CP, *more vile we schul be þan any beste* B, *we schal þan be more uile þan ani best* Ha. For multiple comparison in Middle English, see Mustanoja 1960:281.

**63/18 becomeþ** *comeþ* CPBHa. For the sense, 'comes', see *MED* bicomen *v.* 1 (a); in this sense, however, this verb is usually accompanied by a prepositional phrase indicating destination. Since the other MSS have *comeþ*, H *becomeþ* may have arisen from a miscopying of *he comeþ*; in some hands 'b' and 'h' were confusable. Cf. 97/11 note.

**63/19–20 þenche we in stedfast bileue & woni in gode werkes** *þenche we in stedefast bileue & wake we in good werkes* CPHa, *wake we in stedfast byleue & in gode werkes* B. For H *woni in* (with *in* inserted), cf. CP *wake we in*. Here the CP text is closer to 62/1895: *E veillez en bone fesance* than H, and HCP closer to the AN than B.

**63/23 men sinnes** With the following noun beginning with *s*, *men* here may conceivably be an endingless genitive, but seems more likely to be an error – cf. *mannes* CB, *mennes* PHa.

**65/1–2 al don hii wel her mister** See p. xl.

**65/3–4** Perhaps referring to Ecclesiastes viii.12.

**65/11 angels** So CPBHa, R lacks. The scribe of H wrote *angel*. A horizontal stroke has been added after the final 'l', here accepted as an abbreviation mark for 's' of the required plural *angels*.

**65/12–13 hii han songen** See p. xli.

**65/16 in Gode** Cf. 64/1955 *en De*.

**65/20 suffiseþ** The added *þ* is adopted here as a necessary correction. Cf. *suffiseþ* CPBHa.

**67/1–22** Epiphany. Matthew ii.1–12. In B additional rubrics have been added to divide this sermon into three parts, see 75/17 and 77/20 below.

**67/7 so** So CPR, *so he* B. For ME *so* 'likewise', see *MED* so *adv.* 5.

**67/10–11 þat my folk schul gouernen & kepen of Israel** Cf. p. xl.

**67/14 wite him to say** So CPBR. For the sense 'inform him', see *OED* wit, *v.*1.12. This is a rare idiom; *OED* gives three examples from fifteenth-century texts and suggests an explanation in terms of a possible confusion with the verb witter, 'to inform, instruct'. The added *do* in H suggests confusion of this idiom with *do (to) wit*, 'to make known to, inform', see *OED* wit, *v.*1.9.a.

**67/18 alson** 'immediately'; see *MED* al-sone *adv.* and *conj.* (a), a word found mostly in Northern texts.

**67/27 of water wyne** Cf. 66/2037: *del ewe uin.*

**67/27–28 he schewed him** The reflexive *him* is due to the French, cf. 66/2038: *s'est mustre.* The translator seems to have understood the AN as 'he (i.e. Jesus) showed' rather than 'it was shown'. Cf. 69/15.

**69/2–3 ben comen ... han sen** Cf. 68/2042: *sunt uenuz* and 68/2043: *unt uouz.* See p. xli.

**69/10–13** Numbers xxiv.17.

**69/14 of þat sterre hii maden her giour** Cf. 68/2066.

**69/15–16 Be þat schewed him Ihesus Crist þat he made man & witt etc.** Cf. 68/2070–71.

**69/19–20** Matthew iv.14–16 citing Isaiah ix.2.

**69/19 prophecie** Cf. *prophecie* CPBR and 68/2079. The original reading in H has been altered by changing 'c' to 't' and erasing the final two letters; signs of the erased 'e' are still visible. A corrector in H has sought to make sense of the English by adding *to*, to make *to þe folk etc.* (line 19) parallel with *to hem* (line 20). The whole passage *þat aforn ... gret liȝt* (69/18–20) is re-written in Ha as *þat aforn was prophecied. Þe folk þat ben in derkenes gret liȝt schon vp hem.*

**69/19–20 come gret liȝt** So CBR, *comeþ grete liȝth* P, cf. 68/2081: *uit raier grant luiur.* Confusion of *vit* and *vint*, the *3 sg. pret.* forms of AN *veer* and *venir*, possibly in the translator's exemplar, may have given rise to *come* in the English.

**69/28 Per** An error in H; cf. *þerfore* CPBRHa and 68/2100 *Pur co.*

**71/3 þe syȝt** Cf. *þe liȝt* CPBRHa and 70/2115: *luminaire.* Supplied above the line here, *þe syȝt* is either a bad guess or, conceivably, an addition from a manuscript where *syȝt* occurred as result of the confusion of 'l' and long 's'. Cf. 41/27, note.

**71/9 Loke, lordinges, þat** Cf. 70/2128: *Veez seignurs ke,* UHmOL, with *ke* for W² *cum.*

**73/4–5 bot ȝif he entre wiþ god werkes doinge** An awkward rendering of 72/2185: *Qui n'entret par bone fesance.*

**73/6 Of þe bileue** So CP, *þe bileue* BHa, R lacks, cf. 72/2188: *De la creiance.*

**73/13–14 bitokeneþ þe realtes þat man schal haue in Goddes seruise** So CPBHa, R lacks. The English text appears to mean that gold 'betokens the royal privileges which man shall have in God's service'. This, however, is a curious departure from 72/2205–6 resulting in the omission of any mention of incense from the exposition of the three gifts here.

**73/16 wiþ þat ognement** So CPB, *þerwiþ* Ha, R lacks, cf. 72/2210: *de ceste oynture.* CPB and the AN confirm the addition of *þat* in H as correct.

**73/33 He þat haþ þe flesche slepeand** See pp. xl–xli. A later hand alters this completely to: *He þat haþ cyth þe flesche & slepe.* An addition, interlined above *flesche,* has been erased.

**73/33 o þis liif** *of þis lif* CPB, *on þis lif* Ha, R lacks, cf. 72/2253 *de ceste uie.* Here, as confirmed by CPB and the AN, *o* is a weak stressed form of *of* and not of *on* as assumed by the scribe who added 'n' here.

**75/5 emsample** *–also* **ensaumple 93/35** The *em*-form is quoted for the fifteenth century under *OED* ensample.

**75/9 keuern** Altered to *rekeuern*; 're' has been added twice, once in light ink before the word, then interlined in dark ink.

**75/11 godes** So CP, *gode dedis* BHa, R lacks. The CP reading confirms *godes* as the original H reading restored here.

**75/12 haue in wille** For the infinitive used as a verbal noun, see Mustanoja 1960:511.

**75/13 peyneþ** The added *þ* is adopted; it was possibly intended as a correction to give a *3 sg. pres. indic.* form. However, *he þat ne peyne him etc.* could be plural.

**75/17–31** Matthew iii.13–17. In B (f. 16ᵛ) the rubric *Þe sunday gospel on þe vtas of twefþe* [sic] *day* with a note of the gospel reading has been added in red to the left-hand margin, and a further addition to the right-hand margin notes the liturgical occasion: *Dominica Epiphanie*, in abbreviated form. Another rubric set slightly further up the left-hand margin states: *3e schullyn fynde þe gospel þat is rad on þe sunday wyþinne þe vtas of þe twelfþe day in þe firste chapetle of Ion.*

**75/19 to take cristendome** 'to be baptised', cf. 74/2289: *Pur prendre de li baptire.* See *MED* cristendom *n.* 2. c.

**75/27 wiþ þi gode wille** Cf. 74/2305: *de tun gre.*

**75/32 let** So CPBHa, R lacks.

**77/15–16 ʒif we wil drawe his name of Crist** *if he wil drawe his name of crist* CPBRHa, cf. 76/2357: *Si de Crist uolt dreit nun treire.* The French supports the *he* of the other English MSS where H has *we*. The sense should therefore be: 'if he wishes to take his name from Christ.'

**77/20–33** John ii.1–11. In B (f. 17ʳ) the rubric *Þe firste sunday gospel af[ter] þe vtas of tw[elf]þe day*, has been added in red to the right-hand margin (where some words have been damaged by cropping).

**77/20 fel** For non-expression of *it* in impersonal constructions, see Mustanoja 1960:143 (7).

**77/29 Archetreclin(e** In ME this word as a common noun had the sense 'governor / ruler of the feast' (as in the AV translation of Vulgate *architriclino / architriclinus* in John ii.8–9); it also occurred as a proper name. See *MED* arch(i)triclin *n.* The latter usage arose in some medieval exegetical traditions in which this originally common noun came to be viewed as a name, identified variously with St. Paul, with John the Baptist, and with the bridegroom at the wedding (sometimes thought of as John the Evangelist himself). Others, like Robert de Gretham (see 76/2389–90) took *Architriclin* simply to be the name of the governor of the feast, and this interpretation has been carried over here into the ME text. For a full discussion, see Trotter 1987.

**77/34 Galile** The repeated *Galile* here is an error for *Chana* – cf. *Chana* CPBRHa and 76/2401.

**77/34–35 & þe loue is for passinge** *and þe loue as for passing* RHa, *& loue as for passynge* P, *& þe as for passinge* C, *as for passynge* B. The original Middle English may have read *& in loue as for passinge*, following 76/2402; the archetype of the surviving MSS would appear to have read *& þe loue as for passinge*. By changing *as* to *is* H makes this phrase end the first sentence of this paragraph leaving the following sentence incomplete. B has attempted to arrive at sense by omitting *& loue*.

**77/35 þer** Cf. *þer* CPBRHa and 76/2404 *iloec*; *þer* is restored as the original H reading in place of the alteration *þat*.

**79/11 he** God.

**79/12–14** For example I Corinthians vi.9–10. A later hand has added the instruction 'nota' in the centre margin, probably referring to the quotation from Paul; an addition in the same hand in the top margin is mostly lost through trimming.

**79/14–15** Despite the attribution to Hosea, this biblical quotation has not been located.

**79/16–17 Ac be þe sinne … repenteþ him**. Cf. 78/2440–43 (U text):

> Mais ia n'ert pecche tant lez
> Ne si horribles ne si mesfez
> Q'il ne pus auer amendement
> Quant en sa sancte se repent.

Either the translator's exemplar wrongly had a subjunctive instead of *ert* (fut. indic.) in line 2440, or he misunderstood the AN principal clause as a concessive clause of the *ja* + negative + subjunctive type. Cf. 32/970: *Ia ne seit home …*

**79/24 schuld** *schulde* CPBRHa. In H, *schul* ends a line. Probably 'd' was to be written at the beginning of the next line (such word-division is not uncommon in H), but was accidentally omitted owing, possibly, to the fact that the next word, *drawe*, began with 'd'. The text is emended on this assumption.

**79/25–27** Genesis ii.24 and Matthew xix.4–7.

**79/27–28 þat makeþ departinge þat God makeþ on** See Mustanoja 1960:511 and 569 for ME confusion of the present participle, the verbal noun and the infinitive.

**79/30 him com** For the use in ME of the reflexive *him* with verbs of motion, see Sisam 1955:257, g24.

**81/5 is so muchel holi folke** The interlined *is* is adopted in the text as a verb is required. It should, however, have been inserted after *muchel*; cf. *þer so michel is of holi folk* CPBRHa and 80/2477: *V tant sunt de si seinte genz*.

**81/8 be** The subjunctive here follows *seit* of 80/2484: *E ki k'en seit li seruitur*.

**81/11 þay þat may** After *þay* the scribe formed a single minim (probably the first stroke of the 'm' of *may*); though clearly erroneous the letter has not been erased.

**81/13 and þe water wel betokeneþ** The object of *betokeneþ* is lacking in H. Cf. *and þe water wel hit bitokeneþ* CPBR, *& þat betokeneþ wel þe water* Ha, and 80/2496: *E l'ewe bien co signefie*.

**81/14 in himself** Cf. 80/2499: *par sei*.

**81/14–15 þe flesche þat neuer ne fineþ** i.e. the 'flesh' never ceases to deteriorate.

**81/15–16 bad þe water** Cf. *bad do þe water* CPB, *bad þe water be þat* R, *comaunded þat þe water schuld be don* Ha and 80/2502: *Iesus fist l'ewe mettre*. H lacks the causitive *do*.

**81/20 clere and** There is a small erasure between these two words.

**81/23 flodes** An 's' is supplied to correct an obviously accidental omission in H; cf. *flodes* CPBRHa and 80/2520: *li floz*.

**81/31 haþ bounden hem. O flesche** The preposition *in* of the H reading *haþ bounden hem in o flesche* has been removed from the text here as a corrupt reading which gives nonsense. Cf. *haþ bounden hem o flesch* CPBR, Ha differs, and 80/2539–40. A reviser in H has underlined *makeþ flesche fondinges*, probably indicating the deletion of this phrase, in an attempt to make sense of the MS reading with *in*.

**81/31 flesche fondinges** Under *MED* flesch *n*. 5b, *fleshes fonding* is given as meaning 'temptation to sexual sins'. However there is no connotation of 'temptation' or 'sin' in 80/2540: *charnel leissur*; under *AND* leisur these lines from the *Miroir* are quoted and the sense of *leissur* given as 'pleasure'. Thus *flesche fondinges* here seems rather to be 'sexual pleasures' – cf. *MED* fonden *v*. 5(a) 'to enjoy or indulge in (pleasures, love-making, etc.)'.

**81/36–83/1 God he schewed ... was God** Supplied from C. So PR, *god he schewed ... schewed hym þat he was god* B, om. Ha. The lacuna in H is due to eyeskip.

**85/1–19** 1st Sunday after the octave of Epiphany. Luke ii.41–52.

**85/6 kinde** So PB, *kin* C, Ha differs. For *kinde ne* R reads *kyndome*. The final two letters have been erased in H. This word has been so altered six times in this sermon; erased 'de' is faintly visible in *kinde* 85/8.

**85/6 wist** The apparent extra letter between 'w' and 'i' appears to be a letter-form begun in error by the scribe and not erased.

**85/6 ac** The original reading has been altered to *bot*, then erased, and *þat* written over the erasure in dark ink. A later hand has added a caret after *þat*, and the words *hyt schold be he but* in the margin.

**85/6 vnderstonde** The present tense occurs also in C *vnderstonden*, but the appropriate past tense *vnderstoden* is found in PBR; cf. 84/2568 *quiderent*.

**87/2 to gon** Cf. *to go* CBR, *for to go* P, Ha alters. CBR and P support *to gon* restored here as the original reading of H.

**87/4 God seruise** The 'es' interlined after *God* gives the same form of the genitive as in CPBRHa and in *Godes seruise* in line 2. However, an endingless genitive is possible, especially before a word beginning with 's'. Perhaps also influence from 86/2625: *Deu seruise* is not to be discounted.

**87/9 mouþe wiþ mouþ** Cf. 86/2635: *Buche a buche*.

**87/11** Matthew x.20.

**87/22–23** The fluctuations in number here may have arisen from the ambiguity of the pronoun *he* which in H may be both singular and (sporadically) plural. The singular prevails throughout in the other MSS.

**89/3 do** For the restoration of *do* here, cf. *do* CPBR, Ha differs, and 88/2702: *faire*.

**89/7 hertteþ his fader oþer his moder or smiteþ** *fader oþer moder hirteþ oþer smyteþ* CPBR, Ha differs, cf. 88/2711: *Ki pere e mere fuit e blesce*. In H, *hertteþ* has been misplaced.

**89/9 no kepe to his** The scribe of H has added these words after *ne ȝeueþ no*, thus giving the reading *ne ȝeueþ no no kepe to his*; the repetition of 'no' was doubtless inadvertent and is not retained in the text.

**89/18–26** This section draws upon St. Paul's teaching in Ephesians vi.1–4 and Colossians iii.20–21.

**89/30 and to God and to þe folk** The correction of the word order in H is supported by the other English MSS and by 88/2755: *Cresseit a Deu e a la gent.*

**91/1–24** 3rd Sunday after Epiphany. Matthew viii.1–13. Between lines 2757–58 of the Anglo-Norman text in W² there is a rubric designating the final section of the Epiphany sermon, the part concerning the marriage in Cana of Galilee, for the 2nd Sunday after Epiphany.

**91/6 telle nouȝt** *telle nouȝt* B, *telle not* R, *ne telle nouȝth* P, *ne telle* C, Ha differs. The erased *nouȝt* (of which 'n' and part of 'ȝt' are visible) is restored here.

**91/7 offerende** *offrende* CPBR, Ha differs. Cf. *offerende* 95/3 and 95/6. Clearly the 'g' by alteration replaced an original 'd' restored here.

**91/17 And y say** So C, *I saie* PBR, Ha differs. *And* is restored to the text here since the erased ampersand seems to have been the original HC reading.

**91/21 of þe kingdom** Cf. AN 2802: *del regne* (so W¹HmL). The required sense is 'of this kingdom', i.e. the kingdom of *this* world – cf. *de ceste regne* U.

**93/5 he haue ben** So CPBRHa. The addition of *haue* and the alteration of *be* to *ben* (possibly by H) are supported by the other MSS.

**93/7 þat to whom .. seruen** For the preposition *to* here, cf. 92/2833: *A ki del ciel sert la uertuz.*

**93/13–18 and 93/27–95/7** The comments relating to leprosy in these passages are indicative of contemporary attitudes to the disease. The incidence of leprosy (indeed, disease in general), was associated with past sins, but those so afflicted were regarded as deserving cases for charity and alms; lepers especially were referred to as Christ's poor (*pauperes Christi*) and associated with the biblical Lazarus. Note also the details given here about the physical effects of the disease. See Rubin 1974.

**93/20–21** Psalm cxxxiv.6.

**93/25 he** i.e. *stedfast bileue*. So CBR, *it* Ha, om. P. Cf. 21/3, note.

**93/29 what schal ben of vs** See p. xl.

**93/33–34 him ... he be, he oweþ** *him ... he be he owe* CPBRHa. The pronouns *he* (both by alteration) and the alterations *him* from *hem*, *be* from *ben*, and *oweþ* from *owen*, appear to be valid corrections to the singular number as in other MSS.

**95/1 ac** The faintest traces of this erased word are visible. Cf. *ac* CPHa, *but* BR, and 94/2898: *mais.*

**95/2 þat** Here *þat* comes in the middle of a sentence, not at the beginning of a new paragraph as the capital Þ in blue ink in H would mistakenly suggest.

**95/2 him** So CPBRHa.

**95/8–9 whan man was al brouȝt adoun** So CBR, *whan a man ...* P, om. Ha. The English here differs from 94/2913: *Quant home fu, tut ad grante.*

**95/10 þat** So CBR, *þat who þat* P, om. Ha.

**95/27 himseluen** For *himseluen* as a nominative, see Mustanoja 1960:147–48.

**95/31–32 and bi consail ... is maister** Word order as in 94/2952–3: *E puis par le conseil de sun prestre / Ki desuz Deu de l' alme est mestre.*

**97/11 to centirion** These words are written partly in the margin, and partly interlined above deleted 'orion' which begins the line. This spelling (with medial 'i' instead of the usual 'u') is not recorded in the *MED* or *OED;* presumably a minim has been omitted.

**97/11 besouȝt** So CPBRHa. The H reading *he souȝt* is emended here as an obvious error arising from the confusion of 'b' and 'h'.

**97/13 payne** See *MED* paien, *n.* and adj. As it stands here in H, *payne* is an adjective; it may originally have been a noun if the erased final letter was an 's'. Alterations to this word in H show a preference for the form *paynem,* see *MED* painim(e, *n.* and *adj.*

**97/22–23 alle gode befor God be put forþe** With the corrections H would read: *alle gode dede befor God beþ put forþe* – 'every good deed is set forth before God', with the alteration of *be* to *beþ* probably intended here to give a singular verb. However, the H reading is clearly corrupt and the corrections only partial – cf. *alle good dedes bifore god ben put furþ* CPB, *all gode dedes ben put forth byfor god* R, om. Ha, and 96/2994–5: *Veez, seignurs, tuz bienfaiz / Deuant Deu mesmes sunt retraiz.*

**97/24 help** So CPBR, Ha lacks. The final letter of *help* in H has been touched up in darker ink – perhaps a correction of *helþ* to *help.*

**97/30 him þourȝ** So CPBR, om. Ha.

**99/5 of which God herd his biddyng** Cf. 98/3027: *Dunt Deus oit ses ureisuns.*

**99/9 vsen** The H scribe began this word at the end of a line, but wrote only 'v'; *vsen* is written in full on the next line.

**99/17 to lyue and alway be in** *to lyue alway in* CPBR, Ha alters, cf. 98/3050–1: *a uie / Tut dis en.* The H text is corrupt: the *and* before *alway* has led to the addition of *be* after *alway.*

**99/19 and Seyn Poul seiþ and techeþ** *as seint poul seiþ in his techinge* CPBR, om. Ha, cf. 98/3055: *Cum dist Saint Pol en sun sermun.* The underlining of *and* (indicating deletion?) and the *þat* added after *and* represent an attempt at 'improving' the corrupt H text.

**99/24 for** An erased word above *for* was probably *þi* – cf. *for þi* CPBRHa and 98/3066: *Pur co.* There are other occurrences in H of the erasure of *þi,* see 89/9 and 89/28; *þi* is also occasionally added, see 107/14 and 117/26 (both probably by H).

**99/26 payne** A bar over *e* in *payne* is probably an addition. Presumably the intended form was *paynem* in line with other alterations to this word.

**99/27 to our soules** For *to,* interlined here probably by H, cf. *to our soule* Ha, *to þe soule* CB, *vnto þe soule* PR, and 98/3073: *as almes.*

**99/29 pynynges** The scribe wrote *pynyges,* presumably in error.

**99/29 and his body**  *in his bodi* CBR, *in þe bodi* P, Ha differs, cf. 98/3077: *El cors*. The corrupt *and* for *in* in H may have arisen from the misreading of an abbreviation of *in* as an ampersand. Cf. 21/26 note.

**99/33 þouȝtful**  Cf. 98/3086: *pesante*. The translator's exemplar must have read, or been misread as, *pensante*.

**99/35 bidding**  An erasure above '-ig' has affected both letters and doubtless removed an abbreviation sign for 'n', assumed for the usual ending *-ing* adopted in the text here.

**101/1 mesager**  There is a bar over the 'a', but this appears to be an addition in lighter ink. For the usual ME spelling without 'n', see *MED* messager *n*.

**101/7 what**  So CBR, om. P, Ha alters, cf. 100/3104: *Quant pur sun serf deignat preier*. Presumably *what* was an error for *whan* early in the English MS tradition or, conceivably, a translation from an AN exemplar with *Qe* for *Quant* as Hm (by alteration) appears to read.

**101/8 loued him**  'humbled himself', cf. 100/3106: *s'umiliat*. The alteration to *lowed* was doubtless intended to avoid any confusion with the verb 'to love'.

**101/9–10 schul answer ... misdon**  The H text may represent the original English rendering of AN 3109: *respunderunt* and 100/3110: *mesfunt* where plural pronouns are unexpressed. However the additions of *þai* before *answer* and *misdon* may have been by H; plural pronouns are found in all other MSS.

**101/11 leggen**  The alteration of 'n' to 'þ', rather than the Reviser's usual change to a plural ending in 'þ' (see p. lxi), may here have been intended as a correction to a singular verb. However the plural *leggen* may be explained as bad concord due to the influence of the immediately preceding plural, *tenaunce*.

**101/11 hem longeþ**  For the impersonal construction in this verb, see *MED* longen *v*.(1) 2.

**101/14 anguischen**  *languissen* CPBRHa, cf. 100/3120: *languirunt*. Initial 'l' has been lost in H (or its tradition), possibly by haplography after the final 'l' of preceding *schul*. Cf. 79/24, note.

**101/16 to cristen man**  Cf. *to þe cristen man* CBRHa, *vnto ... man* P.

**101/20 ȝif he haue**  So CP, *ȝif ȝe han* BRHa, and cf. 100/3136: *Si uos auez*. HCP have *he* in error.

**103/1 fro**  The bar over the letter 'o' appears to be written in slightly lighter ink and is probably an addition. The same is true of the second instance of the word later in the sentence and of *fro* (103/3, first instance).

**103/3**  Psalm cxix.155.

**103/6 ben þai**  *ben þe jewes* CPBRHa, cf. 102/3178: *sunt li Giu*.

**103/6 Cananes**  'Canaanites'; see *MED* Canane *n. & adj.* (a).

**105/1–10**  4th Sunday after Epiphany. Matthew viii.23–27. Trimming has caused the loss of letters from the heading.

**105/21–22 he owe ... lowen him ... his miȝt**  So CP, *he owen ... lowen hym ... his miȝt* B, *þai ow ... lowen hym ... þair myȝht* R, *hii owe ... lowen hem ... her power* Ha. The singular number in the second half of this sentence of HCP moves progressively to the plural in BRHa.

**105/22 schewen him** *schewe* CPBRHa. Here *him* appears to be an error, perhaps echoing *him* in preceding *lowen him*.

**107/9 and haþ** Between *and* and *haþ* a letter, possibly 'þ', has been begun but not completed.

**107/20 for** A space has been left before *for* for a paragraph sign which has not been supplied.

**107/21 þar her liif was in present** 'where their life (i.e. Jesus) was present'. Cf. 106/3299: *V lur uie fut en present.*

**107/31–109/4** Aitken 1922:51 notes an analogue to this allegorical reading in Haymo Halberstat, Homily XX, which is also for the fourth Sunday after Epiphany; see *PL* 118.147–54.

**107/33–34 to him þat him loued** 'to those who loved Him'.

**107/34–35 princes and kynges ... and þe phariseues** *of kynges & of princes ... & of þe pharisens* CB, *of kynges & princes ... & of þe phariseus* PR, *of princes & prestes* Ha (which otherwise differs), cf. 106/3320–1: *Des reis, de princes ... de pharisels.* The omission of the preposition *of* (twice or three times) obscures the syntax in H. In the metaphor here, the disciples are thought of as being beset by a tempest of princes, kings, Jews, etc.

**107/37 for þat** H omits the verb here; cf. *for hii leued þat* CPBRHa and 106/3328: *K'il ne crusent.*

**109/2 bileuen** The sequence of tenses here requires a preterite; cf. *bileueden* CPBRHa.

**109/10 his** i.e. 'his followers', cf. 108/3351: *lei sons.*

**109/11–12 & þat dide hit so gret turment; ʒete lasteþ holi chirche** So CBR, *& þat duden so gret* etc. P, *ʒett lasteþ holi chirche* Ha, cf. 108/3354: *Vncore regne seinte eglise.* The lacuna in H results from eyeskip; the missing text is supplied from C.

**109/13–111/8** Aitken 1922:29–30 observes that despite the attribution of this story to St. Gregory, its source is not to be found in either the *Dialogues* or the *Homilies.* She notes however that the *Dialogues* contains a different story which presents the same moral, see *Dialogorum Libri IV*, chapter 36:

> In eodem quoque ponte hunc quem prædiximus Stephanum se recognovisse testatus est. Qui dum transire voluisset, ejus pes lapsus est, et ex medio corpore jam extra pontem dejectus, a quibusdam teterrimis viris ex flumine surgentibus, per coxas deorsum, atque a quibusdam albatis et speciosissimis viris cœpit per brachia sursum trahi. Cumque hoc luctamen esset, ut hunc boni spiritus sursum, mali deorsum traherent, ipse qui hæc videbat, ad corpus reversus est, et quid de eo plenius gestum sit, minime cognovit. Qua in re de ejusdem Stephani vita datur intelligi, quia in eo mala carnis cum eleemosynarum operatione certabant. Qui enim per coxas deorsum, per brachia trahebatur sursum, patet nimirum, quia et eleemosynas amaverat, et carnis vitiis perfecte non restiterat, quæ eum deorsum trahebant. Sed in illo occulti arbitri examine quid in eo vicerit, et nos, et eum qui vidit et revocatus est, latet. Constat tamen, quia idem Stephanus postquam, sicut superius narravi, et inferni loca vidit, et ad corpus rediit, perfecte vitam minime correxit, qui post multos annos de corpore adhuc ad

certamen vitæ et mortis exiit. Qua de re colligitur, quia ipsa quoque inferni supplicia cum demonstrantur, aliis hoc ad adjutorium, aliis vero ad testimonium fiat: ut isti videant mala quæ caveant, illi vero eo amplius puniantur, quod inferni supplicia nec visa, et cognita vitare noluerunt (*PL* 77.385).

Aitken also notes that a story closer to that recounted by Robert de Gretham occurs in a collection of *Miracles of the Virgin Mary* in MS Cotton Cleopatra C.x. (ff. 101–44), a late twelfth-century manuscript which is bound up with other material. The story occurs in Book II, miracle 10, and tells of Peter and Stephen, two brothers in Rome. See Ward and Herbert 1883–1910:ii.607.

**109/14 stede**  So CPBR, *woninge* Ha. Beneath the reading *hows*, added over an erasure by a later hand, the original reading *stede* is partly visible.

**109/14**  Little is known of the life of St. Cecilia, a Roman virgin martyr of the third century. Her supposed relics were translated to the church called the *titulus Ceciliæ* in the Trastevere, Rome, by Pope Paschal I in c. 820; this is presumably the church mentioned in the narrative. Cecilia's feast day is 22 November; she has been known as the patron of musicians only since the sixteenth century. St. Projectus or Præjectus was Bishop of Clermont. His death in 676 was due to palace intrigue and violence. When Emperor Childeric ordered the arrest of Hector, ruler of Marseilles, this was believed to be the result of Projectus's complaints, and he was assassinated. He was immediately venerated as a martyr and many miracles were claimed at his tomb. His feast (25 January), is found generally in monastic calendars after 1100. See Farmer 1978:72, 335–36.

**109/36 he went him**  Cf. 79/30, note.

**111/2 þat þai**  *þat hii* CPB, R lacks, om. Ha. The H reading *þat þat* is a straightforward error for *þat þai*. Cf. 113/12, where the same error was made and then corrected by H.

**113/1–13**  5th Sunday after Epiphany. Matthew xiii.24–30.

**113/3 gode whete**  So CPB, R lacks. In H *sede* before *whete* is an error and expuncted as such.

**113/14 þis**  So CPBHa, R lacks.

**113/14–15 God & skil & resoun**  So CPB, *god* Ha, R lacks.

**113/22–23 þerfor ... vnderstondinge**  These words are added in the margin by H; some letters have been lost by trimming and are restored in the text in line with the readings in C.

**113/25 etc.**  Compare Matthew xiii.37–43 where Christ himself explains the parable.

**115/1–2 and his sede is wykkednes**  So CPB, R lacks, Ha differs, cf. 114/3493: *E sa semaille iniquitez*. The uncorrected reading, *and wykkednes is kokel*, would make sense, but additions are accepted here as elsewhere in this sermon as corrections by H.

**115/7 is vnto man als at**  *is vnto man as at* BHa, ... *to man* ... C, *is* ... *as a* P, R lacks. The erased readings in H can largely be made out; obliterated letters are supplied from C.

**115/10 þus he biddeþ and alle his and liue in almus**  *þus he biddeþ & alle his & lyuen in almes* B, *þus biddeþ ... almes* C, *þus he bid[deþ] on al wise & lyue in almes* P, *þus he biddeþ & alle his þat we schul liue in loue* Ha, R lacks. The P and Ha readings may be attempts at improving upon the HCB text which may itself be a corrupt version of the original ME rendering of the French since it ignores 114/3511: *Li cumande laisser tuz mals*.

**115/13–14 is his sede; þat is bitokened bi þe whete** The corrections here are again accepted as the work of H; cf. *is his sede þat is bitokned bi þe whete* CPB, *is al goddes sede and is ... whete* Ha.

**115/25–26 as ȝif it** *ȝif* in H is a mistake, cf. *as hit* CPB, R lacks, Ha differs.

**115/27–28** Perhaps 2 Corinthians xi.12–15.

**115/32 þurth** H's usual form supplied in line with *þurh* CPB, R lacks, Ha differs.

**117/5 deuelries** 'devilish acts'. This, the sense required here, is given under *MED* debleries *n. pl.* but not under *MED* develri(e *n.* Under devilry, 3, the *OED* first records this sense from Tindale (1533).

**117/7 þat Y clepe kokel** So CPB, R lacks, Ha differs. The original reading may be made out as *þat is y cleped kokel*. This would make possible sense, but the erasures may be accepted as possibly corrections by H.

**117/14 vnderstonden** Supplied from PB; R lacks, om. HC, Ha differs.

**117/16–17 Crist is sede ... Belsabub is sede** After both *Crist* and *Belsabub es* is added, *e* in the interverbal space, and *s* at the beginning of a two-letter erasure. The restoration of *is* after both words seems justified by the nature of the erasure in each case and by the 's' visible in the erasure after *Belsabub*. For the 'his' genitive in ME, see Mustanoja 1960:59–61, and cf. *Ihesu is* (107/37).

**117/20** Small crosses added to the text here, after *gode* and in the margin after *hemseluen*, are presumably the work of a later annotator.

**117/20 þurth wel late of hemseluen** 'through thinking highly of themselves'. Here *late* is an infinitive used as a noun – cf. 75/12, note. For the phrase *leten wel of* 'have a high opinion of', see *MED* leten *v.*15.(c).

**117/21 erne** Originally *ȝerne*; for the correction of *ȝerne* to *erne*, cf. *erne* CPBHa, R lacks.

**117/27 of himseluen** *himsilf* CPBHa, R lacks. Clearly *of* in H is an error.

**117/30 seȝþe** This anomalous spelling (*seþ* elsewhere in H) is doubtless merely one of several copying errors at this point in H.

**119/3 þis heuene her bineþe** So CPB, *þis kingedom her bineþen* Ha, R lacks, cf. 118/3617: *cest ciel ci aual.*

**119/6–7** Compare Proverbs xvii.13.

**119/7 and þe holi suffreþ þe myseis** So CPB, *and þe holi men ben proued þoru misais* Ha, R lacks, cf. 118/3626–7: *Bon or s'esproue en la furneise / E les seinz homes la malaise.* The redactor has spoilt the sense of the proverb by taking *les seinz homes* as the subject of the second clause and supplying the verb *suffreþ*. Ha rewrites to restore the sense.

**119/13 tendrour** 'compassion'. This word is taken directly from the French, cf. 118/3638 *par tel tendrur; tendrour* is not recorded in *MED*.

**119/13 miȝt falle** *fallen* CPBHa, R lacks. The repetition of *miȝt* here is an error in H.

**119/14 to hem** *bi hem* CPBHa, R lacks.

**119/29 goyng** 'departure, going hence'; see *MED* going(e *ger.* 2.(a). This passage has been altered in H. After *entre* (119/27) CPBHa read: *in to his bern þat is þe blisse of heuen* (cf. 118/3669: *En la grange del ciel irrat*); CPB continue this image with *grange* (cf. 118/3671: *grange*) where H has *goyng* (119/29). Ha differs.

**121/1–23** Septuagesima. Matthew xx.1–16.

**121/3 morowenwhile** 'morning'. It may not be mere coincidence that all the *OED* quotations under morn-while are from thirteenth and fourteenth century northern and east Midland texts. This uncommon compound with *while* may have been unfamiliar on account of date or dialect, and *while* may well have been here erased by the southern Reviser. See *MED* morwe *n.*2 (a) and while *n.*4(a).

**121/6 sent hem** So CPB, R lacks, Ha differs.

**121/7 at midday and at non** The canonical hours of sext and nones, at midday and at 3 pm respectively – see *MED* mid-dai *n.*2. and non *n.* (a).

**123/11 þat were** 'those were'; cf. *MED* that *pron.* 3. (b).

**123/20–21** Luke xxiii.43.

**123/30 of** So PB, om. HCR, Ha differs.

**125/3 For in litel tyme, þurth reson, takeþ god seruise ȝeldynge** So CPRHa, *for in litel tyme takeþ seruise þurgh resoun gode ȝeldynge* B. 'For in a short time good service reasonably takes a reward'. The 'þ' added to give *takeþ* is not the Reviser's usual alteration to a plural ending in 'þ' but a correction to give the required *3 sg.* form here. The word order (altered in B) follows 124/3818–19: *En poi de tens, par raisun, / Prent bon seruise guerdun.*

**125/8–9 By þe fyue oures ben oure fyue eldes schewed** So CPBR, Ha differs. The expuncting of *wittes vnder* and deletion of *stonded* in light ink may well have been by H; the deletion in dark ink of *eldes schewed* is clearly a mistake.

**125/9–12 Þe morowenynge ... of þe liif** The exposition of the five hours of the parable is incomplete here whether by virtue of careless translation or textual corruption. HCPB (substantially alike) and R (partly altered) mention four hours: *morowenynge, þe þridde oure, midday*, and *euesong tyme*. Ha differs considerably and mentions only *morwetide, þe þrid houre* and *þe elleuent houre*. The English thus omits the fourth hour (ME *non*, AN *nune*), and wrongly equates *midday* with *mannes state*. Cf. 124/3834–5: *Midi demustre la iuuente; / Nune home parfit presente.*

**125/23 help to holi cherche** So CPBR, Ha differs. Cf. *help holi cherche* (123/21) above, where CPBR also have *helpen to*, and 124/3857: *Poet a eglise mult ualeir*. The preposition *to* in *helpen to* reflects the influence of French idiom.

**125/23 amendeþ** *amende* CPBRHa. The alteration of *amenden* to *amendeþ* was presumably intended as a correction to the required singular. Possibly owing to the potential ambiguity of the pronoun *he* (which could be singular or plural), an original subjunctive singular *amende* was mistaken for a plural and given the optional *-en* plural ending.

**125/28–29** Psalm li.17.

**125/29–32** This is a very common sentiment. Possible sources might be 1 Kings viii.47–48 or 2 Chronicles vi.37–38.

**125/31 repenteþ** *repente* CPBR, Ha differs. Cf. *amendeþ* (125/23) above, and note.

**125/33** Presumably the thin vertical line drawn before *comeþ* is connected with the neighbouring alterations and indicated that the reader was to continue at *comeþ* after *obstinat*, i.e. reading *be ȝou nouȝt obstinat, comeþ etc.*

**127/7 roundehed** 'roundness'. See *MED* roundhed *n.* where only one instance (dated before 1425) is given.

**127/20** Ephesians iv.1.

**129/1–17** Sexagesima. Luke viii.4–15.

**129/2–3 and þai comen** For the superfluous *and* here (also in CPB but not in R) cf. 128/3926: *Et ils vindrent a Ihesu Crist* Hm, *Il uindrent* etc. W²UOW¹.

**129/5 defoiled** 'trampled'. According to the *OED* (*see* defoul, defoil, *v.*) the phonology of the oi-form 'has not been satisfactorily made out'. Under 'foil' (*v.*) 1 it is taken to be an irregular representation of OF *fuler* etc. 'to trample down'; mention is also made of a possibility of confusion with OF *fouiller*. *MED* (*see* foilen *v.* (2)) simply gives it as an 'aberrant form of (1) *fullen* & (2) *filen, foulen*'. For further discussion, see Liedholm 1941:141, and Dobson 1957:§ 260, note 2.

**129/15 wenen** So CPB, om. R.

**131/5 And ech** So CPBRHa and cf. 130/3990: *E si alcuns.* The H reading *In* here is a mistake for *And* doubtless resulting from the misreading of an ampersand as an abbreviated form of *in*. Cf. 21/26, note.

**131/9–10** The words *for euer wite he muchel he mote heren and sen* are underlined.

**131/11 Crist** So R, *cristes* CPBHa, cf. 130/4002: *Veez les deciples Iesu.* The HR reading *crist*, reflecting the endingless genitive of the AN, has been altered to *cristes* in CPBHa. An abbreviation for *-es* has also been added in H.

**131/15 draweynge** 'translation', see *MED* drauing(e *ger.* 4.(b), or 'writings, compositions', cf. 130/4013: *traitiz*, and see 5/12–13, note.

**131/19–20 Nouȝt for þan þa þouȝ it ben so for soþe** 'Nevertheless, however, they are indeed so'. Cf. 130/4022: *Purquant si sunt il ueierement.* The *þa* in *nouȝt for þan þa þouȝ* is a mistake, cf. *nouȝth for þan þeiȝ* PBR, *ne for þan þeiȝ* C, om. Ha. For *it ben* as equivalent to 'they are', see Mustanoja 1960:132.

**131/26 bodilich** 'literally', as opposed to *gostlich*, 'spiritually', in line 3. For this sense of *bodilich* in Biblical exegesis, see *MED* bodili(che *adv.* 3. (b).

**133/5 dorndales** A word, not otherwise recorded in English, taken over from the French, cf. 132/4068–9: *La pere sunt li durendal / Kar tant sunt endurci el mal.* Aitken 1922:95 notes that *Durendal*, the name of Roland's sword, is used here of the hardened ('dur') sinner who refuses to repent, and compares this with a later occurrence of the word in the same sense, W² 6441–6442: *As pieres vindrent li durendal / Ki sunt endurci en lur mal.* Thus AND *durendal*, 'hardened sinner (?)'.

**133/12 bi her liue** 'during their lives'; see *MED* bi *prep.* 4. (b).

**133/14** A later hand has added *'nota'* in the margin, perhaps referring to the sentiment that riches confound the soul.

**133/17** The marginal addition *or dystroyth* was presumably intended as a gloss on *slokeneþ* which, as a northern and Scottish word (see *OED* slocken, v.), would have been unfamiliar to a southern reader.

**133/20–21 þe gret prides and þe ʒiftes** So CPB, *of þe gret prides & of þe ʒiftes* R, om. Ha, cf. 132/4096: *Les granz orguilz e les rauines.* The plural form *prides* is rare in English; see *OED* pride, *sb.* 1 1.b. where the only occurrence quoted before the Douay Bible (1609) is from OE. The plural form and the concrete sense, 'deeds of pride', here follow AN *orguilz* – cf. Godefroy 1880–1902:V, 634a, *orgoil*: 'action outrecuidante'. The sense of *ʒiftes* here is puzzling. A possible sense for this negative context might be 'bribes' (see *OED* gift, *sb.* 5 'Something given with a corrupting intention; a bribe'), but this meaning is uncommon and in no way accords with AN *ravine* 'rapine, robbery'. Corruption at an early stage of transmission (since HCPBR all read *ʒiftes*) may be suspected. Since 'ʒ' and 'þ' were sometimes confused by ME scribes, *ʒiftes* could have replaced an original *þiftes*, a form of ME *þeft* 'theft' (see *MED* theft(e *n.*), and a plausible rendering of 132/4096: *rauines*.

**133/21 euel delit** So CPBR, *medlet* H, om. Ha, and cf. 132/4098: *mal delit.* As the H reading is evidently a corruption of *euel delit*, the text is emended here.

**133/26–7 confounded wiþ his owen turne** 'confounded by his own guile'. For *turne* in this sense, cf. *OED* turn, *sb.* 21 and cf. 20 for the phrase *wiþ his owen turne* in a wrestling metaphor from c. 1325 *Metr. Hom.* 83: *Bot sinful man gers him [the devil] oft schurne, And castis him wit his awen turne.* See also *MED* turn(e *n.* 3.(b).

**133/31–2 þat loueþ to fordon oþer þurth destresse for to don riʒt** *þat leueþ þe on and for doþ þe oþer for any destresse for to don riʒt* C, *þat leueþ for deþ oiþer for any destresse for to done riʒth* P, *þat leueþ for deþ oþer for eny oþer destresse for to do þe riʒt* B, *þat lateþ for drede oþer for ani oþer destresse for to do riʒt* Ha, *þat leues for ded & for any destres for to do ryʒht* R, cf. 132/4116–17: *Kar kikunkes iustise leit / Pur estre murdriz u detreit.* The PBRHa texts appear to represent the original ME rendering of the Anglo-Norman. H and C offer corrupt texts to some extent related.

# APPENDIX ONE

## Emendations to the Anglo-Norman Text

The following minimal alterations have been made in the text of $W^2$ as presented in this volume. They are supported by readings in one or more of the other AN manuscripts except, as noted, at 12/380 and 18/585, and, perhaps, 62/1889.

### (a) Correction of Obvious Errors

| | |
|---|---|
| 6/230 | obscurement] obscuremet MS |
| 10/291 | new paragraph; red paraph in MS mistakenly at 290 |
| 12/380 | sunt] funt MS; *but* funt O, frunt U |
| 14/461 | uraisuns] uraisus MS |
| 18/569 | persone] pesone MS |
| 18/585 | tolt] tost MS; U *om.*, O *lacks* |
| 40/1286 | criminal] crininal MS |
| 62/1889 | orde] orbe MS; orde (d *on eras. of* b) Hm, orbe $W^1$O, vile U, L *lacks* |
| 64/1934 | espelt] esplelt MS |
| 72/2181 | dreiturere] dreiturele MS, 1 *on eras.* |
| 76/2392 | ueneit] ueneneit MS – en *dittography* |
| 78/2463 | Guard] Guadd MS |
| 80/2535 | Que] Quo MS |
| 102/3168 | uenent] uenenent MS – en *dittography* |
| 104/3243 | ke] k MS |
| 116/3561 | furmenz] furmez MS |
| 118/3649 | repentent] repetent MS |
| 120/3719 | vuerames] vue(..)mes MS – *two letters eras.* |

### (b) Restored Readings

| | |
|---|---|
| 38/1201 | uie] u MS, *first minim only; hole in MS*, vie U |
| 40/1243 | en enfern] e....fern (*part of first* e *only*) MS, en enfern $W^1$ |
| 62/1892 | aore cume] ao MS, aore cume $W^1$ |
| 62/1893 | ne] *lost in* MS, ne $W^1$ |
| 62/1893 | confus] c MS, confus $W^1$ |
| 62/1894 | parfite] p MS, parfite $W^1$ |
| 62/1895 | veillez] lez MS, veillez $W^1$ |
| 62/1895 | fesance] *lost in* MS, fesance $W^1$ |

In $W^2$, lines 1892-95 are written in the right-hand margin; text loss is the result of trimming.

## (c) Doubtful Readings

32/992        poait] This reading has been altered and is difficult to make out. Aitken
              (1922:136) reads 'poeit'.

48/1470       Iuielz] This word is difficult to make out. It appears to consist of four minims
              followed by a letter which may be an 'e' by alteration; a letter which may be
              an 'l'; and a final letter, perhaps a 'z'. The faintest oblique stroke over the
              initial minim suggests that it is to be taken as an 'i'. For the reading 'Iuielz'
              ('Jews'), cf. iuelz L, iues O; other readings are: message U, messages Hm, uns
              W[1]. Cf. also Iuels in line 3320.

# APPENDIX TWO
## Checklist of Sermons & Additional Material

The following table lists the prologue and sermons as found in the various English and Anglo-Norman manuscripts, but not always in the order in which they appear. The following divergences in sermon should be noted:

1. The order of sermons 50 and 51 (ie. Trinity 21 and 22) is reversed in HCHaHm. In Hm there are running titles in a later hand. This scribe noticed the wrong order of these sermons, for having first written 'xxi' in the title heading Trinity 22 at the top of f. 114$^v$ he then made an alteration to 'xxii'. Thereafter Trinity 21, following, is correctly numbered 'xxi', even though these sermons remain in the wrong order. That these sermons should appear wrongly ordered in both Anglo-Norman and Middle English manuscripts can hardly have been coincidental and therefore indicates that the misordering of sermons 50 and 51 must have been carried over from the translator's Anglo-Norman exemplar into the original Middle English version.

2. Sermon 54 appears between sermons 3 and 4 in Hm.

3. Sermon 55 appears between sermons 5 and 6 in Hm and O.

4. The order of sermons 57–60 varies in Ha and R: 58, 57, 59, ...60 in Ha; 57, 59, 58, 60 in R.

**Key:** * = lacking; $\underline{H}$ = incomplete; RN = sermon split between R and N; $\underline{RN}$ = sermon split between R and N but still incomplete.

| No. | Occasion | English MSS | French MSS |
|-----|----------|-------------|------------|
| P | Prologue | H $\underline{C}$ P B $\underline{R}$ Ha $\underline{I}$ | * W$^2$ $\underline{O}$ * U $\underline{Hm}$ |
| 1 | Advent 1 | H C P B R Ha | $\underline{W^1}$ W$^2$ O * U Hm |
| 2 | Advent 2 | H$^1$ W$^2$ O * U Hm | W$^1$ W$^2$ O * U Hm |
| 3 | Advent 3 | H $\underline{C}$ P B R Ha | W$^1$ W$^2$ O $\underline{L}$ U Hm |
| 4 | Advent 4 | H C P B R Ha | W$^1$ W$^2$ O L U Hm |
| 5 | Christmas Eve | H C P B * Ha | W$^1$ W$^2$ O L U Hm |
| 6 | Epiphany | H C P B $\underline{R}$ Ha | W$^1$ W$^2$ O L U Hm |
| 7 | Sunday after octave of Epiphany 1 | H C P B R Ha | W$^1$ W$^2$ O L U Hm |
| 8 | Sunday after Epiphany 3 | H C P B R Ha | W$^1$ W$^2$ O L U Hm |
| 9 | Sunday after Epiphany 4 | H C P B $\underline{R}$ Ha | W$^1$ W$^2$ O L U Hm |
| 10 | Sunday after Epiphany 5 | H C P B * Ha | W$^1$ W$^2$ O L U Hm |
| 11 | Septuagesima | H C P B $\underline{N}$ Ha | W$^1$ W$^2$ O L U Hm |
| 12 | Sexagesima | H C P B N Ha | W$^1$ W$^2$ O L U Hm |
| 13 | Quinquagesima | H C P B RN Ha | W$^1$ W$^2$ O L U Hm |
| 14 | Quadragesima 1 | H C P B $\underline{R}$ Ha | W$^1$ W$^2$ O L U Hm |
| 15 | Quadragesima 2 | H C P B $\underline{R}$ Ha | W$^1$ W$^2$ O L U Hm $\underline{Mo}$ |
| 16 | Quadragesima 3 | H C P B * Ha | W$^1$ W$^2$ O L U Hm $\underline{Mo}$ |
| 17 | Quadragesima 4 | H C P B $\underline{R}$ Ha | W$^1$ W$^2$ O L U Hm |
| 18 | Quadragesima 5 | H C P B R Ha | W$^1$ W$^2$ O L U Hm |

| No. | Name | | |
|---|---|---|---|
| 19 | Palm Sunday | H C P B R Ha | W¹ W² O L U Hm |
| 20 | Easter Sunday | H C P B R Ha | W¹ W² O L U Hm |
| 21 | Sunday after Easter 1 | H C P B R̲ Ha | W¹ W² O L U Hm |
| 22 | Sunday after Easter 2 | H C P B * Ha | W¹ W² O L U Hm |
| 23 | Sunday after Easter 3 | H C P B R̲ Ha | W¹ W² O L U Hm |
| 24 | Sunday after Easter 4 | H C P B R Ha | W¹ W² O L U Hm |
| 25 | Sunday after Easter 5 | H C P B R Ha | W¹ W² O L U Hm |
| 26 | Ascension | H C P B R Ha | W̲¹ W² O̲ L U Hm |
| 27 | Sunday within octave of Ascension | H C P B R Ha | * W² * L U Hm F̲ |
| 28 | Pentecost | H C P B R Ha | W̲¹ W² * L U Hm̲ F |
| 29 | Trinity Sunday | H C P B RN Ha | W¹ W² * L U Hm̲ |
| 30 | Trinity 1 | H C P B N Ha | W¹ W² * L U Hm |
| 31 | Trinity 2 | H C P B N̲ Ha | W¹ W² * L U Hm |
| 32 | Trinity 3 | H C P B R̲ Ha | W¹ W² * L U Hm |
| 33 | Trinity 4 | H C P B R Ha | W¹ W² * L U Hm |
| 34 | Trinity 5 | H C P B R Ha | W̲¹ W² * L U Hm |
| 35 | Trinity 6 | H C P B R Ha | * W² * L U Hm |
| 36 | Trinity 7 | H C P B R Ha | * W² * L U Hm |
| 37 | Trinity 8 | H C P B R Ha | * W² * L U Hm |
| 38 | Trinity 9 | H C P B R Ha | W̲¹ W² * L U Hm |
| 39 | Trinity 10 | H C P B R Ha | W¹ W² * L U Hm |
| 40 | Trinity 11 | H C P B R Ha | W̲¹ W² * L U Hm |
| 41 | Trinity 12 | H C P B R Ha | * W² * L U Hm |
| 42 | Trinity 13 | H C P B R Ha | * W² * L U Hm |
| 43 | Trinity 14 | H C P B R Ha | * W² * L U Hm |
| 44 | Trinity 15 | H C P B R Ha | * W² * L U Hm |
| 45 | Trinity 16 | H C P B R Ha | * W² * L U Hm |
| 46 | Trinity 17 | H C P B R Ha | * W² * L U Hm |
| 47 | Trinity 18 | H C P B R Ha | * W² * L U Hm |
| 48 | Trinity 19 | H C P B R̲ Ha | * W² * L U Hm |
| 49 | Trinity 20 | H C P B * Ha | * W² * L U Hm |
| 50 | Trinity 21 | H C P B R̲ Ha | * W² * L̲ U Hm |
| 51 | Trinity 22 | H C P B R Ha | * W² * * U Hm |
| 52 | Trinity 23 | H C P B R Ha | * W² * * U Hm |
| 53 | Trinity 24 | H C P B R̲ Ha | * W² * * U Hm |
| 54 | Annunciation | H C P B R Ha | * * * * Hm |
| 55 | Christmas Day | H C P B R Ha | * * O * * Hm |
| 56 | Birthdate of an apostle | H C P B R Ha | * * * * Hm |
| 57 | Birthdate of a martyr | H C P B R Ha | * * * * Hm |
| 58 | Birthdate of many martyrs | H C P B R Ha | * * * * Hm |
| 59 | Birthdate of a confessor and pope | H C P B R Ha | * * * * * |
| 60 | Quinquagesima [Epistle] | H̲ C * B R Ha | * * * * * |
| 61 | Vigil of St. Peter & St. Paul | * * * B R Ha | |
| 62 | Creed | * * * B N * | |
| 63 | Sermon on Pater Noster | * * * B RN * | |
| 64 | Advent (Christ weeps for Jerusalem) | * * * B R * | |

| 65 | Sermon on 2nd Coming | * * * | B R * |
| 66 | Sermon on Signs of Doomsday | * * * | B R Ha |
| 67 | On the Nativity | * * * | B R * |
| 68 | Prayer to the father, son, holy ghost | * * * | B * * |
| 69 | Sermon on Dedication of a Church | * * * | B RN * |
| 70 | Candlemas (Purification) | * * * | B R * |
| 71 | Assumption | * * * | B R Ha |
| 72 | Michaelmas | * * * | B R * |
| 73 | Sermon on Last Judgement | * * * | B R Ha |
| 74 | Holy Innocents & 10 Commandments | * * * | B * * |
| 75 | On original sin | * * * | * * Ha |
| 76 | On the 10 Commandments | * * * | * * Ha |
| 77 | On the 10 Commandments | * * * | * R * |

# GLOSSARY

This glossary records words and phrases which, despite the help of their immediate contexts, may not be readily comprehensible even to readers with some familiarity with Middle English. The order of the entries follows normal modern practice: **i** as a consonant [dʒ] follows **i/y** as a vowel, **u/v** as a consonant [v] follows **u/v** as a vowel, **þ** follows **t**, **ʒ** follows **g**. Customary grammatical abbreviations are used: *adj.* adjective (including the present participial adjective); *adv.* adverb; *comp.* comparative; *conj.* conjunction; *dem.* demonstrative; *imp.* imperative; *impers.* impersonal; *inf.* infinitive; *intr.* intransitive; *n.* noun (including the verbal noun); *pa.* past tense; *pl.* plural; *pp.* past participle; *pr.* present tense; *pr. ppl.* present participle; *prep.* preposition; *refl.* reflexive; *sg.* singular; *super.* superlative; *v.* verb. Where more than one spelling is quoted, the references follow the order of the variants.

**abayst** *pp.* perplexed 49/9; **abaisched** *pp.* astonished 85/12
**abaten** *inf.* injure, disparage 107/3
**abiden** *inf.* await 41/12; **habitt** *3 sg. pr.* waits, delays 79/11
**ablindeþ** *3 sg. pr.* blinds 71/5; **ablinded** *pp.* blinded 13/3
**aboute** *adv.* **ben ~ to** been disposed to 131/16; **is ~ for to** strives to 71/19
**abreuen** *inf.* record 57/24
**ac** *conj.* but 5/17
**acente** *3 sg. pa.* yielded 111/3
**acorden** *inf.* **~ wiþ** be reconciled with 125/16
**acumbren** *inf.* assail 71/19
**adresce, adressen** *inf.* direct 9/16; make straight 49/8; **adresseþ** *3 sg. pr.* put right, put straight 7/3
**afie** *v. refl. 1 sg. pr.* trust 5/14
**afoled** *pp.* infatuated 39/28
**after, efter** *prep.* in accordance with 3/14, 4/18
**aʒeinsayinge** *n.* contradicting, disobeying 89/5
**aʒaines, aʒeines, aʒenes, oʒain, oʒaines** *prep.* against 27/25; towards 25/13, 111/4; in anticipation of 37/1; facing 25/4
**aknowen** *pp.* **ben ~** acknowledge, admit 29/6
**aliʒten** *inf.* illumine 125/16
**almus** *n.* alms-giving 115/10
**als** *conj.* as 75/35
**alson** *adv.* immediately 67/18
**amonesten** *inf.* admonish 17/2; remind 131/4; **amonest** *1 sg. pr.* urge, exhort 15/2
**and** *conj.* if 9/27
**anoyʒing** *n.* offending 89/4

**anoynt** *pp.* enbalmed 73/16

**anouȝ** *adv.* enough 47/6; fully, abundantly 65/20; completely 69/28

**anoure** *inf.* worship, honour 67/15

**aperceyuen** *inf.* notice, become aware of 71/24

**apertliche** *adv.* openly, manifestly 13/27; in person 47/8; plainly 77/3

**Archetreclin(e), Architrecline** *n.* Master of the feast at the wedding in Cana of Galilee 77/29 *(N)*, 81/24

**arere** *inf.* raise up 43/15

**aresound** *3 sg. pa.* addressed 39/9; **aresoned** *pp.* rebuked 5/11

**asayen** *inf.* try, test 49/19

**asailours** *n. pl.* chastisers 9/11 *(N)*

**asembled** *pp.* united 41/6

**asise** *n.* court of assize 27/26

**asoileþ** *3 sg. pr.* absolves 73/27

**astoren** *inf.* redress (a wrong) 59/32

**atempren** *v. refl. inf.* restrain oneself 27/17

**atendaunt** *adj.* obedient 3/23

**auntre** *n.* **in ~ ȝif.** in doubt whether 11/26

**auter** *n.* altar 99/3

**auaunten** *v. refl. inf.* boast 125/2

**avis** *n.* **saien ~** to give advice 115/9

**avouterie** *n.* adultery 39/21

**bailie, bayly** *n.* control, power 93/14; keeping, custody 99/15

**baudestrotes** *n. pl.* procurers 115/31

**bede** *n.* prayer 53/8

**behoteþ** *3 sg. pr.* promises 19/27; **beheȝt** *pp.* promised 35/8

**benimmeþ** *3 sg. pr.* deprives of 21/17; **benam** *3 pl. pa.* seized 109/9

**berne** *n.* barn 113/13

**bi** *prep.* during 133/12

**biddyng** *n.* prayer 99/5

**biȝeten** *pp.* begotten 51/30

**bigge** *inf.* buy 33/17

**bihoue** *n.* **to our ~** for our sake, benefit 77/2

**biknewe** *3 sg. pa.* confessed 33/37

**beleft** *3 sg. pa.* remained 33/37

**bleþlich** *adv.* gladly 5/30

**bobaunce** *n.* vanity 33/4

**bode** *pp.* invited 77/22

**bodilich** *adv.* literally 131/26 *(N)*

**bones** *n. pl.* requests 53/10

**bordel** *n.* cottage 19/10 *(N)*

**boustouslich** *adv.* simply, without polish 5/18

**bouxsum, buxsum** *adj.* gentle, obedient 85/17, 89/3

**bowes** *n. pl.* branches 29/20

**bridale** *n.* wedding feast 77/21

**breued** *pp.* recorded 57/2

**buxsumnesse** *n.* obedience 89/27

**can** *3 sg. pr* can, is able to 11/20; knows how to 21/22; **cunnen** *3 pl. pr.* 59/19; **couþe** *3 sg. pa.* knew 131/17; *3 pl. pa.* 69/8

**castel** *n.* walled town, small town 25/4
**ceriauntes** see **seriaunt**
**chaimcchipes** *n. pl.* causes of shame 63/7 *(N)*
**charmers** *n. pl.* enchanters, sorcerers 115/31
**ches** *3 sg. pa.* chose 45/7
**clepeþ** *3 sg. pr.* calls 31/19
**clepyng** *n.* calling 127/20
**cler(e)** *adj.* clear, pure 17/29; guiltless 17/32
**clerete** *n.* light, radiance 69/20
**clerke** *n.* person in holy orders 15/5
**cloutes** *n. pl.* swaddling cloths 57/9; rags 63/7
**coloryng** *n.* camouflage 115/27
**coluer** *n.* dove 75/30
**comune** *n.* community 95/4
**conforted, confort** *pp.* supported 5/3; encouraged 53/5
**coniecten** *inf.* misrepresent 5/30 *(N)*
**conninge** *n.* knowledge 11/13
**connand** *adj.* competent 9/30
**consel, counsail** *n.* advice, instruction 21/19, 115/20
**conseil** *inf.* advise 9/31
**contrarious** *adj.* antagonistic 13/16
**controued** *pp.* contrived 3/3
**corious** *adj.* fastidious 129/27
**countour** *n.* nobleman, count 27/26 *(N)*
**couþe** see **can**
**crache** *n.* manger, crib 57/10
**cried** *pp.* declared 39/12 *(N)*
**cristendome** *n.* **to take** ~ to be baptized 75/19
**crudinge** *n.* crowding 31/4
**cunnen** see **can**
**cuntakes** *n. pl.* conflicts 35/18

**ded** *n.* death 43/19
**defaute** *n.* defect 21/10
**defouled, defoiled, yfouled** *pp.* trampled 79/14-15, 129/5 *(N)*, 131/31
**degre** *n.* state, condition 61/1
**dele** *n.* **þe most** ~ mostly 9/17
**delices** *n. pl.* desires, pleasures 9/34
**delicious** *adj.* sensual, luxury-loving 129/27
**deliuer** *adj.* free from encumbrance 81/20
**deluen** *inf.* bury 15/15
**departen** *inf.* share, divide 17/11; separate 79/29
**departinge** *n.* dispensation 27/29; **makeþ** ~ separates 79/27-28
**deposed** *3 sg. pa.* quelled 105/14
**derworþ, derworþi** *adj.* precious, valuable 7/25, 81/5
**derworþilich** *adv.* respectfully 131/14
**desmaien** *v. refl. inf.* be alarmed, frightened 17/2
**despenden** *inf.* spend 21/34
**despense** *n.* means 21/31
**destruen** *inf.* destroy 65/10

**destruinges** *n. pl.* devastations 31/5

**deuelries** *n. pl.* devilish acts 117/5 *(N)*

**diȝt** *pp.* cultivated 123/16; prepared 135/3

**diswarre** *adj.* unaware 41/21

**do** *1 sg. pr.* ~ **of** do with regard to 15/18

**donge** *n.* manure 79/15

**dorndales** *n. pl.* hardened sinners 133/5 *(N)*

**dorst** *3 sg. pa* dared 101/6

**douten** *inf.* fear 31/21; **douted him** *3 sg. pa. refl.* doubted 41/12

**draw** *inf.* translate *or* compose 5/12 *(N)*; **drawen** *inf.* ~ **out** write *or* translate 3/9 *(N)*; **drawen** *pp.* taken 3/18; ~ **out** translated 15/9

**draweynge** *n.* translation 131/15

**drenchen** *inf.* drown 105/5

**drescen** *inf.* prepare 39/13; **dresse** *3 sg. pr. subj.* correct 115/18

**dukes** *n. pl.* leaders 69/12

**eld(e** *n.* age 85/18; old age 125/33

**elded** *pp.* enfeebled from age 61/33

**elders** *n. pl.* forefathers 31/25

**enbreued** *pp.* enrolled 59/1; *3 sg. pa.* enrolled 59/7

**encens** *n.* incense 67/20

**encheson** *n.* reason, grounds (for action) 107/4

**encombringe** *n.* affliction, burden (of sin) 75/21

**enformeþ** *3 sg. pr.* fashions, moulds 3/18

**engendrur** *n.* offspring 79/25

**eniune** *inf.* require, oblige 95/32

**enpairen** *inf.* suffer 31/28

**enquered** *pp.* investigated 3/6

**ensaumple** *n.* **take** ~ **at hem** take an example from them 11/35 *(N)*

**entendaunt** *adj.* engaged, concerned 109/25

**entent** *inf.* give heed 99/2

**entent** *n.* mind 7/23; intention 15/27; **ȝeuen** ~ pay attention 31/7

**ententilich, ententiflich** *adv.* earnestly 5/12, 133/28

**enterliche** *adv.* sincerely, wholeheartedly 15/31

**entermetteþ** *v. refl. 3 sg. pr. ,* ~ **him of** engages in 5/9

**enuie** *n.* malice, ill-will 21/16

**er, er þat** *conj.* before 31/14, 31/5

**ernand, ernynge** *pr. ppl.* flowing 77/1, 81/14

**erninge** *n.* current 77/1

**euen** *adj.* ~ **cristen** fellow Christian 27/14

**euen** *n.* evening 41/8

**euerich** *adj.* every 119/24

**euerildel** *adv.* entirely 71/2

**fable** *n.* **wiþouten any** ~ undoubtedly 115/23

**faile** *n.* **wiþouten any** ~ certainly 135/2

**fayntise** *n.* **wiþouten** ~ without fail 71/33

**falleþ** *3 sg. pr.* appertains to 11/7; ~ **to** accords with 43/7

**fals** *n.* falsehood 5/18

**fantom** *n.* delusion 43/7

**fautes** *n. pl.* faults 5/36

**febles** *n.* bodily weakness 7/1
**feches** see **veches**
**feffed** *pp.* endowed 33/6
**feynt** *adj.* weak, faint-hearted 133/27
**fel** *3 sg. (? pl.) pr. subj.* should feel 87/22
**fel** *n.* skin 41/34
**fend(e, fynde** *n.* fiend, devil 71/4, 19/8
**figure** *n.* appearance 7/15; **þurth ~** figuratively 7/32
**filed** *pp.* defiled 61/34
**filleþ** *imp. pl.* **~ out** pour out 77/28
**fine** *adj.* pure 43/32
**fineþ** *3 sg. pr.* becomes pure, free from corruption 81/15
**flode** *n.* river 75/35
**flumme** *n.* river 75/17
**fole** *n.* foal,colt 25/5
**fole** *adj.* foolish 5/10
**fol(e** *n.* fool 33/22
**folilich** *adv.* wickedly 99/18
**fonde** *inf.* endeavour 3/29
**fondinges** *n. pl.* **flesche ~** sexual pleasures 81/31 *(N)*
**forboden** *pp.* forbidden 63/27
**force** *n.* **it is no ~** it does not matter 117/9
**fordoþ** *3 sg. pr.* dispels 9/7
**fore** *prep.* for 51/9
**foreheued** *n.* forehead 11/32
**forȝeten** *inf.* forget 71/17
**forlernisse** *n.* (= **forlornisse**) perdition 53/29
**forlest** *3 sg. pr.* deserts 27/17; **forlorn** *pp.* forsaken 27/16; lost 99/32
**forþencheþ** *3 sg. pr.* repents 25/28
**forþenchynge** *n.* repenting 125/26
**forþer** *comp. adj.* farther, more remote 91/21
**for þi** *conj.* therefore 5/1; **for þi (þat)** because 27/29, 69/22
**founden** *pp.* trained, grounded 21/7 *(N)*
**frelte** *n.* weakness 15/33
**ful** *adj.* full 9/2; sated, weary 5/22
**fur(e** *n.* fire 103/12, 35/26

**gabben** *3 pl. pr.* lie 3/14
**gestes** *n. pl.* tales, stories 3/1, 3/14
**gyen** *inf.* guide 11/32
**giour** *n.* guide 69/14
**gnaystyng** *n.* gnashing 91/22
**gon** *inf.* **~ oway** perish 11/25
**gost** *n.* spirit 71/17
**goter** *n.* channel for conveying fresh water 17/29
**grenen** *inf.* become green, flourish 7/30
**groching** *n.* complaining, grumbling 89/23
**gruchand(e** *adj.* quarrelsome 5/30; *pr. ppl.* grumbling 13/25
**grutcheþ** *3 pl. pr.* grumble 89/19; **grochedhen** *3 pl. pa.* grumbled 121/16

**ȝede** *3 sg. pa.* went 33/36

ȝeld(e *inf.* give 3/30; repay 111/1; **ȝald** *3 sg. pa.* gave 101/3; **ȝeld** *3 pl. pa.* gave 57/22
ȝeldinge *n.* giving 15/22; reward 125/3
ȝelpyngges *n. pl.* boasting 117/4
ȝeme *n.* **take ~ to** give heed to 19/9
ȝerde *n.* rod 13/31
ȝern *adv.* eagerly, readily 53/19
ȝeue(n, ȝif, ȝiue *inf.* give 17/6, 31/7, 3/10, 29/2; **ȝaf** *3 sg. / pl. pa.* gave 33/17, 27/30;
  **ȝaue** *3 sg. pa.* gave 25/23
ȝeueinge *n.* giving 9/19
ȝif (þat), ȝef, ȝeue, if *conj.* if 3/11, 9/16, 53/6, 10/21, 37/22
ȝif al, ȝef þouȝ *conj.* even though 107/25, 99/11
ȝiftes *n. pl.* gifts 67/20
ȝougþe *n.* youth 87/16

**habitt** see **abiden**
**half** *n.* side 115/7; **on al ~** on all sides 25/15
**halpe** *3 pl. pa.* helped 97/26; **hulpen** *pp.* helped 51/17
**halt** *adj.* lame 41/28
**haluendel** *adv.* to the extend of a half 5/25
**halwen** *n. pl.* saints 19/35
**halowe(n** *inf.* sanctify 75/20, 77/2; **hallowed** *3 sg. pa.* sanctified 75/23;
  **halwed** *pp.* sanctified 11/1
**hardy** *adj.* rash 101/24; bold 109/3
**haue** *3 pl. pr.* possess, hold 9/22
**heiȝe** *v. refl. 1 pl. pr. subj.* hasten 29/29
**heiȝe** *adj.* great 11/8; **on ~** on high 25/16; up 27/2; in a loud voice 129/11
**heiȝed** *pp.* exhorted 39/7 *(N)*
**heiȝen** *inf.* exalt 61/31
**hele** *n.* health 79/18
**heleþ** *3 sg. pr.* conceals 21/16
**helþ** *n.* health 97/12; salvation 103/3
**heberwe** *inf.* take, hold 99/15
**heren** *inf. as n.* hearing 3/25
**herien** *inf.* praise 65/13
**herijnge** *n.* praise 29/16
**hiȝt** *v. intr. 3 sg. pa.* was called 109/13
**hirdmen, herdmen** *n. pl.* shepherds 57/10, 63/16
**hole** *adj.* whole, cured 35/10
**hores** *n. pl.* whores 79/14
**hordom** *n.* harlotry, fornication 79/16
**hoten** *3 pl. pr.* promise 33/28
**hulpen** see **halpe**
**hure** *n.* payment, wages 123/18
**husbandrie** *n.* household *or* farm management 71/14

**ich, ech** *adj.* each, every 3/18, 45/28
**ichon, echon** *pron.* each one, everyone 7/10, 77/26
**iche** *pron.* **þat ~** that very matter, those things 11/7; *adj.* **þat ~** that very 15/27
**yfouled** see **defouled**
**ynouȝ** *adv.* enough 13/8
**ioiand** *pr. ppl.* rejoicing 29/16

**jolifte** *n.* levity 51/2

**kepe** *n.* heed 5/15
**keuer** *inf.* remedy 59/37; **keuern** *inf.* recover, regain 75/9
**kinde** *n.* human nature, humanity 37/1; nature 41/34; lineage, family 57/6
**kynrede** *n.* family, kinship 119/10
**knotty** *adj.* covered with protuberances 93/15
**knowen** *inf.* recognise 63/6; **knowen** *pp.* am ~ confess, acknowledge 15/34
     **knew** *3 sg. pa.* ~ **flescheliche** had sexual intercourse with 87/28
**knowinge** *n.* intercourse 87/33
**kokel** *n.* a weed growing among corn, cockle or darnel 113/4
**kouenont, couenaunt** *n.* agreement, bargain 121/4, 121/16

**late** *n.* **wel ~ of** thinking highly of 117/20 *(N)*
**liggen** *inf.* be placed 63/1
**largeliche** *adv.* generously 21/32
**leche** *n.* physician 33/31
**lechecrafte** *n.* medicine 33/29
**lef** *n.* leaf 53/23
**leiȝer** *n.* liar 3/4
**lemes** *n. pl.* limbs, members 99/31; followers 115/20
**lene** *3 pl. pr. subj.* grant, allow 21/13
**lernen** *inf.* teach 3/21; learn 87/19
**lese** *inf.* lose 119/13; **lest, leseþ** *3 sg. pr.* loses 3/22, 35/30; **lore, lorn** *pp.* lost 53/34, 35/2
**lesinges** *n. pl.* lies 3/17
**leten, lett(e(n** *inf.* desist from 97/1; cease 53/2; refrain from 5/31
**lett** *inf.* hinder, obstruct 115/33
**lett** *n.* **wiþouten ani ~** without fail 91/13
**letter** *n.* text, literal sense 7/22
**letterure** *n.* learning 21/2
**letteinge** *n.* **wiþouten ani ~**without hindrance 5/23; **lettyng** relinquishing 133/16
**leue** *adj.* dear 33/10
**leuen** *inf.* **ben for to ~** are to be believed 3/13
**leuer** *comp. adj.* **him hadde bi ~** he would rather 109/27-28
**leueþ** *3 sg. pr.* puts forth leaves 33/1
**lewed** *adj.* uneducated 5/9; *adj. as n.* layman 15/5
**liȝen** *inf.* lie 61/20
**liȝt** *3 sg. pa.* alighted 75/30
**liȝtlich** *adv.* easily, readily 117/20
**losangerie** *n.* flattery 15/20
**lopen** *pp.* ~ **vp** mounted 29/10
**loude** *adj. as n.* **o ~** loudly 91/16
**loued** *3 sg. pa.* ~ **him** humbled himself 101/8 *(N)*

**make** *1 sg. pr.* write, compose 15/20
**maker** *n.* author 15/24
**manace** *3 sg. pr.* threatens 13/16
**maner** *n.* way 77/12
**manslauȝt** *n.* manslaughter, murder 41/2
**mantel-bond** *n.* fastening, clasp 11/24 *(N)*
**mede** *n.* reward 3/27

**meyne** *n.* household, family 57/6
**mesel** *n.* leper 41/35
**meselrie** *n.* leprosy 93/13
**messe** *n.* mass 51/10
**mester, mister** *n.* undertaking 5/10; office, calling 19/24; duty 65/2; **han ~** need 89/12
**mete** *n.* food 19/26
**midday** *n.* midday, the canonical hour sext 121/7 *(N)*
**misanswarand** *adj.* arrogant 49/24
**morowenwhile** *n.* morning 121/3 *(N)*

**ne** *conj.* nor 113/19
**ne for þan** *conj.* nevertheless 3/19 *(N)*
**neschen** *inf.* soften, 133/6
**nice** *adj.* extravagant 51/4
**nygardes** *n. pl.* misers 133/12
**nigramaunciens** *n. pl.* necromancers 115/32
**nim** *imp. pl.* take 43/19
**noyouse** *adj.* troublesome 5/30
**noiþer, noþer ... ne** *conj.* neither ... nor 9/27, 9/9
**non** *n.* the canonical hour nones 121/7 *(N)*
**note** *n.* nut 7/19
**note** *n.* profit, advantage 3/8
**nouȝt for þanne** see **ne for þan**

**office** *n.* position of responsibility 9/27; **ofices** *n. pl.* required tasks 3/26
**ognement** *n.* ointment 73/15
**oȝain, oȝaines** see **aȝaines**
**oȝainseyd** *pp.* renounced 53/33
**onhed** *n.* unity 107/36
**onyng** *n.* union 81/33
**open** *inf.* interpret, expound 113/23
**or þat** see **er**
**ordre** *n.* religious order 9/26; order of priesthood 95/25; **ordres** *n. pl.* ranks 9/11
**orizoun, orisoun** *n.* prayer 27/8, 75/11
**orrible** *adj.* horrible 51/18
**ostele** *n.* lodging 99/29
**our** *n.* hour 91/24; **oures** *n. pl.* ecclesiastical hours 125/8

**payeþ** *3 sg. pr.* pleases 89/26; **paied** *pp.* satisfied, content 5/2
**payen** *n.* pagan 69/21; **payne** *adj.* pagan 97/13 *(N)*
**paynted** *pp.* adorned 45/33
**palat** *n.* palate 13/14
**pans** *n. pl.* pence, money 35/5
**peyneþ** *v. refl. 3 sg. pr.* endeavours, strives 75/13
**pes** *n.* peace 25/21
**pesiblete** *n.* peace 25/10
**pine** *n.* pain, torment 29/18
**pined** *pp.* tortured 37/5
**pynynges** *.n. pl.* torments, afflictions 99/29
**pleynen** *3 pl. pr.* commiserate with 119/11
**plenteþ** *n.* abundance 59/19

**poynt** *n.* **in god** ~ in good standing 101/18; **in ~ to** on the point of 105/5
**potestates** *n. pl.* sixth order of angels 93/8
**pouer** *adj.* poor 45/5
**pouerlich** *adv.* in poverty 45/7
**pouste** *n.* power 61/8
**predicacion** *n.* preaching 27/7
**prent** *n.* image 127/8
**prenteþ** *3 sg. pr.* stamps 127/8
**pride** *n.* **a** ~ a kind of arrogance 5/8 *(N)*
**priue** *adj.* close 59/29
**pryuyte** *n.* **in** ~ in private 117/14
**putten** *3 pl. pr.* strike, smite 33/3

**qued** *adj.* bad, evil 51/6
**queyntise** *n.* deceptive eloquence 5/18
**queynteliche** *adv.* artfully 3/4
**queme** *inf.* please 47/6
**quikeþ** *3 sg. pr.* enlivens, nourishes 11/6

**radinge** *n.* reading 5/21
**rauisour, rauischour** *n.* ravisher 51/5, 95/28
**realtes** *n. pl.* royal privileges 73/13
**reddur** *n.* rigour 9/15
**rede** *n.* reed 45/20
**rede** *1 sg. pr.* advise, counsel 37/10
**regne(n** *inf.* reign 61/15, 77/8
**renter** *n.* proprietor, landlord 21/36 *(N)*
**reson** *n.* sense, argument 5/16
**respit** *n.* respite, reprieve 43/13
**rested** *pp.* stopped, paused 27/4 *(N)*
**rewele** *n.* manner, form 43/25
**rigge** *n.* back 11/30
**riȝt** *n.* justice 37/8
**riȝt** *adv.* straight, directly 29/8
**riȝteþ** *3 sg. pr.* sets in order 7/9
**riȝtwisnesse** *n.* justice 75/28
**rode** *n.* cross 41/18
**rote** *n.* root 119/14
**roundehed** *n.* roundness 127/7 *(N)*

**saddeþ** *3 sg. pr.* wearies (through satiation) 5/21 *(N)*
**sarrain, sarazin** *n.* infidel, heathen 69/21, 101/16
**sauf** *adj.* safe 45/18
**sauȝtel** *inf.* become reconciled 125/19
**sauter** *n.* psalter 17/4
**schenden** *3 pl. pr.* dishonour, besmirch 127/16; **schent** *pp.* reviled 45/16
**scheweing** *n.* signification 73/22
**schild** *inf.* protect 75/21
**schone** *n. pl.* shoes 49/14
**schrewednesse** *n.* wickedness 19/22
**schrewes** *n. pl.* evildoers 13/13

**schrift(e** *n.* confession 27/7, 25/28
**sclaundred** *pp.* slandered 39/8
**sclaunders** *n. pl.* slanders, calumnies 45/15
**scole** *n.* school, way of behaviour 133/9; **holdeþ his ~** teaches 17/26 *(N)*
**seiȝ (e** see **se(n**
**seke** *adj.* sick 33/19
**semblaunt** *n.* appearance, show, pretence 41/33; demeanour 49/25
**se(n** *inf.* see 7/14, 7/15; **seiȝ (e** *3 sg. pa.* saw 109/22, 47/8
**sentens** *n. pl.* precepts 7/25
**serchen** *inf.* find out by enquiry 21/8
**seriaunt** *n.* officer 109/30; **ceriauntes** *n. pl.* officers 25/13
**sete** *n.* seat 25/10
**seþ(þ)en þat, siþen þat** *conj.* after 21/31 since 41/15, 75/22-23
**sewed** *3 sg. pa.* followed 91/2
**siker** *adj.* sure 37/6; secure 53/26
**skil** *n.* discernment, understanding 113/14; **be ~** reasonably, fittingly 99/28
**slauȝ** *n.* slaughter, murder 31/24 *(N)*
**sleweþ** see **slouþ**
**slokeneþ** *3 sg. pr.* smothers 133/17; **slokened** *pp.* smothered, destroyed 129/9
**slouþ, sleweþ** *n.* sloth 117/27, 115/18
**slowe** *adj.* slothful, sluggish 27/34
**so** *adv.* likewise 67/7
**solas** *n.* joy, pleasure 33/1
**solennite** *n.* celebration 109/18
**somundeþ** *3 sg. pr.* summons 31/20
**sond** *n.* message *or* messenger 39/19
**soþe** *n.* truth 5/17; *adj.* true 3/19; **for ~** truly 7/1
**soþfast** *adj.* very, true 73/7
**soucors** *n.* succour, support 7/11
**spede** *inf.* prosper, succeed 73/30
**spelen** *inf.* save 33/17
**spelleþ** *3 sg. pr.* means, signifies 21/5
**spensers** *n. pl.* stewards 3/26
**spiren** *inf.* breathe 19/13
**spouse-breker** *n.* adulterer 39/20-21
**sposaile** *n.* marriage ceremony 79/8
**sufferable** *adj.* forbearing 89/25
**sustinaunce** *n.* necessities of life 27/19
**swiþe** *adv.* quickly 109/33; **as ~** at once 25/8

**taken** *pp.* undertaken 15/32
**tenaunce** *n. pl.* tenants 101/11
**tendrour** *n.* compassion 119/13 *(N)*
**tenes** *n. pl.* hardships 135/4
**tiffen** *inf.* beautify 7/5
**tiffeinge** *n.* beautifying effects 7/5
**tiþinges** *n. pl.* news, tidings 63/17
**tokne** *n.* sign, token 91/27
**touched** *pp.* interpreted 27/6 *(N)*
**trewes** *n. pl.* trees 7/31

**trowauntes** *n. pl.* vagabonds 115/33
**truage** *n.* tribute 57/22; servitude 61/29 *(N)*
**trufles** *n. pl.* trifles 3/3
**turne** *n.* guile 133/27 *(N)*
**turned** *pp.* ~ **to** directed towards *or* returned to 3/24 *(N)*

**þar** *3 sg. pr.* dares 33/30
**þarwhiles þat, þe whiles þat** *conj.* while 101/17-18, 43/8-9
**þeiȝ (e, þeiȝ þat, þeiȝ al** *conj.* although 5/19, 5/22, 13/3, 17/26
**þencheþ** *v. impers. 3 sg.* it seems 107/10; **þouȝt** *3 sg. pa.* it seemed 109/28
**þes, þis** *dem. adj. pl.* these 3/14, 5/6
**þo** *conj.* when 107/32
**þo** *dem. pron. pl.* those 9/19
**þolemodnes** *n.* patience 135/3
**þouȝ, þouȝ al, þouȝ þat** *conj.* although 81/6, 89/5, 97/13
**þraldome** *n.* constraint 45/31
**þrest** *n.* thirst 51/14
**þurth, þurȝ, þurȝh, þurȝth, þurthȝ, etc.** *prep.* through, by means of 7/32, 5/27, 5/34, 7/24, 3/3

**vnconynge** *n.* ignorance 15/34
**vnderne** *n.* the third hour of day, 9 a.m., the canonical hour tierce 121/5
**vndernomen** *pp.* reproved 5/10
**vndo** *inf.* expound 113/22
**vndoer** *n.* interpreter, expositor 7/34
**vndoinge** *n.* exposition 5/5; expounding, interpreting 7/24
**vnȝulden** *pp.* unrequited 97/9
**vnneþ, vnneþes** *adv.* hardly 21/9, 27/26
**veches, feches** *n. pl.* vetches, plant of the genus Vicia 117/8, 117/13
**vertuz** *n. pl.* mighty works, miracles 51/9
**volage** *adj.* fickle, capricious 51/26
**volaious** *adj.* giddy, volatile 133/1

**wayteþ** *3 sg. pr.* lies in wait for 119/30
**wakeþ** *3. sg. pr.* watches 63/21; **woken** *3 pl. pa.* watched over 57/11
**wane** *n.* place 57/10
**warant** *n.* guardian 111/9
**wesche** *3 sg. pa.* washed 75/22
**wawes** *n. pl.* waves 105/3
**weye** *n.* **in a** ~ in a balance, i.e. in a state of uncertainty 127/4
**weld** *inf.* manage, look after 33/20
**weneinge, wenynge** *n.* supposition, idle fancy 3/15; supposition 87/32
**wer(e)** *n.* **in** ~ in doubt 45/27; in jeopardy 107/37
**weried, waried** *pp.* cursed 43/17, 103/10
**wikke** *adj. as n.* wicked person 117/24
**wild** *adj.* wicked, vicious 107/5
**wildness** *n.* indiscipline 133/4
**wonden, wounden** *pp.* wound, wrapped 57/9, 57/16
**winners** *n. pl.* labourers 9/11
**wislich** *adv.* **as** ~ **als, als** ~ **as** as assuredly as 123/32
**wissen** *inf.* guide, direct 11/32

**wite** *inf.* ~ **him to say** inform him 67/14 *(N)*
**wonen** *inf.* dwell, live 55/4
**wreche** *n.* vengeance, punishment 13/30
**writen** *pp.* enrolled 57/8; ~ **in** enrolled 59/3

**zizannie** *n.* a weed growing among corn, cockle or darnel 117/8

# BIBLIOGRAPHY

Aitken, M. Y. H., *Etude sur Le Miroir ou Les Evangiles des Domnées de Robert de Gretham* (Paris, 1922).

Allen, H. E., 'Two Middle-English Translations from the Anglo-Norman', *Modern Philology*, 13 (1915–16), 741–45.

————, 'The *Manuel des Pechiez* and the Scholastic Prologue', *Romanic Review*, 8 (1917), 434–62.

Avril, F., and Stirnemann, P. D., *Manuscrits Enlumines d'Origine Insulaire VII–XX Siecle* (Paris, 1987).

Baker, A. T., 'A Fragment of the "Miroir" or "Evangiles des Domees" of Robert de Gretham', *MHRA Bulletin*, 1 (1928), 62–67.

Benson, L. D., ed., *The Riverside Chaucer* (Oxford, 1987).

Bossuat, R., and G. Raynaud de Lage, *Evangiles des Domnées* (Paris, 1955).

Campbell, A., *Old English Grammar* (Oxford, 1959).

*Catalogue général nouv. acq. IV* (Paris, 1918).

*A Catalogue of the Harleian Collection of Manuscripts ... preserved in the British Museum*, 4 vols (London, 1808–12).

*A Catalogue of the Manuscripts Preserved in the Library of the University of Cambridge*, 5 vols (Cambridge, 1856–67).

Cavanaugh, S. H., 'A Study of Books Privately Owned in England 1300–1450' (unpublished Ph.D. thesis, University of Pennsylvania, 1980).

Chambers, R. W., and M. Daunt, *A Book of London English* (Oxford, 1931).

*Checklist of Medieval Western Manuscripts Acquired from 1916,* unpublished type-script in the Bodleian Library.

Coleman, J., *Public Reading and the Reading Public in Late Medieval England and France*, Cambridge Studies in Medieval Literature, 26 (Cambridge, 1996).

Colledge, E., '*The Recluse*, a Lollard Interpolated Version of the *Ancren Riwle*', *Review of English Studies*, 57 (1939), 1–15 and 58, 129–45.

Colunga, A., and L. Turrado, *Biblia Sacra Iuxta Vulgatam Clementinam*, 7th edition (Madrid, 1985).

Crane, T. F., *The Exempla or Illustrative Stories from the Sermones Vulgares of Jacques de Vitry*, Publications of the Folk-Lore Society 26 (London, 1890).

————, 'Medieval Sermon-Books and Stories and their Study since 1883', *Proceedings of the American Philosophical Society*, 56 (1917), 369–402.

de Ricci, S., *A Handlist of Manuscripts in the Library of the Earl of Leicester at Holkham Hall, abstracted from the catalogues of William Roscoe and Frederic Madden, and annotated by Seymour de Ricci*, Supplement to the Bibliographical Society Transactions No. 7 (Oxford, 1932).

Dean, R. J., and M. B. M. Boulton, eds, *Anglo-Norman Literature: A Guide to Texts and Manuscripts*, Anglo Norman Text Society (London, 1999).

Deanesly, M., *The Lollard Bible and Other Medieval Biblical Versions* (Cambridge, 1920).

Dobson, E. J., *English Pronunciation 1500–1700* (Oxford, 1957).

Doyle, A. I., 'A Survey of the Origins and Circulation of Theological Writings in English in the Fourteenth, Fifteenth and early Sixteenth Centuries with Special Consideration of the Part of the Clergy Therein' (unpublished Ph.D. thesis, University of Cambridge, 1953).

Duncan, T. G., 'A Transcription and Linguistic Study of the Introduction and First Twelve Sermons of the Hunterian MS Version of "The Mirror"' (unpublished B.Litt. thesis, University of Oxford, 1965).

_____, 'Notes on the Language of the Hunterian MS of the *Mirror*', *Neuphilologische Mitteilungen*, 64 (1968), 204–208.

_____, 'A Middle English Linguistic Reviser', *Neuphilologische Mitteilungen*, 82 (1981), 162–74.

_____, 'The Middle English *Mirror* and its Manuscripts', in *Middle English Studies Presented to Norman Davis in Honour of his Seventieth Birthday*, ed. by D. Gray and E. G. Stanley (Oxford, 1981), pp. 115–26.

_____, 'The Middle English Translator of Robert de Gretham's Anglo-Norman *Miroir*', in *The Medieval Translator: Traduire au Moyen Age 6*, ed. by R. Ellis, R. Tixier and B. Weitemeier (Turnholt, 1998).

Dutschke, C. W., *Guide to Medieval and Renaissance Manuscripts in the Huntington Library* (San Marino, CA. 1989).

Ellis, R., R. Tixier, and B. Weitemeier, eds, *The Medieval Translator: Traduire au Moyen Age 6* (Turnholt, 1998).

Erbe, T., ed., *Mirk's Festial*, EETS e.s. 96 (1905).

Farmer, D. H., *The Oxford Dictionary of Saints* (Oxford, 1978).

Fletcher, A. J., *Preaching, Politics and Poetry in Late-Medieval England* (Dublin, 1998).

_____, 'Compilations for Preaching', in *The Cambridge History of the Book* (forthcoming).

Furrow, M., 'The Author and Damnation: Chaucer, Writing, and Penitence', *Forum for Modern Language Studies*, 33 (1997), 244–57.

Godefroy, F., *Dictionnaire de l'Ancienne Langue Française et de tous ses dialectes du IXe au XVe siècle* (Paris, 1880–1902).

Grabes, H., *The Mutable Glass: Mirror-imagery in titles and texts of the Middle Ages and English Renaissance*, trans. by Gordon Collier (Cambridge, 1982).

Heffernan, T. J., 'Sermon Literature', in *Middle English Prose: A Critical Guide to Major Authors and Genres*, ed. by A. S. G. Edwards (New Brunswick, NJ, 1984), pp. 177–207.

Hervieux, L., *Les Fabulistes Latins IV: Eudes de Cheriton, et ses dérivés* (Paris, 1896).

Holmqvist, E., *On the History of the English Present Inflections particulary '-th' and '-s'* (Heidelberg, 1922).

Hudson, A., *English Wycliffite Sermons*, vol 1 (Oxford, 1983).

_____, *Lollards and their Books* (London, 1985).

Hunt, S., 'An Edition of Tracts in Favour of Scriptural Translation and of Some Texts Connected with Lollard Vernacular Biblical Scholarship' (unpublished D.Phil. thesis, University of Oxford, 1994).

James, M. R., *The Western Manuscripts in the Library of Trinity College Cambridge: A Descriptive Catalogue*, 3 vols (Cambridge, 1900–1904).

_____, *A Descriptive Catalogue of the Manuscripts in the Library of Corpus Christi College, Cambridge* (Cambridge, 1912).

_____, *Catalogue of the Latin Manuscripts in the John Rylands Library at Manchester*, vol. 1 (Manchester, 1921).

_____, *A Descriptive Catalogue of the Library of Samuel Pepys,* Part III, Medieval Manuscripts (London, 1923).

Jordan, R., *Handbuch der mittelenglischen Grammatik*, 2nd edn, revised by H.C. Matthes (Heidelberg, 1934).

Ker, N. R., *Medieval Libraries of Great Britain*, 2nd edn (London, 1964).

_____, *Medieval Manuscripts in British Libraries*, vol. III (Oxford, 1983).

_____ and A. J. Piper, *Medieval Manuscripts in British Libraries*, vol. IV (Oxford, 1992).

Laird, C. G., 'A Fourteenth Century Scribe', *Modern Language Notes*, 55 (1940), 601–603.

_____, 'Five New Gretham Sermons and the Middle English *Mirrur*', *Publications of the Modern Language Association of America*, 57 (1942), 628–37.

Legge, M. D., *Anglo-Norman Literature and its Background* (Oxford, 1963).

Lester, G. A., *Index of Middle English Prose, Handlist II: Manuscripts containing Middle English Prose in the John Rylands and Chetham's Libraries* (Woodbridge, 1985).

_____, 'Unedited Middle English Prose in Rylands Manuscripts', *Bulletin of the John Rylands Library*, 68 (1985–86), 135–60.

Luick, K., *Historische Grammatik der Englischen Sprache* (Leipzig, 1914–40).

McIntosh, A., M. Samuels, and M. Benskin, *A Linguistic Atlas of Late Mediaeval English* (Aberdeen, 1986).

McKitterick, R., and R. Beadle, *Catalogue of the Pepys Library at Magdalene College Cambridge, Volume 5: Manuscripts, Part 1: Medieval* (Cambridge, 1992).

McLoughlin, K., 'Magdalene College Pepys 2498 and Stephen Batman's Reading Practices', *Transactions of the Cambridge Bibliographical Society*, 10 (1994), 525–34.

Marshall, L., 'A Lexicographical Study of Robert of Gretham's *Miroir*', (unpublished M.A. thesis, University of Manchester, 1971).

_____, 'The Authorship of the Anglo-Norman Poem *Corset*', *Medium Aevum*, 42 (1973), 207–23.

_____ and W. Rothwell, 'The *Miroir* of Robert of Gretham', *Medium Aevum*, 39 (1970), 313–21.

Marx, C. W., and J. F. Drennan, eds, *The Middle English Prose Complaint of Our Lady and Gospel of Nicodemus*, MET 19 (Heidelberg, 1987).

Mersand, J., *Chaucer's Romance Vocabulary* (New York, 1937).

Meyer, P., untitled, *Romania*, 7 (1878), 343–47.

_____, 'Notice du MS Douce 210 de la Bibliothèque Bodleienne à Oxford', *Bulletin de la Société des Anciens Textes Français*, 6 (1880), 46–83.

_____, 'Les Manuscrits Français de Cambridge 2', *Romania*, 15 (1886), 296–305.

_____, 'Les Manuscrits Français de Cambridge', *Romania*, 32 (1903), 18–120.

Mooney, L. R., *The Index of Middle English Prose, Handlist XI: Trinity College, Cambridge* (Cambridge, 1995).

Moore, S., S. B. Meech, and H. Whitehall, 'Middle English dialect characteristics and dialect boundaries', *Essays and Studies in English and Comparative Literature*, University of Michigan Publications in Language and Literature XIII (Ann Arbor, 1935).

Morris, R., *The Story of Genesis and Exodus*, EETS o.s. 7 (1865).

_____, *A Bestiary in An Old English Miscellany*, EETS o.s. 49 (1872).

Morsbach, L., *Ueber den Ursprung der neuenglischen Schriftsprache* (Heilbronn, 1888).

Mustanoja, T. F., *A Middle English Syntax, Part I: Parts of Speech* (Helsinki, 1960).

Nevanlinna, S., ed., *The Northern Homily Cycle*, 2 vols (Helsinki, 1972).

*Ninth Report of the Royal Commission on Historical Manuscripts*, Appendix II (London, 1883).

Oakden, J. P., *Alliterative Poetry in Middle English, the Dialectal and Metrical Survey* (Manchester, 1930).

Omont, H., *Nouvelles Acquisitions du Department des Manuscrits 1913–14* (Paris, 1915).

Panunzio, S., *Robert de Gretham, Miroir ou les Evangiles des Domnées: edizione di otto domeniche*, Studi e testi di letteratura francese (Bari, 1967; 2nd edn 1974).

Paues, A. C., *A Fourteenth Century English Biblical Version* (Cambridge, 1904).

Pope, M. K., *From Latin to Modern French with Especial Consideration of Anglo-Norman: phonology and morphology*, 2nd edn. (Manchester, 1952).

Reichl, K., *Religiöse Dichtung im Englischen Hochmittelalter* (München, 1973).

Ross, W. C., ed., *Middle English Sermons*, EETS o.s. 209 (1940).

Rothwell, W., 'The Role of French in Thirteenth-Century England', *Bulletin of the John Rylands Library*, 58 (1976), 445–66.

_____, 'The Trilingual England of Geoffrey Chaucer', *Studies in the Age of Chaucer*, 16 (1994), 45–67.

_____, 'Playing "follow my leader" in Anglo-Norman Studies', *French Language Studies*, 6 (1996), 177–210.

Rubin, S., *Medieval English Medicine* (London and New York, 1974).

Russell, J. C., *Dictionary of Writers of Thirteenth-Century England* (London, 1936).

Samuels, M. L., 'Some Applications of Middle English Dialectology', *English Studies*, 44 (1963), 81–94.

_____, *Linguistic Evolution* (Cambridge, 1972).

_____, 'Chaucer's Spelling', in *Middle English Studies Presented to Norman Davis in Honour of his Seventieth Birthday*, ed. by D. Gray and E.G. Stanley (Oxford 1983), pp. 17–37.

Sauer, H., *Nominalkomposita im Frümittelenglischen* (Tübingen, 1992).

Schmidt, A. V. C., ed., *William Langland: The Vision of Piers Plowman* (London, 1978).

Severs, J. B. and A. E. Hartung, eds, *A Manual of the Writings in Middle English 1050–1500*, 10 vols to date (New Haven and London 1967–).

Sinclair, K. V., *Corset*, ANTS 52 (London, 1991).

_____, 'The Anglo-Norman Patrons of Robert the Chaplain and Robert of Greatham', *Forum for Modern Language Studies*, 27 (1992), 193–208.

Sisam, K., ed., *Fourteenth Century Verse and Prose* (Oxford, 1955).

Spencer, H. L., *English Preaching in the Late Middle Ages* (Oxford, 1993).

_____, 'The Study of Medieval English Preaching: What Next?', *Medium Aevum*, 69 (2000), 104–109.

Stevenson, W. H., *Report on the Manuscripts of Lord Middleton preserved at Wollaton Hall, Nottinghamshire*, Historical Manuscripts Commission (London, 1911).

Stratmann, F. H., *A Middle-English Dictionary: containing words used by English writers from the twelfth to the fifteenth century*, revised and enlarged by H. Bradley (Oxford, 1891).

Tobler, A., and E. Lommatzsch, *Altfranzösisches Wörterbuch* (Berlin, 1925–).

Tolkien, J. R. R., and E. V. Gordon, eds, *Sir Gawain and the Green Knight* (Oxford, 1925).

Toller, T. N., *Supplement to the Anglo-Saxon Dictionary* (Oxford, 1908–21).

Trotter, D. A., 'The Influence of Bible Commentaries on Old French Bible Translations', *Medium Aevum*, 56 (1987), 257–75.

_____, ed., *Multilingualism in Later Medieval Britain* (Woodbridge, 2000).

Turville-Petre, T., *Image and Text: Medieval Manuscripts at the University of Nottingham* (Nottingham, 1996).

Tyson, M., *Handlist of ... English Manuscripts in the John Rylands Library 1928*, Bulletin of the John Rylands Library, 13 (1929), 152–219.

Ullman, B. L., *The Origin and Development of Humanist Script* (Rome, 1960).

Varnhagen, H., 'Die handschriftlichen Erwerbungen des British Museum auf dem Gebiete des Altromanischen in den Jahren von 1865 bis Mitte 1877', *Zeitschrift für Romanische Philologie*, 1 (1877), 541–45.

Vising, J., *Anglo-Norman Language and Literature* (London, 1923).

Wakelin, M. F., 'The Manuscripts of John Mirk's Festial', *Leeds Studies in English, n.s.* i (1967), 93–118.

Ward, H. L. D., and J. A. Herbert, *Catalogue of Romances in the Department of Manuscripts in the British Museum*, 3 vols (London, 1883–1910).

Watson, N., 'Censorship and Cultural Change in Late-Medieval England: Vernacular Theology, the Oxford Translation Debate, and Arundel's Constitutions of 1409', *Speculum*, 70 (1995), 822–64.

Weatherly, E. H., ed., *Speculum Sacerdotale*, EETS o.s. 200 (1936).

Wenzel, S., 'Sermon Collections and Their Taxonomy', in *The Whole Book: Cultural Perspectives on the Medieval Miscellany*, ed. by S. G. Nichols and S. Wenzel (Ann Arbor, 1996), pp. 7–21.

Wright, T., *St Patrick's Purgatory: An Essay on the legends of Purgatory, Hell and Paradise current during the Middle Ages* (London, 1844).

Young, J., and P. H. Aitken, *A Catalogue of the Manuscripts in the Library of the Hunterian Museum in the University of Glasgow* (Glasgow, 1908).

Zettersten, A., ed., *The English Text of the Ancrene Riwle*, EETS o.s. 274 (1976).